# Nonprofit Guide to Going Green

# Nonprofit Guide to Going Green

**TED HART**
**ADRIENNE D. CAPPS**
**MATTHEW BAUER**

**WILEY**
John Wiley & Sons, Inc.

Published by John Wiley & Sons, Inc., Hoboken, New Jersey.
Published simultaneously in Canada.

No part of this publication may be reproduced, stored in a retrieval system, or transmitted in any form or by any means, electronic, mechanical, photocopying, recording, scanning, or otherwise, except as permitted under Section 107 or 108 of the 1976 United States Copyright Act, without either the prior written permission of the Publisher, or authorization through payment of the appropriate per-copy fee to the Copyright Clearance Center, Inc., 222 Rosewood Drive, Danvers, MA 01923, (978) 750-8400, fax (978) 750-4470, or on the web at www.copyright.com. Requests to the Publisher for permission should be addressed to the Permissions Department, John Wiley & Sons, Inc., 111 River Street, Hoboken, NJ 07030, (201) 748-6011, fax (201) 748-6008, or online at www.wiley.com/go/permissions.

Limit of Liability/Disclaimer of Warranty: While the publisher and author have used their best efforts in preparing this book, they make no representations or warranties with respect to the accuracy or completeness of the contents of this book and specifically disclaim any implied warranties of merchantability or fitness for a particular purpose. No warranty may be created or extended by sales representatives or written sales materials. The advice and strategies contained herein may not be suitable for your situation. You should consult with a professional where appropriate. Neither the publisher nor author shall be liable for any loss of profit or any other commercial damages, including but not limited to special, incidental, consequential, or other damages.

For general information on our other products and services or for technical support, please contact our Customer Care Department within the United States at (800) 762-2974, outside the United States at (317) 572-3993 or fax (317) 572-4002.

Wiley also publishes its books in a variety of electronic formats. Some content that appears in print may not be available in electronic books. For more information about Wiley products, visit our web site at www.wiley.com.

*Library of Congress Cataloging-in-Publication Data:*

Hart, Ted, 1964–
    Nonprofit guide to going green / Ted Hart, Adrienne D. Capps, Matthew Bauer.
        p.   cm.
    Includes bibliographical references and index.
    ISBN 978-0-470-52982-9 (cloth)
    1. Green marketing.   2. Nonprofit organizations.   3. Fund raising.   I. Capps, Adrienne D. II. Bauer, Matthew, 1966–   III. Title.
    HF5413.H374 2010
    658.4′083–dc22

                                                                        2009033768

Printed in the United States of America.

10  9  8  7  6  5  4  3  2  1

Ted Hart, Senior Editor, thanks Sanofi-Aventis for providing
funding and support to the development of this
*Nonprofit Guide to Going Green.*

We dedicate this book to the hard work of all charities
around the world and their growing efforts to
help protect our planet.

# Contents

# Introduction
# Let the Revolution Begin:
# Going Green for Good

*Ted Hart*

Going green generally means adapting habits and business practices that will stop or reduce greenhouse gases (mostly carbon dioxide) from forming in the atmosphere. It is this increase in greenhouse gases that causes global warming. The challenge before us is to mobilize the huge charitable sector around the world to reduce its impact on our planet.

In writing this book my fellow editors, authors and I seek to provide practical advice, specifically written by experts, for charities around the world in meeting this global challenge. We approached this first-of-its kind handbook mindful that most organizations struggle to meet their budgets and to fulfill their own goals. Knowing full well that for most organizations going green can be a dream, a luxury that seems out of reach in difficult economic times.

The editors and authors are not suggesting that everything charities do must be seen as a "green" decision. This book does not advocate that all charities must become "crunchy green." What we are saying is that through the adoption of suggestions made in the various chapters of this book, charities can make a difference, and that collectively as a charitable sector we can make a significant positive impact on the environment.

Protecting the environment is not easy, it is not something you do in an afternoon and then go on with your same old business practices. Protecting the environment is not just a good idea. Protecting the environment is important to the future of the charitable sector.

As more and more corporations, individuals and foundations change their day-to-day practices, seeking to reduce their own effect on the environment, by adopting more green business practices, the day will soon come to our charitable sector when our supporters will begin to demand that we join them in becoming a part of the global environmental solution. This handbook is the practical guide to help charities change their practices *ahead* of this challenge that will be made by funders.

The charitable sector in the United States alone is huge; according to *The World Factbook*, the asset base of the charitable sector makes the "US nonprofit economy" comparable to the sixth largest economy in the world, larger than the entire GNP of Brazil, Russia, Canada, Mexico, and South Korea. Combine this with charities around the world and we are talking about a huge economy that has both the opportunity and the obligation to become greener.

This charitable economy was built on the promise that we care for those around us and the communities we serve. We must now add to that community promise a pledge to protect our environment and reverse the damage already done. All charitable organizations around the world are challenged now to do their part to reduce their carbon emissions footprint.

For those who might be skeptics as to the need for this movement, those who might still be clinging to false statements that there is nothing to this whole global warming thing, the unmistakable message from scientists around the world, who devote their professional lives to understanding the effect human activity has on climate change, is that climate change is real, it's caused by humans, and it will create serious risks for our charities, economies, and the quality of life in our communities.

For example, one of the effects of global warming is the gradual melting of the polar icecaps, which in turn raises ocean levels and eventually floods low-level coastal areas around the world. Already the rising seas are swallowing beaches around the world. Right here in the United States there are several city blocks, surrounding inhabited homes, in Key West that regularly flood by some 4–6 inches during high tide every day. This is happening now; it is not a theory, not some prediction of the future. This will only continue to grow and threaten many thousands of communities around the world. This is but one consequence of doing nothing.

Many charitable organizations who began "going green" may have first adopted environmental conservation measures simply as a good thing to do. Now, more and more charities are reaping the positive financial impact of going green, such as reducing costs, improving operations, and raising employee morale and productivity.

In this book we advocate the long-term benefits of small steps taken now, changing business practices, and becoming more aware that decisions made now add up when combined with the collective efforts of charities around the world also dedicated to making a difference.

**This is a charitable revolution.** It will change the way your supporters think about your organization and which charities they choose to support. Like most revolutions it starts slow, with early results that are modest compared to their potential, but it will gain momentum. As more and more charities start changing their practices there will be more opportunities to network with innovative, caring, and astute charity leaders. Making these changes will forever change the way you view your organization and will change the way your community views you.

GreenNonprofits.Org. As nonrenewable sources of energy run thin and the negative impacts of human society on the environment continue to grow, the entire world is seeking to green its efforts and reduce its carbon footprint on the globe. GreenNonprofits.org is a charitable organization that was founded in 2008 on the belief that all nonprofits and NGOs around the world must do the same and be accountable to their communities.

The nonprofit and NGO sector, in general, senior management and board members in specific are in need of practical advice that will lead to concrete action being taken that will positively affect the environment.

Just as corporations and individuals must, the nonprofit sector must take its place in the green movement. *Nonprofit Guide to Going Green: The GreenNonprofits*

*Handbook* is the definitive go-to resource for the charitable community to learn how to most effectively transition into green[er] organizations.

As charities become familiar with these concepts they are encouraged to consider signing the GreenNonprofits Pledge and moving toward becoming a certified green nonprofit, as a public declaration of the dedicated effort each charity puts forth in helping reverse the effects of global warming.

Regardless of the path you take, whether you ever become certified or not, what matters most is that your organization makes all the changes you can practically make and sustain these changes into the future, joining the call to become a more green nonprofit.

# Green Facts

- The average nonprofit office worker discards 175 pounds+ of high-grade paper per year.
- Businesses use 2 million tons of paper in copiers each year.
- In the United States, the average person generates 4.39 pounds of trash per day.
- Every year, Americans make enough plastic film to shrinkwrap the state of Texas.
- Americans receive approximately 4 million tons of junk mail every year—most of which ends up incinerated or in the landfill. Reconsider your direct mail plans.
- Only 1 percent of water on earth is drinkable.
- A faucet with a slow leak can waste more than 10 gallons of water a day. A single leaky toilet can waste as much as 100 gallons per day.
- Outdoor lighting provides an excellent opportunity for energy savings, as these lights often remain on for a long time. By using efficient lights (compact fluorescents, etc.), your nonprofit can reduce wasted energy and your monthly bill by up to 15 percent.
- ENERGY STAR monitors have power management features and consume up to 90 percent less energy than conventional monitors. Fax machines can reduce their annual electricity costs by about 50 percent.
- A sample tune-up can increase the energy efficiency of your furnace by 5 percent. You can save up to 10 percent by insulating and tightening up ventilation ducts.
- Each commuter driving alone to work creates more than 2 tons of auto exhaust annually.
- If a commuter car in the United States carried just one more passenger, we would save 600,000 gallons of gas and reduce air emissions by 12 million pounds of carbon dioxide every day.
- An improperly tuned car produces 10 to 15 times more pollution than a tuned one.
- If every American home replaced just one light bulb with an ENERGY STAR qualified bulb, we would save enough energy to light more than 3 million homes for a year and more than $600 million in annual energy costs, and prevent greenhouse gases equivalent to the emissions of more than 800,000 cars.

# About the Editors

**Ted Hart** is founder and chief executive of the international nonprofit environmental movement called GreenNonprofits (http://greennonprofits.org), dedicated to helping nonprofits and nongovernmental organizations (NGOs) around the world to learn how to become part of the much-needed global environmental solution. He is considered one of the foremost experts in online fundraising and social networks for charities around the world, having founded the ePhilanthropy Foundation and P2PFundraising.org.

Ted is sought after internationally as an inspirational and practical speaker and consultant on topics related to nonprofit strategy, both online and offline. He serves as CEO of Hart Philanthropic Services (http://tedhart.com), an international consultancy to nonprofits/NGOs. He has served as CEO of the University of Maryland Medical System Foundation and before that as chief development officer for Johns Hopkins Bayview Medical Center. He has been certified as an advanced certified fundraising executive by the Association of Fundraising Professionals. Ted is author of several published articles, an editor, author of the books *Major Donors—Finding Big Gifts in Your Database and Online*; *Nonprofit Internet Strategies Best Practices for Marketing, Communications and Fundraising Success*; and *Fundraising on the Internet: The ePhilanthropyFoundation.Org's Guide to Success Online*, and a contributing author to *Achieving Excellence in Fund Raising*, 2nd ed., and to *People to People Fundraising: Social Networking and Web 2.0 for Charities*. He has also served as an adjunct faculty member to the Master of Science in Fundraising Management program at Columbia University. He resides in the Washington, DC, and New York City areas with his daughter, Sarah Grace, and son, Alexander Michael.

**Adrienne D. Capps** is currently the senior director of development for the Graduate School of Management at UC Davis in California. Over the past 10 years, Adrienne has raised nearly $20 million for a variety of causes, including at-risk youth, mental health, and higher education in Virginia, New York, and California. Prior to her move to California in 2007, she served as the head of fundraising for Dyson College of Arts & Sciences at Pace University in New York City. A certified fundraising executive since 2004, Adrienne has published several articles in *Advancing Philanthropy*, the most recent of which is "Gastronomy and Giving," which discusses the unique intersection of her two passions: fundraising and food. She continues to travel the United States speaking on the topic of green fundraising; her most recent speech was at the CASE 2009 Summit for Advancement Leaders. Adrienne has been an active participant in the fundraising community as a member of the Association of Fundraising Professionals for nine years, having served on the board of directors of the Greater New York Chapter. Adrienne also serves on the board of directors and as treasurer of S.W.i.S.H, a New York City–based gay-straight alliance.

**Matt Bauer,** president of BetterWorld Telecom, has worked to improve communities in the United States and abroad in both the for-profit and nonprofit sectors for more than 20 years. Before cofounding BetterWorld Telecom in 2002, Matt served in a series of leadership roles in the telecommunications and power industries, including AES Corp and NETtel. He has helped to start or grow a number of nonprofits over the past 10 years, including the Charleston, South Carolina–based Lowcountry Local First, the Sitar Center for Children and the Arts in Washington, DC, and Atlanta-based True Colors Theatre Company. Matt now serves on the board of directors for the Business Alliance for Local Living Economies, GreenNonprofits, the Noisette Foundation, and the Charleston Regional Alliance for the Arts. He holds a BA in Telecommunications from Indiana University and an MBA from the George Washington University.

# Nonprofit Guide to Going Green

# PART I

# Green Management

## CHAPTER 1

# Raising Green by Being Green—Charity Fundraising

## Adrienne D. Capps

## What Is "Green Fundraising," and Why Do It?

Green fundraising is the concept that even the fundraising activities of the charitable sector should incorporate techniques, which reduce carbon footprint, are friendlier to the environment, and promote sustainability. But is this really needed? The fundraising efforts of an organization are typically lean and represent just a portion of its overall operations. Examining your organization's fundraising efforts and transitioning them to include green techniques can contribute to increasing revenues and reducing expenses and serve as a communications tool to build awareness of your organization and present it as a sustainability leader in your community.

There are more than 1.5 million nonprofit organizations in the United States[1] alone and easily more than 2 million worldwide. Combined, the charitable sector is an economic powerhouse. In 2006, the U.S. nonprofit sector was large enough to rival the sixth largest economy in the world,[2] surpassing the economies of Brazil, Russia, Canada, Mexico, and South Korea. In the same study, total expenditures of all 501(c)(3) nonprofit organizations examined (U.S. designation), together numbering more than 835,000, was nearly $945 billion.[3] For the entire U.S. nonprofit sector, the annual total expenditures are estimated to be approximately $1.8 trillion.

It is estimated that a well-run charity will spend approximately 20 percent of its budget on fundraising. Using this measure, nonprofit spending, on average, totals more than $360 billion annually. Fundraising activities specifically and charitable spending generally make significant impacts on the economy.

Environmentally conscious charities are encouraged to examine, understand, and make improvements to the way they fundraise, utilizing more environmentally sustainable methods. Given the total expenditures of this industry around the world, combined efforts will result in a more sustainable future for our planet.

The discussion to follow and the organizations used as examples for this chapter were chosen because they are making changes in a systematic and thoughtful manner. These organizations are formally and informally surveying their staff, donors, volunteers, and board members for their input and feedback. They are researching articles and discussing the greening of their fundraising programs with colleagues.

When they make changes, they are being thoughtful in their planning over a longer time horizon, not attempting to do it all at once or all overnight. A process that is thoughtful, deliberate, and has both staff and leadership support will most assuredly put your organization onto a smoother road toward success.

This chapter is organized into four sections that address the main techniques a nonprofit uses to raise funds:

1. Annual fund/direct mail
2. Grant writing
3. Fundraising Events
4. Major/planned gifts program

Appendix A presents lists of resources and tools that will help in the transition to a greener fundraising program

## Greening Your Annual Fund/Direct Mail Program

### Traditional Fundraising Method

A typical direct mail program consists of, at a minimum, these components: a compelling letter, a pledge form, and a return envelope mailed together in bulk to current and lapsed donors as well as prospects several times per year. Depending on the size of and resources available to the nonprofit organization sending these letters, the annual fund or direct mail program can be highly sophisticated and creative by using list segmentation, premiums or small tokens given with the letter or after a donation is made, irregularly shaped packages to draw attention or call to action, a promise or other compelling language used on the outer envelope to encourage the receiver to open it immediately. It is hoped that the organization, no matter its size, keeps statistics on response rates in order to more effectively analyze and test different packages, premiums, text, and other variables.

The history of direct mail is older than one might think—historians have dated its earliest examples back to the twelfth century in Japan. More recently, abolitionists in Great Britain used direct mail in the eighteenth and nineteenth centuries.[4] In the United States, however, the modern form of the direct mail program that we all know today began after World War II, when national nonprofit organizations, such as the National Easter Seal Society, were looking for new donation streams. Direct mail did not truly catch on until after the creation of the national zip code system in the 1960s. The popularity and success of direct mail continued to thrive as computers came on the scene in the 1970s. Before that, maintaining and utilizing lists was costly and time consuming.

The growth of the nonprofit sector, both in the number of organizations and in their individual sizes, over the next couple of decades continued to fuel the fire in the rapid development of the direct mail industry. Today direct mail fundraising makes up at least one-fifth of the more than $250 billion contributed annually to the 1.5 million+ nonprofit organizations in the United States.[5]

According to a survey published by Target Analysis Group, a Boston-based consultancy firm, donations made to nonprofit organizations in 2007 did not even keep pace with inflation, growing by an average of 1.4 percent.[6] The number of donors declined by a median 1.4 percent from the previous year, and organizations acquired a median 6.2 percent fewer new donors. The only silver lining was that the 72 organizations surveyed still raised more money with individual donations growing by a median 3.9 percent from the previous year. Target Analysis Group gave several reasons for the downward trend, including the fact that the number of people who grew up around the time of World War II is dwindling, as is the growth of direct mail fundraising in the United States.

## Fundraising Challenge

The challenge for direct mail fundraising is plain on one front: how to acquire and keep a large base of supporters who make annual gifts. On a second front, with the advent of social media and the increased use of technology such as BlackBerry And the iPhone, how do nonprofit organizations reach prospects who are not responding to direct mail efforts?

Greening your direct mail program offers some unique answers. Many organizations have already become greener without realizing it.

## Transition to a New, Green Paradigm

In the last few years, has your organization sent an e-mail solicitation as a cost-cutting method? Have you tried to sell tickets to an upcoming fundraising gala by posting to Facebook or LinkedIn? If so, you have started to transition toward becoming more green without realizing it (or maybe becoming green was one of many reasons you made the change) while reducing expenses at the same time.

If your organization is at a stage of considering using social media, the Internet, and e-mail to raise annual fund dollars, this section will help you. The key, once again, is transition. Implementing new techniques too quickly or changing your program too radically will not only be difficult for your organization to handle and potentially not sustainable but may confuse or even anger your donors. Slow and steady change wins the race. Take time to talk internally to staff and volunteers and externally to donors and prospects about the changes your organization intends to make in its direct mail program. Get their input, and incorporate it into your plans.

In a phased transition to greening your direct mail program, your organization may start by streamlining its direct mail package before jumping right into e-mail or social media solicitations. This method may be particularly relevant to larger, national organizations that need time to make large changes or whose volunteers, staff, and donors are concerned about the success of such online campaigns.

When you are planning your next mailed annual fund appeal, take a look at each piece of the package. Are there parts or whole pieces that can be eliminated, made smaller, or otherwise streamlined? Are you using recycled papers and other materials? Is your printer or print shop using environmentally friendly inks, dyes, and other chemicals?

Before making changes, however, talk to your board members, volunteers, donors, and staff. What are their thoughts on changing the look of your direct mail packages by downsizing or eliminating pieces? Is it meaningful to them for your

FIGURE 1.1    Table tent example from the United Way of York County, SC.

organization to use recycled paper and natural dyes? If so, you should let them know by printing the message "100 percent recycled paper" on the outer envelope or pledge form. Doing this may even serve as an example in your community and garner increased support by demonstrating that your organization is a thoughtful, environmentally-focused leader. Note that eliminating pieces or making them smaller may result in cost savings, but use of environmentally friendly inks and dyes and recycled paper may increase expenses slightly. However, over time as more and more of us move in this direction, these costs will come down.

*CASE STUDY:* UNITED WAY OF YORK COUNTY, SOUTH CAROLINA    The United Way of York County, South Carolina has incorporated a number of greening techniques into its fundraising program, including its direct mail campaigns. The competitive advantage, however, has come from taking the time to talk to external constituents before it made a change.

You may be familiar with your local United Way, which represents other non-profit organizations in the community and solicits donations for them through work-place campaigns. Representatives from the United Way make brief presentations, generally 10 to 15 minutes in length, to a roomful of employees at a corporation and distribute pledge forms, brochures, and other materials with information about giving, the United Way mission, and the organizations it represents. Employees take the information and, with luck and motivation, return a pledge form or donation by mail or designate a recurring gift through payroll deduction.

The United Way of York County, South Carolina, "greened" this process by eliminating informational brochures that usually got left behind on chairs after the meeting. At the suggestion of a company employee, the organization created a table tent that could be displayed in a break room, lobby, or kitchen. It had specific information about the United Way campaign that could be read easily and quickly. The organization also reduced a three-page pledge form to a one-page, black-and-white, self-mailing return device (see Figures 1.1 and 1.2). This actually streamlined

Your privacy is important to us. We do not sell or distribute personal information for any reason.

☐ Mr.  ☐ Mrs.  ☐ Ms.  ☐ Dr.

First Name _____ Initial _____ Last Name _____

Home Address _____

City _____ State _____ Zip _____

Home Email _____ Phone _____

Employer _____

---

**My gift to my community** - *pledged amount will begin January 1, 2009*

**Easy Payroll Deduction** - I want to contribute the following amount each pay period:

☐ $5  ☐ $10  ☐ $25  ☐ $50  ☐ Other (_____)
My pay period is: ☐ Weekly (52)  ☐ Bi-weekly (26)  ☐ Semi-Monthly (24)  ☐ Monthly (12)  ☐ Other (_____)

**"LIVE UNITED" gift**                **Palmetto Leadership Society gift**
($5 week/$260 year or more)          ($11.54 week/$600 year or more)
Pledge $260 or more and receive a    If your family's pledge is $600 or more, you will be recognized in
discount card for local businesses   our annual registry and invited to our exclusive thank you event!

**Other Payment Options**

☐ Cash (enclosed) $_____

☐ Check (enclosed, payable to United Way of York County, SC)  $_____

☐ Bill Me *$50 minimum* $_____  ☐ One time (give date: _/_/_)  ☐ Quarterly  ☐ Monthly

☐ Credit or Debit Card $_____     ☐ VISA     ☐ MasterCard     ☐ American Express

Name as it appears on card _____

Credit Card Number_____ Exp Date _____

Bill my card    ☐ One time (give date: _/_/_)    ☐ Quarterly    ☐ Monthly
Please allow 30 days for processing. Please include home address above.

| My Total Gift: |
| --- |
| $_____ |
| *Thank you for supporting your local United Way!* |

---

**Signature to authorize your pledge:**

Sign: _____ Today's Date: _____

*I understand that nothing has been provided in return for this contribution and that my gift is fully tax deductible, subject to IRS regulations*

---

**Gift Recognition** - United Way of York County, SC recognizes individuals and families giving at $600 and above

Names as they should be published:_____     ☐ Please acknowledge my spouse with our joint leadership gift.
                                                                 Spouse's name _____
☐ I (we) wish to remain anonymous                                Spouse's place of work _____

---

Optional

AGE: ☐ 18 - 25 years old   ☐ 26 - 35 years old   ☐ 36 - 50 years old
     ☐ 50 - 65 years old   ☐ 65 years old and up

Have you given to United Way for more than 25 years?
☐ Yes, I am a Diamond Donor

*Please send my gift to:*
Optional Designations ($50 minimum for each designation)

☐ Meeting basic needs &   ☐ Promoting health   ☐ Creating safe   ☐ Promoting life
   building self-reliance     & wellness            communities        long learning
$_____              $_____         $_____      $_____

☐ Other United Way or Specific Partner Agency (see back)
$_____
            Agency or United Way name

United Way of York County, SC   PO Box 925, Rock Hill, SC 29731   803.324.2735 or 803.684.9847   www.unitedwayofyc.org
Please retain a copy of this pledge form for tax purposes. United Way of York County, SC did not provide any goods or services in exchange for this donation.

FIGURE 1.2    Revised one-page pledge form; printed back and front from the United Way of York County, SC.

Our mission:

*Our United Way will be the non-profit leader in identifying needs,
facilitating collaboration and maximizing resources to
positively impact our community.*

United Way of York County, SC

## United Way of York County, SC

When we reach out a hand to one
we influence the condition of all.

That's what it means to

# LIVE UNITED.

2-1-1 is an easy to remember
telephone number connecting
callers to information
about health and human
service agencies.

Call 2-1-1. It's easy,
confidential and free!

United Way of York County, SC

## 2-1-1

Get Connected. Get Answers.

**Help Starts Here.**

### Suggested Gift Guide

| Your Annual Income | Weekly 1% Gift |
|---|---|
| Up to $19,999 | Up to $3 |
| $20,000 - $29,999 | $3 - $5 |
| $30,000 - $39,999 | $5 - $7 |
| $40,000 - $69,999 | $7 - $12 |
| $70,000 - $79,999 | $12 - $13 |
| $80,000 and up | $13 and up |
| "LIVE UNITED" level | $5 a week/ $260 a year |
| Palmetto Leadership Society level | $11.54 a week/ $600 per year |

### United Way of York County, SC Partner Agencies

Alston Wilkes Society
A Place for Hope
American Red Cross of York County
Boy Scouts - Palmetto Council
Boys & Girls Clubs of York County
Catawba Care Coalition
Children's Attention Home School
Clover Area Assistance Center
Clover Rescue Squad
Early Learning Partnership of York County
Florence Crittenton Services, Inc.
Fort Mill Care Center

Fort Mill Rescue Squad
Girl Scouts - Hornets Nest Council
The Haven Men's Shelter
Hickory Grove Lifesaving Squad
Hospice and Community Care
International Center of York County
Keystone Substance Abuse Services
P.A.T.H. (People Attempting To Help)
Pilgrims' Inn
Rock Hill Rescue Squad
Rock Hill School District Foundation
Safe Passage

Salvation Army
Serenity Club of York County
Speech & Hearing Center
Teen Health Center
Tega Cay Rescue Squad
YMCA - Upper Palmetto
York County Adult Day Care Center
YC Board of Disabilities & Special Needs
York County Council on Aging
York County First Steps
York County Literacy Association
Youth Development/Clemson Extension (4-H)
York Rescue Squad

FIGURE 1.2    (*Continued*)

its internal office procedures just in the ease of handling one page instead of three.
In addition, the organization began promoting the opportunity to make donations
and fulfill pledges online at its Web site. These three small changes have added up
to big savings in paper and printing costs.

The organization first made the change in 2008 after informally surveying volunteers and donors over the course of a few months. People reported that the forms were long and cumbersome and that the brochures did not provide any additional useful information beyond the presentation and the United Way's Web site address. In the last year, the United Way of York County, South Carolina, reports that the changes have been so well received that it will continue using the one-page form and information table tents and plan to be more aggressive about promoting the Web site for online donations and pledge fulfillment.

Organizations can eliminate mailed annual fund appeals and conduct them wholly online in any number of creative ways. Your organization can send an e-mail solicitation, also called an e-solicitation, using virtually the same text and techniques as a direct mail package. If your organization has never sent a mass e-mail to its constituents, you will need to consult your information technology department or a consultant. Technology issues that may arise from ensuring your message does not end up in a junk folder, formatting e-mail addresses, and using images, among others, will need to be considered. See Appendix A for a list of organizations that can help in this area, including Grassroots.org and the Taproot Foundation.

A great deal of attention is being paid to the subject of how to use social media networking sites, such as Facebook and LinkedIn. Creating a Facebook group or cause can build awareness about a fundraising campaign (and events) and drive prospective donors to your organization's Web site for more information and to make gifts online. An individual's Facebook friends can see the person's involvement with your organization, and he or she can receive updates to fundraising efforts through messages you can post to the group or cause page. Starting a discussion about your fundraising campaign on your organization's page(s) is similarly effective.

*CASE STUDY:* SAN DIEGO CHAPTER OF THE YOUNG NONPROFIT PROFESSIONALS NETWORK
The local San Diego Chapter of the Young Nonprofit Professionals Network (YNPN) has had the opportunity to start a green annual fund program from its inception. With a budget of about $10,000 annually, YNPN San Diego is run by an all-volunteer group of nonprofit professionals just getting started in the nonprofit sector. The group quickly recruited 15 board members and organized themselves into eight committees. Board members and volunteers stay connected on e-mail and, increasingly, via social media sites like Facebook and LinkedIn. What the organization quickly discovered after its inception in April 2008 was that a network of emerging leaders in the nonprofit sector in and around San Diego was virtually nonexistent. To build awareness and to fundraise for YNPN San Diego, they turned to the tools they had been using themselves to communicate—namely social media sites. First, they created a Facebook group and in January 2009, after receiving their 501(c)(3) status, started a cause. The goal was to raise $1,000 on Facebook within four months, by their first anniversary in April 2009—and people started to get creative. One of the volunteers pledged $100 if 100 people joined the organization's cause. A few board members paid their board dues of $100 per year through Facebook, either by paying it themselves or raising the funds through friends in order to raise awareness and publicize their support of YNPN San Diego to their Facebook friends. The first donation for the campaign came in on January 19, 2009, and YNPN

San Diego surpassed the $1,000 goal on March 18, 2009, one month ahead of schedule. As of April 29, 2009, YNPN San Diego had 224 members in its group, and 105 people joined its cause with a fundraising total of $1,204.

YNPN San Diego completed its first fundraising plan in April 2009. It includes many references to conducting their fundraising program in a 100 percent green manner, including continuing to raise funds in creative ways through Facebook. An excerpt from the "About YNPN San Diego" section outlines the group's commitment to green fundraising: "YNPN San Diego continues to use its listserv, Facebook, LinkedIn, and Twitter as its primary modes of communication focusing on being a 'green' organization." An excerpt from the "Online Networking & Resources" section explains their goals in greater detail:

> *YNPN San Diego uses the latest and greatest technology to help manage our internal communications and network with our members. This multi-faceted strategy is fun and green, as well as time and cost-efficient. YNPN San Diego continues to examine new communications technologies and at this time you can find YNPN San Diego using the following tools: listserv, blog, Facebook, LinkedIn, Twitter, Idealist and more. The use of social media has helped YNPN San Diego spread like wildfire and become a model organization for nonprofit social media use. Through its website, YNPN San Diego also provides pages on resources related to next gen nonprofit issues as well as career information. We believe that these resources provide support to our members by creating a small clearinghouse of information for our membership that helps to strengthen the San Diego nonprofit community.*

Whether your organization has the opportunity to start an annual fund program from the ground up in a green manner or needs to transition to a greener program, these examples demonstrate creativity and entrepreneurial spirit while securing buy-in from constituents. Appendix A can help you in your exploration of greening your annual fund program and provide more ideas and techniques.

## Greening Your Grant Writing

### Traditional Fundraising Method

The traditional process many of us are familiar with involves researching potential grant makers, finding potential matches between our organization's programs and the grant makers' giving interests, making contact with potential funders and communicating with them for a period of time, and then, it is hoped, being invited to submit a proposal or completing a grant form. The procedure continues with grant proposal review on the part of the foundation or corporation with possible site visits at any time and ending in success when a funder provides a grant of funds. Although this is a great oversimplification of the relationship between a nonprofit organization and a foundation or corporate grantor during grant making, it generally describes how the two interact with each other.

In conversations about the topics and content of this chapter, many nonprofit leaders expressed doubt at being able to do anything to green their grant-writing programs. They thought that they were beholden to the requests and requirements of the foundation or corporation funder and their chosen grant-making program. If a particular foundation's giving guidelines included submitting five copies of a proposal together with annual reports, brochures, and other printed materials, that was what the nonprofit had to do, even if most of the paper would, after a brief review period by the foundation, end up either in the trash or in a big file drawer, wasting space. If a corporate funder required printed copies of 990 Forms in triplicate be mailed to its 30 corporate foundation officers, then a nonprofit had no choice in the matter. Some enlightened foundations and corporations are beginning to make use of technology and allowing potential grantees to submit proposals online or by e-mail, but for the most part, corporations and foundations still require nonprofits to mail in grant proposals.

## Fundraising Challenge

If a nonprofit organization is truly at the mercy of a potential grant maker, can anything be done to green its foundation and corporate relations and grants program? Can a nonprofit effect change on these grant makers so that the process of submitting proposals and other communications is greener? And if so, how?

In continued discussions with nonprofit leaders and in research with foundation and corporate grant makers, I am convinced that a nonprofit *can and should* work with its funders and help *them* green their grant-making process. As more and more funders adopt a green grant-making process, your organization will in turn enjoy the benefits of a green grants program.

The key in greening this aspect of your fundraising program will be buy-in and persuading funders that it is advantageous for them to change their process. Starting with its most long-term grant-making partners, a nonprofit can leverage its relationship and community position to influence these funders' grant-making process. A nonprofit could approach a funder, perhaps in between funding cycles when the grant maker is less busy, about making its grant-making process be greener. Emphasis on costs savings, streamlined operations, and providing a leadership example in the community are all great points to make in the case for greening to foundation and corporate funders.

## Transition to a New, Green Paradigm

There are myriad options for greening the grant-making process that you can discuss with your foundation and corporate partners. Could the funder ask for proposals to be submitted by e-mail? That e-mail then could be forwarded to decision makers on the board instead of being printed. Could the funder access 990 Forms and annual reports online? Could the funder send award notification by e-mail—and even make award payments by direct deposit instead of a check by mail?

It is advisable that nonprofits begin to have these conversations with their closest funders—those with whom the organizations have had a long-term relationship and commitment. Those funders probably will be the most open to the conversation and to changing their operations. In the end, not only may the funder's process become more environmentally friendly, but it is quite likely to save the funder a good deal of money in printing and mailing costs.

## *Case Study:* Community Foundation for Palm Beach and Martin Counties

The example for this section is unique. It is not a story of a nonprofit that has succeeded in helping one of its foundation partners transition to a more green grant-making process. It is a foundation that did it itself—without prompting from one of its grantees. It is a foundation with a goal to be a national model for other foundations in being green—the Community Foundation for Palm Beach and Martin Counties. The Community Foundation has included an environment funding category as a part of its regular grant-making activities for many years. In 2008, the advisory committee making the funding decisions began to discuss asking the nonprofit organizations it funded in the environment category about the state of their operations and how green they were. The nonprofit grantee may be making a great, positive impact on Palm Beach and Martin counties' environment, but what about their fundraising, administration, and management activities? Was the nonprofit operating in a green, sustainable way, or just their environmental programming?

The committee thought about including a requirement for a certain level of a grantee's operations to be green and sustainable as criteria for grant making, but then they worried about it turning into more of a stick than a carrot. Would nonprofits stop applying for grants and have a harder time finding funding just because their administrators used too much paper or left their computers on at night? And more to the heart of the matter: What was the Community Foundation doing to be green? How could it regulate its grantees' behavior while not being green itself?

Instead of that approach, the Community Foundation searched for best practices in being a green nonprofit. It surveyed, by e-mail, its grantees, the community, and other constituents about what other nonprofit organizations were doing to green their operations. And out of the survey and subsequent discussions, the Community Foundation's "Nonprofits Going Green" program was created. The objective of the initiative was threefold: "(1) to raise awareness, capacity, motivation within the nonprofit community in Palm Beach and Martin Counties, (2) to improve the environmental sustainability of their operations, and (3) to raise public and corporate awareness and support for the nonprofit community."[7]

The main component of the Nonprofits Going Green program is a contest that provides donations of cash and in-kind gifts to nonprofit organizations in the community that are greening their operations and programs. The Community Foundation created a panel of judges with experience and expertise in both the nonprofit sector and environmental issues and created categories that were fun and approachable so nonprofit organizations of all sizes could participate. In 2008, the categories were "Most Green with the Least Green," "Most Sustainable," "Judges Green Harvest Award" (for the most dedication and commitment to going green two awards), "Most Creative Use of Recycled Materials," and a listing of runners-up. The Community Foundation received 25 nonprofit applications and distributed more than $8,000 in cash and in-kind gifts to the winners (see Figure 1.3).

**Most Green with the Least Green:** Awarded to organizations with an annual budget of $500,000 or less for greatest ncrease in energy savings accomplished through the most cost-efficient means.

> Grand Prize Winner ($4,000): Quantum House for its holistic and cost effective approaches of involving board members, volunteers and families served in energy efficiency, waste reduction and water conservation efforts.
> First Runner Up ($2,000): Ann Norton Sculpture Gardens for comprehensive efforts to restore native habitats, conserve water, and eliminate need for pesticides on their property.
> Honorable Mention (Starbucks Green Basket): Annie Appleseed for their minimal impact operations and outreach on healthy environmentally sustainable lifestyles.
> Honorable Mention (Starbucks Green Basket): Dress for Success for their dedication to putting one person's waste to work for those less fortunate.

**Sustainability Leader:** Awarded to organizations with an annual budget of more than $500,000 for greatest increase in energy savings accomplished through the most cost-efficient means.

> Grand Prize Winner ($4,000): Palm Beach Zoo for taking a comprehensive strategic planning and implementation approach and particular innovation in waste reduction throughout operations, sustainability in retail items
> First Runner-Up ($1,500): Norton Museum of Art for also a comprehensive and consistent approach including with a high priority on employee incentives, waste reduction, water conservation and ensuring a healthy indoor environment.
> Honorable Mention (Starbucks Green Basket): Planned Parenthood of South Florida and the Treasure Coast for involving all staff in their "greening" initiatives.
> Honorable Mention (Starbucks Green Basket): St. Peters Catholic Church for a truly astounding comprehensive effort led by two high school youth members of the church

**Least Wasteful:** Awarded to an organization that has demonstrated most comprehensive efforts for reducing, reusing and ecycling waste.

> Grand Prize Winner ($2,000): Habitat for Humanity of South Palm Beach County for reducing the disposal of construction related debris
> First Runner Up ($750): Lighthouse Center for the Arts for their creative re-use of materials as well as comprehensive recycling and reduction initiatives.
> Honorable Mention (Starbucks Green Basket): Aid to Victims of Domestic Abuse for their comprehensive paper reduction initiatives that resulted in a reduction of over $2,200 in office expenses over a 7 month period.
> Honorable Mention (Starbucks Green Basket): Summit Christian School for involving the whole school – headmaster, operations, teachers, parents and students in waste reduction and recycling efforts that has resulted in a 1/3 reduction of waste generation.

**Energy Saver:** Awarded to organizations for greatest increase in energy savings accomplished through the most cost-efficient means.

> Grand Prize Winner ($1,500): St. Peters Catholic Church for the comprehensive approach to energy conservation and efficiency led by two high school student members.
> First Runner Up ($500): Legal Aid Society of Palm Beach County for their combination of low-cost efficiency retrofits and consistency and creativity in reminding staff to turn off lights and office equipment.
> Honorable Mention (Starbucks Green Basket): Take Stock in Children for a focus on saving money through no cost behavior changes.
> Honorable Mention (Starbucks Green Basket): Summit Christian School for its combination of low cost retrofits and "Hit the Switch" poster contest.

**Greenraiser:** Awarded to organizations for most successful efforts to market their organization and/or raise money while promoting environmental sustainability (e.g., green events or auctions).

> Grand Prize Winner ($1,500): American Heart Association for a focus on green events from choosing green venues and caterers to invites to awards and recycling logistics.
> First Runner-Up ($250): Council on Aging of Martin County for engaging more donors in a capital campaign by making it a LEED certified facility.
> Honorable Mention (Starbucks Green Basket): Peer Support Network for launching its seed card fundraiser.
> Honorable Mention (Starbucks Green Basket): Big Brothers Big Sisters of Palm Beach County for its "Think Big, Go Green" awareness-raising through green activities and education month.

**Judges' Harvest:** Awarded to organizations that the Judges' feel deserve recognition for their dedication and commitment o going green.

> Grand Prize Winner ($500): Boys & Girls Club of Martin County for the launching of its "Green Certified Club" at each of its locations

FIGURE 1.3 Categories and winners from the Community Foundation for Palm Beach and Martin Counties' 2009 Going Green Contest.

Momentum grew. In 2009, the Community Foundation received 57 applications for the contest and announced its winners during a luncheon at their offices. In total, the Community Foundation secured $18,500 in cash and in-kind gifts from continuing and new corporate and foundation partners in the community. It also secured a media sponsorship from a local television station. Three new categories were added to the contest: "Least Wasteful," "Energy Saver," and "Green-raising" (for an organization that greened its fundraising event or program).

Through the Nonprofits Going Green program and the contest, the Community Foundation hopes to get nonprofit organizations to understand the process of becoming greener, to learn and examine themselves, and then to be motivated to make changes. It seems to be working. In the contest applications, the Community Foundation is seeing organizations use their greening initiatives to attract new donors and reengage past donors. Nonprofits are also greening their fundraising events, including offering green products and services in auctions, providing a green fashion show, or moving away from big events in general and looking more to neighborhood and Internet-based fundraising efforts. The Community Foundation also sees nonprofit organizations capitalize on the multiple benefits of greening by, for example, reducing printing and mailing budgets while simultaneously greening their marketing and fundraising efforts.

As a companion to the contest, the Community Foundation also has offered an introductory workshop for nonprofits on going green and offered its grant-seeking training using webinars. The foundation has seen record participation in the webinars; many nonprofits are using them in their own organizations. Their grant-making process is also green. All grant seekers must submit a letter of inquiry, which is downloadable from its Web site and can be submitted by e-mail. The letter of inquiry must be printed double-sided on recycled paper, and proposals are only by invitation. The Community Foundation Web site (www.cfpbmc.org) also provides a detailed list of tips, tools, and resources for nonprofits going green.

When the Community Foundation created the Nonprofits Going Green program, it set out to be a national model for other community foundations that want to support nonprofit organizations in their greening efforts. The contest, the foundation's Web site, its own grant-making process, and the training the foundation provides are examples of its leadership efforts. However, the Community Foundation is also leading by examining itself and its greening efforts. The organization is well aware of GreenNonprofits, Inc., a nonprofit organization created to support the global movement that both educates and assists nonprofits in becoming green and to make its green certification process available to nonprofits. By April 2009, the Community Foundation had completed over 75 percent of the steps needed to be certified. Its board of directors also adopted the GreenNonprofits pledge at its spring meeting. Once the organization is certified, it plans to offer financial and technical support to nonprofits interested in going through the process as well. In a survey at the beginning of 2009, more than 92 percent of nonprofits indicated that they would like to be certified green by GreenNonprofits, Inc. More information about GreenNonprofits, Inc. and its green certification process is included in Appendix A.

## Greening Your Fundraising Events

### Traditional Fundraising Method

We have all been to them and most of us have organized them— fundraising events. There are dinners, galas, luncheons, auctions, cocktail parties, golf tournaments, and the list goes on. The fundraising event, in whatever form, is usually labor intensive and time consuming and sometimes is executed with very little reward (i.e., dollars raised). But we nonprofit leaders soldier on organizing events year after year.

Fundraising events are also quite heavy with regard to consumption and resources needs compared to other types of fundraising. Consider a gala event. A nonprofit must contract with a venue, typically a hotel or other event space. Then there is food and beverages, linens, china, lights, sound, a save-the-date mailing, invitations, gift processing, phone calling, a printed program, menu cards, awards, tables, chairs, podium, a script for the presenters, often videotaping—and the list can go on. These events often cost tens of thousands of dollars to put on. All of these requirements do not sound very green, do they?

Chapter 5 addresses all types of nonprofit-run events, including trade events, conferences, and festivals, in much greater detail. This section addresses the events nonprofit organizations run for the specific purpose of raising funds to support their mission.

## Fundraising Challenge

The challenge is quite clear: More often than not, fundraising events are wasteful and resource intensive in just about every way. Think about all the leftover food when people do not attend; the elaborate, multi-insert save-the-date cards and invitations that end up in the trash; the printed programs left on the chairs; the energy used in lighting, sound, washing dishes, and cleaning linens; the staff time executing all the contracts, gift processing, details, and follow-up needed; the travel costs of everyone getting to and from the venue. It sounds like an overwhelming list. How would you even start greening a fundraising event?

Besides the obvious use of energy and production of waste, another challenge may arise from your board of directors, staff, donors, clients, volunteers, or other constituents who may resist the event's change. If the event is successful every year, what is the incentive to make any changes? There can be a great deal of risk in altering a profitable recipe.

A final challenge may come from the vendors and venues themselves. Their operations may not incorporate a green approach. The caterer, sound and lighting company, and/or events space management might not see the value in offering organic, local foods, using energy-saving lighting, or washing linens and dishes in water-saving machines.

## Transition to a New, Green Paradigm

Alas, do not become overwhelmed and either give up or not try. The key again is transition. How can your organization transition its current fundraising events program into *a greener one*—not necessarily a green one? In theory, and it probably should be in practice as well, this transition could take place over years with each year incorporating more green techniques.

Transition over a period of years will also help with buy-in from staff, clients, donors, and volunteers who have been involved with your event in the past. Greening your event often will save on expenses that can be used as a marketing message to attract more attention—and possibly ticket sales and advertising revenue. Your organization can be seen as a leader in your community for incorporating green techniques into your fundraising event—for "being green while raising green."

With regard to your vendors, if they are longtime partners, talk to them. Similar to the approach in raising the issue with foundation and corporate grant-making funders, find out what your vendors have the interest and capability to do. Certainly they do not want to lose your business so it is in their interest to try to work with you. And unfortunately for them, if they are not willing to make the transition with you, there are many other fish—or vendors and event space—in the fundraising events sea.

*CASE STUDY:* THE ABINGTON-ROCKLEDGE DEMOCRATIC COMMITTEE    One nonprofit organization in Pennsylvania is successfully making this transition, taking it one step at a time. The Abington-Rockledge Democratic Committee (ARDC) in Abington, outside of Philadelphia, has organized a spring banquet for the past 18 years. In 2009, it wanted to start moving to a greener format. With an all-volunteer base, the ARDC knew it could not do it all at once—it was too overwhelming to make all the changes necessary to run a truly green event in just one year.

The spring banquet is a typical fundraising event held at a local country club. It is traditionally the ARDC's largest fundraising event of the year. During the formal dinner program, which typically draws about 200 people, the organization distributes a series of awards to local people in the community.

Besides its ticket sales, the spring banquet also raises money by selling advertisements in a printed program. This piece is a traditional booklet program printed in color, bound in the center, and put on every chair at the event. The program has a typical layout of information about ARDC and the honorees with advertisements from businesses and individuals on the back pages.

In 2009, the ARDC went green by eliminating the printed program altogether. It was noted in years past that, as is the case with many fundraising events, a majority of these programs were left behind, wasting paper, printing costs, staff time, and money. So the ARDC decided to take a small step with a virtual advertising program that would be projected on a white wall of the room during the event. The computer presentation used the same logos and messages that would have been printed in the program but each advertisement had its own slide or page that was displayed on the wall. The looping presentation started at the cocktail hour and continued throughout the event. It also gave the ARDC the opportunity to create pages for the award winners.

The presentation was created and organized by a volunteer, and the projector used to display it was donated in exchange for an advertisement. Following the event, the ARDC plans to send a quarterly e-mail newsletter that includes a link to the presentation. The link will be included for the next four newsletters (over the next year), so that advertisers gain exposure not only among event attendees but the wider ARDC database of supporters and constituents.

Altogether the ARDC spent zero dollars putting the presentation together, saving $1,150 from the 2008 spring banquet's printing and setup costs. The organization also raised slightly more money—bringing in $4,310 in advertising revenue in 2009 over $3,465 in 2008. Besides the obvious increase in revenue, the cost savings from not printing a program also boosted ARDC's bottom line.

# MARCEL & BERNICE GROEN
## congratulate the

ABINGTON+
ROCKLEDGE
DEMOCRATIC
COMMITTEE

## on their
# GREEN PROGRAM

―HONORING― ―EMPOWERING―
THE PAST           THE FUTURE
Spring Banquet 2009

## SUNDAY, APRIL 19, 2009

A slide from the Spring Banquet presentation: Donors congratulated the ARDC or the Virtual Green Program.

―HONORING― ―EMPOWERING―
THE PAST           THE FUTURE

## DONORS, SPONSORS, AND MATCHING SPONSORS

### DONORS

*Democratic Citizen:* State Senator LeAnna Washington
John L. Spiegelman

*Benefactors:* Steamfitters Local Union #420 • Marilyn and Martin Yarmark

*Supporters:* Michael Baurer • Joan Bachman • Alex and Belinda Glijansky • Leroy Lowenstern • Caren Moscowitz • Peter Stern and Joan Johnston-Stern

*Contributors:* Bettie and Robert Beall • Philip Chapalas, M.D. • Michael Kernicky • Lois Koff • John Oldynski • Joy Pollock • Elizabeth Smith

### SPONSORS
Joan Bachman • Anne Baumann • David Floyd • Susan and Tony LaDuca • Jeannette Maitin • Marge Sexton

### MATCHING SPONSORS
Burns, White, and Hickton
Barry Stupine

A slide from the Spring Banquet presentation: The ARDC thanked its donors and sponsors.

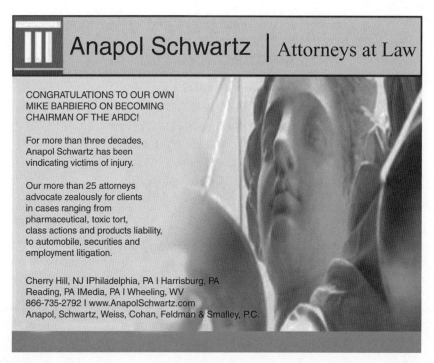

A slide from the Spring Banquet presentation: A sample paid advertisement.

The ARDC raised more money in 2009 than it had in the event's 18-year history, and it is thrilled with the results. There was no paper waste, no printing and layout costs—and the organization received no complaints about the change in program formats. In fact, people seemed to like the change. For 2010, the ARDC hopes to take the next step. It plans to make another virtual presentation for the program and a switch to organic food for the banquet.

The ARDC represents just one successful example of a transitioned approach to green fundraising events. The change was simple to make, and it saved the organization money while increasing its income. The ARDC created a plan that was easy and that its constituents approved of. The one step the organization took in 2009 helped it secure buy-in and support for the greening effort and will allow it to take further steps in the future.

## Greening Your Major/Planned Gifts Program

### Traditional Fundraising Method

Historically a major and planned gifts program is focused on developing long-term relationships with individuals who have both capacity and willingness to financially support a nonprofit organization in a significant way. What dollar amount constitutes a major gift varies from organization to organization, but typically a major or planned gift differs from an annual gift in that the gift is made through multiyear payments or by a vehicle that involves the donor's estate.

Popular methods have defined and organized the process of building and maintaining these long-term relationships in many ways, including the Five *Is* of Donor Cultivation,[8] the Donor Cultivation System,[9] and the Donor Commitment Continuum,[10] among many other techniques to cultivate individual donors for gift solicitation. Whether you are asking for a donation that provides funds now through a major gift or via a deferred plan (in the case of a planned gift), the techniques teach you and your organization to engage individuals and move them through a process whereby they become emotionally invested in your mission and want to financially invest. The stewardship or thanking process usually starts the cultivation process for future gifts.

## Fundraising Challenge

The focus of the major and planned gifts program is, however, always on building relationships through face-to-face visits. Cultivation can be supplemented with phone calls, e-mails, letters, notes, event attendance, and social media, but the most meaningful relationship development with a gift prospect occurs through in-person meetings. A development officer may bring a faculty member, an executive director, a dean, a board member, a client of the nonprofit, a colleague, or other individual(s) who can best make the case for support and/or influence a prospect at various times during the process. A conference call or even video chat online simply cannot replace the interactions of meeting face to face, nor will it in the foreseeable future.

## Transition to a New, Green Paradigm

Until we can be beamed around the world in real time, the continued strength and focus of a successful major and planned giving program is in-person meetings. How do we "green" those? How can the process of identifying potential major or planned gift donors, cultivating them, soliciting them, and stewarding them become more environmentally friendly? This section focuses on the latter three stages of this method: cultivation, solicitation and stewardship of major and planned gift donors.

The face-to-face meeting and communications leading up to and after it are the crux of the discussion in greening a major and planned gifts program. Certainly these days we have naturally moved to a greener process simply because of the technology available to e-mail, text, instant message, and otherwise just about eliminate the need for mailing letters, annual reports, and invitations and even phone calls. Use of these technologies has become standard practice and has significantly reduced costs and had a positive effect on becoming greener.

The second step then is to consider transportation. If we are committed to the in-person meeting as the most effective way to build a relationship, getting to and from these visits is the heart of the matter. Transportation is discussed in greater depth in Chapter 9; the section below describes and provides a commonsense way to reduce the carbon footprint and organizational expenses in your major and planned giving program using a personal example of streamlining transportation.

*CASE STUDY:* **UC DAVIS** Greening your major and planned giving program through car transportation can be articulated through the personal experience of my current position at the University of California, Davis (UC Davis). My colleagues and I are fortunate enough to have significant advantage in the area of transportation because the university has invested in a fleet of cars, which include many hybrid vehicles. Fleet Services, a department of the Offices of Administration, has the mission to: "Provide high-quality, efficient and cost effective services by offering safe, reliable, economical and environmentally-sound transportation and related support services that are responsive to the needs of the campus community."[11]

As a staff member of the Graduate School of Management, the Master of Business Administration program on campus, I can call, or more recently go online, and reserve a car for use when conducting official UC Davis business, such as visiting major and planned gift prospects and donors. The fleet includes both hybrid and plug-in vehicles along with traditional sedans, trucks, and vans. In fact, it so useful, convenient, and cost effective that I do not own a personal car. It costs my school less money for me to use a campus car than it does for it to pay me a per-mile rate if I used a personal vehicle.

During fiscal year 2007–2008, I used a Fleet Services car for 20 trips, for a total of 2,231 miles driven. The reimbursement rate UC Davis pays its employees for driving their personal cars for official business purposes is 58.5 cents per mile, which includes gas and maintenance. Those 20 trips then would cost $1,305.14 if I were driving my own car. By using Fleet Services, the Graduate School of Management paid just $1,198.26 in car rental and gas fees—that is a savings of nearly 9 percent. Over years of travel among many staff and faculty, the savings are significant.

In addition to saving money simply by using a campus car, my greening methods for prospect and donor visits also include requesting hybrids each time I use a car, using public transportation (Amtrak and the Bay Area Regional Transit) as much as is possible, and also "stacking" my time. This is how this method works. Davis is about 72 miles to Oakland at the north of the Bay Area, about 106 miles to San Jose at the south, and just about 105 miles to Silicon Valley farthest west. Once or twice each month, I plan one-to-two day trips into the Bay Area and "stack" my day, meaning I schedule appointments from about 10:00 A.M. through dinner. Instead of scheduling one or two appointments on many days across the month and making many trips, I schedule the meetings as closely together as possible over a short amount of time. Juggling things logistically does take some time and effort, but online map services come in handy. Traffic is always a factor to consider as well, but generally the technique is successful.

Sometimes these trips happen organically, where either I or a prospect or donor requests a meeting on a particular day and then I designate that a Bay Area day. Then I can fill up the rest of the day with other appointments or set aside multiple days and work to fill them with appointments. Being organized and knowing the area are the keys to the success of this method. Also, over time you will learn about your constituents, their likelihood of responding to your meeting request, and scheduling. For example, historically the school's alumni located in one area are not as responsive to introductory meetings; in other areas, I receive a very high response rate from alumni interested in meeting with a school representative. This information is extremely helpful when I try to "stack" a day with appointments so as not to over-schedule or disappoint potential donors (see the example in Figure 1.4).

Stacking is not a difficult technique to implement or master and may seem like common sense. However, it is a tremendously efficient and effective method to green your major and planned giving program.

| Thursday, March 5 | |
|---|---|
| 8:30am | Pick up car<br>Fleet Services, UC Davis Campus<br>Davis, CA |
| 10:00am | Meeting: School alumnus<br>Starbuck's<br>Lafayette, CA |
| 11:00am | Meeting: School alumna<br>Peet's Coffee<br>Walnut Creek, CA |
| 1:00pm | Meeting: School alumnus<br>Suisse Italia<br>San Francisco, CA |
| 4:00pm | School Event: Peer-to-Pier<br>The Waterfront Restaurant<br>San Francisco, CA |
| 8:00pm | Overnight Stay<br>Club Quarters<br>San Francisco, CA |

| Friday, March 6 | |
|---|---|
| 10:00am | Meeting: School alumnus<br>His Office<br>San Jose, CA |
| 12:00pm | Lunch, Tour and Meeting: School alumnus with Faculty<br>Blackhawk Grille<br>Danville, CA |
| 2:30pm | Return to UC Davis Campus<br>Davis, CA |

FIGURE 1.4   Example of a schedule from "stacked" two-day trip to the Bay Area.

Alas, many organizations are not large enough to support a fleet of cars, or your prospects may not live in concentrated geographic locations. Nevertheless, using your own vehicle and stacking your days for travel to locations, say, farther than 30 miles each way, can make a significant impact. The key here is, in essence, doing the best you can to be efficient in scheduling and travel. The Green Car Institute (listed in Appendix A) provides green driving tips to further assist your environmentally friendly transportation efforts.

This section would be remiss without discussing air travel. Many fundraisers working in international organizations or with prospects and donors across the globe may find it very difficult to green their major and planned giving program efforts. One could spend much time and effort greening annual fund programs, events, and even the traveling by car portion of major gift programs, and turn around and use up all the energy and pollution saved in one international flight.

Check the Carbon Fund (www.carbonfund.org) to determine your personal impact on the environment. Even if you do not fly enough to have a significantly negative impact on the environment, you can always work to reduce pollution.

The solution to air travel is a bit complicated. You cannot do a tremendous amount to green your air travel at this time. However, a few commonsense techniques can help you reduce your impact. For example, make sure to stack air travel so that a trip to Asia includes two or three stops rather than taking two or three separate trips. If you are traveling across the country for vacation or to speak at a conference, set aside time to visit with prospects and donors even for just a stewardship call.

Another effort, and maybe the most significant, is to ask whether the trip is needed in the first place. Because there are no fuel-efficient or hybrid planes, we should think twice before hopping on a plane. Many of my colleagues and donors who practice energy- and pollution-saving techniques at home tend not to have a second thought about air travel. Is it that the air travel is really necessary, or could one or two of the trips be done by e-mail, webinars, or conference calls?

I know questioning the face-to-face meeting is counter to my earlier discussion, but my point is to think before using the energy and money to fly. If you pause and decide that the trip is indeed necessary, do not feel guilty. However, if the flights can be stacked, replaced, or otherwise greened, please make that choice. Contributing to the greening of the nonprofit sector is valuable in and of itself. Transition, effort, and change are the keys.

## Conclusion

The main message of this chapter about greening your organization's fundraising efforts has been about transition. It is hoped that you and your organization will be inspired to take a step, not a leap, toward greening. As you prepare your next annual development plan, take a deeper look at one aspect of your fundraising portfolio—whether it is the annual fund, grant writing, events, or major and planned gifts. Next, think about how you and your organization can make changes toward being greener. If you do not feel confident that your organization's board of directors will embrace changes in a successful fundraising event, try looking at the annual fund program.

Could you organize an e-solicitation instead of a paper, mailed one? Could you use social media sites to motivate donors? If you are working to deepen relationships between your foundation and corporate funders but do not feel that you could broach the subject of their changing their grant process, try examining your next scheduled fundraising event. Could your organization create a virtual program or an e-invitation?

The idea is to take small steps continuously over a long period. This approach will help ensure success by creating buy-in from your constituents, allowing for changes to the course if things are not working out, and will make everyone feel in control of the process. It will also allow you and your organization time and room to communicate changes with donors, volunteers, staff, and others, to seek their input and feedback and make them feel connected to your organization. The resources in Appendix A will help you get started toward greening your fundraising program.

## About the Author

**Adrienne D. Capps** is currently the senior director of development for the Graduate School of Management at UC Davis in California. Over the past 11 years, Adrienne has raised nearly $20 million for a variety of causes, including at-risk youth, mental health, and higher education in Virginia, New York, and

California. Prior to her move to California in 2007, she served as the head of fundraising for Dyson College of Arts & Sciences at Pace University in New York City. A certified fund raising executive since 2004, Adrienne has published several articles in *Advancing Philanthropy*, the most recent of which is "Gastronomy and Giving," which discusses the unique intersection of her two passions: fundraising and food. She recently launched a company, Vintners Charitable Cooperative, where people can drink charitably by joining a wine club that gives 50% of profits to their nonprofit partners www.charityvintner.org. Adrienne also maintains a food blog, www.vegetarianized.com, and teaches cooking classes. She has been an active participant in the fundraising community, frequently speaking on the topic of green fundraising and as a member of CASE as well as the Association of Fundraising Professionals, having served on the board of directors of the Greater New York Chapter. Adrienne also serves on the board of directors and as treasurer of SWiSH, a New York City–based gay-straight alliance. She holds a B.S. in Business Administration, with honors, and B.A. in Leadership Studies from the University of Richmond, a Certificate in Fundraising Administration from New York University and an M.B.A. in Financial Management, with honors, from Pace University in New York City.

## CHAPTER 2

# The Green Bottom Line

## Glenn Croston

Nonprofits are all about making a difference in the world, working to help people and the planet we all share. They are not, however, immune from the need to spend money carefully and effectively. While their goal is advancing a cause rather than making a profit, paying attention to the bottom line is still central to accomplishing their mission. In the tight financial conditions being experienced today, close attention to a budget is more important than ever. Regardless of their mission, going green is an effective strategy for nonprofits to get more out of their money. Although many people assume that going green is an expensive proposition, greening your operations can save money, reduce overhead, and allow more money to be spent on your core mission, all while helping the environment at the same time.

This green strategy for success is not unique to nonprofits. In the for-profit world, some of the largest businesses, such as DuPont and 3M, have saved billions of dollars by making themselves more resource efficient, as related in the book *Green to Gold* by Dan Esty and Andrew Winston.[1] These savings are large enough that they could be responsible for keeping these businesses profitable.

The same methodologies that increase resource efficiency and help people do more with their money in the for-profit world can improve the bottom line in the nonprofit world. The real question is not whether you can afford to go green; the real question is whether you can afford *not* to.

## Your Budget, Before and After Greening

To look at the potential impact of going green on your organization, your budget is a useful starting point. Consider the example budget in Table 2.1 for an organization that works primarily from an office space. Whether its mission is related to the environment or not does not really matter here. What does matter is how the organization goes about pursuing its work. Many environmentally friendly choices conserve resources and save money. Some green choices can cost slightly more but increase productivity, improve your brand, increase visibility, and further demonstrate your commitment to doing the right thing, whatever your mission is.

TABLE 2.1    Example of an Operating Budget before and after Greening

| Expense | Before ($/year) | After ($/year) |
|---|---|---|
| Rent/Lease | $ 40,000 | $ 41,000 |
| Salaries | $225,000 | $250,000 |
| Advertising | $ 15,000 | $ 7,000 |
| Travel | $ 30,000 | $ 15,000 |
| Utilities | $ 7,000 | $ 4,000 |
| Cleaning Service | $ 2,000 | $ 2,200 |
| Legal | $ 10,000 | $ 10,000 |
| Meetings | $ 30,000 | $ 20,000 |
| Office supplies | $ 4,000 | $ 4,000 |
| Printing | $2 0,000 | $ 24,000 |
| Vehicle | $ 6,000 | $ 4,500 |
| Insurance | $ 4,000 | $ 3,600 |
| Total | $393,000 | $385,300 |

Every organization is different and your results may vary, but this example is a useful way to highlight the potential impact of going green. Whether they are green or not, a major expense for most groups is salaries, the cost of paying people. Green policies toward people such as providing daycare and good healthcare may increase costs but help employees become more productive, getting more done. Policies like these can also retain experienced employees, avoiding the cost of recruiting and training new employees, which is a drag on overall productivity.

Another significant expense is often the space your organization works in. Your lease may cost a bit more in a green building, but your utility bill will be lower. A green building may cost up to 2 percent more, according to the U.S. Green Building Council (USGBC), but this increased cost more than pays for itself with reduced utility bills. In some cases the utility bill in a green building can be reduced by 50 percent or more.

Additional savings may come from reduced spending on advertising and travel. Many green groups and businesses have found that they can spend less on traditional advertising than their peers by harnessing the energy of the environmental community through green events and blogs. Traveling less and using tools like Web collaboration or video conferencing for meetings saves both money and the environment.

Even the green steps that do not immediately reduce spending may build value for your group in other ways. Working with a printing business that uses eco-friendly printing methods may cost a little more but delivers a valuable message about your commitment to helping the environment. Green promotional materials contribute to your brand in a similar way. In considering the bottom line, it is important to remember that the cheapest solution may not always be the highest value answer that helps your nonprofit achieve its goals.

The rest of this chapter examines more closely opportunities like these to green your operations and the impact this will have on your bottom line, productivity, and reputation.

## Looking for Opportunities to Improve: The Green Audit

Before starting a campaign to improve the environmental impact of your nonprofit, you need to know where you stand today. A complete green audit provides this information by examining the impact your organization has on people and the planet. An audit can be performed on your own, as a self-audit, or by professionals who can visit your site to review your operations.

Do not be afraid if the audit reveals that you are not perfect. No group can realistically claim that it has no environmental impact yet. If you turn on the light switch, use water from the tap, take the bus to work, you are having an impact. It is not necessary to be perfect to green your operation as long as you are taking solid steps to make a real improvement and being honest and open about where you stand today. Having the information from a green audit can get you started on the right path. Without this information, you will not be able to tell how your environmental efforts are paying off. With the results in hand, you can target initiatives that will have the most impact for both your budget and the environment.

To be useful, the audit needs to be kept alive and repeated. Do not file the results away; rather pull them out to review frequently and stay on track. Repeat the audit at least once a year, record the results, and see how you are progressing. The more you document your eco-improvements and their impact, the more apparent their value will be, and the more motivated you and your colleagues will be to continue with these efforts.

## Green Buildings

Buildings have a massive environmental impact, consuming three-quarters of the power we produce, but they also provide an important opportunity for environmental improvement by building and retrofitting them to waste less energy, water, and other resources. Wasted energy consumed by buildings contributes to climate change, necessitating greater use of coal-fired power plants. Wasted energy also wastes money year after year, draining resources that could be spent more productively elsewhere. The buildings we work in also can affect our health with potentially hazardous chemicals, such as formaldehyde, released into the air.

Although people often assume that green buildings must be very expensive, the initial cost of green buildings is just 0 to 2 percent higher than other buildings according to the U.S. Green Building Council (USGBC).[2] Investment in energy efficiency in green buildings often pays for itself through greatly reduced utility costs, slashing energy costs by 50 percent or more. The greener the building, the lower the power bill will be for the life of the building.

For nonprofits that have an environmental focus, taking up residence in a green building can also make a strong statement to the world about their mission, reaffirming their commitment to the environment.

What makes a building green? The definition of green can be murky, but when it comes to green buildings, certification standards such as the LEED system (Leadership in Energy and Environmental Design) of the USGBC have set clear criteria for what makes buildings green. LEED scores buildings in categories such as location, energy efficiency, water use, and materials used. The more points scored, the higher the LEED rating a building can earn, from Silver, Gold, to the highest level, Platinum.

Some of the features of green buildings that certification standards look for include:

- Greater use of natural sunlight for indoor lighting.
- Use of lighting control systems that automatically turn off lights when they are not needed.
- Energy-efficient lighting, delivering more light with less heat and wasted energy.
- Better insulation for buildings and a better building envelope, saving energy for heating and cooling.
- Passive ventilation for cooling and air exchange.
- Energy-efficient windows and shading.
- Use of building materials that are sustainably produced and that do not release hazardous materials into the indoor air environment.
- Water conservation fixtures.
- Greater comfort, due to improved environmental control.
- Renewable energy production, such as from solar panels on the rooftop.
- Cool roofs or green roofs, cutting down on air-conditioning needs.
- Locating near mass transit.
- Accommodations for bike riding.
- Space for recycling bins.

Many of these features are good for the environment and save money. Not everyone can buy or construct a brand-new green building, though, and new building construction is only a small part of the story compared to the millions of existing buildings that are less efficient than they need to be. To meet this challenge, the USGBC has created LEED for Existing Buildings: Operations and Maintenance to certify how existing buildings are used by their occupants to improve energy efficiency and reduce waste. Energy Star is another certification standard for buildings, focused on energy efficiency.

Certification is an easy way to measure and verify the green steps taken in buildings, but it is not the only way to go. Not every green building gets certified; many building owners take steps to improve efficiency on their own, without certification. And whether a building is certified or not, anyone can implement easy, low-cost steps such as changing the thermostat, adding weather-stripping, and changing light bulbs.

One of the challenges for leases in buildings with other tenants is that the connection between who conserves energy and who pays the bill is not always clear. In a traditional lease, the landlord owns the buildings and all of the improvements made to it while those leasing the space pay the utilities. Often neither party is very motivated to make changes. One solution is a green lease that creates incentives to encourage efficiency for everyone involved. Wendel, Rosen, Black & Dean is a law firm in Oakland, California, that is pioneering green leases to change this situation. Aleka Eisentraut, a lawyer with Wendel, advises consulting with a lawyer before signing a letter of intent for a lease, particularly a green lease, since they are quite specialized.

## Lighting

One important energy cost is lighting, accounting for about 35 percent of the electricity bill in commercial buildings. A great deal can be done to save money with more efficient lighting. The potential for savings through increased efficiency is so great that governments around the world are phasing out the use of incandescent light bulbs in favor of more efficient lighting solutions, such as compact fluorescent bulbs and light-emitting diodes (LEDs). Changing light bulbs is one of the lowest of the low-hanging fruits, saving energy and money for only a few dollars a bulb. One of the benefits of more efficient lighting is that it generates less waste heat, saving money on air conditioning as well. To encourage more efficient lighting, the U.S. government has passed legislation requiring the phasing out of inefficient incandescent bulbs starting in 2012. Other governments around the world are also taking action to phase out incandescent bulbs in favor of more efficient technologies, including the European Union, Australia, and Brazil.

Introducing natural light into a business area with skylights, solar tubes, or other means can pay for itself through reduced energy costs. The more natural lighting can be used, the less electricity is needed.

Another strategy is to turn the lights off when they are not needed. Changing behavior to remember to switch off the lights is one way to accomplish this. Another method is making the process automatic by installing timers or occupancy sensors from companies like Wattstopper or Leviton to turn lights off automatically when nobody is around. Some building codes, such as Title 24 in California, now require the use of occupancy sensors in new commercial construction or remodeled buildings. Their cost ranges from about $30 to $100 per light switch. They are easy to install and reduce energy use up to 45 percent. For help with your lighting, consult with experts such as EnvironmentalLighting.com, to get the lighting solution with the highest quality and value.

## Heating and Cooling

Heating and cooling are also important expenses. According to the U.S. Department of Energy,[3] commercial buildings spend about 40 to 60 percent of their energy bills on heating, ventilation, and air conditioning. When it comes to heating and cooling, the low-hanging fruits to save money and energy include sealing the building envelope, taking care of weather-stripping, sealing cracks, and improving insulation. Fixing air ducts can be a surprisingly easy and cost-effective fix; air ducts frequently leak 30 percent or more of the air going through them, meaning that sealing the ducts can reduce your heating or cooling bill by 30 percent. Insulation, preferably with an eco-friendly material, can also produce a surprisingly large impact on your utility bill.

The opportunities to save money do not stop there. Additional ways to save money on heating or cooling includes installing fans, using window shades to block the sun, and changing filters in your air-conditioning system. Adjusting your thermostat higher in summer and lower in winter by a few degrees is an easy way to save money and energy. It is hard to please everyone, but changing the thermostat even two to three degrees can save money without producing a big change in the general comfort level. Also, changing your thermostat to a programmable digital version helps automatically to turn off the heat at night or on weekends so you do not have to.

Many of these steps pay for themselves quickly through reduced energy bills and continue producing savings for years down the road. Although the initial expense required for insulation or more efficient air conditioning can deter businesses or nonprofits, an increasing variety of grants and loans are available to encourage these changes. One place to look for money to fund energy-efficiency projects is your local utility, many of which have extensive programs to encourage and support such improvements. A variety of grants and loans are also available from state governments, and the Database of State Incentives for Renewables & Efficiency (DSIRE) database located at www.dsireusa.org lists more about these for every state. The economic stimulus package approved by Congress in February 2009 includes a variety of measures to encourage energy efficiency, including block grants being distributed to local and state governments (see recovery.gov).

## Saving Money by Saving Water

Water is increasingly precious in many parts of the world, and as populations grow and the climate changes, this trend is likely to continue. Many people already lack sufficient water, and the United Nations estimates that by 2030, half of the world's people will live in areas without sufficient water.[4] Many nonprofits are focused on helping the world's people deal with this important issue, so taking steps in your own facility to use water wisely sends a message in tune with these efforts as well as saving money.

Fixing water leaks is a low-cost place to start saving water. A leaky faucet or toilet may not seem like a big deal, but a steady drip from a leaky faucet can waste thousands of gallons a year. Stepping the conservation measures up further, consider installing low-flow toilets or waterless urinals. Landscaping is another big drain on water. If you are selecting a space to lease or have your own landscaping to take care of, look for drought-tolerant plants from the Mediterranean, Australia, or South Africa or your local region. Change your irrigation schedule, the type of sprinkler heads you use, and the timing for your watering schedule.

## Transportation

Transportation is one of the largest contributors to global climate change as well as to causing pollution. It costs a great deal of money to move goods and people around the globe, making the travel budget a target for both saving money and helping the planet. Whatever your motivations are, traveling less and traveling more efficiently will squeeze more out of your budget.

One transportation expense is vehicles that your nonprofit buys, if any. If a car is needed, small used cars can save fuel with increased efficiency and save money on both initial outlay and operating expenses. Used cars can provide a great value, driving more consumers to go with used vehicles as the economy has tightened. Used cars also have the eco-advantage of not using any new resources in production, unlike new cars.

Looked at more broadly, the environmental impact of your group includes not just the direct impact while working but the environmental impact employees have while commuting. The choice for commuting is up to the employee, but businesses or nonprofits can encourage environmentally friendly choices without spending a lot of money. Encouraging ridesharing with a business like PickupPal (www.pickuppal.com) is one way to do this, helping both employees and nonprofits without costing a business anything. PickupPal helps to match up those who need rides with others who can give them, including those who want to share a ride to work in the morning. Started in Canada, PickupPal is now also found in a growing list of cities in the United States, Australia, the United Kingdom, and New Zealand. PickupPal also works to green transportation to events in the same way.

"In these economic times, providing a carpooling option can boost employee productivity, making it easier and more cost effective to get to work," said Brent Drewry, executive vice president of business development at PickupPal. Joining with PickupPal is one way for groups to achieve progress toward sustainability goals they report, helping to measure environmental impacts for groups that sign up.

Other than biking or walking, the greenest commuting option is staying home and collaborating at a distance by telecommuting. More and more the workplace has less to do with having people sit in a room together and more about assembling teams of high-quality people who can collaborate and innovate together no matter where they are located. Employees appreciate the lack of a commuting hassle, and a nonprofit can benefit from less need for office space

Air travel has a large environmental impact but at times it is necessary. To reduce the impact of air travel that cannot be avoided, you can buy offsets from Terrapass (www.Terrapass.com), Nativeenergy (www.nativeenergy.com), or Carbonfund (www.carbonfund.org). Offsets provide the means to indirectly reduce greenhouse gas emissions from somewhere else in the world, funding such projects as methane capture from dairy farms or landfills. The cost of offsets can be surprisingly small—less than $12 for a round trip from Los Angeles to New York, for example. This is less than the luggage fee many airlines are charging now, or lunch in the airport. Third-party verification of offset projects ensures that a real reduction in greenhouse gas emissions is produced.

## Meetings and Events

Greening events and meetings can save money and help make events successful. Professionals like Midori Connolly, chief executive and founder of Pulse Staging and Events in San Diego, can make this happen. Reducing the impact of events is a growing field, in part because of the opportunity to save money. "There is undoubtedly a business case for greening events," Connolly said, suggesting close review of venue selection, transportation, food and beverage, office procedures, and communications. "Generally a budget must be more closely monitored and each dollar maximized.

"Think carefully about the site you choose," said Connolly. Minimizing transportation to and from the meeting helps to reduce the environmental impact. "Venues situated at or very near airports are an ideal choice. Most airport hotels are willing to negotiate more on pricing for meetings and events."

When arranging the event, guests may expect organic food, but there are ways of providing this without busting your budget. "When choosing menus, work with the caterer to source seasonal, organic ingredients locally," said Connolly. "Rather than individually wrapped meals, use tray-passed or buffet where possible. Finger foods and/or sandwiches eliminate the expense of cutlery altogether."

Reducing waste can also save money. "One study showed that collecting name badge holders for reuse at an event of 1,300 attendees can save approximately $975 for the event organizer," Connolly said.

When organizing a green meeting offsite, you can look for a green hotel as a venue. Hotels can have a surprisingly large environmental footprint, but a growing number of hotels are saving money and attracting business by going green. Kit Cassingham, who has many years of experience as an environmental consultant to the hotel industry, has assembled a database of over 3,800 green hotels around the world to search for a venue (environmentallyfriendlyhotels.com).

For consulting on green hospitality and hotels, you can contact Cassingham at www.sageblossom.com.

## Reduce, Reuse, Recycle

You might not be a regular Dumpster diver, but looking through your trash can reveal opportunities to reduce waste and save money. Whatever is in the Dumpster is by definition a waste, something you paid for once when you first bought it and then paid for again to have the waste disposal company haul it away.

The easiest and most obvious items to recycle are cans and bottles with a deposit or redemption value. You can save hundreds of dollars a year easily by saving these bottles and returning them. In the absence of a recycling program, they could easily end up in the trash, throwing away money.

Buying water in disposable plastic bottles is a big eco no-no these days because of the resources consumed in the production of bottled water as well as its transportation. An easy alternative to bottled water is water from filtration devices offered by businesses such as AquaPure4Me (aquapure4me.com) to eliminate waste and provide cool, clean water. A system like this can also save money, avoiding the cumulative cost of large numbers of water bottles purchased each year.

In addition to recycling and reusing materials, you can reduce waste by not using something in the first place. Use hand towels instead of paper towels, and use mugs, plates, and cups instead of disposable kitchenware. The disposable stuff may sound cheaper at first, but the cost of disposable items adds up easily to hundreds of dollars, even in a small organization.

Reducing your quantity of mailings is a big opportunity to help both the bottom line and the environment. I routinely receive bulky bulk mailings from environmental nonprofits, a practice that seems counterproductive. Electronic delivery and personalized contact may be a better way to go, wasting fewer of your resources and acting in a manner more consistent with your mission.

## Human Capital

In addition to saving money by wasting less, another way to go green and improve your budget is by increasing productivity, getting more out of each dollar you spend. The people in your group are your most valuable resource to boost productivity. According to Jim Hartzfeld of InterfaceRAISE, going green engages employees, improves retention, and helps recruit high-quality talent, all of which increases productivity. Attracting and energizing people who are excited about your mission and its impact on the environment can produce much more value out of your tight budget without increasing costs.

The question is not just what workers cost or how they add to overhead. Employees add value, and the more engaged they are, the more innovative and productive they are. Thinking of employees not just as costs or overhead but as the key to productivity helps to unlock their true potential.

Several steps can be taken in human capital policies to go green on a budget without sacrificing productivity:

- Be flexible about work hours.
- Provide good medical benefits.
- Consider telecommuting, where appropriate.
- Listen to employees.
- Encourage participation in community events.
- Encourage exercise.
- Provide healthy snack options.
- Encourage transparency and openness in communications.
- Encourage green efforts within your company.
- Avoid too much hierarchy.
- Provide educational support and training.
- Invite employees to participate in "green teams," committees of employees who want to get involved in greening the workplace.

Human capital is also found in people everywhere, not just in your employees. In executing your mission, whether it is environmental or not, looking at your impact on people globally is one aspect of greening your nonprofit.

When talking about the human element, it is also important to remember the value of getting buy-in from people throughout the organization. Getting buy-in can make the difference between having a successful transformation of your whole organization to perform in a more environmentally sensitive manner, or not. Although people generally are inherently receptive to doing the right thing for the planet, they also are busy and may have many of the common misconceptions about what going green means, such as the idea that going green is always hard and expensive. Forming a green team helps get others involved, and brings in more great ideas for how best to implement green projects.

## Green Cleaning

To green your operations, you can reach out to work with businesses that provide green services, solidifying your green brand. If you need insurance, why not partner with a green insurance provider? You need a bank, so why not deposit your money with a green bank, helping other green businesses and communities in the process? Doing so also can provide powerful connections, helping you plug into the community of green businesses in your local area and in the rest of the world. Green cleaning is an easy place to start.

Conventional cleaning products can seem cheap but come with a hidden cost. The chemicals they contain may affect the health of cleaning workers and others as well as affect the environment. The health impact can lead to lost work and lost productivity. Although people assume that green cleaning products are expensive, their cost is decreasing as they compete with more traditional products. In addition, green cleaning products avoid the negative health impacts of other products and may improve productivity as a result.

Hiring a green cleaning service like Ecoclean Services in San Diego can take care of green cleaning for you, providing an alternative to traditional cleaning services. As the owner of Ecoclean Services, Carrie Cortazzo provides cleaning that helps the environment, buildings, and the people who work in them. "Eco-friendly products are not harmful to pets or human health while conventional cleaners do cause problems over time to our skin and lungs," Cortazzo said. The cost of a green cleaning service is about the same or slightly higher than for conventional cleaning, Cortazzo reports.

## Green Insurance

Businesses of all types have risks and require insurance, and nonprofits are not any different in this respect. Green Business Insurance (GreenBusinessInsurance.com) is an independent insurance agency run by Pat Thompson of Dublin, Ohio, providing insurance for nonprofits as well as for-profit businesses. When Thompson looks at the insurance industry, he sees it as one of the industries with the most to lose with climate change and the most to gain by encouraging green alternatives. "We really need to get a handle on this," said Thompson. He believes that green businesses present a lower risk in many ways, and he works with underwriters to translate that lower risk into lower costs by brokering better insurance policies. "The insurance industry has everything to gain by giving businesses and individuals an incentive to reduce carbon emissions and reduce waste," said Thompson.

## Clean Energy

Although almost everyone knows that solar power is clean and green, most people also think that it is expensive. But the benefits are not just for the planet. Solar can also save you money, and no matter how you feel about hugging trees, most people like saving money. Depending on where you live, the power from solar panels can be cheaper than what you pay your utility. Many states have extensive solar incentive programs, and with expanded federal tax credits for renewable energy passed by the U.S. Congress in October 2008, solar will be cost effective in more states than ever before.

Like most solar power providers, SolarCity sells panels and installation services to homes or businesses, but it also offers an alternative to paying cash for photovoltaic systems. As another option, SolarCity maintains ownership of the panels and sells customers the power they produce on a per-kilowatt-hour basis in an arrangement called a power purchase agreement. In addition to installing the panels, SolarCity monitors and maintains the systems it installs to ensure that they keep working. The clients SolarCity works with are not just green businesses; they include a broad spectrum of enterprises as well as schools, churches, and other groups.

The power purchase agreements for businesses do not require any money up front and can help businesses save some money immediately and more money in the future. "They are small savings," said Lyndon Rive, chief executive of SolarCity in Foster City, California, "but if you have a choice of clean power versus dirty power, and you save money as well, then people will sign up." The locked-in rate can be lower than what customers pay their utility today, particularly in certain states on the East Coast and California. While utility rates are predicted to continue increasing on average 6 percent in the years ahead, the rate with SolarCity increases only 3.5 to 3.9 percent annually, depending on the region. As time passes and the cost differential increases, the savings grow larger.

## Carbon Offsets

There is a broad range of steps you can take to reduce your environmental impact, but you probably will not be able to eliminate it altogether. For those with more aggressive environmental goals, doing better by reducing their environmental impact is not enough. They want to go all the way to zero, having no negative impact on the environment. After adopting all possible energy efficiency steps, businesses and other groups can use carbon offsets as a low-cost means to reduce their carbon footprint all the way to zero.

Carbon offsets are an indirect way to reduce greenhouse gas emissions by paying someone else to reduce theirs. If I need to fly on an airplane from Los Angeles to Boston and cannot avoid the trip, I can pay a farmer to collect the manure from his pigs and ferment it into methane that is captured. (If you did not pay the farmer to do this, and the manure produced methane on its own that escapes into the atmosphere, the methane contributes to climate change.) The net result is the same as if I had not flown, offsetting the impact of flying on the plane or any other climate change impact I might be responsible for.

Terrapass provides offsets for a wide variety of for-profit and nonprofit groups to eliminate the impact of air travel, vehicle fleets, buildings, commuting, or other activities. The cost of offsets from Terrapass per ton of carbon dioxide avoided is $13.12 currently, and the more you can reduce your greenhouse gas emissions with other efforts such as energy efficiency, the fewer offsets you need to become carbon neutral.

Offsets will cost a small amount of money, but the question is not just what they cost. You also need to consider what they are worth. As a sign of your deep commitment to fighting important issues like climate change, offsets can provide real value and attract donors.

## Green Printing

The United States consumes 85 million tons of paper products each year, according to Your Green Guide to Living (greenyour.com/office). There is a great deal you can do to change this, such as using less paper, using recycled paper, and using Forest

Stewardship Council (FSC)–certified paper products. Recycled paper is available with up to 100 percent post-consumer content, and at a price only slightly higher (about 5 to 10 percent higher in some cases) than conventional paper from virgin material. Recycled paper also works well for all printers today, despite the assumption many have that recycled paper does not work as well.

For print jobs that you send out to a service, greener printing services provide an alternative to the bigger name chain stores. Dave Michaels directs sales and marketing for Ecoprint (www.ecoprint.com), based in Washington, DC. Ecoprint gets its power from wind, in addition to being carbon neutral and using recycled and FSC-certified paper and low-impact inks for a wide range of printing services. He finds that the cost of green printing depends on the job but is generally within 5 to 10 percent of what other printers charge.

Another green printing option—the greenest option—is to avoid printing when possible. Handling documents electronically is a step in the right direction in this regard. Think about reports and whether they really need to be printed at all. The less you print, the more you save trees and money.

## Green Bank

Although working with a bank is necessary, not every bank is the same when it comes to providing services and holding your deposits. With branches in Oregon and Washington, ShoreBank Pacific is a community bank that supports sustainable businesses and the communities they reside in. To ShoreBank Pacific, helping to build sustainable businesses is the right thing for the people who live in the community. Its mission is closely aligned with that of many nonprofits. By putting money in "Eco-deposits," their customers know that that the money is helping communities and green businesses. Eco-deposits are competitive bank accounts with all of the services you would normally find at a bank but with the added benefit of knowing that your deposited money is being put to good use by the bank in their community. While they lend primarily in their local region, their depositors come from a wide range of locations, attracted to working with a bank aligned with their own values. When you work with a bank like ShoreBank Pacific, you can support other green businesses with your deposits, knowing that this essential service is also helping others fulfill their own dreams of helping the environment and local economies.

## Green Computing

Computers are everywhere in the workplace today, and so is their environmental impact. Computers can help businesses save money by replacing business travel with Web conferencing. By increasing worker productivity, they can allow a business to get more done with fewer resources overall. Computers themselves use a surprising amount of energy, though, and the mountains of obsolete computers and monitors filling storage spaces create a massive environmental headache. Luckily, there are straightforward ways to reduce the environmental impact of computers, including those in the office, and the impact your Web site has on computing.

No matter what the mission of your nonprofit is, you probably have at least one or two computers involved in it. Your computers may not look like energy hogs, but they waste a surprising amount of energy and resources. According to the Web site for Climate Savers Computing Initiative (www.climatesaverscomputing.org/), "In a typical desktop PC, nearly half the power coming out of the wall is wasted and never reaches the processor, memory, disks or other components." A typical desktop PC will use over 100 watts of power. This costs nonprofit organizations as well as the planet.

The trick is finding simple, low-cost ways to use computers more efficiently with less of an environmental impact. There are several ways to use less energy, reduce e-waste (discarded electronic hardware such as PCs and monitors), and reduce the carbon footprint without sacrificing the power of computing to move your business forward. Activating hibernation can save $60 a year (Climate Savers Computing Website) for a computer. Buying energy-efficient PCs may cost a little more than other computers but save money in one to two years. One way to find more efficient PCs is to look for the Energy Star label. Energy Star–rated computers use 15 to 25 percent less energy than other computers. Laptops usually consume less power than desktops. Another place to find a greener PC is at www.EPEAT.net, the Green Electronics Council. The council evaluates computers from major manufacturers using environmental criteria and gives products a ranking of gold, silver, and bronze based on their environmental impact.

## Green Offices

No matter what the mission of your nonprofit is, you still use office supplies, often in significant quantities. These supplies include paper, pens, ink cartridges, coffee, binders, and many other items. The environmental impact, or the cost, of one pen or one package of paper is tiny, but with millions of pens, the impact adds up. Businesses like The Green Office (www.thegreenoffice.com) help to green this aspect of your efforts and in doing so add another piece to the greening of your overall efforts and image.

There are many preconceptions about green office products, such as the belief that green products are always a great deal more expensive compared to other products or that they do not work as well, but this is not necessarily the case. "Depending on the product, the price of a green alternative compared to its conventional counterpart will range from being slightly cheaper to slightly more expensive," said Jesse Gibbs of The Green Office. "For instance, a remanufactured toner cartridge is greener than a new one since materials are being reused, and it costs significantly less. One hundred percent post-consumer recycled copy paper, another popular green product, will typically cost 10 to 25 percent more than paper with no recycled content."

And as for the assertion that "green products do not work as well"? "This is a common misconception," said Gibbs. "Green office products work just as well as their conventional counterparts. The average person would not be able to tell if a given document was printed on 100 percent post-consumer recycled paper using remanufactured toner versus conventional paper with a new toner cartridge. Green products have come a long way in the past few years and are now just as functional as their conventional counterparts."

Office supplies are not a big budget item for most small businesses or nonprofits, so greening your office supplies will not have a big impact on your budget. As a visible sign of your commitment, however, they can add value to the rest of your efforts as well.

If you find the idea of greening your office overwhelming, you can get help with the job by working with eco-consultants from a business like Green Irene. Green Irene Eco-Consultants can come to your office and provide the Green Office Makeover, with detailed recommendations for the low-cost steps to reduce your environmental footprint (http://greenofficemakeover.com).

## Promotion and Publicity

Who has not gone to a conference and come home with pens, mugs, shirts, and other promotional gear? These promotional items are a good way to raise awareness of your business or organization but they could pose a dilemma. Although your organization can benefit from promotion, your image could be damaged if the promotional items hurt the environment. To solve this, companies such as Proforma Simonetta Freelance (www.proformagreen.com) and Eco Imprints (www.ecoimprints.com) provide promotional items that are greener than other promotional items, including shirts from organic cotton, soy candles, and pens made of recycled material. One benefit of these promotional items is not just what they are made of but the fact that often they are better made and will last longer. A durable promotional product will have a much more favorable impact than a cheaply made, ungreen pen or key chain that quickly falls apart.

Green business leaders such as Gary Hirshberg, CE-Yo of Stonyfield Farm, have pioneered creative steps to spread the message of their business while on a tight budget. In his book *Stirring It Up: How to Make Money and Save the World*, Hirshberg describes the innovative ways they have connected with customers, ensuring their loyalty.[5] This connection is often called "the handshake," that moment when a lasting connection is made. For Hirshberg, the handshake was often a literal one while giving out samples. For your nonprofit, the handshake may take some other form.

Rather than sending out mass mailings, a fairly nongreen activity, think about electronic ways of connecting or how to make more connections in the local community directly at events and meetings. In his book *The Gort Cloud: The Invisible Force Powering Today's Most Visible Green Brands*, Richard Seireeni provides a series of valuable case studies of how green entrepreneurs have connected with their markets.[6] As Seireeni describes how Seventh Generation, Green Key Real Estate, ShoreBank Pacific, Earth Friendly Moving, and others have spread their message, a common thread emerges in their stories. One is the importance of having someone who gets out and tells their story. Another common element is how they tell it.

As much as possible, these green entrepreneurs are out actively and directly connecting with people. To achieve broader visibility, they are actively using the power of the interconnected green community. Whether people work in for-profit green businesses or nonprofits, they all share a common interest in doing the right thing for the world. They are receptive to messages that are in alignment with this. When you have a message about how you are greening what you do in your nonprofit, they love to hear about it, blog about it, Facebook about it, and Twitter about it. Such publicity takes some work on your part but can be an invaluable asset.

## Conclusion

All of these green steps help the environment and can help your nonprofit, although they also come with varying price tags to get started, effort, impact on productivity, and impact on brand. Some of these changes are easy to implement and can save money quickly, such as replacing inefficient light bulbs with more energy-efficient lighting. Other changes, such as replacing your furnace or air conditioning, require more of an investment. Changes such as fixing air ducts save money, but since they are hidden away in the walls, they probably do not have a large impact on your overall reputation or brand. Highly visible green steps, such as a green building, events, or printed materials you distribute, are central to your image. Greening these brings value by greening your overall brand.

It might seem unusual to describe brand value of nonprofits, but the term is applicable here. A nonprofit's brand is an overall perception of what your organization has to offer the world, and greening this brand by taking steps like these can attract more attention, increase your positive perception, and attract greater funding. For nonprofits, your brand is inevitably tied to how well you communicate your mission and how effectively you carry out your mission. Greening your nonprofit can help accomplish both of these.

In the end, providing for sustainable living on our planet is a universal concern, but this does not mean we must abandon other pursuits. Whatever our work is, wherever we work, we can integrate the environment into our work lives and benefit from it. Nonprofits are an important part of our economy and our society, and an important part of environmental solutions. By implementing measures such as those described in this chapter, nonprofits can help themselves, and by helping themselves they can do a better job of helping us all.

### About the Author

**Glenn Croston** is the author of *75 Green Businesses You Can Start to Make Money and Make a Difference* (Entrepreneur Press, 2008), describing green business opportunities for people from almost any background to pursue. Through talks and workshops, he opens the door to green for people from many backgrounds. He is also the expert blogger on green business for Fast Company and the founder of Starting Up Green (www.StartingUpGreen.com), helping green entrepreneurs with resources, business listings, strategies, and opportunities to succeed. His most recent book, *Starting Green* (Entrepreneur Press, 2009), is a how-to guide for green entrepreneurs, laying out the path to start and build a profitable business that does the right thing for the planet.

## CHAPTER 3

# Developing a Green Management and Employee Plan

## Matthew Bauer

## Overview

> Sustainability . . . is not an individual property but a property of an entire web of relationships. It always involves a whole community. This is the profound lesson we need to learn from nature. The way to sustain life is to build and nurture community. A sustainable human community interacts with other communities—human and nonhuman—in ways that enable them to live and develop according to their nature. Sustainability does not mean that things do not change. It is a dynamic process of co-evolution rather than a static state.
>
> —Fritjof Capra

This quote from the best-selling author of *The Tao of Physics* and *The Web of Life* and the cofounder of the Center for Ecoliteracy in Berkeley, California, sums up both the complexity and opportunity facing nonprofits considering building and managing a comprehensive green management and employee plan.

What is "green"? Define what makes an organization "green." Interview 100 people passing by on a street corner and you will most likely get 100 distinctly different answers, but all the answers most likely will share many common themes and threads. From these common threads come two distinct categories, the environment and social justice, and from these two categories will emanate the essence of planning, implementation, and ongoing monitoring of your green management and employee plan. The reasoning behind the evolution of these two categories coming to symbolize "green" in the organization is that, when looking at the environment and sustainability, the human element is intrinsic to any efforts to green self, family, community, an organization, or the world. Focusing on one without the other will only cause any plan to be hollow and without meaning. For instance, how silly is it to have a top-notch internal environmental plan for an organization whose employees have no benefits, whose hiring practices are biased, that does not participate in its community in a positive way, and whose view of social justice is not on a plane with its environmental commitment? This realization and dynamic is sweeping

41

both in for-profits and nonprofits, as the calls for transparency and holistic practices become more the norm.

In fact, the lines are blurring between for-profit and nonprofit models, with terms such as "social enterprise" and "social entrepreneur" becoming commonplace. Minus the relatively few lines of tax code and some compliance rules, the core difference between nonprofits and companies tends to be much more in the soul and how they see themselves as well as their relationship and role in society. Dating back to the early 1980s, through early pioneers such as Green America (formerly Co-Op America), the Social Venture Network, and Business for Social Responsibility, business began a process of looking inward as well as outward to its effects on the environment and society. Although there is no need or platform to debate which category has more or less commitment to a better world, many companies large and small have an official process of looking inward to at least their internal environmental policies and efforts; many nonprofits, however, even the most ardent environmental nonprofits, do not publish their internal/organizational environmental impacts, goals, and progress.

This is a great opportunity and goes to the core purpose of this book, providing a road map and categorical assistance for the nonprofit to establish, hone, or further commit to a comprehensive environmental plan that is inclusive and that can be reported on and accurately measured.

With many nonprofits morphing more and more into businesslike activities, the timing could not be better to address the development of a green management and employee plan, especially by looking at the best-of-breed concepts and structures from both for-profit and nonprofit sectors.

There are not much data out in the public domain, nor a complete playbook as to how to implement a green management plan and employee plan (the green plan), and surely it differs from somewhat to a great deal for each organization. Nevertheless, there are models out there, such as the Green Nonprofit Audit (Chapter 17) developed by Ted Hart and the Friends of the Earth Scotland, that serve as great starting points for any nonprofit. As there are many common elements of the green plan that cut across any type of organization, we can and will look in this chapter to both for-profits and nonprofits for examples to follow. We also will examine case studies of both to provide real-world examples of where organizations are inspiring change and putting significant results on the board.

So many elements are interchangeable whether the organization is a corporation or a nonprofit that we will study and learn from both in this chapter as examples of how to create the ideal blueprint for nonprofits to follow. When looking at designing, implementing, and managing the green plan, it can be divided into the tactical (how to, context), human (buy in, motivation, continuity), and elemental (measurement, impact).

One of the keys to success is effective partnering. Partnerships are key for many reasons. In the for-profit sector companies have to be careful about colluding, sharing data, and appearing to rub up against anti-trust rules; in the nonprofit world anti-trust rules do not apply and it is actually in the nonprofit's best interest to collude, collaborate, and share data on common goals. Reduce G&A as much as possible by either replicating or sharing resources and practices with other non-profits. In this model, the community and village helps its own—whether regional or in the same sector or both, there are always lessons, mistakes, and successes to be learned from other nonprofits, and creating and managing the Green Plan should be no exception. One of the best examples of nonprofit collaboration and community sharing is the NetHope Consortium (www.nethope.org), which we discuss in greater detail in the section titled "Phase One: Developing the Green Plan."

Transparency is another key to success—as you begin to put the lens on your organization and its operations, it only begs that you keep opening and widening the lens. As noted by Jeffrey Hollender, chief executive officer of Seventh Generation: "By exposing problems, transparency begins to solve them. When a company begins to make itself transparent, it essentially conducts an unblinking audit of all its activities."[1] It only follows that when formulating the green plan, input from all stakeholders is crucial as the organization must solicit feedback from employees, its board, its funders, suppliers, and general community.

That which is measured is improved. Just as important as any of these keys to success is proper reporting and measurement, which is critical to transparency and buy-in from all stakeholders. One way to accomplish this is to weave the green plan into existing annual reporting and/or into its own report. Once goals are set, it is imperative that progress be demonstrated and highlighted at least annually by category, explicitly stating the goal and progress made that year or for the period of time. Otherwise, the green plan will appear hollow and not become a long-term part of the organization day to day.

Developing an impactful and lasting green management and employee plan requires nothing less than that the organization perform a complete soul search. As the areas of environmental and social justice have morphed and lines have blurred, a proper plan must account for both people and the planet. As they are linked in nature, so are they linked in nonprofit and corporate management.

Meaningful programs are both ground up and require the buy-in and participation of all levels of the organization; otherwise, any program will most likely look and feel like window dressing. Developing this type of management plan is an opportunity to define and codify the soul of the organization. What do we really stand for? What are our priorities? What programs and practices will we adopt and work toward to define us and our mission? The most successful programs involve regular participation from everyone in the organization as well as constant adjusting, measurement (remember, *that which is measured is improved!*), and regular messaging as to progress areas and opportunities.

But focus is everything. Search and find that one thing in your organization that represents your essence and revolve the green plan around it. While most thoughts of greening an organization go to simple changes, such as reduction in paper, water, and energy use or recycling, it is far more complex because of the human factor. It is just unrealistic and very difficult to be fighting for a cause or set of causes, and to advocate environmentally responsible practices and programs, and not give equal or more weight to the human capital in the organization, as well as consideration of all external stakeholders as part of a comprehensive program.

The three areas of concentration in this chapter are: Phase One: Developing the Green Plan; Phase Two: Implementation of the Green Plan; and Phase Three: Ongoing Management, Measurement, and Improvement. The chapter focuses heavily on Phase One as that is where the soul-searching, planning, development, and actual creation occur. Phases Two and Three are much more tactical, comprised mostly of plan execution, tweaking, measuring, and reporting. Examples and success stories, of both for-profit and nonprofit organizations, are interspersed throughout and can be used guides and benchmarks for implementing some of the techniques and topics featured in the chapter.

## Phase One: Developing the Green Plan

### Development Planning

Each organization should strive to find a unique and passionate way to approach developing its green plan. Let us focus on the general areas and some success stories regarding the main concepts mentioned earlier in this chapter, as opposed to a connect-the-dots approach. We give each organization artistic license to craft the green plan that works for it specifically instead of trying to shoehorn itself into someone else's plan. As we have seen in countless cases, especially in nongovernmental organization (NGO) circles, this concept does not work toward creating lasting value. The time spent and invested in the up-front planning and development cycle is crucial to long-term success. This phase of the process is by far the most time intensive, but it is a real opportunity to almost reinvent the organization with new ideas around 360-degree participation, democracy in the workplace, creating meaningful and tangible environmental impacts, and new partnerships that could end up bearing fruit in unforeseen ways down the road.

### Environmental Checklist and Planning

When gauging your organization's pure environmental impact, a great starting point is to consider a comprehensive checklist, such as the GreenNonprofits Certification and Registration form, available at www.greennonprofits.org/greening (see Figure 3.1).

As an example, the GreenNonprofits form is an exhaustive list of the areas of impact that your plan should include in the formation stages. We will return to the form in more detail as we discuss certifications and ongoing monitoring of the

FIGURE 3.1   GreenNonprofits Web site.

*Source:* Green Nonprofits Web site, www.greennonprofits.org.

green plan. The high-level categories covered in the form, and also covered in detail throughout this book, include:

- Reduce solid waste disposal and promote recycling.
- Become energy and water efficient.
- Purchase products that are less harmful to human health and the environment.
- Minimize pollution contributions to the environment.
- Help improve indoor air quality and reduce smog formation.
- Educate customers, employees, and other nonprofits about GreenNonprofits' practices.[2]

In addition, the GreenNonprofits form suggests "mandatory" categories and practices and option areas for improvement that are helpful in establishing the environmental impact portion of the green plan. Also, there are pages and pages of suggested categories and changes that organizations can make, providing a universe of possibilities from which to draw for your green plan. Figure 3.2 is an excerpt

---

**Green Nonprofits Certification (GNPC) Application**

**TRANSPORTATION**

NOTE Each measure in this section is worth 2 points once completed.

Choose a minimum of 5 New or Existing Measures (earning a minimum of 10 points):

- Provide a secure location for staff to store bicycles or install a bike rack in or near facility.
- Cover rideshare programs at new employee orientations.
- Provide Bus and Metro maps and information (where available)
- Encourage alternative modes of transportation via incentives. For example, bus pass or small bonus.
- Provide ridesharing information on carpooling, vanpooling, bicycling, walking and public/mass transportation on a bulletin board.
- Distribute rideshare information monthly.
- Offer telecommuting opportunities and/or flexible schedules so workers can avoid heavy traffic.
- Incorporate a "How to get here via alternative transportation" page into your employee manual and provide information to employee upon hiring.
- Perform local errands on bike or foot.
- Shop at local businesses within close proximity.
- Maintain fleet to optimize miles per gallon, including adjusting tire pressure, filter, oil, etc.
- Provide company commuter van.
- Provide shower facilities for employees who walk, jog, or bike to work.
- Consider contracting with a nearby health facility for the use of their showers.
- Provide preferential parking for alternative modes of transit such as carpools, electric, hybrid or biodiesel vehicles.

Total Points Earned (Transportation): _____ (min 10 points)

*Source*: www.GreenNonprofits.org

**FIGURE 3.2** Green Nonprofits certification application.

*Source:* Green Nonprofits Certification Application and Checklist, from www.greennonprofits.org.

of the Green Nonprofits Certification Application from the section dealing with the category of transportation:

Typically, most larger metropolitan areas have local organizations that provide hands-on certifications similar to those in the Green Nonprofits Checklist, focusing more on the particulars and opportunities presented in each area. The certifications also support the organizations based in or headquartered in those regions. One example is the Sustainable Business Network of Washington (SB NOW). Based in Washington, DC, SB NOW works with organizations to help them integrate environmental and social responsibility principles into their operations and strategy. They are a community of businesses, nonprofits, and individuals dedicated to realizing a common goal: helping Washington, DC, become a more sustainable place to live and work now and in the future. SB NOW's *Essential Guide to Greening Your Business* (see Figure 3.3) helps make organizations more environmentally sustainable while also reducing operating costs.

The comprehensive guide covers water conservation and quality, energy conservation, waste reduction and recycling, pollution prevention, environmentally friendly procurement, and training. It offers checklists, practical steps, ideas, and resources to help users "green" organizations. In addition, SB NOW offers a third-party validation of organizations' commitment and achievements in the area of environmental programs and sustainability.

Start with a checklist and process like Green Nonprofits or SB NOW, and then boil it down to your organization's top-priority issues. The long-term goals, though, should be as far reaching and comprehensive as those presented on the checklist,

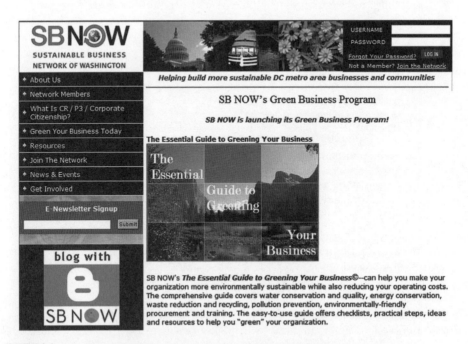

FIGURE 3.3   Sustainable Business Network of Washington Web site.

*Source:* Sustainable Businsess Alliance of Washington Web site, main page, from www.sbnow.org.

but it is important to determine early on what your largest areas of impact will be. For example, some organizations generate a lot of paper, some a lot of transportation, use a lot of building space use, and so on. Focus on areas where impact can be swift and fairly painless.

Now that we have filled up the left side of the brain with the checklist and you are thinking of all the hard choices that your organization is going to have to make to set up physical short- and long-term goals by checklist item and category, it is time for some right-brain, creative brain food. If you are truly serious about creating impact and lasting change through your organization's activities and the green plan that you create, then let us take off the blinders for a bit and consider some potentially deep changes but ones that are all really rooted in common sense. Many would call them the vanguard of green management and employee relations, but now we will just consider them as potential parts of your green management and employee plan. At the end of the day, for the green plan to stand the test of time, employees must have buy-in, be motivated to make changes and, most important, be the change that they seek. Let us look at some ways to shake things up and motivate the troops and organization.

## Alternative Work Arrangements that Affect Stakeholders, the Environment, and an Organization's Overhead in a Positive Way

Another consideration when developing the radar screen of issues is that sometimes the most immediate and impactful possibilities might be obvious but require a new kind of thinking, redesigning the organization in a more modern, freer framework that takes location-centric and nine-to-five work out of the equation. In their study, *The Time Clock Revolution*, students from the Bainbridge Graduate Institute, in partnership with BetterWorld Telecom, consider the positive social and environmental effects of open work (remote anytime/anywhere work methods) on the organization and on organizational planning:

*CASE STUDY:* BETTERWORK™—A NEW STRATEGY FOR WORK    The traditional concept of "work" is changing rapidly. Both small and large organizations face increasing pressure from fierce competition, aggressive pricing, regulation, and social and environmental concerns that make business and nonprofit endeavors ever more challenging. Twenty-first-century enterprises must have the ability to respond rapidly to changes in markets, technology, and stakeholder needs. In addition, the typical office environment now includes a cross-generational workforce made up of baby boomers, Gen X, and Gen Y. Organizations must respond to these varied demands to stay competitive. A number are adapting by exploring radical approaches to workplace structure—not by asking for more hours from employees, increasing rigid processes, or adding more buildings and infrastructure, but by using technology and the Internet to create a new work culture that includes a mobile workforce working on a flexible schedule. The outcome of employing these new workplace philosophies is a more nimble and agile company with highly productive, dedicated workers and real savings for the bottom line.

Flexible work schedules are not new and have been given many names, such as telework, telecommuting, and flex time. Each of these terms has the common element of removing "time in the office" as the basis of employee measurement and enabling mobile employees to work from any location, giving them the freedom to choose that location as long as client needs and company objectives are met. At the core of a mobile program is an employee's ability to access data and information from anywhere, easily connect with team members and colleagues, and participate in the work flow remotely. A few companies have taken this concept of freedom of choice to a new level, measuring employee performance not by how many hours worked but by results delivered.

This concept of measuring only results and not time spent is so new that it has no universally recognized label. The term "BetterWork" has been coined by BetterWorld Telecom and the Bainbridge Graduate Institute in their 2009 white paper series and seems to best capture the philosophy of democracy, choice, and personal engagement in addition to the concept of flexible work locations (see Figure 3.4). At the forefront of this revolution are the Results Only Work Environment (ROWE) at BestBuy Electronics and the OpenWork Platform at Sun Microsystems. Both of these programs are much more than telecommuting. They have created cultural and operational changes in the company as a whole and have had dramatic, positive impacts on the bottom line and the environment.

The growing landscape of high-speed Internet penetration and the rise of technologies such as Internet telephony and unified communications have removed much of the need for the traditional office. By removing the need to be in the office to be working, organizations can dramatically reduce their real estate expenditures and associated costs of heating and cooling buildings. Removing the requirement to travel to an office also decreases commuting and travel-related carbon dioxide ($CO_2$) emissions. And, from the results from BestBuy and Sun, employees appear to like having the choice of where and how to work, which can have a direct impact

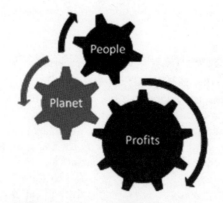

# BetterWork™
## A New Strategy for Work

FIGURE 3.4  BetterWork™ telegreening concept.

*Source:* BetterWork Logo, from BetterWorld Telecom Web site, www.betterworldtelecom.com.

on company financials. If every U.S. worker who could telecommute did so 1.6 days per week, 1.35 billion gallons of gasoline would be saved, preventing 26 billion pounds of $CO_2$ from being released into the atmosphere. Add that to the statistics about productivity, and changing our commutes from down the interstate to down the hall looks pretty compelling.[3]

Even though the examples provided in the *Time Clock Revolution* and *BetterWork*™ white papers (see Figure 3.5) mostly involve for-profit enterprises, these concepts can and do apply to all categories of organizations, regardless of size and number of employees and/or locations. These examples, coupled with the WorldBlu democratic workplace discussion to come, are presented to get your creative juices flowing through the planning and development part of the process. Don't make your focus just a green plan checklist; take the opportunity to reinvent your organization through this process.

Finishing up BetterWork concepts, many organizations rightfully consider whether to seek LEED (Leadership in Energy and Environmental Design Green Building Rating System™) certification for their existing or new building. As a society, we need to start considering "need" before LEED. This mentality could change your whole decision process and have profound impacts on your organization's

# The Time Clock Revolution

Creating sustainable work through engagement and choice

Libby Johnson McKee

Desiree Williams Rajee

Manan Shukla

Stephen Yogi Rueff

FIGURE 3.5 "Time Clock Revolution" cover.

*Source:* Libby Johnson McKee, Desiree Williams Rajee, Manan Shukla, and Stephen Yogi Rueff, "The Time Clock Revolution: Creating Sustainable Work through Engagement and Choice," www.betterworldtelecom.com.

carbon footprint. Sun Microsystems saved tens of millions of dollars and tens of thousands of tons of $CO_2$ in 2007 by employing Open Work techniques. Taking people and cars off the road even just a few days a week on a rotating basis, cutting down on travel and substituting more efficient video, voice, and data conferencing are the building blocks for true change. In the BetterWork study, a small organization of 25 employees saved almost $60,000 per year in operational costs and over 30,000 pounds of $CO_2$ just by having five people telecommute and cutting back on travel, substituting off-the-shelf technologies such as Voice Over IP, Virtual PBX, and voice/audio/video conferencing. The numbers are just too drastic to say that your organization would not benefit from another look at how it works; do you need all the space, cars on the road, planes in the air?[4]

## Organizational and Cross-Functional Employee Support

One tendency when developing a green management and employee plan is not to include all parts of the organization. The executives, board, and management need not only to buy in but to participate on a regular basis, as do the rest of the employees, volunteers, and community members if possible. Just as important is that all levels are brought into the fold. The best example of this process is a holistic system developed by Act Now Productions (now Saatchi and Saatchi S), in its Personal Sustainability Project (PSP) framework. This groundbreaking system takes the concept of sustainability and weaves it into the psyche of the organization, making sustainability more of a daily life force for all employees.

To quote from the "What Is the Personal Sustainability Project?" document:

> *[T]he Personal Sustainability Project is a bottom-up, grassroots effort that helps [an organization's] employees incorporate the principles of sustainability into their personal lives. PSP is built by listening to employees—their hopes, dreams, and desires—and recognizing that real and meaningful change begins at home. It starts with simple things, like a Personal Sustainability Practice—one small action that tangibly brings sustainability into a person's daily life.*
>
> *The PSP Methodology Background: The underlying methodology of PSP is based on the field of research known as Positive Psychology. Where the science of Psychology has been focused on learning what makes people unhappy and sick, Positive Psychology studies what makes people happy. Actions that lead to gratitude, service to others and a state of self-fulfillment are key contributors to lasting happiness.[5]*

Information on PSPs is easy to find on the Web; a great place to start is www.actnowproductions.com.

## People Are the X Factor: Democracy in the Workplace

With the PSP framework still fresh in our minds, what a great time to explore one of today's more progressive and long-overdue systems of organization: democracy in the workplace. Just as you cannot make a peanut butter and jelly sandwich without jelly, so you cannot design a sound green management and employee plan without considering how you treat your employees and all stakeholders. How transparent is your organization? Do you have more of a top-down, hierarchical, and outmoded structure? Having operated both for-profits and nonprofits in the green space for many years, I can unequivocally say that how you treat green and how you treat people are completely intertwined.

One proven method of increasing the performance and focus on people in your organization is to infuse true democracy into your organizational policies and structure. According to one of the leading voices in organizational democracy, Austin, Texas-based Worldblu:

> *Organizational democracy is a system of organization that is based on freedom, instead of fear and control. It's a way of designing organizations to amplify the possibilities of human potential—and the organization as a whole. The concept of democracy comes from the Greek words "demos" and "kratein" which mean "the people rule."*
>
> *So the core of organizational democracy and political democracy is the same— allowing people to self-govern and determine their own destiny. What is different is the context—one is in the political arena, the other is in the realm of organizations.*[6]

Founded in 1997 as a 501(c)3 nonprofit, tax-exempt social enterprise by Traci Fenton, the purpose of WorldBlu is to unleash human potential and inspire freedom by championing the growth of democratic organizations worldwide.

Their vision is to build a more democratic world, one organization at a time, and our goal is to see the creation of 20,000 democratic workplaces around the world by 2020. They inspire and support this global movement by offering a range of programs and services that enable business leaders to design, develop, and lead the most successful democratic organizations in the world.

## The WorldBlu 10 Principles of Organizational Democracy™ (see Figure 3.6).

1. *Purpose + Vision.* A democratic organization is clear about why it exists (its purpose) and where it is headed and what it hopes to achieve (its vision).
2. *Transparency.* Democratic organizations are transparent and open with employees about the financial health, strategy, and agenda of the organization.
3. *Dialogue + Listening.* Democratic organizations are committed to having conversations that bring out new levels of meaning and connection.
4. *Fairness + Dignity.* Democratic organizations are committed to fairness and dignity.
5. *Accountability.* Democratic organizations point fingers, not in a blaming way but in a liberating way.
6. *Individual + Collective.* In democratic organizations, the individual is just as important as the whole.
7. *Choice.* Democratic organizations thrive on giving employees meaningful choices.
8. *Integrity.* Integrity is the name of the game, and democratic companies have a lot of it.

FIGURE 3.6    WorldBlu Web site.

*Source:* WorldBlu Web site, from www.worldblue.com.

9.  *Decentralization*. Democratic organizations make sure power is appropriately shared and distributed among people throughout the organization.
10. *Reflection + Evaluation*. Democratic organizations are committed to continuous feedback and development.[7]

***CASE STUDY:* ORGANIZATIONAL DEMOCRACY IN PRACTICE: TAKINGITGLOBAL.ORG**    Based in Toronto, Ontario, nonprofit TakingITGlobal (see Figure 3.7) is the world's most popular online community for young people interested in making a difference.

FIGURE 3.7    WorldBlu Web site, TakingITGlobal case study.

*Source:* www.worldblu.com/worldblu-list/worldblu-list?company=takingitglobal.

TakingITGlobal cofounder and executive director Jennifer Corriero notes: "As a youth-led organization driven by the collaborative power of Internet technologies, we strongly believe in democracy. Our online community is a vibrant network of socially engaged youth leaders who embody the WorldBlu principles in their daily lives and through their actions to address global issues. It is thus imperative that TakingITGlobal practices democracy as a fundamental guiding principle."[8]

Below are two organizational democracy best practices from TakingITGlobal:

1. *Decentralization.* At TakingITGlobal, project managers are often given just the basic outline and final objective of their projects. How they actually achieve their goal is up to them. TakingITGlobal's staff structure is very flat, and what little hierarchy there is exists for operational efficiency.
2. *Transparency.* Documents and organizational memory at TakingITGlobal are stored in a freely accessible database, while Web 2.0 tools such as wikis and instant messaging software are used for communication on a daily basis.[9]

## Putting Social Networking to Work for Your Organization

One of the true benefits and long-term appeals of sites/tools such as Twitter, Facebook, LinkedIn, Care2, and JustMeans is that they can be put to use to supercharge many different elements of your nonprofit, especially input and feedback surrounding your green management and employee plan. There are many, many examples now of this taking place, where nonprofits are opening the kimono to their constituents for input and feedback. This topic is probably a book in itself, and because there are a host of easy-to-find examples out there, there is no need to ramble on. Just make sure you include social networking in your master strategy.

PARTNERSHIPS    Another category for consideration when in the green plan formation stage is looking to peers, other nonprofits in your region, nonprofits with similar missions outside of your region, as well as for-profit companies that are tied to the organization as donors, board members, and the like.

One area where there are strong examples of nonprofit cooperation and information sharing is international relief and the environment. The NetHope Consortium (www.nethope.org) provides a sterling example of NGOs coming together to share best practices and helping each other to achieve their respective goals. NetHope is a nonprofit information technology (IT) consortium consisting of some of the largest international NGOs, collectively serving tens of millions of beneficiaries each year in over 150 countries on all continents. NetHope, which began as an informal collaboration, now operates as a separate nonprofit organization that is operated and governed by its NGO members. The leading mantra of NetHope is built around sharing, collaboration, and facilitation between the various IT departments and needs of the member organizations. The model has been wildly successful, allowing each organization to function better, faster, and cheaper.

With the NetHope example in mind, you can use the green plan as an opportunity to cooperate, sharing best environmental and management practices regarding programs that work and that do not work. In this way, your organization and other nonprofits can to get up to speed and make a positive impact on the environment and people with a cost-effective and quickly formulated green management plan. Cooperation on this level is a great excuse to reach out to a host of colleagues and other nonprofits to establish and learn best practices and forge new partnerships.

## Structuring the Team to Get the Work Done

In the past, many organizations established a dedicated person or department to handle internal sustainability efforts. This structure can be effective but sometimes lacks the teeth or buy-in from the rest of the organization and can be difficult to get off the ground, especially on a limited budget. One alternative is to establish a cross-functional committee made up of representatives from across the organization and rotate in new people on a rolling, regular basis from those different departments. It is critical then to make the teams representative of the entire organization, top to bottom, side to side. If you have a small nonprofit, then all hands should participate in the process and contribute to the overall goals. The process is great for team building and the environment.

## Planning for Measurement, Certifications

As discussed in some detail in the Green Nonprofits and SB NOW examples, the final planning category sets the stage for ongoing measurement of goals and impacts and the resetting of goals. Certifications are critical to benchmarking where the organization stands at the beginning of the process as well as the short-, mid-, and long-term opportunities for improvement. In addition to the initial certification, plan for regular checkups at least annually to be able to report and reset goals effectively.

## Ready, Set . . . Creating the Green Plan

Now that you have determined all the elements of your plan and its focus, established the initial team, and planned the process for the short and long term, the next phase is probably the most painstaking of the entire plan development. Now it is time to roll up your sleeves and put it all down on paper, organized so that it can be communicated to the stakeholders by the person or team that will be shepherding the process. The process for creating the green plan should center on three success elements:

1. Focus on the 20% that will make 80% of the difference.
2. Incorporate best practices and advances into the green plan.
3. Ensure the plan is comprehensive but manageable.

# Phase Two: Implementation of the Green Plan

Once the green plan is ready for prime time, regardless of how large or small your organization is, make sure that the process and product are launched with a big bang. Make sure that everyone's roles and responsibilities are clear and that targets are clearly communicated and demonstrable, setting expectations and responsibilities across the organization early and clearly.

## Benchmarking and Scheduling

The schedule for updates, progress, and meetings should be set at least a year out. The cross-functional team or a dedicated person must present progress and update reports on dates set in advance. The initial benchmarking, whether you are using an external or internal source, should be completed and highlighted prior to the launch and included in the green plan.

## Communication Is Everything

The green plan must be visible and easily accessed from the organization's Internet and/or intranet, with other examples such as signs, posters, and information in visible places. Meetings should take place both via online webinars and visibly throughout the organization. This ties in well with the next stage.

## Celebrate and Have Fun with the Green Plan

Celebrate any victories and progress on a regular basis. As noted, there are a number of ways to create buzz through easy-to-update technologies, such as Twitter, Facebook, Care2, blogs, and RSS feeds. Encourage individuals to add postings to the Web-based channels—the best feedback is when everyone is truly participating in both the inputs and the outputs and a true discussion ensues that becomes its own living, breathing entity. When this is achieved, when the flywheel is spinning on its own, as Jim Collins says in his classic *Good to Great*,[10] progress comes much easier and the green plan becomes less dependent on specific people but rather on the whole organization's ecosystem.

# Phase Three: Ongoing Management, Measurement, and Improvement

## 20 Percent Makes 80 Percent of the Difference: Achieving Early Success Is Key

As we discussed earlier, now that you have embarked on your plan and the machine is off and running, nothing is more important than registering some early victories and progress. The low-hanging fruit, enhanced recycling, employee policies such as commuting and flex time, water use, reduction of paper use—progress can come quickly, and these victories are part of the early success story, so yell from the mountaintop when there are tangible results. As the green plan is being run by humans, the tendency will be to relax after the effort of developing and launching the plan. It is key to keep the rhythm and schedule in the first few months, or the green plan will fall behind and people will start to lose interest.

## Technology Makes a Difference: Putting It to Work for Your Plan

Many organizations are finding blogs and social networking tools to be perfect for input and output, tracking, and reporting on many facets of the organization. This could actually end up being the most useful facet for many of the social networking tools, especially as we explore and implement more Open Work and democratic work philosophies and methods. Utilize resources such as TechSoup Global and

NetSquared to help enable your technologies. Keep the communication regular: weekly or more for the blog and perhaps Facebook pages, daily or more on Twitter. The key is to make sure that the frequency is regular, relevant, and dependable, or the flock will lose interest. Once you utilize these forums, it is amazing how long the tail of the Internet is and how you can build a true following of interested parties in your organization and what you are trying to achieve.

## Is the Green Plan Really Making a Difference?

This is a great question to insert into your ongoing plan and meetings. Be objective: Is the effort worth the output, or does it need to be adjusted, restarted, redesigned? If the results are not credible or tangible, the troops will not stay motivated and the green plan will quickly die on the vine. These questions should be asked at every meeting and forum: Is change happening, are we having impact? This whole exercise is really about self-reflection for the organization, creating a lens and awareness for the impact the plan is having on people and planet through its direct activities. As many nonprofits are mission driven to make changes in a host of areas, including health, education, children, disaster relief, the environment, and policy, the green plan serves as an extension of those missions and makes the services delivered even more true. Without our own houses in order, how can we help or tell our communities or the world to do things better?

## Ongoing Independent Certification

As mentioned earlier in this chapter and elsewhere, nothing drives results like an independent source providing feedback, criticism, and opportunities for improvement. Because this interaction drives new ideas and especially the ongoing reporting on program success, any long-term plan must account for regular auditing and outside supervision to be truly credible. A host of local, national, and international resources provide appropriate certifications for your green management and employee plan.

## Reporting

While there are sure to be examples of nonprofits reporting on their internal greening efforts out there, we were not able to find any publicly available examples at the time we went to press, so it does not seem to be a pervasive practice in the NGO space. Obviously this is a great opportunity for change. That being said, there is plenty of room to make an impact in this area. Many ongoing efforts are published and updated by environmental leaders in the for-profit space, such as Patagonia, REI, Green Mountain Coffee, and Seventh Generation, all readily available on their Web sites. One great example of a transparent, thoughtful report is Seventh Generation's annual Corporate Consciousness Report, available at www.seventhgeneration. com/corporate-responsibility/2007. The mantra of the company's head of Corporate Consciousness and CEO, Jeffrey Hollender, is to take sustainability and transparency to a new level—make it personal, make it real. "Transparency is a process, not a prophecy," Hollender notes in the 2007 Seventh Generation Annual Report.

# Conclusion

Make it personal, make it real... with those words echoing in our minds, and we hope with many new ideas and a sense of empowerment about creating the green plan for your organization, go out there and start turning the tide in the nonprofit world. As nonprofits/NGOs have been outwardly focused on changing the world in a positive way for decades, now is the time to look inward. With approximately 2 million nonprofits globally, with assets nearing $2 trillion, and with expenditures in the $1 billion range, the opportunity for greening the sector is tremendous. All organizations must do their share if we are truly to start turning the tide on climate and social change. Starting with a meaningful plan to get there is the first step; take the step now!

## About the Author

**Matt Bauer,** president of BetterWorld Telecom, has worked to improve communities in the United States and abroad in both the for-profit and nonprofit sectors for more than 20 years. Before cofounding BetterWorld Telecom in 2002, Matt served in a series of leadership roles in the telecommunications and power industries, including AES Corp and NETtel. He has helped to start or grow a number of nonprofits over the past 10 years, including the Charleston, South Carolina–based Lowcountry Local First, the Sitar Center for Children and the Arts in Washington, DC, and Atlanta-based True Colors Theatre Company. Matt now serves on the board of directors for the Business Alliance for Local Living Economies, GreenNonprofits, the Noisette Foundation, and the Charleston Regional Alliance for the Arts. He holds a BA in Telecommunications from Indiana University and an MBA from the George Washington University.

## CHAPTER 4

# Creating Your Green Marketing and Communications Plan

## Gabe Roth and Alex Slater

## Introduction

When it is done right, going green and promoting those efforts can have distinct marketing, communications, and public policy advantages for a nonprofit charitable organization.

Let us be clear: *Going green* often remains an amorphous and subjective notion. But in this chapter, we offer some concrete steps you and your organization can take to implement sincere environmental practices and policies that improve how you market—among your own staff, among current and potential donors, and in the media.

Selling the notion of a green charity might seem counterintuitive. You may not automatically think that your organization, for example, would need to espouse sustainability practices, but there are plenty of instances in which charitable causes, regardless of type, can intersect with environmental progress.

In this chapter, you will learn how to put the intersection of your mission and the green movement to work for your nonprofit's communications. There is much to be learned from the corporate sector's approach to "green" marketing.

## Green Marketing in the Corporate World

It seems there is no single act of environmental conscientiousness that a marketing department somewhere does not immediately seize upon. Once a company makes the decision to use less energy or reuse more raw materials, say, it is often quick to send out a press release or to air a commercial with the fundamental message of: "Buy our product—because we're *green.*"

Going green can be seen as trendy (just note the proliferation of "It's Good to Be Green" T-shirts from H&M, Urban Outfitters, and the like), not only in merchandising but in print, broadcast, and online communications. Local news stations seem to tease their green stories as much as they promote their hard news pieces ("Coming up at 11 on NBC 4, how to green your routine...."). Local newspapers have begun adding "how to green your life" sections in print and on their Web sites, and magazines such as *Newsweek* and *Ladies' Home Journal* have followed suit, telling readers where to buy compact fluorescent light bulbs and how to buy carbon offsets.

Another example: On the Eurostar train between Paris and London, you will find this statement printed in the menu:

> *As part of our Tread Lightly initiative to reduce our environmental impact, we use organic produce sourced in the country of departure and Fairtrade products in our food wherever possible. What's more this menu is printed on FSC approved paper and will be reused again and again to minimize its environmental impact.*

## Green Marketing in the Environmental Movement

The Alliance for Climate Protection (www.RepowerAmerica.org) "We" Campaign started in 2008 with the goal of raising $300 million to bring the message of the urgency—and the solvability—of the climate crisis to the American people. The organization began fundraising intensely and hired powerhouse ad agencies to promote this message on a broad platform. The Martin Agency, known for its Geico gecko ads, produced a TV spot comparing the challenge of stopping global warming to the great generational challenges of decades past, such as World War II and the civil rights movement. In addition, Crispin Porter + Bogusky, of anticigarette "Truth" campaign fame, enlisted Academy Award–winning filmmakers Joel and Ethan Coen to satirize the coal industry—and point out its role in the climate crisis—with the tagline "In reality, there is no such thing as clean coal" (www.ThisIsReality.org).

# Greenwashing

Clearly, being seen as environmentally conscious has become central to the marketing efforts of corporations, new media, politicians, and some organizations. The term "triple bottom line" is often used to express a company's ability to generate profit, develop its people, and reduce its impact on the planet. Thousands of companies are using this model to look more attractive to an ever-growing segment of environmentally conscious consumers.

The popularity of green merchandising and marketing has even pushed into the realm of green *rebranding*—but in an unfortunate and sometimes dangerous way.

Some publicly traded companies that incur significant environmental impacts, such as Chevron and BP, are choosing to "greenwash"—meaning they are vigorously trying to portray themselves as leaders of the green movement. Greenwashing deflects criticism from a company's practices by showing images of environmental consciousness that is just on the surface.

For example, BP is no longer British Petroleum; it is now "Beyond Petroleum," and invests some money in alternative energy development. Many would argue, however, that the actions of such companies reveal a less-than-earnest approach to sustainability.

(As a response to energy companies' greenwashing during the 2008 U.S. election cycle, a number of environmental groups produced satirical television and online ads. In the Alliance for Climate Protection's "Smudge" ad shown in Figure 4.1, the chief executive of mock energy company "Coalergy" professes, "The fact is, coal isn't dirty; it's clean. Smells good, too!")

# Why Green Marketing and Communications Matter to Charities

Although it may be too early to put exact figures against this rise in environmental awareness, environmental consciousness is beginning to affect the way

FIGURE 4.1 Alliance for Climate Protection's "Smudge" ad.

individuals and organizations decide how to give donations and grants. And it does not matter what type of organization—arts and culture or health and human services; international development or community benefit. There are active steps that your organization can take that will give you an advantage—both in how many trees you are saving and how much green you are raising.

In July 2008, the U.S. Green Building Council (USGBC) and McGraw-Hill Construction released a survey of potential homebuyers. It showed that the *lower-income* individuals—and *not* the wealthier individuals—were more likely be able to afford solar panels, efficiency upgrades, and other green home improvements. (See Appendix B for the press release; speakers at the event, held at an affordable housing community in the Bronx, are pictured in Figure 4.2.)

Just as the survey finds that those whose household incomes are tight are placing an emphasis on solar energy, efficiency upgrades, and other improvements, so should charitable organizations be looking at instituting green practices. Every dollar saved goes directly to the bottom line.

As these changes are being made at your organization, you will need to learn how to insert sustainability and sustainable practice messaging into your internal and external communications. These strategies are most effective when used in tandem

FIGURE 4.2   Affordable housing community speakers.

From left to right: USGBC Senior Vice President Michelle Moore; Mt. Sinai Medical Center Researcher Dr. Elizabeth Garland; McGraw-Hill Construction Vice President Robert Ivy; Bronx Borough President Adolfo Carrión Jr. (now an Obama administration official); New York Secretary of State Lorraine Cortés-Vázquez; and Yolanda Gonzales, executive director of the Bronx housing nonprofit Nos Quedamos.

with sustainable practices in fundraising strategies (i.e., marketing your nonprofit as environmentally conscious will help your fundraising efforts) and public policy strategies (i.e., engaging in public policy goals that improve the world we live in can raise your nonprofit's profile, so long as they are consistent with your status as a 501(c)(3) U.S. charitable organization or nongovernmental organization).

The saying "imitation is the highest form of flattery" applies when trying to turn sustainable practices into a marketing advantage. Take inventory of what other nonprofits and even corporations are doing to green their business practices.

## Ladder of Engagement

Creating a green marketing strategy should not happen in a vacuum. Before outlining the way in which you would like to present your organization as green both to coworkers and the outside world, it is imperative that you have a cohesive set of marketing and communications goals that stem from your organization's mission and ethos.

There are different levels at which you can engage your existing communications resources to create positive outcomes through your green marketing efforts. Green issues are top of mind for many journalists and publications, a fact that provides ample opportunities for your organization to gain traction by highlighting your green initiatives. You just have to be realistic in what you can achieve.

How do you make sure you are not biting off more than you can chew? The answer lies in the planning process—anchored in the creation of a communications plan.

But before you even get there, it is important to identify the willingness of your staff, board, and other stakeholders to engage in different activities levels.

Here we have identified three potential levels of engagement—remember, no size fits all here. This process is about finding what works best for your organization.

**"Ladder of Engagement" for Green Nonprofits/Green Organizations**
1. Basic engagement (e.g., willing to green your routine, create communications plan around sustainability initiatives)
2. Active engagement (e.g., basic engagement plus a willingness to use sustainability initiatives as a means of raising funds and applying for grants)
3. Very active engagement (e.g., active engagement plus a willingness to participate in discussions of public policy within your organizations and among other like-minded organizations)

Our recommendation: Start small and increase engagement over time.

As you get started, it is not necessary to decide which of these engagement levels applies to your organization—that will become apparent as you further engage in the planning process. But you should use the Ladder of Engagement as a guiding strategic template during the planning process.

As you begin working up the ladder, we suggest a deliberately incremental approach that will help your organization find the appropriate level of communications engagement around green issues, without disappointing or letting down your key stakeholders—staff, leadership, members, supporters, your community, and, of course, journalists.

## Five Elements of Your Green Communications Plan

Crafting a green communications plan is not just about creating a well-written document. It is about mapping out strategies and tactics that not only align to your organization's mission and dedication to environmental causes, but also speak to the audiences you will be engaging. We will help you answer this important question: What is interesting, unique, and marketable from your organization's story, and how do you tailor it to make it interesting to your key stakeholders?

Communications professionals understand that the impetus driving external communications is to fill the marketplace with positive impressions about the individual, community, or organization you are promoting. People and groups that can afford to do so utilize advertising; another effective way to promote your group or position is with "earned media"—news stories that portray your organization in a positive light.

A communications plan does not have to be complicated. It does not even need to be very long. But it should include some clear steps that take you from your broad strategic goals to specific and achievable tactics that will help your organization achieve its goals.

Many organizations have some type of communications plan or strategy in place before they embark on a green initiative. It is important to review and consider how your new green communications/marketing efforts will alter the original before writing your new plan.

---

### Five Elements of Your Green Communications Plan

1. Objectives
2. Audience
3. Message
4. Strategy
5. Tactics

---

### Objectives

Objectives are your overarching goal for your green communications plan. What does success look like? In the case of charities engaging in a green marketing strategy, there may be multiple answers.

For example:

- Distinguish your organization from others in the nonprofit space by highlighting your deep commitment to environmental efforts.
- Make key donors and members aware of your environmental efforts.
- Raise new donations from existing donors by highlighting your environmental efforts.

- Develop your thought leadership (i.e., other groups that think of your group as *the* expert on issues relating to, for example, the intersection of healthcare and sustainability) with stakeholders and specialists by showcasing your dedication to sustainability and related initiatives.

Although you, no doubt, will have multiple objectives, remember the green communications rule: Keep your objectives tight, focused, and disciplined.

## Audience

So often, nonprofits try to be all things to all people. However, a catch-all approach works only for the best-funded and staffed organizations.

The key to determining an achievable communications plan is making sure you understand, identify, and keep a laserlike focus on the audiences that matter. Whatever you do, avoid the notion that you are targeting everyone with everything— answering "the general public" to the question "Who are your targets?" in most cases will not result in success.

Keep focused. For example, your targets might more appropriately be:

- Donors, current and/or prospective, high level or grassroots
- Foundations, grant-making bodies, federal or local government
- Members, current and/or prospective, high level or grassroots
- The charitable community: competitors, experts, and others in the nonprofit "echo chamber"
- Internal audiences: staff, vendors, contractors, potential partner's organization

## Message

Communications strategists often talk about the "main message" or the "message hierarchy" in hushed, reverent tones. In fact, less is much, much more in this department.

As Joe Lockhart, press secretary to President Bill Clinton, points out: "Your message should be short enough to fit on a small index card. If you can't communicate it faster than that, you'll lose the attention of the audiences you're trying to reach."

Part of your communications plan must be to boil down a main message for each audience you plan to reach. Try summarizing it in one sentence—you can always add subheadings or proof points later.

A common pitfall is to overcomplicate the main message. So, instead of saying . . .

"Green issues are more important than ever to anyone, and that's why our organization is dedicated to the environmental cause by undergoing a series of important initiatives that will inspire and help other nonprofits follow our lead in this important area"

. . . say . . .

"Our organization is at the cutting edge of a new wave of environmentalism sweeping the nonprofit world."

## Strategy

Strategy is often the hardest part of the communications plan. It is the section that links the high-minded objectives and messages just outlined with the nitty-gritty tactics to be discussed next. Basically, it is the link that makes your wish list become reality before you get to specific ideas.

Strategy will vary enormously according to the objectives you outline, but let us use an example from earlier. Imagine your main objective is: "Distinguish our organization from others in the nonprofit space by highlighting our deep commitment to environmental efforts." How are you going to do this? What is the strategy to illustrate your thought leadership?

Some examples might be to:

- Embark on a targeted reporter education campaign to make them aware of your efforts.
- Engage your members in an online campaign to have them validate your efforts with key audiences.
- Convene a major event with other charities in your sector and/or community designed to prompt action and highlight your leadership in this area.
- Leverage your efforts with Green Nonprofits (www.GreenNonprofits.org) to highlight your leadership in this space.

## GreenNonprofits

These are just four examples. You will think of more. The important part is to identify distinct streams of activity—strategies—that will help you achieve your goals. The specific tactics can come later.

## Tactics

This is where the rubber meets the road. Different organizations approach the tactics part of the communications plan in different ways. In our experience, there is nothing like a traditional brainstorm, bringing all sorts of players (not just key communicators) into one room to explore a host of tactics that might help advance your plan.

Others prefer tasking specific individuals with different pieces of the plan. If you are seeking to get the buy-in of your board or key stakeholders—even your members—why not issue a plea for their help coming up with tactics they would like to see be initiated? There is nothing better than asking advice if you are seeking buy-in.

These days, the press—and the public—can have environmental fatigue. That means that while their antennae are up for interesting environmental stories, the bar for catching their interest and inspiring their imagination is high. For this reason, you have to work hard at identifying the types of tactics you want to include in your communications plan.

## Three Ways to Break through the Green Clutter

Generally speaking, there are three ways to break through the clutter—to grab the attention you need. As you evaluate each of these three tactics, make sure it meets at least one, and preferably more, of the six criteria:

1. You should be doing something new, at least in your sector or community.
2. Tactics should be creative, unheard of. Even try something wacky.
3. You should position yourself—credibly—as the authority on this subject. Keep in mind being an expert is something you just cannot fake.

## Six Criteria for Evaluating Each Tactic

Tactics must meet your internal goals laid out earlier in your green communications plan. However you choose to do it, you should evaluate each tactic through a filter—a lens that evaluates each potential initiative by six important criteria:

1. Do they help further your fundamental objectives?
2. Do they deliver your message?
3. Are they realistic, given your resources?
4. Do they fit under at least one of the strategies you have outlined?
5. Do they genuinely help you break through the clutter to reach the audiences you have identified?
6. Do they play to your organization's brand strength and/or expertise?

For organizations that are strapped for time—and money—it can be tempting to skip the strategic planning and get right to the exciting part—tactical execution. Time and time again, we have seen busy nonprofits fail to engage the press successfully or, even worse, harm their reputations by failing to make their efforts part of a comprehensive and worthwhile strategy.

Next we outline a number of categories for activities you should consider as you plan to engage your audiences in execution of your green communications and marketing strategies.

# Outreach to Press

## Briefings and "Collateral" Material

To influence the news through briefings and "collateral" material means to influence the individuals reporting, producing, and editing the news.

Take the example of a community development nonprofit, which we will call CDN for short. This nonprofit has plans to make a positive impact in your city or town by promoting new commercial development in general and, more specifically, say, stricter efficiency standards for small businesses that move to your city or town. In promoting its message, a CDN communications professional could work with a production company to make commercials for local TV stations about its current projects, but that would take a considerable amount of time and money.

Instead, the staffer could produce fact sheets and brochures, called collateral material, about how CDN would have a positive impact in the community—and then he or she could use these materials as discussion guides when meeting with the local print, TV, radio, and online reporters who cover community development and related issues. These reporter briefings do not frequently generate positive news stories (although they may), but they start to create important relationships that pay dividends in the future. For example, the next time the local city hall reporter has a question on how a proposed tax increase or a new solar power initiative would affect small business, he may call CDN for a reaction.

More germane to this chapter in particular, be sure to include local and regional environmental reporters when you begin briefing reporters about your upcoming activities—and do not forget to tell the reporters you typically would speak with, such as the city hall reporters, about your environmental initiatives. Just because CDN management may be focusing more energy and fundraising dollars toward building code enforcement, say, over environmentally friendly construction, does not mean that your environmental policies are not important or that a reporter would not find that aspect of your work noteworthy.

In general, the energy and environment beat is one of the few beats that have increased the number of dedicated staff at media outlets across the country. Take advantage of that fact and introduce yourself and your nonprofit to your local environmental reporter. Set up a briefing in his or her office or in a local coffee shop, and do not forget to provide informational background or collateral material.

## Thought Leadership

Billing your organization as a resource for the media would further a second important communications goal: positioning your group as an expert, or *the* expert, in its field. In addition to being a resource for the press (see Appendix B for a skeleton media advisory), you should try to put forth your organization and its leadership in front of influential people, whether at conventions, meetings, or the like. Check out idealist.org and similar Web sites for such opportunities.

## Partnerships

To continue with the example of our community development nonprofit, or CDN, the creation of a partnership or coalition around a certain policy position (e.g., the Create a Sustainable Building Code coalition) or charitable imperative (e.g., the Partnership to End Construction Waste in Central Ohio) would also be a time in which you should try to make news. Again, these specific policies and programs do not have to relate to an environmental initiative, but it helps.

# Online and Social Media

On a local level, it can be difficult to measure the breadth and depth of your reach and impressions online. Blogs may have hit-counters and online advertising vendors might record "click-through rates," but on the local level, including an Internet strategy as part of your communications strategy should be just one component of a well-organized effort, not a strategy by itself. That being said, using online media effectively is one of the easiest ways in which to create a sense of immediacy. Creating a blog on your Web site, sending an e-newsletter to members or donors, or frequently posting articles on a sector-wide nonprofit Web site creates the impression that there is a lot of action in your organization.

Although social media is strong and growing (Facebook has over 200 million members), do not view Facebook, Twitter, and the like as anything more than one part of an overall strategy. We are not saying do not do it, but too often we have seen nonprofits put too much faith in the power of social media when, in reality, few things beat a phone call, in-person visit, or personal letter (or e-mail) to get members, donors, or members of the community at large excited about a specific event or initiative.

Certainly there are notable exceptions, and you should ask yourself: Are you an exception? Or more the rule? If you work for a charity embroiled in a critical court case with unpredictable twists and turns, and no cameras are allowed in the courtroom, it may make sense to send hourly updates to members and donors via Twitter. If you are trying to attract college students to an event at a local student union or student hangout, then starting a Facebook page or sending an e-vite to monitor RSVPs may be smart, but expecting you will be the one to create the next "viral video" that will get a million hits on YouTube—and then trying to produce and promote the video—is not recommended as a serious strategy for most organizations.

# Taking Advantage of Opportunities

The launch of a new initiative, the execution of an organization or community-wide event, green or otherwise, presents a great opportunity to take advantage of your media contacts to generate positive coverage of your organization and its activities. Such an event can even include your annual fundraiser or the receipt of a much-sought-after grant or donation. Steps on how to publicize this event or occasion are described in Appendix B.

Imagine the additional attention your annual gala dinner would get from your key stakeholders if you were able to hold it completely green. Or try selling tickets with an upcharge with that additional money going toward reducing the carbon footprint of the event.

# Communications and Public Policy

Just as it may take a lot to gain favor from a local reporter for your sustainable initiatives, lawmakers, too, are looking for real action and tangible results—results for which, down the road, they may even want to claim credit. A general, nonprofit-wide resolution to go green likely will not gain a public official's attention. But a concerted effort to donate funds to environmental refugees in East Asia, or to encourage all contemporary art museums to exhibit "installation art" made from re-cycled materials across a certain congressional district, or even an initiative for local hospitals to reduce paper and thereby create more health information technology jobs are all green initiatives worthy of lawmaker attention.

Aside from lobbying—which is legal for a nonprofit in the United States, so long as it has an established 501(c)(4) organization, which is discussed in Chap-ter 16 in more depth—an effective way in which to promote your nonprofit's environmental agenda with local and national policy makers is to set up "infor-mational" or "educational" meetings in their offices.

Just as with events touting your sustainable initiatives, these meetings will be more effective if you join forces with like-minded groups—for example, if you work for a Catholic nonprofit, coordinate lawmaker visits with your counterparts at a Protestant nonprofit. These meetings will be even more interesting should you be able to find a similar-minded unlikely ally—such as if your Catholic nonprofit formed an environmental alliance with an atheist nonprofit. (We are still looking into whether those exist.)

## Whom to Talk to

Although different countries have different approaches to governing, in general, you should start the process of reaching out to government officials (both elected and appointed) by contacting communications directors, press secretaries, or legislative assistants of the specific lawmaker or government agency with whom you would like to meet.

Briefly explain your sustainability initiative or event in an e-mail or phone call, and be sure to follow up with your contact, as they likely receive dozens of meeting requests per week.

Whether these meetings are public should be up to the public official with whom you are meeting. For example, if you are a Catholic organization meeting with the state senator from a largely Catholic region of your state, and you are meeting to discuss the U.S. Conference of Catholic Bishops' new nationwide campaign on climate change and poverty, it may be in the state senator's interest to promote that meeting by putting out a press release and snapping a picture with you to post on her Web site.

## Keeping Communications Open

These meetings ideally should become starting points for ongoing relationships between policy makers and your organization. Add lawmakers' environmental policy advisors to your press list. Invite these lawmakers to your sustainability-related events and to your annual meetings. Send them your annual report (electronically), highlighting the creation and/or progress of your sustainability initiatives. In short, do not be ashamed of efforts on the part of lawmakers on both sides of the political spectrum to look green. Use that as an opening, and tell your sustainability story as appropriate.

## Note of Caution: Public Officials

We would advise that public officials can, sometimes, act like politicians, and neither you nor your organization would want to be seen as a political football. "Why did Congressman Smith meet with *that* health advocacy group instead of *our* health advocacy group?" is not a question you would like swirling around a lawmaker's office or in the press.

Best advice: Be cautious and well informed about a lawmaker's reputation and his or her position on environmental issues. Lawmakers can be just as guilty of greenwashing as corporations.

## Case Study: *Mother Jones* Magazine

For *Mother Jones* magazine (www.MotherJones.com), sustainability runs in the bloodstream. Readers of the most widely read liberal publication in the United States simply expect the nonprofit[1] publication to be environmentally friendly, according to Steve Katz, *MJ*'s vice president for Strategy and Development.

# Mother Jones

"Given the intensively green values of our readers," Katz says, "if we didn't [act environmentally], we'd be running into big trouble." Of course, successful sustainability practices begin among a nonprofit's employees, and *MJ* uses a number of traditional strategies to reduce office waste—including buying energy-efficient computers and using recycled carpet tiles. It uses online conference tools in place of frequent flights among the Washington, DC, New York, and San Francisco offices, and it donates old computers, books, and paper to other nonprofits.

Even though *MJ* produces a paper product, it has been using a number of strategies to reduce its environmental impact. "For years, *MJ* has been printed on partial percentage recycled paper," Katz says. "With our September/October 2008 issue, we moved to 100 percent recycled paper. An added bonus of this paper change is that the actual weight of the paper is lower than our previous stock, allowing us to reduce our shipping emissions."

*MJ*'s printer, Quad Graphics, has won numerous awards for its sustainability initiatives, including the American Forest & Paper Association's 2005 Business Leadership Recycling Award and the Rainforest Alliance's 2005 Sustainable Standard-Setter Award.

*MJ* is even trying to "better estimate sales of the magazine [...] meaningless waste at the newsstand" and deliver complimentary copies digitally.

"Now that we have a digital version of the magazine that we like, we will be promoting it online via our Web site, e-mails to our lists and our e-newsletters. We'll also start testing to see how the digital version plays with our print subscribers." *MJ* is even working to get current issues uploaded onto Amazon's Kindle reader.

The magazine has taken advantage of readers' interest in environmental issues, and the national interest in the subject at large, and has become a national leader in environmental journalism—which in turn has led them to sell more magazines and improve their reputation nationwide.

Katz says:

> MJ *has a long and deep history of environmental journalism. Beginning with our very first issue in 1976, which featured Paul Jacobs' path-breaking exposé on how U.S. corporations exported faulty nuclear technology to third world countries,* MJ *has covered the environment like no other magazine.*

> *Since 2004 alone, we have published 53 feature stories on the environment from a roster of freelancers that reads like a "who's who" of American environmental journalism. Over the years, we've published writers such as Michael Behar, Wendell Berry, David Case, Al Gore, Frances Moore Lappé, Jacques Leslie, Judith Lewis, Bill McKibben, Paul Roberts, Orville Schell, and many more.*

## Case Study: Habitat for Humanity of Metro Denver

Founded on the belief that "every man, woman and child should have a decent, safe and affordable place to live," Habitat for Humanity International may be the world's best-known nonprofit home builder, having built more than 300,000 homes for low-income families since it was established in 1976.

One affiliate chapter in Colorado, Habitat for Humanity of Metro Denver (HFHMD; www.habitatmetrodenver.org), is taking that mission a step further by "striving to be good stewards of our environment, implementing green building practices into our home construction for over a decade," says HFHMD's Communications and Marketing manager, Robyn Burns, in an interview in April 2009.

> *These sustainable building practices allow for the homes to be affordable for low-income families to purchase and maintain. In fact, HFHMD homeowners saved hundreds of dollars each year on utility costs due to these responsible building practices.*

*In addition to the standard green building practices that are incorporated into every HFHMD home, Habitat strives to stay at the forefront of sustainable building done affordably.*

Recent green projects include:

- A Net-Zero Energy home built in 2005 in partnership with the National Renewable Energy Laboratory (NREL). This Wheat Ridge, Colorado, project included numerous modern green building techniques, including use of solar power and energy-efficient insulation. The home was built in partnership with the Department of Energy's Building America program, Outreach Colorado, Xcel Energy, and the Colorado Governor's Office of Energy Management and Conservation. According to the NREL, the house exceeded expectations and *produced* more than twice the energy it consumed in one year. The *Denver Post* took notice, writing up a positive feature story on the house in February 2006.
- A 2008 project to equip an entire Habitat community with solar photovoltaic panels. The Aurora, Colorado, community features 11 Habitat homes, each fitted with a 2- to 3-kilowatt solar array. "With the help of for-profit partnerships, grants from the governor's office, professional pro bono installation and the granting of an energy rebate, the organization was able to install these panels and reduce its carbon footprint at little additional cost," Burns says.

HFHMD markets its green building practices, Burns says:

*to demonstrate its responsibility and environmentally conscious approach to its home construction. This provides a great marketing advantage, in that HFHMD can gain additional media exposure for unique green projects and also engage other local companies and organizations for funding and support of its solar, green, and affordable building projects.*

Case in point: HFHMD will begin work on a 24-townhome project in 2010 that is a recipient of the Enterprise Community Partners' (www.enterprisecommunity.org) Green Communities Grant. Says Burns:

*This partnership will allow Habitat to integrate a variety of green building strategies that will reduce the negative impact on water quality, air pollution, global warming and the depletion of natural resources—while also lowering operating costs and maintenance needs. This grant will also allow for an increase in sustainability and affordability for the future homeowners.*

# Enterprise

Consistent with this message of sustainability, HFHMD even runs a used building materials outlet in Denver. According to the *Denver Post*:

*The store, which sells everything from windows and doors to light fixtures and paint, will send deconstruction crews to homes and commercial buildings to collect the salvageable materials. "A lot of people don't realize that they don't have to throw this stuff away. It can be reused," said Roger Krapfl, director of the Habitat store. The 14,000-square-foot store attracts dozens of contractors and do-it-yourselfers looking for products that sell for as much as 80 percent off retail prices.*

Whatever advantages HFHMD may have gained for building green, Burns is quick to point out the very premise of environmental stewardship is closely tied to Habitat's mission as an organization.

"Habitat's implementation of green building practices is done through a matter of conscience and responsibility," she says. "These practices are also done so that the homes are affordable for low-income families to purchase and maintain well into the future."

## Introduction to the Appendixes

In Appendix B at the end of this book, you will find step-by-step instructions on conducting your own press outreach, in addition to a range of sample materials you can customize for use in your area.

### Step-by-Step Instructions on Planning a Green Press Event
- Inviting the press to your nonprofit's event
- Submitting an op-ed to your local newspaper
- Submitting a letter to the editor
- Pitching local radio talk and news stations

### How to Work with the Media
- The press today
- Preparing for interviews
- Interview techniques
- Your media list/pitching the media

### Sample Media, Marketing, and Communications Materials
- Journalist pitch phone scripts
- Sample media advisory

## About the Authors

**Alex Slater** is a managing director of the public affairs division at the Glover Park Group, a Washington, DC–based public affairs, research, and government relations firm. He brings a wealth of experience in reputation management and crisis communications.

An award-winning communications strategist, Alex has been with the Glover Park Group since its inception and has directed a range of important advocacy and nonprofit communications efforts. He has provided strategic communications counsel, tactical media support, and integrated campaign management for the Center for Constitutional Rights, Constitutional Accountability Center, National Air Traffic Controllers Association, People for the American Way, ACLU, and Election Protection. A strong leader and creative force, Alex has been awarded four Pollie awards, two Tellie awards, and four Bulldog Reporter awards honoring his contributions to advertising, campaign management, and media relations.

Alex holds an MA in communications from the Annenberg School of the University of Pennsylvania, where he researched corporate and political communications strategies. Originally from Edinburgh, Scotland, he received BA and MA degrees in history from Cambridge University, where he was president of the Cambridge Union.

**Gabe Roth** is a senior associate at the Glover Park Group, a Washington, DC–based public affairs, research, and government relations firm. Since joining GPG in 2007, Gabe has worked with environmental, legal rights, technology, and issue advocacy clients on providing communications strategy, messaging, media placement, and op-ed and speech writing.

Gabe has managed or coordinated a number of extensive media campaigns aimed at raising awareness for key policy issues—from implementing sustainable building practices nationwide, to ensuring all registered Florida, Wisconsin, and Indiana voters were able to cast ballots successfully in the 2008 general election. Additionally, Gabe worked on coordinating media efforts for the Alliance for Climate Protection, the nonprofit group headed by former Vice President Al Gore that advocates for bold solutions to the climate crisis.

Before joining GPG, Gabe worked as a journalist in Florida, Illinois, and Washington, DC. Originally from Nashville, Tennessee, Gabe holds a master's degree from Northwestern University's Medill School of Journalism and a bachelor's degree from Washington University in St. Louis.

## CHAPTER 5

# Green Events

## Georgia Malki

## Yesterday and Today

The event industry has always been a powerful platform for communicating the cause of social and political movements. In both cases, the central tenet is the sustainable survival of a hospitable environment supporting the diversity of life-forms, not just our own species. This goes right to the core of the event industry's impact on energy, resources, and habitat.

Aside from the massive waste and energy footprint, the positive potential of our event industry can help inform decision makers, provide clarity around the complexity of environmental issues, even change hearts and inspire minds.

It is becoming clear that the crest of the next wave of community, business, and government innovation, and investment opportunity, is rapidly transforming the way commerce is happening. Market trends indicate that sustainable natural products and renewable energy and services will continue to climb steadily. Today more organizations are shifting from the "take, make, and throw away" assumptions of the Industrial Age to ecological models that vest profit and funding with environmental wisdom. Nonprofits, governments, and businesses are finding more freedom, resources, and profits through adaptation and reinvention than by retaining the status quo—an indication that a profound transformation is under way. The depth and breadth of evidence indicates that we are witnessing and participating in a societal transition as large in scope as the agricultural and industrial revolutions.

This transition is becoming apparent in the events sector as a catalyst for communicating values by adopting an ecological model using a triple-bottom-line approach (profit, planet, people) in the planning and production of events. From intimate, simple, and local, to large, complex, and global, event planners and producers, especially those in the public sector, have an inherent responsibility to adopt sustainability as their event guide. As a nonprofit, you have an opportunity to lead a demographic of consumers, businesses, and governments with beliefs about the importance of ecological health and social responsibility. Furthermore, by adopting an environmentally responsible and socially respectful (eR/sR) position in event production, nonprofit organizations will improve financial performance through sponsor, exhibitor, and attendee loyalty while fortifying leadership in the public sector.

Committing to producing a state-of-the-art green event informs public opinion, increases confidence among stakeholders, and capitalizes on a target demography's vision of a more just and sustainable world.

## Triple-Bottom-Line Event Planning

### Typical Day on Planet Earth: Imperative, Real, and Dramatic

Henry Thoreau wrote in *Walden*: "Goodness is the only investment that never fails."

A typical day on Planet Earth draws your breath away. The world is filled with very real, dramatic, and imperative changes that leave us feeling helpless. Today, as so many days before and so many to come, we are witnessing diminishing natural resources and air and water quality affecting our social fabric and tonal quality of life. On a typical day on this planet, it is estimated that:

- 15,000,000 tons of carbon dioxide ($CO_2$) are released into the atmosphere[1]
- 72 to 100 square miles of desert are created[2]
- 50 species are added to extinction[3]
- 170 million tons of topsoil are lost[4]
- 27,000 tons of chlorofluorocarbons are added to the atmosphere[5]
- 263,000 humans are born[6]

This challenges us to think, "What can we do, and how can we shape our events to reduce any harmful impact on natural resources while contributing positively to the local community and global planet?"

### Typical Trade and Consumer Event Facts

When we take into account that there are 1.2 million meetings and conventions held annually to the tune of $107 billion per year providing experiences to an estimated 136.5 million persons in the United States each year, we can extrapolate the event industry's implications.[7]

When we consider special events, such as music concerts, festivals, sporting events, weddings, parties, reunions, and birthdays, the impact of the event industry is staggering. This industry has one of the largest environmental footprints related to carbon and waste. A single 200-person conference event can produce as much waste in an hour as a family of four will produce in one year.[8] A study conducted by the Environmental Protection Agency (EPA) in 2000 analyzed a typical meeting/conference attendee staying at a conference hotel. The finding showed that the average attendee produces nearly 16 more pounds of trash per day, compared to the 4.6 pounds of trash produced at home. Extrapolated estimates calculate that meeting/convention attendees will produce nearly 730,000 tons of landfill per year.

## Atypical Opportunities and Responsibilities of Event Planners

As an organization dedicated not only to greening its events but also influencing the event industry, you are in the ideal position to invest in Thoreau's value proposition of goodness as a guideline: to shape and mold a more sustainable world without the assumed sacrifices. Green events are not a sacrifice; you can have chic, glamour, elegance, and be an eR/sR change agent, a captain of influence.

People muse at this notion of influence. However, I have found that my passion for event greening is fueled by what is often invisible to most people; it is in the science of sustainability that we find small changes creating great differences in the world. Through one green event at a time, you can improve the health of individuals, affect hunger, influence the long shadow of livestock and the diminishing seafood marketplace. Your green event can reduce landfill $CO_2$ and methane gases, connect deeply with a community through volunteerism, inspire others to recycle, and dramatically reduce energy and oil consumption. Your green event decisions will help shape the green economy by your support of businesses, venues, hotels, and caterers that practice eco and social ethics. This is not the challenge it sounds like; rather it is a journey of research, clear planning, and attention to making changes, one green event at a time.

## Seven-Star Steps to Success

In 1999, our company, Seven-Star, began a journey of creating the most successful green events in the trade, entertainment, conference, and exposition industries. Since the beginning, our operations incorporated solutions for the greening of every scale of event as well as the commercial facilities in which they were held. Our mission has always been twofold: to transform the event into a model of environmental responsibility and to deliver to our teams of volunteers the powerful experience of creating huge impacts on their communities and our planet.

In order to convey the philosophy by which we produce events and manage our business, we coined the phrase, "eR/sR," short for Environmental Responsibility and Social Respect. eR/sR is how and why we produce events, and events such as Green Festivals™, Green Cities™, Investor Circle, and Green Business Conference all reflect the best practices in the event production business consistent with this philosophy.

In addition, we make public awareness a top priority, highlighting the events' eR/sR initiatives and educating everyone associating with an event of its ecologically mitigating attributes. We found that by working closely with venue management and the city, what seemed challenging becomes an opportunity to provide green education and awareness centered on training and leading by example.

As an official U.S. EPA Waste Wise sponsor and Gold Star award recipient, our track record is the best in the nation and has set the standard for large-scale events. Seven-Star averages over 94 percent waste diversion for the 180,000-attendee Green Festival events around the country. Venues, facility managers, and cities all benefit from these results and realize that adopting eR/sR practices can lead to significant benefits, whether other events attract a demographic of consumers with deeply held environmental beliefs or not. When this level of commitment meets amazing results, loyalty increases among sponsors, attendees, volunteers, and exhibitors as an eco-friendly, socially responsible culture is cultivated.

# Seven Steps to Best Practices in Greening Events

## Step One: Determine Your Event's Footprint

Our approach to low-impact event production is to begin by reviewing an event's ecological footprint, taking into account energy and water use, waste stream, and the quality of products used. We see event greening falling into four major variables connected to each other generating various degrees of impact. We refer to these four categories as the Four Pillars of Greening. To understand and develop an effective greening plan, we begin by asking simple questions, then drill down into the specificity of what is being consumed, what is thrown away, and how we can improve systems to minimize negative impact.

**PRODUCT USAGE**  Do our products benefit, leave unchanged, or worsen the environment? Do they support the local economy? Can we reuse or recycle them? Are they U.S. made?

An audit of product usage and analysis of a conversion strategy to eco-friendly/sustainable products is a process. It takes time to lay a strategy of what we can affect today and what we will pursue tomorrow. Consider this checklist of product categories in your analysis:

☐ Cleaning products
☐ Product giveaways
☐ Consumable products
☐ Disposable products
☐ Show floor décor products
☐ Operational products
☐ Structural products
☐ Sales and marketing products, including all printed materials, signs, banners

**LANDFILL CREATION**  What is being thrown away that can be recycled, reused, or composted? What do we use that is disposable that could be reusable or bio-degradable?

An analysis of what is landfill is dependent on available regional resources in the secondary marketplace for recyclables. Often it is not obvious or even clear what services are available in a community for landfill diversion. Time spent researching on the Internet and good old-fashioned phone calling to determine waste haulers, recyclers, and compost collectors is time well spent. Starting with the venue and onto the host city, nonprofit and private organizations, farmers, and even military bases will eventually lead you to a supplier. The next checklists are the considerations and questions you will need to analyze to coordinate what we call a landfill diversion program.

### Resource Recovery System
☐ Identify opportunities for recycling and landfill reduction.
☐ Identify opportunities for reduction of supplies and products consumed.

☐ Analyze food waste and opportunities for composting.
☐ Consider input from attendees.
☐ Consider input from exhibitors.
☐ Consider input from the general service contractor (GSC), set designer, stage designer, and decorator.

**Energy Consumption**

Is my energy use smart? How do products and people get to my business? Where are the areas of conservation? What is in my control?

☐ Perform an energy audit to assess strategies to reduce consumption.
☐ Identify opportunities for alternative energy sources.
☐ Analyze attendees'/exhibitors' travel- and hotel-related carbon expense.
☐ Analyze overall energy expenditure.
☐ Analyze secondary energy usage.

**Water Consumption**

Is my water use smart? How do we influence water consumption by producing this event? What is in my control?

☐ Perform a water audit to assess strategies to reduce attendee consumption.
☐ Perform a water audit to assess strategies to reduce venue operations and production consumption.
☐ Perform an analysis of opportunities to eliminate single-use serveware.
☐ Consider input from attendees.
☐ Consider input from exhibitors.
☐ Consider input from food service providers.

## Step Two: Assess the Venue and Negotiate with the Vendor

Before developing an event's green plan, budget, vendor relationships, and the team to execute the plan, you need to determine what the venue's best practices are and the extent to which the venue is willing to work with you. If you have the option to select a venue that is actively pursuing sustainable practices, this will improve your execution and communication to your audience and participants. The venue selection and its level of commitment to sustainable practices will lay the groundwork for selecting vendors and the green guidelines you enforce. Appendix B provides an extensive questionnaire for venue and vendors that will help you identify opportunities for:

☐ Material reuse and recycling
☐ E-waste recycling
☐ Food composting
☐ Food and product donations
☐ Energy conversation
☐ Water conservation
☐ Carbon emissions neutralizing
☐ Product conversion to no volatile organic compounds (VOC), reusable, recyclable, biodegradable, and/or earth friendly
☐ Food and beverage conversion to local, fair trade, and/or organic products

Appendix B also contains our venue and vendor best practices questionnaires.

Negotiate with the venue your requirements based on your assessment of the venue's practices and your green goals. Request that your contract have an addendum added to indicate practices that are agreed on. From donation of food to charity, to bulk service condiments and beverages, to composting of food waste and biodegradable food service ware, spell out your expectations. Adding an environmental clause into the contract with consequences for noncompliance is always a good measure. Be sure to have your legal counsel review and approve all stipulations you add to your contract.

## Step Three: Develop a Green Plan

I cannot say enough about the benefits of adopting an ecological model using a triple-bottom-line approach in the planning and production of events. Whether your demographic of attendees shares beliefs about the importance of ecological health and social responsibility or not, your example and leadership will be respected.

Developing the green plan for your event requires integrating your goals with overall operations, logistics, procurement, coordination, and staffing. Greening an event successfully results from a coordinated communications and operations effort. Through this process, your greening guidelines will be in concert with the plan's change to event's overall production. Green plans need to be integrated into the architecture of the event for it to be effective and adhered to.

This step starts with establishing your goals for greening; whether they are in the form of a manifesto, policy, or wish list, they need to be drafted and distributed to all levels of your event planning organization. There needs to be top-down and bottom-up buy-in. The more the goals take the shape of organizational policy, the easier it is to align all decision makers and provide congruent, transparent messaging.

Table 5.1 presents an example of greening goals created for Seven-Star's Green Cities conferences, 2007. Examples abound online from event producers going green. Budget, bandwidth, staff, venue, vendors, and timing all influence how broad and deep your green goals are. Recognize that it is a process, a journey that takes time to perfect, and that at the end of that road there will remain more to do.

### FOUR PILLARS: ESTABLISH GREENING GOALS TO IDENTIFY ACTION PLANS AND COMMUNICATION

**Pillar 1: Identify Product Replacement to Earth- and People-Friendly Products**   There are dozens of Web sites with checklists and suggestions on best practices for transforming products and their use. Product use directly influences an effective landfill diversion recourse recovery program. Products are tied to energy consumption and waste. Listed below are the suggested best practices questionnaires and guidelines provided for downloading or viewing at www.sevenstarevents.com/greening;

- Venue Best Practices Questionnaire
- Event Venue: Landfill Diversion Objectives Questionnaire
- Event Venue: Energy Usage and Conservation Questionnaire
- Event Venue and Convention and Visitors Bureau (CVB): Public Transportation Questionnaire

TABLE 5.1    Example Green Cities Conference Goals

| I. Energy: Conserving and Neutralizing Sourcing | II. Water Conservation |
| --- | --- |
| On-site generation and transport | Public usage |
| Solar for outdoor features | Water canteens for all attendees |
| Biodiesel motor coaches | |
| Hybrid energy transport | Venue conservation best practices |
| Carpooling organization | Hotel conservation best practices |
| Bike valet | |
| Venue conservation best practices | |
| GSC conservation best practices | |
| Vendor conservation best practices | |
| Carbon offsets based on International Organization for Standardization (ISO)-certified restoration projects | |
| Electrical, paper, and office | |
| Travel, freight | |
| Renewable energy credits | |

| III. Products: Replacement to Earth- and People-Friendly Products | IV. Landfill: Diversion through Resource Recovery |
| --- | --- |
| **Food and Beverage** | Waste diversion |
| Local-sourced foods when possible | Resource recovery education |
| Organic foods when possible | Green team hosts |
| Fair trade beverages | Greening information campaign |
| Nondisposable service ware | Product recycling |
| Biodegradable service ware | Reuse |
| Biodegradable trash bags | Signage donation |
| **Venue and GSC (Show Decorator)** | Food donations |
| Organic fair trade soaps | Floral donations |
| No VOC inks for printing | Food composting |
| Green signage | Product conversion |
| No VOC cleaners | Electronic recycling |
| Recycled-content papers | Leave-no-trace policies |
| No vinyl banners | |
| **Marketing and Program** | |
| Memory sticks instead of large? | |
| **Conference Program Guide Printing Requirements** | |
| No promotional print mailing | |
| All electronic communications | |
| 100% recycled content and soy ink for business cards and print | |
| Collateral [print collateral refers to marketing materials—standard reference in the event industry] | |

- Event Venue: Public Water Usage and Conservation Questionnaire
- Event Venue: Product Usage for Custodial and Maintenance Questionnaire
- Event Venue Caterer: Product Usage Food, Beverage, and Services Questionnaire
- Decorator (General Service Contractors) Practices Questionnaire
- Exhibitor Practices Questionnaire

- Hotel Best Practices Guidelines
- Exhibitor Best Practices Guidelines
- Decorator (General Service Contractors) Best Practices Guidelines
- Food Service Providers Best Practices Guidelines
- Audio-Visual Best Practices Guidelines
- Marketing, Promotion, and Communication Best Practices Guidelines
- Special Event Planners' Best Practices Guidelines
- Set Designer Best Practices

**Pillars 2 and 3: Reduce Energy Use and Conserve Water**   Reducing and conserving our energy and water use in event production is the first imperative. Actual savings are seen through simple conservation methods alone. Although the carbon market's "carbon offsetting" products are valuable in helping the climate crisis, such products should be employed only after all efforts are made to reduce and conserve. I will leave carbon neutralizing through retiring carbon credits to offset carbon emissions to the many experts serving this market.

Use the Venue and Vendor Best Practices questionnaires provided for downloading or viewing at www.sevenstarevents.com/greening to determine what programs and efforts are already in place. Also identify some of the more visible programs and operations that focus on reduction, conservation, and alternative considerations using the next list.

- ☐ Identify and promote car rentals that offer energy-saving cars (hybrid, electric) to attendees and participants.
- ☐ Work with the city to arrange for electric, hybrid, or biodiesel public transportation.
- ☐ Arrange for all speaker, artist, and very important person transport service in alternative fuel vehicles.
- ☐ Identify and promote ride-share and carpool programs.
- ☐ Identify and promote a park-and-shuttle to a city event location.
- ☐ Identify and promote all city public and mass transit services to the venue.
- ☐ Work with the city traffic safety department on stop light pattern changes to reduce traffic idling to reflect the inbound and outbound traffic patterns for the event.
- ☐ Provide all vendor and exhibitors with best practices guidelines containing energy reduction tips.
- ☐ Identify and coordinate with venue all energy-saving opportunities and integrate them into event specifications and promotions.
- ☐ Work with all vendors using freight services to consider the biodiesel option or to offset freight and shipping transportation.
- ☐ See Venue and Vendor Best Practices Questionnaires
- ☐ Work with the venue to establish an alternative to individual beverage servings whenever possible.
- ☐ Provide attendees with canteens to eliminate single-use water bottle consumption.
- ☐ Work with the venue to reduce wastewater consumption in public area bathrooms and operations.

☐ Work with the hotel to promote best practices to reduce water in operations, housekeeping, and landscaping systems.

☐ Work with the hotel to promote energy conservation practices in guest rooms, back-of-house operations, and housekeeping.

### Pillar 4: Begin the Planning Process for Your Landfill Diversion through Resource Recovery

Landfill diversion resource recovery success is dependent on the elimination of all waste receptacles in the event venue and the placement, in their stead, of selected resource recovery satellite stations with volunteer hosts who make up the Green Team. The hosts monitor the stations to ensure that all materials are properly sorted into their respective bins. The hosts' role is to ensure that the recovered materials are sorted into recyclables, compost, trash, and liquids. This system can be set up throughout all the public areas where attendee traffic is concentrated and food service is provided. Where public stations are undesirable, a larger station is set in back-of-the-house areas where collected waste brought in by wait staff is transported to Green Team sorters.

Regardless of location, all collected waste is transported to a back-of-the-house area adjacent to the recyclables, compost, and landfill debris boxes and gray water collection tanks. This is where a final quality control sorting is done by Green Team sorters to ensure the highest level of landfill diversion. Steps involved in a classic public event are presented in the next checklist and illustrated in our case study of Live Earth Concert Greening for Johannesburg, South Africa (later in this chapter).

#### Pre-Event Planning

☐ Estimate the volume of recoverable materials to determine hauling and collection units.

☐ Develop a "landfill diversion-resource recovery" (LDRR) plan including all pre- through postsorting logistics.

☐ Develop an LDRR staffing matrix: position, schedules, and duties for volunteers.

☐ Coordinate volunteer recruitment with the appointed volunteer recruiter.

☐ Work with the creative services designer to develop signage for LDRR satellite separation stations.

☐ Plan for the integration of any sponsorship deliverables related to signage.

☐ Plan the composting system—from incorporation of biodegradable products with food service providers and exhibitors to the collection and delivery to the contracted compost collector.

☐ Provide LDRR guidelines to the food service provider to ensure compliance.

☐ Create green guidelines for all vendors—production vendors, designers and decorators, food service providers, and exhibitors.

☐ Coordinate the LDRR plan with the venue for collection and quality control sorting in the back of the house.

☐ Plan benefits for volunteer teams.

#### Pre-Event Operation and Production Management

☐ Prepare a detailed floor plan of the LDRR satellite separation stations and compost/recycling/trash collection centers.

☐ Procure a vendor, and coordinate delivery and placement of all satellite separation stations.

☐ Coordinate with the venue the location of debris boxes, compactors, roll-offs, or gondolas.

☐ Finalize the quantity of signage for visibility and education.

☐ Coordinate the delivery and installation of signage.

☐ Procure and coordinate the delivery of LDRR volunteer support items (T-shirts, equipment, supplies).

☐ Coordinate local area composting center and procure needed compost supplies.

☐ Liaise between the venue and contractors to ensure clear communication and fulfillment of expectations.

☐ Coordinate with the LDRR volunteer recruiter all staffing needs with related job descriptions and time slots.

☐ Review execution procedures with venue management and other participating contractors.

☐ Ensure that appropriate details of LDRR operation are incorporated into information handouts, as needed.

### On-Site Setup of LDRR Operations

☐ Participate in a pre-conference meeting prior to beginning the setup.

☐ Ensure that vendor deliverables for satellite stations, collection centers, and movement equipment are delivered and/or installed.

☐ Ensure that all LDRR signage is installed.

☐ Manage receipt and setup of delivered volunteer support items at the LDRR volunteer check-in (T-shirts, equipment, supplies, etc.).

☐ Set up the LDRR volunteer check-in.

### On-Site Management and Fulfillment of LDRR Operation

☐ Manage all LDRR program logistics/operations.

☐ Manage composting collection and delivery schedule to composting center.

☐ Manage LDRR volunteer check-in.

☐ Provide on-site training of LDRR volunteers during the event.

☐ Manage staffing for the LDRR throughout the event.

☐ Respond to requests and troubleshoot problems regarding LDRR operations.

☐ Document the LDRR at the close of each day and close of the event.

☐ Provide close-of-festival LDRR tear-down, packing up, final cleanup, and move-out.

☐ Provide volunteer support and management.

☐ Assist with troubleshooting.

## Step Four: Mitigate the Green Event Investment

The implementation of your green plan has the potential to create a new source of revenue. There are two steps for mitigating costs and potentially generating revenues: green plan sponsorship and green plan sponsorship rights and benefits for sponsorship.

### Green Plan Sponsorship

Select companies can be sold sponsorship in approximate alignment with the rights and benefits packages created for existing, successful sponsorships. Sponsorship opportunities come from a number of sources.

☐ Existing sponsors whose vision and mission integrates sustainability can continue to sponsor the event.

☐ Upgrade existing exhibitors whose vision and mission integrates sustainability to green sponsors.

☐ Enlist companies new to your event whose primary focus is on green and sustainable issues.

☐ Acquire media partnerships with companies whose primary or secondary focus is on green and sustainable products and services for marketing support for your green plan.

### Green Plan Sponsorship Rights and Benefits

Based on your proposed green plan, what you offer to sponsors is a very rich marketing, branding, affinity, and public relationship opportunity. The objective is to provide highly effective visibility that markets a company's products, enhances its public relations, and taps into the growing market of consumers who want healthy, earth-friendly products and services. Some rights and benefits that a marketing director may find appropriate and effective are listed next.

☐ Brand resource recovery center tents with a sponsor logo and tagline.

☐ Brand resource recovery station bins with a logo and tagline.

☐ Brand resource recovery station banners (used to visually locate and identify each station) with a logo.

☐ Resource recovery hosts at recovery stations may offer a sponsor-approved gift to each attendee coming to the station.

☐ Print a logo and tagline on organic cotton "Green Team" staff T-shirts.

☐ Make a 5- to 10-minute presentation at the Green Team volunteer orientation focusing on the company's sustainability mission and goals.

☐ Post a logo on the Green Team volunteer recruitment registration Web page.

☐ Place a logo on all greening-associated signage in all indoor, outdoor, and back- and front-of-the-house operations.

☐ Send a onetime e-mail communication from the sponsor company to all volunteers.

☐ Mention the sponsor in all public relations and media activities as the greening sponsor of the event.

☐ Sponsor logo-branded Green Team transport: Segways, electric carts, vans, and the like.

☐ Complete a documentary of the event's greening report including landfill diversion percentages and weights, public and volunteer experiential interviews, photo documentary, testimony, and so on.

☐ Host a Green Team volunteer thank you/appreciation party.

☐ Provide a gift bag with sponsor goodies to all Green Team volunteers.

## Step Five: Provide Best Practices Guidelines for Vendors

How do I know if this vendor or product is green or socially responsible? Some of the best and most trusted resources that I endorse are Green America, Global Exchange, Marketplace Transformation to Sustainability, and B Corporation. Many organizations vet products, vendors, manufacturers, and services. Appendix A provides Web site resources to provide guidance. However, by asking some significant questions, you can determine whether a product or vendor should be included in your green plan. Does the product or vendor . . .

☐ Eliminate toxic pollution or waste?
☐ Conserve and/or restore natural resources and habitats?
☐ Have no effect on or minimize climate change and ozone depletion?
☐ Support fair trade and socially responsible practices?
☐ Support sustainable business practices in its plant, operations, or culture?
☐ Follow a sustainable economic and ecological life cycle?
☐ Support its local community—"give back" to the community?

## Step Six: Establish an Educational and Awareness Campaign

Your green plan needs to be clearly communicated not only to your event's audience but to venue, vendors, staff, volunteers, sponsors, and exhibitors as well. Provide education, facts, and the drive for these changes in how your event will be different. Share your expectations in all your communications strategies.

As for media, consider developing a case study story of your event or providing a postevent audit report with photo documentary and testimonials from Green Team volunteers, participants, and attendees. Many audiences and stakeholders are involved in most events, from the planning process through execution. Consider some of these green education and communication strategies:

☐ Create a Green Resource Directory and Guidelines for participants.
☐ List recycling and composting facts for signage designed to educate guests and event participants.
☐ Provide press release content to a public relations agency contact announcing the launch of the pillars of greening your plan is executing.
☐ Provide press release content announcing LDRR Green Team volunteer recruitment information.
☐ Provide digital photographs of the LDRR program execution.
☐ Provide testimonials of venue, vendor, hotel energy and water conservation new initiatives and existing best practices.
☐ Establish an "Event Greening Pavilion" with information on the event's greening goals and lists of participating sponsors, exhibitors, vendors, and so on.
☐ Provide press release content quantifying and qualifying the program's success.
☐ Establish a green event competition/recognition program.
☐ Enter the EPA's Waste Wise Program.

**SUGGESTED STRATEGIES FOR EDUCATING YOUR AUDIENCE**   Events are, at their core, communication and experience devices. Consider all these communication outlets as places for writing, announcing, speaking, or presenting the active green initiatives happening at the event and your future green goals.

☐ Pre-event information
☐ Web site

- ☐ Exhibitor and sponsor information kit
- ☐ Hotel check-in
- ☐ Program guide
- ☐ Event menu
- ☐ Registration
- ☐ Event e-newsletters, Twitter, blogs
- ☐ Event welcoming reception
- ☐ Opening plenary session
- ☐ Breakout or concurrent sessions
- ☐ Plasma screens and signage
- ☐ Off-property events
- ☐ Post-event surveys
- ☐ Follow-up thank-yous

## Step Seven: Green Message in Marketing and PR: Creating Lasting Legacy with Green Events

As you articulate your adopted state-of-the-art green event, it stands poised to develop into a great story and organizational legacy. The increased targeted and national media coverage for a leading-edge event will leverage more investment into your organization and increase awareness of your mission and culture. It also will create a wave of excitement and invigorate enthusiasm among your attendees and participants.

Remember that developing an organizational culture around sustainability will strengthen your marketing message. Adoption of this green event model by your organization can effectively articulate the message to:

- ☐ National and regional media
- ☐ Other nonprofit organizations
- ☐ National trade publications
- ☐ Associations
- ☐ City and county agencies
- ☐ State environmental departments
- ☐ Sponsors and stakeholders

### What Defines Your Content?
- ☐ Identify environmental achievements by reporting on your benchmark achievements for use in all public relations.
- ☐ Relate your adopted strategies to enroll exhibitors, attendees, and guests in green goals through participation opportunities.
- ☐ Identify next year's goals.
- ☐ Identify the experiential impact on Green Team volunteers, guests, and exhibitors.
- ☐ Identify the experiential and operational impact on the venue and/or hotel and its personnel.

## Measuring Success of Your Green Improvements
- ☐ Create an environmental impact report and assessment on product conversion, water and energy conservation, landfill diversion, and so on.
- ☐ List costs and savings.
- ☐ Describe the quality of the experience.
- ☐ Assess its long-term impact.
- ☐ Offer an evaluation survey for attendees, sponsors, and exhibitors.
- ☐ Offer an evaluation questionnaire for vendors and suppliers.
- ☐ Report on the normalized event output of energy, landfill, and water compared to your event's reduced resource consumption.

    (An example of this report might say: "A typical event of the same size conference as ours would traditionally produce 2,400 pounds of waste stream. Our event produced only 500 pounds of waste stream. Of that 500 pounds, only 7 percent was landfill and 93 percent was compost, gray water, recyclables, cardboard, and donated food.")

## Accomplishment Reporting
- ☐ List the total number of volunteers per event and the total person-hours dedicated to greening.
- ☐ Describe the material waste stream captured by the description overview.
- ☐ List the material diversion by type, weight, and volume.
- ☐ List materials donated and delivered to community for reuse.
- ☐ List materials donated and delivered to local area food banks.
- ☐ Describe hotel participation values on waste diversion and energy and water reduction.
- ☐ Present an ecological impact analysis of:
    - ☐ Energy conservation activation
    - ☐ Alternative fuel conversion and renewable energy usage
    - ☐ Hybrid fleet usage
- ☐ Present an ecological impact analysis of:
    - ☐ Water conservation activation
    - ☐ Reusable water bottle program
    - ☐ Filtered water sales
- ☐ Present an ecological impact analysis of:
    - ☐ Construction materials conversion
    - ☐ Sustainable furnishing and furniture used
    - ☐ Imprinted substrate conversion of banners, scrims, signs, and uniforms
- ☐ Present an ecological impact analysis of:
    - ☐ Food and beverage conversion to organic, local, fair trade
    - ☐ Food and beverage service ware conversion to bioware

## Interviews and Image Documentation
- ☐ Present the Green Team volunteers' unique human stories.
- ☐ Describe vendor and subcontractor special contributions to the greening.
- ☐ Present digital photos of the greening process, volunteer action, and greening results.
- ☐ Present testimonials from the public and vendors.

## Case Study

### Building a Story: Legacy Case Study, Live Earth 2007, Johannesburg, South Africa

When Live Earth awarded us in May 2007 the contract for greening four concerts in four countries to be held on July 7, 2007, the Seven-Star team wondered how we were going to pull this off in eight weeks. South Africa, Brazil, Japan, and China had such different challenges, opportunities, resources, languages, and even time zones. However, we discovered that this work of greening events is all about the approach and attitude. We needed to approach each country from humility using our expertise to respectfully nudge existing practices into a system that could be replicated by the local communities. Enrolling the community, receiving advice, and engaging volunteers were the cultural processes needed to secure trust and desire that the legacy was for them to perpetuate. We were reminded every day in those fast-paced eight weeks that we were there not to just get the mission done but to pull together the community in a new way that could be replicated when we left.

## Conclusion

### Green Is Powerful

The convention and tourism industry in the United States, along with its hospitality industry partners, is one of the major contributors to local landfills. Trade and consumer shows, meetings, special events, festivals, and concerts are notorious for waste and until now have been poorly designed to include ecological and social responsibility. For-profit and nonprofit event planners are vested in creating an event that is successful, but we often fail to consider the triple-bottom-line costs of our event's environmental performance. If you are not paying to green your event, you also are not contributing to saving money in high-cost obligations. We incur societal considerations, ecological repercussions, and financial costs when we do not consider the larger picture of the impact of event production on our community and nation's welfare. We pay for negligence, if not directly out of our event budget, then ultimately by passing on the costs through higher health insurance, higher oil prices, and diminishing natural resources.

According to the Organization for Economic Cooperation and Development, if current trends continue, the industrialized nations will produce between 70 and 100 percent more waste by 2020 than we do now. The developing world will produce 200 percent more. Today we face a huge problem. The only way that we can overcome it and contribute to a sustainable solution is to practice what we know in our hearts and witness daily through media: Leave the world in a better place than you found it. I like to say that everything you need to know about sustainability you learned in kindergarten and from your grandmother. Eat everything on your plate, hold hands crossing the street, share, be kind, and put your toys away.

The central teaching of ecology is that everything in the world is connected. With each green step you take, you help solve planetary problems. When you buy fair trade products, you contribute to fair wages for farmers and producers who can in turn contribute to a balanced global economy. When you choose to host organic foods and organic cotton products, you contribute to putting an end to pesticides. When your office or facility chooses to recycle and compost, you contribute to reducing the next generation's despair concerning what to do with landfills. When your organization chooses to reduce energy consumption and increase energy efficiency, you create a more secure energy future. When management takes the steps to become sustainable, it sets in motion a culture that employees will rally behind. And that investment's return on investment is more than dollars; it is the valuation of public endorsement, new business, and leadership recognition. This word "green" is powerful. It is our next societal transition.

I invite and encourage you to lead your organization in the green economy parade. You will find that, one step at a time, you can march with the thousands of businesses and over 50 million Americans in this new wave of sustainable practices.

## About the Author

**Georgia Malki** is the President of Seven-Star, green experts to the event industry. Ms. Malki has over twenty years of event production experience and is deeply committed to the transformation of her industry to one that engages sustainability and socially just practices. Born in *Madrid, Spain*, Ms. Malki was educated at California State University in Sacramento, California, where she earned a Bachelor's in Public Administration and has done graduate work for a Masters in Art Education. She began her event career with Whole Life Exposition and Conferences in San Rafael, CA where she rose to Chief Operating Officer. Her implementation of the first recycling policy in 1996 helped lay the foundation for Seven-Star and its commitment to operating as a green company with a deep commitment to green all its events. Georgia co-founded Seven-Star, Inc. in 1999 as an eco-evolution of an event contracting consultancy with life partner Alan van de Kamp, and brother Joseph B. Malki. Seven-Star is considered the nation's leader for green event production and green education.

## CHAPTER 6

# Greening Your Organization's Travel

## Chris Seek, Brian Mullis, and Peter Krahenbuhl

## Introduction

Travel is an essential element of conducting the business of most organizations. Whether commuting to work, attending meetings and conferences, participating in trade shows, or delivering services to communities away from the organization's home office, travel expenses are often one of a nonprofit's highest controllable expenses. In addition to financial costs for the organization, travel also contributes greatly to its environmental footprint. Travel is a significant contributor of greenhouse gases, such as carbon dioxide ($CO_2$), which contributes to climate change. According to the Organization for Economic Co-operation and Development, these gases account for almost one-third of worldwide climate damaging emissions.[1]

Further, when we consider the resources used and waste generated by hundreds of thousands of nonprofits around the world at hotels, conferences, and business meetings as well as the $CO_2$ generated by rental cars, shuttle buses, taxis, and other forms of transportation, it becomes clear that nonprofit organizations have an opportunity to make a positive impact on the environment by carefully considering the decisions they make in the area of travel.

Nonprofits interested in being green are leading the way to help green the business travel industry by demanding "greener" travel options and searching for opportunities to minimize their environmental, sociocultural, and economic impacts. A recent survey from the Association of Corporate Travel Executives demonstrates how the business traveler is looking to "green" the industry.[2] The survey asked managers whether their companies were measuring social responsibility in the form of published, quantifiable data. Nearly two-thirds of the respondent said yes, and 48 percent of those who said yes also said this was affecting their relationships with travel-related suppliers. In addition, 29 percent said they had either switched to suppliers that offer green business travel options or anticipated that they would switch.

Travel agencies that offset their clients' greenhouse gas emissions, rental car agencies that offer hybrid vehicles, conference centers that host green meetings, and hotels that use renewable-sourced energy, reduce waste, and utilize fair employment practices are increasingly becoming primary considerations when companies negotiate business travel deals with travel suppliers. Nonprofits wishing to become greener are offering employee incentives to carpool, bike, or use public transportation to get to work. The use of renewable energy as well as environmentally preferred and locally produced products and services is also on the increase; this form of sourcing can reduce the need for travel both in delivery and pickup of items needed for services offered.

Many organizations are learning that by creating a green travel policy, the resulting positive public relations and productivity gains, as well as other associated benefits, often outweigh any cost differences. However, despite the willingness and interest of nonprofit managers to adopt green travel policies, limited resources and misinformation can impede this process.

This chapter is designed to help managers identify green travel companies, adopt carbon-neutral travel policies, and take sustainable trips while encouraging their staff to do the same, both for business and leisure. Collectively, these actions provide the foundation for green travel policies and procedures and in doing so help to ensure that your organization is doing its part to lessen the detrimental impacts of its travel.

## Carbon-Neutral Travel

Transportation is a major contributor of manmade greenhouse gas emissions and has a significant impact on global climate change. The U.S. transportation sector accounts for a substantial percentage—33% of the nation's carbon dioxide emissions (Congressional Research Service Report for Congress: Climate Change: Action by States to Address Greenhouse Gas Emissions, January 2007, http://fpc.state.gov/documents/organization/80733.pdf).

Case in point, an Oxford-based ecological footprinting company, Best Foot Forward, points out that a return flight from London to Brazil produces 5,271 pounds of carbon. This means in this one trip, a traveler uses twice the average *annual* carbon emissions of an average African (2,645 pounds) and more than half the average *annual* carbon emissions per person globally (8,818 pounds). An average American who takes one or two trips abroad emits 19,841 pounds of carbon a year. If everyone in the world emitted this much carbon, we would need two and a half planets to support us all.[3]

### Alternatives to Air Travel

Teleconference and video conference technology have come a long way and provide many of the same advantages as meeting face to face. In many cases, it can even be better, as colleagues are not arriving to an event after many long hours of travel. Also, consider alternatives to flying, such as taking a train or choosing a relatively green air carrier. Ask any potential air carriers about their environmental policies and carbon efficiencies.

### Carbon Offsets

Carbon offsets are mechanisms by which the impact of emitting a ton of $CO_2$ can be negated or diminished by avoiding the release of a ton elsewhere or by absorbing a ton of $CO_2$ from the air that otherwise would have remained in the atmosphere.

Keep in mind, though, that offsetting energy is not an excuse to pollute. It is a way to take responsibility for the pollution that cannot be avoided. Organizations should increase energy efficiency and reduce waste production as much as possible and then offset the rest of the energy used with clean and sustainable sources of energy.

Some emissions are unavoidable, and that is when carbon offsets can be a good option for nonprofits interested in becoming greener. Investing in carbon offsets and renewable energy is a great way to compensate for the $CO_2$ pollution you create when driving, flying, or using electricity. Your offset contributions stimulate demand for renewable energy, increase energy efficiency, and provide incentives for increases in the production of renewable energy.

Quality carbon-offset projects will:

- Diversify our power supply and reduce dependency on imported fuels.
- Support the development of resources and technology that does not pollute, helping communities reduce air and water pollution.
- Contribute to sustainable development, improved quality of life, transfer of knowledge and technology, and local job generation.
- Increase demand for renewable energy technology and energy-efficient products.

## Choosing a Carbon-Offset Partner

Organizations interested in purchasing carbon offsets will need to partner with a carbon-offset provider that will help you calculate your carbon footprint using a carbon calculator. Depending on the organization, the provider also may help educate your staff and provide marketing and public relations support to help communicate your commitment to carbon-neutral travel.

Ask these questions in four areas in order to select a credible offset provider:

1. **Cost efficiency.** How much of your investment actually goes into a given project? Is the percentage of funds allocated to projects divulged publicly? Typically, nonprofit offset providers allocate an average of 80 percent of gross revenues in the project portfolios they support; some for-profit offset providers allocate as little as 20 percent of gross revenues to their project portfolios. Bottom line: You get what you pay for—lower costs typically equate to lower environmental benefits.
2. **Credibility.** Are any, all, or only some of the company's projects certified by an independent third party? This is critical to the process in order to properly validate that the offsets you are paying for are certified and measurable projects. High-quality, high-impact carbon-offset projects are verified and/or certified by independent third parties in a way that addresses issues related to accounting, accountability, and true environmental benefits. Currently, the most respected certifiers include the Gold Standard (www.cdmgoldstandard.org), Green-e (www.green-e.org), and the Climate, Community and Biodiversity Alliance (www.climate-standards.org).
3. **Transparency.** Do the offsets support environmental "additionality"? When we ask whether a carbon offset is "additional," we are asking if it would happen

in the absence of whatever incentive we have applied. According to the logic of additionality, if the reduction would have happened anyway, then we have wasted our money.

The cost of the additionality tests is far lower in the renewable energy credit market than in the carbon-offset market. Simpler, cheaper additionality tests set a lower bar, allowing more projects—both "good" and "bad"—to get through. More complex, expensive additionality tests screen out more of the bad projects but inevitably shut out some of the good ones as well.

4. **Philanthropic benefits.** Does the project provide any philanthropic or humanitarian benefits? Although offset projects support renewable energy, energy efficiency, and reforestation, the secondary benefits—such as environmental conservation and community and sustainable development—are equally important.

Next we present an alphabetical list of top-performing retail offset providers (separate from the third-party certifiers listed earlier), according to a 2006 report titled "A Consumers' Guide to Retail Carbon Offset Providers."[4]

- AgCert/DrivingGreen™ (Ireland) www.agcert.com
- atmosfair (Germany) www.atmosfair.de
- CarbonNeutral Company (U.K.) www.carbonneutral.com
- ClimateCare (U.K.) www.jpmorganclimatecare.com
- Climate Trust (U.S.) www.climatetrust.org
- co2balance (U.K.) www.co2balance.com
- NativeEnergy (U.S.) www.nativeenergy.com
- Sustainable Travel International (international) www.carbonoffsets.org

In addition to this list, Carbon Concierge, a project of the Social Venture Network and Bainbridge Graduate Institute, recently published the Carbon Offset Provider Evaluation Matrix. It can be found at www.carbonconcierge.com.

# Green Travel Policies

A green travel program will educate employees on how to travel responsibly, recommend green travel providers, and introduce ways they can support destinations through travel philanthropy and "voluntourism." The next section provides green travel guidelines and an overview of travel philanthropy to help managers green their travel and encourage their staff to do the same.

## Before Traveling

These tips help employers and their staffs prepare for trips and make informed travel choices that are aligned with the organization's mission and values.

### Packing Tips
- Apply the golden rule of packing: Organize everything you want to take with you, and then cut it in half. Additional weight requires more fuel and produces more $CO_2$ emissions. With new airline rules in place, extra baggage and weight may cost you more money. It is more convenient and more eco-friendly to pack light.
- If you need items you do not have, consider borrowing them, buying them used, or purchasing them from a company that specializes in green gear.
- Leave behind just-in-case items. You can borrow or buy them locally, if necessary.
- Instead of packing an extra duffel bag for the trip home, take some items that you would be willing to donate to the local community at the end of your trip. Pack items that will be useful and green. Bring a reusable water bottle to avoid buying bottled, pack reusable utensils so you do not need plastic ones, and add bandanas or washcloths to use as tissues and napkins.
- When packing, remove any extraneous packaging of products that you may not need. For example, take your travel-size tube of toothpaste out of the cardboard box and remove the plastic wrapper from your deodorant. It is easier to recycle packing materials at home.

### Consider Your Transportation Options
Smart transportation choices are an essential aspect of traveling sustainably, but you do not have to limit your destination options based on emissions. With careful consideration, you can get easily from point A to point B without breaking your carbon budget.
- Flying is a quick, easy way to reach almost any destination, but as mentioned, air travel significantly increases your carbon emissions. Choose alternative methods when possible. For example, train travel requires half as much energy per passenger per mile as an airplane. However, there are things you can do to reduce your airline emissions:
  - Pick direct flights instead of ones with multiple stopovers (most emissions are released on take-off and landing).
  - Fly with a responsible airline dedicated to increasing fuel efficiency and decreasing emissions.
  - Offset your emissions every time you fly.

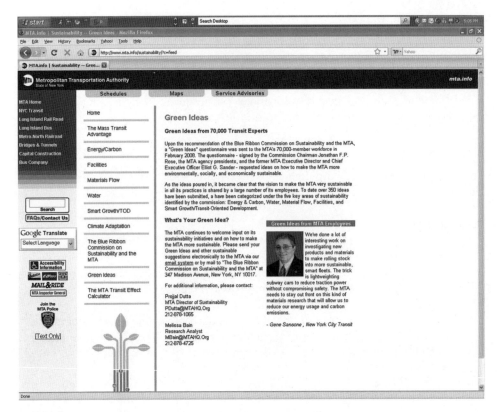

FIGURE 6.1    New York MTA Subway Web site (www.mta.info).

- Biking and walking are alternatives to oil-based transportation. Instead of renting a car, rent a bike for each traveler. This will lessen or eliminate transportation-related carbon emissions and offers excellent health benefits. If a car is required, rent a biodiesel or hybrid-electric car, if possible. If none is available, choose a small, fuel-efficient model; you will spend less money on fuel and release fewer greenhouse gases. Make sure the tires are properly inflated to improve gas mileage.
- Public transport is a fun way to interact with locals and is better for the environment than driving. Often it is also cheaper. Ask the tourist office or your hotel manager for information (one favorite online resource is www.hopstop.com)—they should be able to provide you with a map or point you in the direction of the nearest metro or bus station. Many public transportation companies also have Web sites so you can do research before you leave home (see Figure 6.1).

## Learn about Your Destination

Foster a true understanding of the natural and cultural environments visited before, during, and after the visit. Read up on the communities you plan to visit ahead of time (i.e., review travel guides, travelogues, blogs, local newspapers), chat with the locals, and try to speak their language. Be prepared to share your own culture and foster opportunities for cross-cultural exchange. Being prepared often reduces unnecessary additional trips and travel.

## While Traveling

The next sections are designed to help employers and their staffs do their part to reduce the size of their footprint and to make responsible decisions during their vacation while ensuring that both the traveler and the destination benefit.

### Reuse and Recycling

Here are some tips to help travelers reduce waste while away from home.

**Reduce**
- Buy a reusable bottle and refill it for drinks.
- At restaurants, drink tap water or refuse water if you do not want any. Drink fountain soda or draft beer to save wasteful individual packaging.
- Choose to eat-in at restaurants or grocery-shop instead of getting food to go in disposable containers.
- Decline any services you do not need, such as housekeeping services at the hotel (e.g., reuse sheets and towels).

**Reuse**
- Reuse disposable bottles, cups, flatware, bags, and other containers.
- Instead of throwing out books or other useful items that are no longer needed, leave them behind for another traveler or donate them to locals in need.
- Instead of disposable batteries, buy reusable batteries and a solar-powered battery charger.
- If you need something on the road, buy it used or borrow it from another traveler.

**Recycle**
- Ask the tourist office or hotel staff how to recycle in the area you are visiting.
- Bring an extra bag for recyclables that you cannot dispose of properly. Carry them with you until you encounter an acceptable receptacle.
    Note that many developing destinations have inadequate waste disposal systems and lack recycling programs. Make it easier on destinations by choosing the items you carry in carefully.

### Local Economy, Spending Money, and Bargaining

Travel has the potential to be exceptionally beneficial or unnecessarily harmful to local communities. By spending responsibly, travelers can support disadvantaged artisans and craftspeople in developing countries. With increased local revenue, communities can begin the process of sustainable development, which preserves cultural heritage and helps local people find alternative sources of income.

- **Shop responsibly.** As a traveler, you play a vital role in how the industry operates. As a consumer of tourism services, you can make a statement about responsible travel by spending money with businesses and organizations that focus on the triple bottom line: environmental, sociocultural, and economic sustainability.
- **Bargain respectfully.** Although bargaining is expected in many cultures, do not pinch pennies when negotiating. You may get carried away when trying to find the best deal possible, but keep in mind how this affects others.
- **Be thoughtful of your purchases.** Spending money with community or locally run/owned businesses benefits local people, their families, and communities. The money you spend on local artists and performers also encourages the preservation of their cultural heritage.
- **Avoid endangered species.** Never buy items made from endangered species, such as ivory or tortoise jewelry. Ask whether products are made from renewable resources or if local authorities approve the trade.

## Animal Welfare

When engaging in wildlife observation activities, visitors must be respectful of local species and their environments in order to preserve the destination for wildlife and for future travelers. For example, keeping the recommended distance from wildlife is important to the survival of species because animals lose considerable breeding and feeding energy while fleeing from humans. Voluntourism conservation projects offer great wildlife experiences while also protecting those species. In addition, many animals serve travelers by carrying baggage and humans. Sadly many are overworked and/or overloaded. Travelers can promote animal welfare by awarding their patronage to tourism providers who take care of their animals.

## Visiting Protected Areas

Travelers should visit protected areas because revenue from visits helps keep those areas secure and can help garner support for protecting new areas. Land and marine protected areas represent 12.65 percent of Earth's surface; of that, 11.5 percent is strictly land, leaving little more than 1 percent of Earth's water protected (2003 United Nations List of Protected Areas, www.unep.org/PDF/Un-list-protected-areas.pdf). This is a staggering statistic considering that 80 percent of Earth is covered in water. More marine and terrestrial areas could be protected with the support of travelers.

## Engage in Local Culture

Some ideas to help travelers successfully absorb and respect local cultures are presented next.

- **Observe local standards of dress.** Be respectful and dress smartly. Be sure to know the cultural norms so as not to offend anyone. As a general guideline, dress modestly, especially at any religious sites.

- **Speak the language.** Trying out just a few words of the local language will win you favor with most people you encounter.
- **Be aware of body language.** Many gestures have different meanings in other cultures; try to learn about these gestures before you depart.
- **Learn and abide by local laws.** Local laws apply, wherever you are. Do not expect your embassy to be able to bail you out if you get into trouble.
- **Understand the local concept of time.** The locals may value time differently: Some cultures are more hurried while others are more relaxed. Be patient and courteous.
- **Celebrate like a local.** Every region of the world has its own festivals and holidays that locals enjoy.
- **Stay local.** Instead of staying in a chain hotel or hostel, try a locally owned bed and breakfast, hostel, hotel, or inn. Another option is a homestay with a local family. This is a wonderful opportunity for travelers to make local friends.
- **Shop at local markets and befriend the sellers.** Buying locally leads to meaningful cultural experiences and supports the economy.
- **Support local guides.** When booking a tour, choose a local guide rather than a foreign one. You will be supporting a member of the local community and making a new local friend.
- **Make friends.** Be bold. Engage in conversation with the person next to you on the bus or at the bar. Try to introduce yourself in the local language, and then ask if they speak yours. Even if they do not, you can try to communicate with common phrases you may each know and lots of gestures.
- **Be a respectful photographer.** Ask before taking pictures of people. Some people do not want to be photographed. Good travel photographers are sensitive to the desires of their subjects and accommodate refusals gracefully.

## Voluntourism

Volunteer tourism, or *voluntourism*, is a type of travel philanthropy. Specifically, it is a field of tourism in which travelers visit a destination and take part in projects in the local community. Projects are commonly nature based, people based, or involve such things as restoration or construction of buildings, removal of invasive species, planting trees, and so forth.

According to a 2006 article in *Time* magazine, the number of volunteers in 2005 was 65.4 million; it is expected to reach 75 million in 2010. Thirty-three percent of baby boomers volunteer, and among those age 65 and up, there is a 24 percent volunteer rate. Of this total, approximately 300,000 U.S. citizens engage in volunteer tourism each year. Those under 25 and over 50 are the primary market, but a growing number of 25- to 50-year-olds are starting to get involved.[5] As an example of a for-profit introducing voluntourism, Unilever Corp. designed part of its annual meeting to allow employees time to help build housing with Habitat for Humanity, refurbish Boys & Girls Club facilities, and participate in the restoration and beautification of a National Recreation Area. Unilever spent roughly $150,000 on all three projects, and 2,600 hours of voluntary service were logged by the 600 participants.

There are, however, some pitfalls to avoid. Many nonprofit organizations do not have development experience, so it may be difficult for them to select appropriate partners and projects. In addition, travel philanthropy and voluntourism should not foster dependency in the communities they strive to help. These types of initiatives are most likely to succeed when they focus on individual and/or community achievement and where they reward personal and/or collective initiative and self-reliance.

## Selecting a Green Travel Company

Choosing a green travel company can feel like a daunting task. How do you choose from the hundreds of tour operators, hotels, transportation companies, restaurants, and activities available? What makes one hotel more sustainable than another? How do you distinguish true green from "greenwash"? Written environmental policies can read like legal agreements that provide travelers little or no insight into company policy. The next questions are designed to help you identify the most sustainable company to meet your green travel expectations.

- Is the company's environmental or sustainability policy clearly visible on its marketing materials?
- Is the travel provider actively involved in supporting environmental issues and contributing to the well-being of local people, particularly in the areas visited?
- Does the provider distribute environmental or sustainable tourism guidelines to consumers in order to raise environmental awareness among its clientele?
- Does the travel provider practice responsible waste management? Does it purchase or produce items that use less material, have a longer life, and are readily recycled? Does it reuse items when possible?
- Is the travel provider ethical from a conservation perspective? By selecting this provider, will your trip strengthen the conservation effort for, and enhance the natural and cultural integrity of, the places you visit? Does it encourage locals to proactively support the preservation of their environment?
- Is the travel provider efficient in the use of natural resources, such as water, energy, and building materials? For example, does it use water sparingly, taking into consideration that local people may not have a sufficient clean water supply?
- Are low-impact, energy-efficient technologies utilized in operations: for example, fluorescent or other low-energy lighting, renewable and sustainable building materials, rainwater showers, composting toilets, and solar electricity?

Eco-label and green certification programs are designed to help travelers pick out the most sustainable, responsible travel providers in the industry. Businesses are awarded an eco-label based on their environmental impact. Ask businesses if they are certified, and try to select certified businesses. Doing this helps create a demand for businesses to go through a certification process.

## Sustainable Travel Award Winners

In addition to certification programs and eco-labels, many green awards are given out to sustainable travel providers and destinations every year. These awards highlight the best and worst destinations, travel companies, and more. Try these resources to find some award-winning ideas for your trip:

- Condé Nast Traveler's Green List
- *National Geographic* Traveler Destination Scorecard
- Responsible Tourism Awards
- Tourism for Tomorrow Awards
- *Travel & Leisure* Responsible Travel Section

If your current providers are not engaging in these types of initiatives or are not willing to make improvements, drop some hints about taking your business elsewhere. This may provide them with the incentive they need to explore greener options and improve their efforts.

## Conclusion

Most nonprofit organizations already have travel policies in place. These policies describe the organization's rules and guidelines for how staff should research, book, and travel. Someone in the organization is appointed to develop and monitor compliance of the travel policy. However, the only way to ensure that green travel is encouraged and followed by employers and employees alike is through the organization's adoption of a green travel policy.

This is the perfect opportunity for organizations without a travel policy to establish a responsible policy that benefits both the traveler and the destination to be visited. By incorporating the guidelines and strategies described in this chapter, a nonprofit manager can ensure that his or her organization is contributing to minimizing the negative environmental and social impact caused by travel. Imagine if every nonprofit organization adopted green travel policies—this collective movement could help green one of the largest industries in the world.

### About the Authors

**Chris Seek** serves as president of Solimar International. He is a marketing consultant and international tourism development specialist with over seven years of experience. During the past five years of work in tourism development, Chris has provided marketing and consulting services to over 300 tourism micro-, small- and medium-size enterprises and tourism associations in over 17 countries. Services included business planning, Web site development, graphic design, Internet marketing, photography, virtual tours, video production, international representation, cluster development, business development training, sustainable tourism certification, cross-promotion advertising campaigns, and travel trade seminars. Chris holds an MBA in Marketing and Sustainable Tourism from American University in Washington, DC, and a BA in Communications from Wake Forest University.

**Brian Thomas Mullis** cofounded Sustainable Travel International (STI) in 2002. Brian has over 20 years of experience in the travel and tourism industry. He began his career working in national parks in Wyoming, Montana, and Utah. More recently, he was the president and owner of the World Outdoors, an international travel company specializing in active and eco-travel. During his career, he has assisted numerous travel companies of all sizes in the areas of sustainable and business development, sales, marketing, finance, and management. Brian has a bachelor's degree in Psychology with a focus on Business from Auburn University and holds a master's degree in Recreation Management from Springfield College.

**Peter D. Krahenbuhl** cofounded STI as the first global Sustainable Tourism nonprofit organization and Eco-Certification Program (STEP) in order to help companies measure and manage their triple-bottom-line impacts. He currently manages STI's European operations and its internationally recognized Global Warming and Carbon Offset program. He developed and operated an eco/adventure travel company and simultaneously authored the *Hunter Travel Guides Adventure Guide to Ecuador and the Galapagos Islands* (Hunter Publishing, 2003). Peter holds a BA in Economics and Environmental Studies from the University of California, Santa Barbara, and a Master of Public Affairs from Indiana University's School of Public and Environmental Affairs with an emphasis in International Affairs and Environmental Policy.

# PART II

# The Green Office

## CHAPTER 7

# Building Green and Greening Your Building

## Danielle Brigida and Kristin Johnson

Nonprofits and the people who work for them are always aiming to make the world a better place, which is why it is a natural fit for them to be willing and ready to incorporate better environmental practices throughout their work life—and throughout the very building where they work. No matter if your nonprofit owns its entire building, or if your staff of four shares two desks in a corner of a basement, this chapter aims to show you that there are things you can do—big and small—that can have a positive impact on both the world outside your walls and the environment of the office inside.

Yes, you may have a big challenge to overcome—that, as a nonprofit, you must spend every penny of every donation in the most efficient manner possible. However, you have two things on your side:

1. Sustainable building options have become cheaper, more accessible, and easier to incorporate.
2. Once you get past the initial cost of a green enhancement, it will most likely save your organization money in the long run.

Green building is transitioning further and further away from being an optional detail into being an essential part of the construction process. Even though your nonprofit might not have the same resources as the for-profit next door when it comes to choosing more sustainable methods of building, there are achievable ways to reduce your environmental impact.

Commercial buildings carry a hefty footprint when it comes to greenhouse gas emissions. In the United States, they accounted for 38 percent of all carbon dioxide emissions in the country.[1] Big ideas and strategies are needed to reduce this percentage and change the culture of how people work.

As you start making your nonprofit's building more sustainable, you will begin to notice people there making more sustainable choices. Maybe it is just easier to recycle because of how the building's waste collection stations are set up. Maybe the motion sensor on your conference room lights reminds staff to turn off lights in other rooms. One green action can have a ripple effect throughout an entire community.

# Getting Started

## Setting Goals and Expectations

Once you begin to look at ways to incorporate green practices into your building's construction, maintenance, and overall operations, you may find what seems to be an endless world of opportunities. To help focus your energy, you will need to make sure you set clear goals.

Talk with your organization's decision makers, budget managers, building managers, and any outside consultants to get everyone on the same page with your green building expectations. Who is guiding the effort? Who else is involved? Whereas one employee might be able to lead a crusade to stop people from printing on only one side of the paper, modifying building designs and construction practices will most likely require involving certain people in the organization as well as potential outside advisors.

As you start looking at ways you might make your nonprofit's new or existing building more sustainable, a good place to start is looking at existing green building certification programs. The next two, LEED and BREEM, are two of the better known.

**LEADERSHIP IN ENERGY AND ENVIRONMENTAL DESIGN**    Developed by the United States Green Building Council, the Leadership in Energy and Environmental Design (LEED) Green Building Rating System™ provides benchmarks for how to build green. The rating systems apply based on whether your organization's building is a new structure, an existing structure that your organization owns, or a structure you are renting. LEED looks at sustainable building through five lenses:

1. Energy savings
2. Water efficiency
3. Carbon dioxide emissions reduction
4. Improved indoor environmental quality
5. Stewardship of resources and sensitivity to their impacts

Based on the points scored in each of these categories, buildings can achieve LEED Certified, LEED Silver, LEED Gold, or LEED Platinum status.[2]

**BUILDING RESEARCH ESTABLISHMENT ENVIRONMENTAL ASSESSMENT METHOD**    Established by the Building Research Establishment in the United Kingdom in 1990, Building Research Establishment Environmental Assessment Method (BREEM) ratings are based on eight different categories:[3]

1. Management
2. Health and well-being
3. Energy
4. Transport

5. Water
6. Material and waste
7. Land use and ecology
8. Pollution

As a nonprofit, pursuing certification might be a bit of a challenge, as the process not only can be lengthy but tends to add costs up front. The process usually includes hiring an accredited professional to oversee your building's application. Make sure your organization is willing to invest the time and that it is understood that it might take a few years to recoup the additional cost through energy savings.

If your organization decides LEED, BREEM, or another certification is not the goal, at the very least, these programs are great places to find in-depth resources and breakdowns of how to tackle various aspects of sustainable construction.

## Hiring Green Professionals

Depending on the goals you flesh out and what investment your organization is willing to make, you will need to consider what architects, consultants, designers, or building managers should be employed for the project(s) you are undertaking.

For some projects, hiring a professional who specifies in green building might not be the way your organization chooses to go. Do not let this stop you from communicating your organization's desire to incorporate sustainable practices into all facets of the design and construction, however.

If you are looking to pursue an outside professional based on his or her "green" background, a number of tools can help you find a qualified, experienced contractor. The Green Building Certification Institute's Web site, www.gbci.org, includes a search engine for LEED professionals. Make sure to look beyond various green accreditations, however, and make sure the person you hire has produced solid results.

## Sustainable Building Design

The overall design of your building and its systems can play a huge role in the energy, water, and raw materials that are used throughout the structure's lifetime. If the building is designed well, the end result should be not only better for the environment but also better for your workers. Good design means creating a workplace that is comfortable and healthy and that helps the productivity of your staff.

The six principles of sustainable building design are:

1. Optimize your location.
2. Use environmentally preferable products and materials.
3. Enhance indoor environmental quality.
4. Optimize operational and maintenance practices.
5. Reduce nonrenewable energy consumption.
6. Protect and conserve water.[4]

Whether you are helping with the construction of a new building, moving into an existing building, or just looking for ways to make the building you are currently in more sustainable, these principles will help guide your efforts and help you achieve your goals.

## Picking a Green Location

Optimize your location

The location your nonprofit chooses to rent office space or build a new building can have a dramatic impact on your organization's overall environmental footprint. No matter how sustainable the inside of your office is, if a wetland was paved over to construct it, the benefits may be outweighed by the damage caused.

If you are in the market for a new building, no matter whether you are renting or buying, take a look at these areas:

- **How does your building fit into the surrounding ecosystem?** Avoid selecting a site that might harm natural wetlands, floodplains, or other fragile areas.
- **How will people be traveling to your office every day?** Location scouting must involve understanding employee needs. Know where the majority of your employees live and how they travel to work. Look into public transportation options for the sites you are considering as well as alternative methods of travel, such as being near a bike path or waterfront.
- **What is the community like?** Look for areas that offer many amenities in a compact area, where employees can walk to lunch and other businesses.
- **Consider a site in already developed areas.** Will you have to clear a lot of old-growth trees to build? How much will you have to modify the land? One type of area to look into is a "brownfield land," a vacated industrial space that needs cleaning up due to pollution. Infrastructure is likely available already, and you may be able to get funding assistance from the government to clean the space.

## Material and Appliance Purchasing

**Use environmentally preferable products and materials**

Using sustainable materials with everything from the carpet, paint, and insulation to the structural support that goes into your building can help conserve Earth's natural resources. Look at the materials that go into making every aspect of your office, as many things can be overlooked.

### Things You Can Do When Considering Materials

- Whenever possible, buy recycled materials.
- Purchase renewable, natural, or abundant materials.
- Make sure your chosen materials can be recycled at the end of their life.
- Buy local materials to reduce a product's carbon footprint.
- Use materials that are manufactured in an efficient way.
- Use materials that have a very long life span.
- Buy ENERGY STAR®-labeled appliances.
- Buy furniture, carpeting, flooring, and paint that are free of volatile organic compounds (VOCs) and other hazardous chemicals.[5]
- Buy items that have a green-certified harvesting process. Certification exists through many organizations, including the Forest Stewardship Council®, Cradle to Cradle, GreenGuard®, and Green Seal. As you hunt for green materials, make sure you verify their sustainability using resources such as the Scientific Certification Systems.[6]

### Consider Sustainable Options for These Materials

- **Flooring.** Carpet, wood, bamboo, tile, and laminate are just a few examples of the flooring options that can be sustainable under the right conditions. Flooring that is replaceable in sections (especially carpet) can be useful so that when the time comes to replace a stained or damaged piece, removing the whole carpet is not necessary.
- **Construction materials.** If you are building your office from scratch, use salvaged or composite wood wherever possible. Keep in mind that everything

from the fastenings, brackets, roofing, siding, and trim to the masonry, insulation, and sheathing can be made "greener," so be sure to read labels, verify with professionals, and check local resources.

- **Paints.** Choosing paints that have low or no VOCs will improve the air quality of your office and make it much safer. VOCs turn into a harmful gas that can cause problems for both humans and the environment.
- **Countertops.** There are several sustainable countertop options, such as recycled glass and concrete. Many of these options can be recycled again after you use them.

Of course, it would be a book in itself to talk about all of the sustainable materials on the market these days, but it is good to know that your options are only growing when it comes to the sustainable market. Get comfortable reading labels, asking questions and doing your research regarding sustainable materials.

## Indoor Environmental Quality or Indoor Air Quality

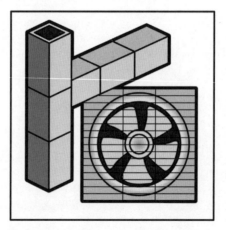

Enhance indoor environmental quality

With staff spending so much time inside your building, it is extremely important that the air quality and internal environment remain very safe. The quality of the air will affect not only the health of staff but also comfort and productivity. Pollutants within the building and a lack of ventilation are two contributors to poor indoor environmental quality. The trick is to build and renovate with safe and sustainable materials while also allowing for proper ventilation.

### Things to Improve Indoor Environmental Quality

- **Limit the use of materials with high VOCs.** These are harmful fumes that are often found in painting supplies.
- **Think through your ventilation and filtration system.** Work with a professional to make sure workspace is properly ventilated.

## Operating and Maintaining a More Sustainable Building

Optimize operational and
maintenance practices

Whether you are able to outfit your building with lots of green features or not, how you maintain your systems is an area of huge opportunity when it comes to making your building more sustainable. The person or people who do this for your nonprofit should be very detail oriented, and willing to know every inch of your building.

- **Start low-maintenance.** When you are purchasing heating, ventilation, and air-conditioning (HVAC) systems and other materials, consider the life span of the products, and choose low-maintenance, low-impact solutions.
- **Keep track of your energy use.** Compare monthly performance rates to the expected performance, and identify places where energy is not being used as efficiently as possible.
- **Know what needs maintenance when.** Establish a master calendar that includes monthly filter changes, tune-ups for HVAC systems, and so on. Whenever a new appliance or product is introduced into your building environment, incorporate the recommended maintenance time periods into that master calendar.
- **Adjust and tweak your systems regularly.** Look at your equipment's operating schedule on a regular basis to identify where things might be running when they do not need to be. Install automatic timers and adjust them based on employee behavior and the changing seasons.[7]

## Greening Your Building's Waste Management Practices

Chapter 13 goes more in-depth about the three *R*s and how you can apply smart waste management techniques throughout the operation of your office. However, when looking at the upkeep and design of your building, think of ways to minimize what your nonprofit sends to the landfill.

CONSTRUCTION AND DEMOLITION WASTE   Whether you are building new or retrofitting old, look at ways to divert waste created by construction and demolition from ending up in the landfill. This "C&D" waste includes concrete, glass, wood, bricks, asphalt, drywall, and items that can be salvaged as a whole, such as windows or doors.

Talk with your contractors about how they normally dispose of waste during construction projects. Work with them to identify areas where materials can be recycled, donated, or even resold. Contact a local builder's association, your county's solid waste department, or a local environmental agency for listings of what can be recycled where.[8]

**DESIGNING YOUR BUILDING FOR EFFECTIVE WASTE MANAGEMENT**   The opportunities your building provides for reducing, reusing, recycling, and buying greener can add tremendously to the solid waste your employees produce.

- **Map your waste.** Sketch the layout of your office through the lens of the waste produced by employees. (See Figure 7.1 for an example.) Flag obvious hot spots, such as the kitchen or mailroom, and look for less apparent heavy waste areas, such as an information technology department that may be unpackaging a plethora of electronic equipment. Doing this can help you ensure that enough collection bins are in place and identify ways to deal with big-ticket items that are not collected by your regular waste pickup.

Your nonprofit's staff make numerous decisions every day that impact the waste stream of your organization. Your building can be a key place to inspire greener actions.

## Greening Your Building's Energy Use

Reduce nonrenewable energy
consumption

When identifying ways to make your building greener, a major area to look at is how your structure uses energy.

- **Your goal.** Reduce the amount of fossil fuels your building needs to operate.
- **Your reward.** Major long-term cost savings (not to mention a healthier planet).

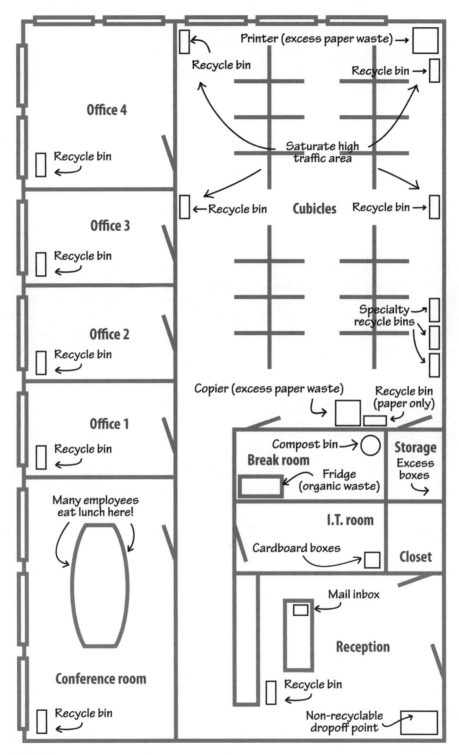

FIGURE 7.1   Designing your building for effective waste management.

*Source:* Illustration by Chris Broz.

**ASSESSING YOUR ENERGY**   Before you start, get an idea of how much energy your building uses now. Doing this involves some research and access to old utility bills and meter readings. The more in-depth you can take this assessment, the more you will be able to pinpoint and prioritize places where energy can be saved.

- Find out how much energy you are using on a monthly basis.
- Break down your building by area (kitchen, copy room, etc.) and by system (lighting, heating and air conditioning, appliances, electronics, etc.) to pinpoint areas of high usage.
- Consider installing power meters on certain outlets to track targeted areas.

Once you gain a strong insight into the energy your building uses on a normal day, put together a plan of attack for how you will be implementing efficiencies.

**HEATING, VENTILATION, AND AIR CONDITIONING**   The most important thing you can do when considering your heating and cooling systems is to carefully calculate what you need. Knowing these numbers can help implement the most energy efficient air-conditioning units and furnaces, keeping the amount of energy your building wastes to a minimum. It is also very beneficial to have the heating and cooling set on timers so that the temperatures will not be adjusted after normal work hours.[9]

- Install programmable thermostats, zoned systems, and motion sensors to regulate thermostat settings.
- Insulate your building with eco-friendly options.
- Use ENERGY STAR–labeled HVAC units.
- Schedule regular maintenance to ensure your HVAC system is always performing to its maximum efficiency.
- Use sealant around the wall outlets.
- Incorporate fans to help employees regulate the air temperature of their personal workspace.

**LIGHTING**   In the United States, an estimated two-thirds of electricity consumption comes from residential and commercial buildings. Reducing your electricity use involves a combination of efficient lighting fixtures plus the use of natural light. How your building is designed, what fixtures you use, and how your windows are covered can make a huge difference.[10]

**Use Natural Light.**   If possible, look to design your building in a way that allows for the use of a large amount of natural light. For example, in the United States, it is best to make use of south- and north-facing windows to minimize glare from direct sunlight. Even if you cannot modify window size and location in an already established location, look at what blocks light from getting in. What types of window coverings are used? Is furniture standing between natural light and certain workspaces in your office?

**Use Energy-Efficient Light Bulbs.** Energy-efficient light bulbs have also earned their name through more effective lighting than incandescent bulbs. Here are a few common options that are easy to find and highly energy saving:

- **Compact fluorescent lights (CFLs).** CFLs use 70 percent less carbon than regular incandescent bulbs and use the energy more effectively, too. They are less expensive than LED lighting and can be found everywhere. One thing to note: They must be disposed of properly because of the small amount of mercury they have in them.
- **Light-emitting diodes (LEDs).** Also known as solid-state lighting. These bulbs last over 10 times longer than CFLs but tend to be more expensive. They are best used for track lighting and recessed lighting and can be combined nicely with solar energy due to the small amount of energy they need.

**Incorporate Other Electricity-Saving Techniques.** If you look at every room of your office, you will probably find many areas that are often active only for portions of the day, such as meeting rooms, shared workspaces, and copy rooms. Think of where, how, and when the staff of your nonprofit uses light, and consider a few of the next energy-saving tips that might be suitable for cutting back on unneeded light.

- **Install ENERGY STAR light fixtures.** Along with the use of CFL and LED lights, consider installing or retrofitting your light fixtures and Exit signs with more efficient options.
- **Use motion detectors.** For areas that are used only a few times a day, install motion detectors that are triggered by movement.
- **Install timers.** For areas that need to be lit only at certain parts of the day (e.g., outdoor areas) put lights on timers. Remember to adjust these as the seasons (or clocks) change.
- **Post reminder signs.** Hang signs and display stickers that say "Please turn off the lights" next to light switches that should be off when not in use.
- **Use task lighting.** Instead of always using overhead lighting that illuminates a large area, incorporate smaller lamps and light sources.

**INCORPORATING RENEWABLE ENERGY** No matter how much you are able to reduce the energy needed to operate your nonprofit, most likely you still will need some type of electricity to function. For most buildings, fossil fuels are probably the default energy source. Fossil fuels are not only a finite resource, but their mining and production is harmful to natural resources and human health. Burning fossil fuels is also one of the largest contributors to the heat-trapping atmospheric gases that cause global warming. So if you cannot reduce this energy use, replace it!

The more you can incorporate renewable energy, the better. When investigating your renewable opportunities, consider these questions:

- What renewable energy sources are the most cost effective for your location?
- Are there any government programs and incentives to help cover the cost?
- Does your energy provider offer any renewable energy options?
- Does your nonprofit have any funds to purchase carbon offsets, even if it is just for a smaller chunk of your energy needs (an event, special types of travel)?

Tapping into the world of renewable energy might seem like a big step for many nonprofits, but do not count it out. The technologies are getting cheaper and more accessible by the minute. Here are a few of the basic options you should look into:

- Solar photovoltaic and solar thermal
- Geothermal heat pumps (GHPs)
- Wind power

**SOLAR PHOTOVOLTAIC AND SOLAR THERMAL**    Solar energy is one of the most affordable options to incorporate in your building. It can offset electricity (solar photovoltaic panels) and provide energy for heating air and water (solar thermal panels). Your building's capacity to make solar an effective option depends largely on your location and building placement; most likely you will need an outside expert to assess your location. The assessment, installation, and maintenance can be somewhat expensive, but solar panels are a long-term investment that generally last about 30 years. If solar is not feasible for your nonprofit today, remember that the technology is constantly becoming cheaper and more accessible to consumers.

**GEOTHERMAL HEAT PUMPS**    Another potential option to look into is a geothermal (or ground source) heat pump. These pumps tap into the constant temperature of the Earth instead of conditioning the air aboveground. Again, they carry a more expensive price tag up front but will pay off within 5 to 10 years.[11]

**WIND POWER**    Can't picture a wind turbine in your parking lot or on your roof? That does not mean your organization cannot tap into the wind market. Although wind energy has a number of limitations, ranging from installation and upkeep costs to potential zoning restrictions, it still can be feasible for your nonprofit. From 1980 to 2006, electricity generated from wind saw a sevenfold decrease in price.[12]

## Greening Your Building's Water Use

Protect and conserve water

Since only 1 percent of the water on Earth is drinkable, it is definitely important to conserve this precious resource when possible. The first step is finding out how you use water now. A good way to check is through previous bills. Some important ways you can cut back on water use while not having to give up convenience are listed next.

- **Sensor faucets.** Install touch-free faucets or add sensors to your existing faucets so that they release water only when someone triggers them. (Bonus: This also enhances personal hygiene.)
- **Faucet aerators.** These low-cost metal cylinders can be screwed into the water output of your faucets, easily reducing water flow by thousands of gallons a year.
- **Instant hot water delivery systems.** When hot water is needed, the faster a faucet can deliver, the less water is used. This feature can be put under the sink to deliver hot water instantly.
- **Low-flow showerheads, faucets, toilets, and urinals.** Install low-flow options that are more efficient than regular water appliances. Low-flush toilets average 1.6 gallons per flush compared to the 3.5 to 7 gallons or more that older toilets use.
- **Dual-flush toilets.** The user gets two options: half tank or full tank. A dual-flush toilet saves up to 26 gallons a day. These toilets are common in Australia and Europe. Figure 7.2 is an example of a dual flush toilet. These buttons allow the user to determine how much water is really needed on a case-by-case basis.
- **Waterless urinals.** Going the waterless route can save thousands of gallons of water; however, be sure they can be maintained properly by cleaning staff. They require that a cartridge is removed on a regular basis.
- **Old-fashioned brick trick.** Placing a brick in the tank of a toilet displaces some of the water. You can also order products to do a similar task.[13]

**GREENING YOUR BUILDING'S LANDSCAPING**  When investigating ways to reduce your nonprofit's water use, it is important not to forget the water used outside the walls

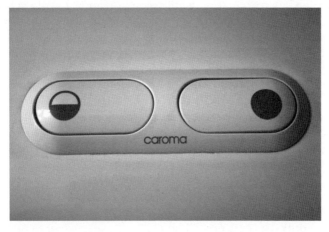

FIGURE 7.2   Low-flush toilet example.
*Source:* Photo by Kristin Johnson.

of your building. While this fits in the water section for a number of reasons, landscaping also touches on how much energy is needed to maintain your outdoor spaces and how your building fits in with the surrounding ecosystem. Landscaping decisions can impact:

- How much water your nonprofit uses
- The health of the storm water runoff that filters into the ground and water supply
- How much energy you expend maintaining your outdoor space
- The habitat available for wildlife to live in

Your landscaping is not only how you present yourself to outside world, it is how your building touches the outside world.

- **Reduce your lawn, go native.** By choosing to plant a flower bed of native plants rather than laying down rolls of sod, you not only can reduce the amount of water needed for irrigation (native plants require less watering because they are well adapted to the climate), but you also cut down on the energy needed to keep the lawn up. It also helps diversify the vegetation and provide food and cover for wildlife. The less lawn, the more likely there will be places for wildlife to live, eat, pollinate, and find shelter.
- **Capture the rain.** Look at how rainwater flows through your landscape and figure out ways to collect and reuse it. One option is to purchase or build a rain barrel. When placed under a gutter downspout, rain barrels collect water that can be used for irrigation purposes later. Also use mulch wherever possible to retain soil moisture and improve soil quality.
- **Choose plants wisely.** One of the easiest ways you can make a difference with your landscaping is by using native plants. Native plants greatly reduce the need for pesticides, watering, or fertilizing because they are accustomed to the local conditions. Native species often provide food for wildlife, such as birds and insects, and will enrich the environment surrounding your building. Planting native species will save you time and money when caring for your landscape. Make sure that when you make the decision to plant native flowers and grasses, you also diversify the species so that it makes for a healthier ecosystem.
- **Think before you pave.** Before you pave using asphalt or cement, consider newer permeable and semipermeable options. These newer options help reduce storm water runoff by allowing rainwater to soak into the ground.
- **Use natural pest removal.** One way to help avoid pests altogether is to go the native route. (They are more resistant to infestations.) However, if you find yourself in need of pest control, natural workarounds avoid the use of harsh chemicals. It is most important to identify the pest. From there, research should be done depending on your location so that you can find alternative means of dealing with the unwanted guest. Very often it is best to attract the pest's natural predator. If you go the "spray 'em" route, look at alternative herbal pest sprays, which can be very effective and will reduce the risk of harming plants and the surrounding habitat.
- **Compost, compost, compost!** Composting is a great sustainable alternative to sending food scraps and other compostable scraps into a landfill. Very often the discarded food sent to a landfill will be so compressed that natural

decomposition cannot occur. But there are benefits to having a compost as part of your building's landscape for other reasons as well. Composting can create great natural fertilizer and useful soil for gardening purposes.

■ **Create habitat for wildlife.** Habitat fragmentation is one of Earth's most pressing environmental threats. Residential, commercial, and industrial buildings continue to encroach on natural areas, dividing up wildlife corridors and reducing the amount of habitat range species have to exist in. Incorporating wildlife-friendly gardening techniques into your landscaping can help replace what your building might have taken away. No matter how big an area you might have to play with, providing food, water, cover, and a place for wildlife to raise young—while also incorporating sustainable gardening practices—can help wildlife find a place in the modern world. Incorporating these components can also help you earn the designation of being a National Wildlife Federation Certified Wildlife Habitat™. See www.nwf.org/gardenforwildlife for more information.

## Conclusion

No matter where you start when greening your building and your landscape, you will find that the opportunities seem to never end. New technology and improvements are introduced every day and are becoming more and more accessible for nonprofit organizations to implement. Do not get overwhelmed. Get empowered.

### About the Authors

**Danielle Brigida** is social media outreach coordinator of the National Wildlife Federation, the nation's largest member-supported nonprofit conservation organization. NWF is at the forefront of confronting global warming and protecting America's wildlife and habitat. Danielle is a part of NWF's internal Cool-It!™ committee, which was formed in an effort to reduce the organization's carbon footprint and create a more sustainable work culture at their headquarters and nine regional centers. She is responsible for communicating the NWF's mission and message across the social media world. She has a BA in Technical Writing from Christopher Newport University.

**Kristin Johnson** is Web producer of the National Wildlife Federation and is responsible for the development of engaging online content that communicates the organization's message. She too is a member of NWF's Cool It! committee, which strives to make their workplace and culture more sustainable. Kristin graduated from the University of Florida with a BS in Journalism.

CHAPTER 8

# Green Purchasing

## Britt Tang Sørensen

## Introduction

"Green purchasing" is defined as products and services where environmental impacts and energy consumption are considered side by side with other issues, such as price, quality, and delivery. All products have some kind of impact on the environment from the raw material, during the production process, through transportation, and to waste management. An example of a typical manufacturing chain is shown in Figure 8.1. It presents the crucial steps in a product's life cycle according to its environmental and health impacts.

By choosing green purchasing, an organization will contribute to reducing environmental load. In so doing, it may improve health conditions and also may lower energy consumption. When an organization demands green products, it motivates manufacturers to develop and produce more environmentally friendly products and services. The overall purpose of green purchasing is to reduce environmental impacts; promote greener products, services, and technologies; and be a good example to other consumers.

Before the organization buys a green product, it must consider some issues.

- What is the use of the product? Is the product necessary?
- Can an existing product in the organization replace the needed one?
- Is the same product found elsewhere in the organization?
- Could a recycled product do the job? Or does an even greener alternative exist?

Many questions need to be asked in the purchasing process in order to identify the exact product needed. Then, when the product is determined, green labels may be guidance to green purchasing.

## Green Labels: A Guide to Green Products

The term "environmentally friendly" is a classification of eco-friendly and nature-friendly abilities of a product. Certified "environmentally friendly" labels are primarily

## Life Cycle of an Ordinary T-shirt

A T-shirt's path from the cultivated field, to a store, and finally to disposal has several levels of possible impact on the environment and human health.

The life of the T-shirt begins in a cotton field, probably in China, India, or the United States. Cotton crops need lots of water to grow. Growing 1 kilogram of cotton requires from 8,000 to 29,000 liters of water. Therefore, irrigation is needed, and water is withdrawn from surrounding lakes and rivers. To prevent crop diseases, pesticides are spread in the fields, mostly in spray form by planes. Pesticides usually are damaging to the environment and, in some cases, also to the health of people working in the fields. One-quarter of pesticide sprayed worldwide is used in cotton fields.

After the cotton is harvested and cleaned, it is spun to make thread. At this stage, oils and chemicals are added. Often these oils and chemicals, which are damaging to the environment, will be released into water in the next processing stage, washing.

Then the textile must be cut and sewed. This is usually done in factories in low-wage countries, such as in Asia or Eastern Europe, where working conditions can be harsh.

The T-shirt probably needs bleaching (raw cotton is not completely white) and coloring. Chlorine or peroxide are used to bleach the fabric. Dyes containing different chemicals, including heavy metals, which have an adverse impact on the environment and human health, are used. The dyes may also be allergenic and/or carcinogenic and leave residues in the material. T-shirts that are sized may contain polyvinyl chloride (PVC), which includes small amounts of phthalates; these chemicals are suspected to be endocrine disrupters and carcinogenic to humans and animals.

Finally, the T-shirt is transported from the factory to the store. During shipment, chemicals are added to the container to prevent degradation of the fabric.

When the T-shirt finally is disposed of, it probably will be incinerated, releasing heavy metals and other compounds into the atmosphere.

It is clear that high environmental and health impacts occur at all stages of a T-shirt's life.

FIGURE 8.1    Description of the life cycle of a T-shirt.

called eco-labels. Besides this, a product may, for example, be "organic" and may be awarded an "organic" label. These labels and others are called "green" labels. In this chapter, the terms "eco-label" and "organic label" are used in these ways. The term "green label" is used to refer to a broad range of labels that pertain to issues of sustainable resources and use in general.

A broad range of green labels exists to communicate information about the health and environmental specifications of a product. The product properties are controlled and certified according to the label used. The purpose of the label is to guide consumers in buying green, nonallergenic, or healthier products. The green label guides consumers to the greenest products in a given category.

Before a product is approved for green labeling, it must meet several requirements. The requirements are based on studies that predict the product's environmental impact throughout its life cycle.

Green labels contribute to more sustainable production and consumption through stepwise improvements. The idea is to affect both production and consumption in a more environmentally friendly way. The criteria required for green-labeled products are reassessed every third to fifth year and go further than the environmental legislation. In that way, innovation is assured.

The price of products awarded a green label is not necessarily higher than nonlabeled products serving the same purpose. But the use of special higher-quality materials or special environmentally friendly production methods may lead to higher production costs. At times, manufacturers also add costs for the compliance verifications required for the award of a green label, such as product emission test results. Still, these higher costs are not reflected automatically in the product's sales price. Conversely, green products may save costs thanks to a longer lifetime, lower energy and raw material consumption, or simple product return. Buying green computers, for example, may save money by lowering energy consumption, enabling longer lifetime and easier recycling. In other words, green purchasing is not only an advantage for the environment; it may also support the economy and image of an organization.

Products that are not labeled still can meet the requirements for green labeling. However, lack of a label makes it more difficult for consumers to recognize these green products; therefore, the easiest way to go greener in purchasing is to look for the green labels.

## Certification Process

The manufacturer may apply for the green label if requirements exist for the group of products in question. If not, requirements are developed in a new group of products in an ongoing process, and a manufacturer may suggest a new group of products if no requirements exist. If the given requirements are present, the manufacturer fills out an application, typically found on the Web site of the green label organization. Then the manufacturer must document that the product fulfills all requirements set in the given product group. This is the crucial step of the application. Documentation of test data must verify that the environmental and performance requirements are met. Before the product is awarded a green label, usually an inspection will be made. The purpose of the inspection is to substantiate that the production procedure follows the outlines described in the manufacturer's documents.

In most cases, manufacturers applying for a green label eventually are awarded one because they are willing to adjust the production to match the requirements set. Sometimes the documentation may need changes or adjustments to substantiate that all requirements are meet. Usually this process is a dialog between the certificate organization and the manufacturer.

Products are awarded a green label for a period of three to four years. During that time, the certificates are controlled through unannounced inspections and product tests to verify that they have not changed in composition or content. This testing is done to ensure that the product offered for sale continues to meet the requirements of the green label. Noncompliance may result in termination of the right to carry the green label. When the time has run out, the manufacturer must apply for a renewal of the certificate.

The label is always awarded to a product with a specific trade name that has been specified in the application. In the final permission, this trade name is given a specific certification number, which is for that exact product. A green label may be used on the product itself, on packaging, in advertising, in promotional materials, and in product descriptions. However, it may not be used in general marketing of the manufacturing company.

Manufacturers pay an evaluation fee when they apply for the green label. They also cover the costs of product tests and documentation to verify that the product meets the requirements of the product group. When the certification needs to be renewed after three to four years, the requirements are reviewed and may be changed to match an ongoing developing process of the manufacturing. If the requirements have been changed, the manufacturer must again cover the costs of supplementary documentation and tests.

Also, the manufacturer pays an annual fee. The amount of such fees depends on the total annual sales of the respective green-labeled product or service. Some certification organizations give discounts for smaller manufacturers. Also, discounts may be given if additional products from the manufacturer are awarded the green label.

## Green Labels in Use

This section describes some well-established green labels in detail to show the principles of the different labels. In that way, readers are able to look a label up and get exact information without reading the entire chapter. The green labels described in this text do not encompass all the green labels that exist on the global market.

### Environmentally Friendly Labels

Eco-labeling is a voluntary method of environmental performance certification and labeling that is practiced around the world. An eco-label is a label that identifies overall environmental preference of a product or service within a certain category based on life cycle considerations (see Figure 8.2). An eco-label is awarded by an impartial third-party in relation to certain products' or services' environmental impacts. This is in contrast to "green" symbols or claim statements developed by manufacturers, which are not always documented.

Eco-labeling originated in a growing global concern for environmental protection by governments, businesses, and the public. Businesses realized that environmental concerns may have market advantages for certain products and services that purchasers are asking for. Therefore, environmental declarations, claims, or even labels now appear on products. Although the labels attract consumers who are environmentally aware, they also have led to confusion.

In 1994, Global Eco-labeling Network (GEN) was founded as an association to improve, promote, and develop the eco-labeling of products and services. According to the GEN, principles for eco-labeling are:

- Voluntary participation.
- Compliance with environmental and other relevant legislation.

FIGURE 8.2   Eco-labeling participants.

*Source:* Global Eco-labeling Network Information Paper, 2004.

- Comparable quality and reasonable performance in relation to product alternatives.
- Substantiated on sound scientific knowledge based on life-cycle considerations.
- Requirements must distinguish leadership of a product category from the rest of the category.
- Requirements must be credible, relevant, attainable, and measurable.
- The eco-labeling process including determination of award requirements should be operated by an independent organization.
- The eco-labeling must be an open and accountable process.
- The process must be flexible. This requires, for example, periodic reviews and updates of the award requirements.
- Consistency with ISO (International Organization for Standardization) 14020 and ISO 14024 or other relevant documents.

All eco-labels described below are part of GEN, among others. To become a member, the eco-labeling organization must share the objectives and basic requirements of GEN.

**THE SWAN**    The Swan is the official Scandinavian eco-label introduced by the Nordic Council of Ministers. A product labeled with the Swan is among the least environmentally hazardous within its group. A Swan label shows that a product fulfills strict environmental requirements. The aim of the requirements is to reduce the use of substances that are harmful to health and environment; the requirements also ensure long lifetime and recyclability of the product. The Swan considers the product's impact throughout its life cycle and also sets criteria for product quality and performance. Products marked with the Swan must be at least as good as other similar but noncertified products on the market.

Before a product can be certified with the Swan label, the manufacturers have to document that the product fulfills the requirements set. Some overall principles may be followed, such as:

- All requirements in the criteria are to be met and verifiable during the period of the license.
- The product must be traceable through the entire production, and any changes in the production have to be reported to Nordic Eco-labeling immediately if the changes have any impact on health or environment.
- There has to be a specified person in the organization responsible for guaranteeing that the criteria of the label are fulfilled.

Necessary environmental requirements could be:

- No or very low content of heavy metals.
- Substances may be easily degradable in the environment.
- Reduced packaging to minimize waste.
- Low noise levels of the product.

The Swan label has specific requirements for each group of products. Swan-labeled groups of products are broad, ranging from paper supplies and personal care products, to furniture and paints. An example could be candles. Candles that are labeled with the Swan must not use phthalates or compounds for the purpose of fragrance. No packaging materials containing polyvinylchloride or other chlorinated materials are allowed. Swan-labeled candles are made of more than 90 percent stearic acid instead of the usual material, paraffin. Stearic acid is an environmentally friendly compound that comes from renewable materials. In fact, if all European candles were Swan-labeled candles, there would be 841,000 fewer tons of carbon dioxide in the atmosphere per year, which could help to counteract the climate changes. More information on Swan labeling is available at www.svanen.nu.

**THE FLOWER**    The Flower is a European Union eco-label. The EU label was established in 1992 to encourage the manufacturing and consumption of green products in Europe. Requirements are set by the European Union Eco-labeling board, which includes the European Commission, national organizations that are responsible for the Flower, and representatives from business, consumers, environmental organizations, and unions. These participants ensure an open process and that all interested parties are heard about the chosen requirements.

The Flower label is used for several different product groups, except for food, drinks, pharmaceuticals, and medical devices. The purpose is to guide consumers to find the greener products and services. Products awarded the Flower need to fulfill environmental, health, and performance requirements that are specified considering the product's life cycle. Requirements may vary according to the concerned product and generally include:

- No use of substances that deplete the ozone layer
- Reduced use of hazardous chemicals
- Low energy consumption
- Minimized waste

Paint and varnish, for example, comprise one group of products, defined as full-covering material with specific properties. The requirements set by the Flower for this group, are, among others, reduced emission of volatile organic compounds; no use of mercury; and no use of substances that are classified as endocrine disrupters. Requirements according to the quality of the product could be a specific hiding power of the paint or varnish and some resiliency to water. Another important requirement is that the correct usage of the product must be described in detail on the outside of the packaging.

More information is available at http://ec.europa.eu/environment/ecolabel.

**BLUE ANGEL**   The Blue Angel (Der Blaue Engel) is a German governmental eco-label. The Blue Angel was established in 1978 and is believed to be the oldest eco-label for products and services. It is the best-known eco-label worldwide with thousands of products labeled in more than 80 different categories. The Blue Angel covers a wide variety of products from paper and toys, to construction machinery and electrical devices. The label considers both environmental and health protection.

The requirements for awarding the Blue Angel are based on the environmental impact of the product throughout its life cycle and the product's quality. The label is awarded to the greenest products in a group. The Blue Angel label always provides two types of information.

1. It distinguishes the green product from nongreen products in a similar group.
2. The label clearly refers to the environmental benefit, such as "The Blue Angel because low in emission" on wall paint products. Wall paint awarded the Blue Angel contains far fewer solvents and other pollutants than other paints.

The German Federal Environmental Agency decides the requirements for a given product and reviews and, if necessary, revises the requirements every third or fourth year. This period can be shortened for product groups where more rapid techno- logical innovation is expected. At the end of a period, the agency resubmits the requirements for award of the Blue Angel to the Environmental Label Jury for deci- sion. This jury is appointed by the German minister of environment for a three-year term and includes representatives from environmental authorities, environmental organizations and unions, as well as industries and other relevant experts.

Examples of requirements are:

- Recycling
- No use of hazardous chemicals, such as heavy metals or bleach
- No use of sprays
- Low emission of volatile organic compounds

A product, for example, could be printing paper. Printing paper awarded the Blue Angel fulfills these requirements:

- A certain minimum of waste paper is used in the production of new paper.
- The waste paper treatment is done without use of chlorine, halogenated bleach- ing agents, and poorly biodegradable agents.
- Colorants used in the production of printing paper may not contain heavy metals or azo dyes.
- The original timber used must be verifiable.

More information is available at www.blauer-engel.de/en/index.php.

**GREEN SEAL**  Green Seal is an independent organization with the mission to cre- ate a more sustainable economy by identifying and promoting environmentally responsible products and services. In particular, Green Seal is devoted to setting environmental requirements and certifying products in a wide variety of product groups. Green Seal began in 1989 and receives support for its program from certi- fication fees, foundations, donations, and government grants and contracts. Green

Seal requirements reduce the environmental impacts associated with the manufacture, use, and disposal of a product. The requirements have to be technologically and economically feasible.

Green Seal sets requirements for products based on the best available scientific data and market information, expert consultation, and stakeholder input. All parties of interest are consulted and involved in the setting of requirements. In making general requirements for product groups, an advisory group of stakeholders is formed with the purpose to help identify potential environmental impacts and issues. Then the Green Seal organization gathers and analyzes the data, often in cooperation with outside experts, to find the areas of greatest environmental impact in the product's life cycle. The proposed requirements from Green Seal are commented on by interested parties, and finally the requirements are approved by the Environmental Standards Committee of Green Seal's board of directors. Examples of requirements are:

- Reduced energy consumption
- Reduced emission of solvents
- Reduced use of hazardous substances
- Recycling

Specific requirements are associated with each product. Industrial hand soap, for example, may have to meet these requirements in order to be awarded the Green Seal:

- The product must show equivalent or better performance compared to a conventional product, such as rinsing.
- The soap must not be a skin irritant in three testing scenarios.
- The hand soap must not contain halogenated organic compounds or EDTA.
- The hand soap must be formulated with only food-grade dyes.
- The packaging of the product must be recyclable.

If a given hand soap is awarded the Green Seal, it will carry the label and this statement: "This product meets Green Seal's environmental standard for industrial hand cleaners based on its reduced human and aquatic toxicity and reduced smog production potential."

More information is available at: http://greenseal.org/findaproduct/index.cfm.

## Energy Labels

Energy labels guide users to products with lower energy consumption. Furthermore, the labels state that higher initial costs of a product are paid back by lower energy costs throughout the product's lifetime. Energy labels may be awarded to office equipment, household appliances, buildings, and others.

According to the European Climate Change Programme (ECCP), office equipment accounts for a significant share of total electricity consumption. Also, it accounts for increasing costs on the electricity bill in private homes, business, and organizations. Together, this means that office equipment is the group of products with the highest potential of saving energy. The ECCP indicates that if appropriate measures are taken, over 50 percent of the energy used by office equipment today could be saved.

Some eco-labels may have requirements to reduce a product's energy consumption. Energy labels, as the name implies, have focused requirements set to reduce energy consumption. Two energy labels are described in detail next.

**TCO**   The TCO label is developed by the company TCO Development and is specified for electronics such as laptops, desktops, printers, mobile devices, and office furniture. Products bearing the TCO label can be found globally. Approximately half of all displays, like TV and computer screens, in the world are TCO-labeled. Depending on the product, the requirements may be:

■ Reduction of radiation
■ Low emission of chemicals

- No use of environmentally hazardous substances
- Recycling of the product

The requirements are based on the product's life cycle with a focus on environmental impacts and consequences to indoor climate. Therefore, TCO-labeled products not only are environmentally friendly but also contribute to a better indoor climate compared to non-TCO-certified products.

The requirements are established through dialog among users, manufacturers, researchers, and other experts. It is the manufacturers' responsibility to ensure that the TCO-labeled product fulfills the requirements continuously. In order to use the label, the product must be tested in an approved laboratory. A TCO certificate is valid for three years.

Several TCO certifications with different corresponding labels exist. Each certification lists the year of issue and the specified product. Four different certifications are shown in the graphic. Desktop computers, for example, may get a standard TCO'05 Desktop certification. TCO-labeled desktops have to meet certain requirements, such as substantial reduction of magnetic and electrical fields, low energy consumption, and reduced emission of heavy metals and brominated flame retardants, and they must be easy to recycle. Finally, the amount of chemicals used is controlled in order to minimize impact on the environment.

For more information, see www.tcodevelopment.com.

**ENERGY STAR** ENERGY STAR is an international voluntary labeling program for energy efficiency started by the U.S. Environmental Protection Agency (EPA) in 1992 to identify and promote energy-efficient products and to prevent air pollution. The ENERGY STAR label is awarded to over 50 product groups, such as office equipment, lighting, and home electronics. Through an agreement with the U.S. government, the European Community is participating in the ENERGY STAR program in matters related to office equipment.

The ENERGY STAR program focuses on energy consumption of office equipment during product life. Most studies conclude that, for an office computer, primary energy consumption during use is three to four times higher than the primary energy needed for manufacturing and production of materials. This is true for the life of both laptop and desktop computers. For an office computer, the energy costs of waste disposal and recycling are less than 15 percent of the production energy. The fraction of primary energy used by PC/monitors is illustrated in Figure 8.3.

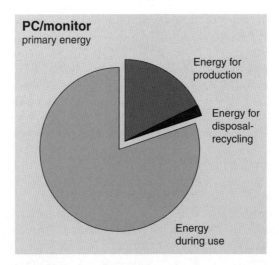

FIGURE 8.3    View of relative energy consumption.
*Source:* European Commission.


The ENERGY STAR guidelines are distinct in three operating modes of the equipment: standby, active, and sleep modes. Requirements for each type of equipment are set according to these modes. This distinction ensures reduction in energy consumption when the equipment is in use and on standby. Additionally, ENERGY STAR–labeled products must have a more efficient internal power supply than non-labeled products.

To develop or change ENERGY STAR requirements, an evaluation process is established involving such stakeholders as manufacturers, environmental groups, and different government agencies. The EPA and Department of Energy follow some key principles to determine whether to label a product group. If a product is awarded the ENERGY STAR, it meets these overall requirements:

- Significant energy savings are realized on a national basis.
- Product performance is maintained or enhanced with increased energy efficiency.
- Purchasers recover their investment in increased energy efficiency within a reasonable period of time.
- Energy efficiency can be achieved with several technology options to avoid competitive distortions.
- Product energy consumption and performance is measured and verified by testing.
- The label effectively differentiates products and is visible for purchasers.

To become an ENERGY STAR partner, the manufacturer agrees to follow a specific partner agreement with obligations such as providing clear and consistent labeling and educating users in power management. As an ENERGY STAR partner, the manufacturer is self-responsible for ensuring that the product follows the exact product requirements set. EPA or the European Commission may conduct tests on products to verify that the product is ENERGY STAR qualified continuously. There is no fee to join the program and use the label.

The requirements are set for each group of products. A computer, for example, awarded the ENERGY STAR meets key requirements, such as use of energy-efficient power supply and efficiently operating in standby, sleep, and idle modes. Also, it may include and enable system power management features and provide user education about these features. Regarding computer performance, requirements could be a certain minimum of system memory and automatic sleep mode after 15 minutes of inactivity from the user.

For more information, see www.energystar.gov.

## Wooden Products

Some overall considerations regarding wood purchases include the quality, strength, and appearance that the wood must have. Is a particular wood needed, or could several kinds be used?

"Green wood" means legal and sustainable wood. However, it is difficult for consumers to determine the accuracy of the claim. If a manufacturer claims a product is green, potential buyers may consider some general principles to prove the greenness. Potential buyers may look at statements from authorities, suppliers, and secondary suppliers, or documented environmental management that substantiates the greenness. Also indications of principles and criteria in the forest management, developing process, and control methods will indicate the greenness of the given product.

The easiest and most reliable way to purchase a green wood product is to use the existing certificates as guidance. Several wood certifications exist, including Forest Stewardship Council (FSC), Program for the Endorsement of Forest Certification (PFEC), Malaysian Timber Certification Council (MTCC), and Lean Enterprise Institute (LEI). Two well-established certifications, FSC and PFEC, will be described in detail.

**FSC**  The Forest Stewardship Council is an international nonprofit certification given to sustainable wood and paper. All types of forests can be FSC labeled, from tropical rain forests to Siberian conifer forests. In an FSC-labeled forest, a limited amount of trees are harvested to ensure that the forest will reproduce itself. Endangered species and vulnerable areas are saved against deforestation. To secure a better environment for plant and animal species, untouched forest areas are larger in FSC-labeled forests than in regular ones, and some specified trees may never be harvested to ensure natural conditions. Also the use of hazardous pesticides and genetically modified trees is forbidden in FSC-labeled forests.

The FSC looks closely at the local population and workers when issuing certificates. Workers must be educated and have the correct equipment, earn a decent salary, and have decent working conditions. Also, workers may have the right to organize unions. The local population receives a part of the profit to use for schools, clinics, and the like. Traditional access and use of the forest are ensured for indigenous peoples. Areas with cultural or religious heritage are mapped and protected. Indigenous peoples are involved in the forest management and receive economic compensation if their know-how or resources are used (see Figure 8.4).

Since different countries have different types of forests, the FSC board defines national standards for the specific country, in addition to the general standards. More than 20,000 products are FSC labeled globally, and the FSC certification is found in 84 countries worldwide. All FSC certifications are controlled by independent companies. All FSC-labeled products are reviewed a minimum of once every year. Also, the certification body makes unannounced control visits if needed.

For more information, see www.fsc.org.

**PEFC**   The Program for the Endorsement of Forest Certification council is an independent, nonprofit, nongovernmental organization. PEFC originated as a European

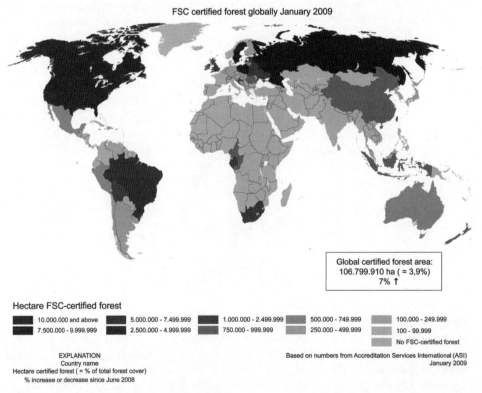

FIGURE 8.4   Global FSC-certified forest area by region.

*Source:* FSC Denmark.

certification in 1999. Now the certification is in use worldwide, including 35 independent national forest certification systems. The assessment process for each certificate involves public consultation and independent parties.

The purpose of the program is to encourage sustainable management of forests. Compared to other existing wood certificates, PEFC focuses especially on ensuring that small-scale forestlands can get certified. It is possible to certify groups of forestlands instead of individually. Various requirements must be met for both individual and group certificates. Requirements vary in each country with different kinds of forests. The requirements are set based on social and economic conditions in the given country and to maintain the natural forest conditions, such as protecting biodiversity and vulnerable or endangered species. Requirements include:

- Limiting cultivation of soil in the forest
- Protecting native species in the forest
- Enlarging areas of untouched forest
- Reducing use of and phasing out fertilizers

To obtain a PEFC label, the wood must be traceable every step through the chain. This demands that the company have a so-called chain-of-custody certification, which is controlled in certain ways to ensure that certified raw material is clearly identified and separated from noncertified material. PEFC covers wood and paper products from all types of forests. The certificates are controlled by annual inspections of the certified forests and manufacturers by third-party companies.

For more information, see www.pefc.org/internet/html.

## Textiles

Green purchasing of textiles such as T-shirts, tablecloths, and banners is possible as well. A number of certifications cover this topic. Most of the certifications follow the Global Organic Textile Standard (GOTS).

**GOTS** Overall, the Global Organic Textile Standard lays down requirements for organic textiles, from harvesting to the end product, including standards for environmental and socially responsible manufacturing of the product. The standards cover the production, processing, manufacturing, packaging, labeling, exportation, importation, and distribution of all natural fibers. The final products could be fiber products, yarns, fabrics, and clothes.

GOTS has two label grades. The first is organic and organic—in conversion. In the organic—in conversion grade, 95 percent or more of the fiber content of the products must be certified organic or from an "in conversion" period. Up to 5 percent fibers can be nonorganic fibers including regenerated and synthetic fibers.

The second grade says "made with x% organic materials" or "made with x% organic—in conversion materials." Here no less than 70 percent of the fiber content of the product must be certified organic. Up to 30 percent may be nonorganic fibers, but GMO (genetically modified organism) fibers are not permitted.

The organic fibers must be separated from conventional fibers in all stages of the production to prevent mixing of the different fibers.

According to general GOTS requirements, in all production stages, some substances are prohibited and some are restricted. For example, the use of biocides and aromatic solvents is prohibited. Examples of restricted substances are the use of the heavy metals iron and copper—iron in general and copper compounds, which are allowed only in trace quantities in blue, green, and turquoise dyestuffs. All other heavy metals are prohibited in all processes.

Also, GOTS has specified criteria for each processing step. Some examples are listed next.

- Only paraffin and substances of natural origin are allowed in the spinning process.
- Manufacturing processes may be only mechanical compaction, webbing, and entangling.
- In the wetting process, bleaching must be based on oxygen only, such as peroxides and ozone.
- Azo dyes that release carcinogenic amine compounds are prohibited.
- Printing methods that involve aromatic solvents, phthalates, and polyvinylchloride (PVC) are prohibited.
- Finishing methods involving mechanical, thermal, and other physical methods are allowed.

The manufacturer must have a written environmental policy for the production process. The policy should include procedures to minimize waste and discharges and documentation of staff training in the conservation of water and energy, the proper and minimal use of chemicals, and their correct disposal. Also, GOTS has requirements for handling waste water and for product storage, packaging, and transportation. The packaging material must, for example, under no circumstances contain PVC. The GOTS standard has basic requirements for the social circumstances for all employees. This includes fair treatment and wages for employees and healthy work environments.

Several companies certify textiles according to the requirements and principles set by GOTS. Some well-established certification companies are Oregon Tilth and One Cert, both American certificates, and IVN, an international union of companies.

For more information, see www.global-standard.org.

## Examples of Green Purchasing

Three examples of ways to consider green purchasing in an organization are provided next.

- A charity organization is about to buy office desks for its personnel. In the general process, the buyer decides requirements for desk stability, strength, and look. In addition, green requirements are selected, such as an FSC- or PEFC-labeled table and production without use of harmful compounds.
- A charity organization wants to buy mattresses for camping children. The buyer has general considerations about mattress size, color, and thickness. To purchase green, the buyer also sets criteria regarding reduction of environmental and health impacts from the mattresses. Here green requirements could prohibit use of ozone-depleting substances in the foam, PVC, and harmful compounds in the coloring. The easiest way to make sure these criteria are fulfilled is to choose mattresses that are eco-labeled with, for example, the Flower.
- A charity organization has a campaign coming up and needs T-shirts for the occasion. The organization decides that the T-shirt must be white, made of cotton, and with a logo printed on the front. In effort to purchase green, the organization decides to buy T-shirts made of organic cotton with prints that do not contain PVC. To make sure that these requirements are met, the T-shirts chosen may bear the Oregon Tilth or IVN label.

## Conclusion

Green purchasing defines products and services where environmental impacts and energy consumption are considered side by side with other areas, such as price, quality, and delivery. If an organization chooses green purchasing, it will contribute to reducing the environmental load and thereby improve health conditions and may also lower energy consumption. Also, green purchasing may enhance the image of the organization. "Green labels" encompass a broad range of labels, including eco-labels, energy labels, and organic labels. Products awarded a green label meet specific requirements set for a group of products. Examples of requirements are no use of specific hazardous substances in the production and documented recycling of waste materials.

This chapter has described some well-established green labels. An eco-label is a label that identifies the environmental performance of a product or service within a certain category based on life-cycle considerations. Energy labels are guides to products with lower energy consumption. Wooden products may have wood certificates to document sustainable forest use with good local forest management practices and proper working conditions. Green textile labels indicate that the textiles are produced with low environmental impacts and with considerations to workers' and consumers' health.

## About the Author

**Britt Tang Sørensen** is a Danish environmental chemist and science journalist. She is the owner of a green Web shop selling organic clothes for children. She is recognized in Denmark for her engagement in environmental issues.

## CHAPTER 9

# Making the Move to Green Transportation

## Jim Motavalli

D oes it matter what kind of car we drive or, for that matter, which vehicle gets to wear our nonprofit's colorful logo? After all, a lot of huge 17-miles-per-gallon (mpg) Chevy Silverado pickups are on the road with green stickers all over them, right?

The fact is that transportation matters a lot, both for your personal travel and for your nonprofit organization. There is a huge difference between that Silverado and a tiny Honda Fit, with its 28-mpg city and 35-mpg highway. The Fit has clown-car cargo and passenger capacity with its second row of seats folded flat, but there are still many fleet operators—even green ones—who think the motor pool has to be filled up with big pickup trucks.

## The Cost of Cars: An Environmental Toll

Even if your group can afford the gas, your vehicle choices matter. A recent PHH Arval survey[1] of fleet managers found that 80 percent had been asked by someone in their organization about the environmental impact of the company's car and trucks—and with good reason: According to the Environmental Protection Agency (EPA), cars and trucks cause almost half of the smog-forming volatile organic compounds, more than half of the nitrogen oxide emissions, and about half of the toxic air pollutant emissions in the United States. The same motor vehicles, when polluting off-road vehicles are added, also account for 75 percent of carbon monoxide emissions nationwide.

An increasingly large U.S. population is contributing to more and more cars on the road—new registrations have outpaced population growth by more than 50 percent since 1970. Before leveling off and starting to decline at the end of 2007 (because of, first, $4 a gallon gas, and then the recession), vehicle miles traveled in the United States increased steadily 2 to 3 percent each year—178 percent between 1970 and 2005 alone—and continues to increase at a rate of 2 to 3 percent each year.

There are well over 200 million cars and light-duty trucks on American highways. Their impact is aggravated by the rise of the sport utility vehicle (SUV). By 2000, the "light duty vehicle" (a category that includes SUVs) accounted for half of new vehicle sales. And many SUVs pollute three to five times more than cars. Their poor fuel economy makes them particular global warming aggravators. Since carbon dioxide emissions directly correlate to fuel use, the only way to improve a vehicle's climate profile is to make it more efficient. (This is why California's tailpipe greenhouse gas standards are basically fuel economy by another name.)

Worldwide, there are more than one billion vehicles, and that figure could double over the next two decades. According to Daniel Sperling and Deborah Gordon, "Today's billion vehicles are pumping extraordinary quantities of greenhouse gases into the atmosphere, are draining the world's conventional petroleum supplies, are inciting political skirmishes over oil, and are overwhelming city roads."[2]

Given all this, green nonprofits should do all they can to walk the talk and get as many cars off the road as possible. Encouraging employees to use mass transit is, then, a prime order of business. But the picture is clouded in the United States, where few commuters have access to a range of options.

Mass transit, a major people mover in Europe, Asia, and most of the rest of the world, is a small part of American commuting. More than 90 percent of all U.S. travel is by car and truck, and only 4 percent by all forms of transit. And we are making slow progress. In 2007, Americans took 10.3 billion trips on public transportation, according to the American Public Transportation Association. Just about every mode was up, including rides on trolleys and streetcars, commuter rail, elevated trains, and buses.

It sounds impressive, but in 1946 (with Americans emerging from World War II restrictions, including a ban on new car manufacturing), a much smaller population of 141 million took a record 23.4 billion transit trips. With our modern light-rail systems and even high-speed trains on the Acela route, the population of 305 million in 2009 musters half that many.

Although there are early signs that the Obama administration will foster a dramatic change, transportation politics has been long dominated by the highway lobby, an alliance of road builders and automakers that spends heavily on congressional races. The American Association of State Highway and Transportation Officials declared that transportation infrastructure spending should total $375 billion from 2010 to 2015, with transit having to make do with $93 billion and intercity passenger rail just $35 billion.

## Subsidizing Mass Transit

Enlightened employers subsidize their employees' alternative commuting, and some transit agencies encourage that. Miami-Dade Transit, for one, offers group discounts to employees of organizations that purchase monthly passes through payroll deduction. Also in Florida, the University of Miami pays 100 percent of the transit costs of any employees making less than $35,000 per year and 50 percent for those with salaries between $35,000 and $100,000. There are many advantages to this, including a reduction in the need for employer-provided parking and less absenteeism due to traffic conditions.

Surely, these types of subsidies would be easy to justify at a green nonprofit. Of course, subsidies would not even be necessary if transit was free, as Irwin Kellner suggests in a provocative *MarketWatch* column.[3]

Washington, he writes, wants to reduce our dependence on foreign oil and is trying to get cities to clean up their air. When transit raises fares and cuts service, he says, it does a disservice to the communities it serves. Says Kellner:

> *Not only should fares be lowered and service improved there is a good case that can be made to eliminate fares altogether.*

> *This is not as far-fetched as it looks. On average, the fare box covers only one-third of the cost of a typical mass transit ride. The rest is made up with dedicated taxes, subsidies from state and local governments, and tolls. Clearly, if these sources cover two-thirds of a ride, how much do you think taxes, subsidies and tolls would have to rise to take over the remaining third? The answer: not much.*

## Walking and Biking: The Scenic Route

While we are waiting for transit to be free—and even train-loving Europeans have not gone that far—nonprofits can also encourage their employees to walk and ride their bikes. That option might seem obvious to people working at a green nonprofit, but American society puts a surprising number of obstacles in our way.

American roads are obstacle courses without sidewalks or bike paths, and office parks are often in distant suburbs only accessible by car. Remedying this situation requires some advance planning.

If it is at all feasible, a downtown office location near transit stops makes the most sense, but high rents may put that out of reach. Portland, Oregon, is the poster child for bike and pedestrian friendliness. Downtown businesses are required to provide bike racks, and downtown gyms open their showers to bicycle riders. City buses offer nose-mounted racks for bicycles, and Tri-Met trains carry them, too.

The city is a center of transit-oriented development, which means that new housing complexes (Orenco Station is a standout) are built within walking distance of Tri-Met light-rail stops. What is more, the new developments are designed to allow residents to walk to shopping, schools, and recreation.

Portland's bicyclists are well organized through groups such as BikePortland and a powerful force in municipal affairs. Chances are you lack that in your city, but nothing stops your organization from becoming the focal point of bicycle activism. The steps necessary to build an interest group are well known to activists: Create a citizens' committee, print up stationery (or just create it on your computer), send out press releases, hold public meetings, and make appointments with the mayor and both state representatives and the congressional delegation.

Your agenda should include:

- New roads should have sidewalks and bicycle lanes or paths added to existing ones.
- All transit, including rush-hour trains (*especially* rush-hour trains), should allow bicyclists to bring their bikes on board.

- Your city or town should require permanent bike racks in front of large buildings and evenly spaced on sidewalks.
- "Traffic-calming" measures—roundabouts, speed bumps—should be built into major thoroughfares to slow cars down and make it safer for both pedestrians and cyclists.
- Legislation, sponsored by friendly city council people and state representatives, can make it easier for employers to subsidize commuting alternatives to the single-occupant motor vehicle.

That last point is particularly important, because your office needs to be proactive in encouraging its employees to try the alternatives. If your company provides "free" parking, for instance, why not also offer a subsidy for people who choose not to park 3,000 pounds of metal?

Donald Shoup, a professor at the University of California at Los Angeles and a determined biker, has written engagingly about the need for equity with America's favorite fringe benefit. "While we all want to park free," he said in an interview, "we should not elevate this wish into a social judgment that charging for curb parking is unfair, especially when we compare it with the alternative—off-street parking requirements that impose a heavy burden even on those with the least ability to pay. Almost everyone will be better off by paying only for the parking they use."

An innovative office can offer a monthly subsidy to walkers and bikers or a free or half-price commutation ticket to transit passengers. Awards also can be given to long-term walkers and bikers. California actually mandates what is called "parking cash out," meaning that employers have to provide certificates to their nondriving (or carpooling) employees that can be used for transit or exchanged for cash.

The state program is poorly enforced, but according to the California Air Resources Board, a study of eight firms that did comply with the law found carpooling had increased by 64 percent and transit ridership by 50 percent. Walking or biking to work was up 39 percent.

Another idea is a free company van to pick up passengers at rail stations and bring them back at night. Of course, there is always the carpooling option, but even high gas prices have not done much to get Americans to make those arrangements. (An interesting fact about carpooling is that 30 percent of new immigrants ride with their neighbors, but after 10 years in the United States, immigrant carpool use has dropped to 20 percent. After 15 years, immigrants have adapted to the "American way of life," and most are driving to work alone.)

Pitney Bowes, a major corporation with headquarters in Stamford, Connecticut, leads the way in encouraging auto alternatives among its employees with a variety of subsidies. Among other things, it offers free vanpools to the Stamford railroad station (400 employees ride them on any given day), bike racks where possible, and a commuting account so that workers can pay for their transportation to work on a pretax basis.

NuRide helps employees hook up for ride sharing. At a Pitney Bowes location in Spokane, Washington, the company provides subsidized bus passes and covered parking for carpoolers and encourages telecommuting and use of flextime schedules. Green nonprofits should be setting an example here, because transportation is and always will be a major environmental issue.

FIGURE 9.1    Zipcar offers small cars, and a good alternative to owning or leasing fleet vehicles.

## Car Sharing: Surrendering Your Keys

There are hidden costs to car ownership. Most people think only of the basics—purchase price, gas, insurance—when assessing the bottom line, forgetting depreciation, taxes, maintenance, and more. Federal estimates put the cost of owning a car at more than $8,000 a year, far more than most people think. The typical American household actually has two cars, paying more than $15,000 every year for the privilege.

An increasingly popular option to ownership is car sharing, a concept that took root in Europe and is now catching on in the United States through national companies such as Zipcar, shown in Figure 9.1 (which merged with former rival Flexcar in 2007).

Here is the idea: Instead of owning a car or renting one, join a sharing service and pay to borrow one when you need it. Car-sharing services locate their cars (often hybrids as well as economy cars, pickups, and even the odd luxury vehicle) in parking garages and lots around a city and its suburbs, and members can unlock them using smart cards. Reservations can be made online.

Car-sharing services have more than 350,000 members worldwide. World leader Zipcar has 5,000 cars and operations in 24 states, plus Washington, DC, Canada, and England, and is expanding rapidly. Some car-sharing services, including Mint in New York City, are locally based and offer great perks to users—such as $2-an-hour weekday rates.

This is another opportunity for nonprofits that want to green themselves. Your organization can, as many already do, dispense with a motor pool entirely and simply use car-sharing services when necessary. The benefits to the environment are hard to refute. Each Zipcar car-sharing vehicle in operation takes 15 to 20 other cars off the road, the company says. And car-sharing is a major opportunity to cut costs. Why not use the money saved to plant a few trees, or make a donation to a worthy environmental cause?

## Charging Around: The Electric Car Infrastructure

As I am writing this, it is not practical for green nonprofits to field fleets of electric vehicles (EVs), but it may be by the time the book is published. The obstacle today, as it has been since the first EV hit the road more than 100 years ago, is a lack of widespread charging networks. Limited by the range of even the latest lithium-ion battery packs, EVs need to plug in every 100 miles. And when they run out of juice and leave you stranded, a hike to the nearest gas station with a jerry can will not fix the problem.

But after decades of plans that went nowhere, the EV infrastructure is finally moving forward. Led by pioneer Better Place, a number of companies are signing up municipalities, states, and even countries to EV wiring contracts. Players include Coulomb, ECOtality, the Renault-Nissan Alliance (which is also providing the EVs itself), and (in an advisory role) the nonprofit Project Get Ready.

These efforts are embryonic: Wiring the world for EVs is comparable to installing fiber optic lines for cable television. It is not digital; it is a bricks-and-mortar project, and will both take years and cost many billions of dollars. But it is under way.

Practically, this will mean EV recharging at home (we have 54 million garages for the 247 million registered cars in the United States, and cars parked there can plug into house current or, even better, high-voltage fast chargers), at work, and while shopping. According to ECOtality, the charging vision includes 15-minute fast charging at big-box retailers such as Home Depot, Wal-Mart, and Best Buy. You will not be left waiting for your car to finish its business: Even waiting for, buying, and then drinking a fast cappuccino at Starbucks will likely consume 15 minutes.

Home recharging is intimately tied into the Obama administration's ongoing work (including an initial $11 billion in stimulus money) to create a nationwide "smart grid" enabling considerable interaction between consumer and electric utility. Tomorrow's EVs (and even some of todays) will come with software enabling them to automatically recharge at the lowest demand times—say, 3 A.M. In an orderly process, EV recharging will be staggered over the course of a night to avoid overload (and the need to build new power plants). Can you imagine the mess if everyone plugged in at 6 P.M. when they arrived home from work?

The smart grid will also enable vehicle-to-grid (known as V2G). While your car is plugged in, a stressed utility experiencing peak loads will be able to draw power from its batteries and credit your account for the electricity it has drawn. Later it will replace the energy it took out by recharging your batteries. This sounds like a Buck Rogers fantasy, but the necessary technology is already built into new EVs from Bright Motors and Aptera, among others. And an alliance among Coulomb, V2Green, and eTec is just one of the combines (with funding from the U.S. Department of Energy) developing smart-charging protocols for the smart grid. The city of San Jose, California, working with Coulomb, is one of the first to build smart-charging stations into streetlights, curbs, and parking lots.

EV home recharging will be a bigger challenge in cities such as San Francisco, where only 16 percent of vehicles are parked in garages overnight. As China adds a city the size of Chicago every few months, it will be easy to incorporate EV recharging into its urban plan, but wiring existing ones will take longer.

EV recharging should be a painless process—software incorporated into the car could interact with the fast recharger to automatically debit your account for a sub-$1 charge, without the need for a card swipe.

One of the best things about all this from the green nonprofit standpoint is the very low operational cost of EVs. Battery cars have very few moving parts to replace, and a charge to travel 100 miles or more is likely to cost no more than 50 cents.

Even if your company has to field conventional cars and trucks now, its next vehicle purchases could well be plug-in EVs and plug-in hybrids. High battery costs will undoubtedly mean these vehicles will cost a bit more, but the tax breaks already in place or coming from federal, state, and municipal authorities should offset the pain considerably. There will be major incentives to purchase or lease EVs. Many are in place already, as discussed in the section titled "How to Use Incentives for Green Transportation."

## Your Fleet: Available Green Cars and Trucks

Let us set aside EVs for a minute and focus solely on cars and trucks that are available in the 2010 model year. Even without many battery cars, there are plenty of available options.

### Hybrids

The hybrid combines a small gas engine with an electric motor and a large battery pack to optimize the performance of both. It is not a new concept: Primitive hybrids were on the market in the 1910s. U.S. companies had the lead then, but they abandoned the technology. Sad to say, if buying American is a priority, you will find that the best value and performance is delivered by vehicles made in Japan: Toyota and Honda had a five-year head start in building hybrids.

The first hybrid on the U.S. market was the two-passenger Honda Insight in 1999. At the time, the Big Three (which had, amazingly enough, spent billions of government money developing market-ready hybrids under the Partnership for a New Generation of Vehicles) did not think the concept was viable.

The Insight was followed by the Toyota Prius, a more impressive and family-capable car, in 2000. The car soon caught on as a practical environmental car that proclaimed its owner's status as a dyed-in-the-wool green.

Today, the hybrid market is crowded. The early Insight was replaced in 2010 by a much more impressive five-passenger model of that name. It is, in fact, the cheapest hybrid on the U.S. market at an entry-level price of $19,800. The Insight, particularly in the down-market LX form, would make an ideal fleet car.

The Prius, too, was redesigned in 2010 and is a technological tour de force. Features include everything from a touch-sensitive display and advanced crash-protection technology to a built-in solar panel that can keep the car's interior from frying on a hot day.

Much of the new tech is optional, however, and Toyota is thoughtful enough to provide a stripped-down introductory model (Prius I) for $21,000, specifically for fleet use. Your folks will have to do without that touch display, a rear wiper, and the EV mode that lets the car run briefly in battery-only mode, but the stellar fuel economy of 50 mpg combined is unaffected.

The first U.S. hybrid was the Ford Escape, introduced in 2004. With some Prius technology onboard, the Escape, a small SUV, is a very credible entry. And it is becoming popular with fleets, seeing daily use as a taxi on the streets of New York. The Ford Fusion hybrid sedan is an excellent new addition, and the Nissan Altima is worth considering.

If you need a larger vehicle or a truck, the pickings are slimmer. The Lexus RX400h SUV is an ungainly beast, but it does offer both good fuel economy and excellent emissions. The Chevy Silverado is a mild hybrid pickup ("mild" in that it relies mostly on the gas engine and uses its electric drive as a relatively minor assist), but it offers only very modest fuel advantages (21 city/22 highway mpg in two-wheel-drive form, compared to 14/20 as a nonhybrid). And with a price that can reach $50,000 with options, it is expensive.

## Plug-in Hybrids (and Conversions)

Thanks to the hard work of a visionary, Felix Kramer of CalCars.org, plug-in hybrids are no longer a dream but real cars from mainstream manufacturers. The starting point is the standard hybrid, with a battery pack, an electric motor, and a small gas or diesel engine. Now add a larger battery pack and the option of plug-in charging and up to 40 miles of electric-only range. Under optimal conditions, a tank of gas will last for months because you will do most of your around-town runs on electricity from the grid—the equivalent of 100 mpg or more.

Toyota is fielding plug-in versions of the Prius it introduced in 2010 for limited fleet trials (see Figure 9.2). If you are lucky, you might be able to snare a few. General Motors has a plug-in hybrid version of its Saturn Vue hybrid, but that will migrate to another brand as Saturn leaves the GM fold. Fisker has a super-fast plug-in hybrid sports sedan and convertible. And start-up Bright Motors, a for-profit spinoff of Amory Lovins's nonprofit Rocky Mountain Institute, is fielding a plug-in hybrid utility truck targeted at large fleet customers.

General Motors' Chevrolet Volt is a form of plug-in hybrid, also known as a series hybrid, that uses a very small gasoline engine not connected to the wheels to generate electricity for the electric motors that actually power the car. The Volt can also be plugged in to recharge its onboard battery pack for a 40-mile all-electric range. Ford is planning a plug-in hybrid for 2012.

Several firms offer plug-in conversion services of such vehicles as the Toyota Prius and the Ford Escape hybrids, but this is expensive at $10,000 to $15,000. Such conversions qualify for a federal tax credit, though (see Figure 9.3).

FIGURE 9.2    The 2010 Toyota Prius, with 50 mpg overall, is the most fuel-efficient hybrid on the market.

*Source:* Jim Motavalli photo.

FIGURE 9.3    The Chevrolet Volt: A $7,500 federal tax credit is available.

*Source:* Jim Motavalli photo.

## Electric Battery Vehicles

We have to be imaginative here, because the battery EV field is evolving rapidly. The Tesla Roadster was one of the few available options in 2009, but this $109,000 two-seat electric sports car (with more than 6,000 individual lithium-ion batteries!) is hardly appropriate for fleet use. Tesla soon complemented the Roadster with the more practical Model S sedan, which boasts seven-seat capacity with two removable child-friendly jump seats. But both Teslas are performance cars with zero to 60 times under six seconds, not practical haulers.

Today, EV companies look like the Internet startups of the 1990s. Many are located in Silicon Valley, many are headed by former software entrepreneurs who cashed out (Elon Musk of Tesla, for example, was a founder of PayPal), and many are seeking cash investors to get from a single prototype to full-scale production. This is happening as the mainstream industry contracts, so the industry of tomorrow may resemble that of 1910: with dozens, if not hundreds, of automotive competitors.

Battery players in addition to Tesla include Aptera (a Jetsons-style pod car that looks like an airplane without wings) and Norway-based Think Global (a small EV commuter vehicle that was developed with a cash infusion from Ford, which bought and then sold the company).

Chrysler's ENVI division developed a range of electric cars, and Ford says it will have a Focus-size battery car, built in conjunction with Magna International, on the road in 2011. This author drove an early version of the Ford battery car and found it impressive. Nissan is deeply invested in battery cars and in their recharging networks. Its zippy battery hatchback, which could serve worldwide markets, starts down the Japanese assembly line in late 2010.

Other companies, Atlanta-based Wheego being just one example and the Chrysler-owned GEM Peapod another, are building what are called neighborhood electric vehicles (NEVs). These vehicles, which benefit from a 10 percent federal tax credit, are limited, in most states, to roadways with speed limits of 35 mph or less. Given that, they have won favor in gated communities, military bases, resorts, sprawling factory complexes, and more.

The advantage of NEVs is relatively low cost and, in some cases, full features. Many NEVs look like golf carts, but the Wheego Whip, for instance, is an under-$19,000 two-passenger subcompact with remote keyless entry, air conditioning, and an MP3 stereo system as standard equipment. Wheego says it costs three cents per mile to operate.

NEVs are unlikely to be practical for green nonprofits unless they operate in a defined space—on the former Presidio military base in San Francisco, home to many environmental groups, for example.

## Fuel Cells

The fuel cell revolution looked imminent in 2000, when I wrote *Forward Drive: The Race to Build Clean Cars for the Future*.[4] Ferdinand Panik of Daimler-Benz had confidently predicted that his company would have 100,000 hydrogen-powered cars on the road by 2004. Other automakers were putting big resources into the technology, too.

But hydrogen has not become affordable, and despite brave talk about the "hydrogen highway," there were still only 65 refueling stations around the country in mid-2009. And the cars themselves, while great fun to drive and offering unparalleled performance, are still far too expensive for the mass market.

The bottom line for the fleet is "wait and see." A lucky few probably will be able to score hydrogen-fueled cars in special test arrangements, but the hydrogen energy economy is probably 20 years off.

In May 2009, Energy secretary Steven Chu attempted to "zero out" funding for hydrogen research (although there is still $68 million specifically for fuel cells), but Congress thought otherwise. Chu's comment at the time: "We asked ourselves, 'Is it likely in the next 10 or 15, 20 years that we will convert to a hydrogen car economy?' The answer, we felt, was 'no.'" Among the carmakers lobbying to restore hydrogen funding were GM, Honda, Toyota, and Daimler. Two groups, the National Hydrogen Association and the U.S. Fuel Cell Council, also got involved.

## Natural Gas Cars

The picture is better here. More environmental groups should investigate natural gas for their fleets, since it is the best fossil fuel for both local and global warming emissions. There is only one natural gas production car on the market, but it is a very good one: the Honda Civic GX. For $25,190 you get the cleanest internal combustion car in the world. It runs on compressed natural gas (CNG) and is an exceptionally clean Partial Zero Emission Vehicle in the California ratings.

In many states, you can drive the 113-horsepower, 1.8-liter GX in the high-occupancy vehicle lanes. The driving range is approximately 170 miles.

Another alternative is to have your existing cars and trucks converted to natural gas. According to About.com:

> *Converting a conventional gasoline car to CNG is complex, but not necessarily difficult, and quite do-able. And if you are mechanically inclined, it could feasibly be done in your own garage. The other option is to find a willing mechanic who will install a CNG kit for you. One potential hoop to jump through could be emissions certification for your particular state—some states require special conditions since you'd be changing the vehicle's "engineered" fuel type.[5]*

The next Web page offers a list of CNG converters. You can also use it to locate CNG stations in your area. Prices for a conversion run $1,000 to $1,500.

## Diesel, Biodiesel, and "Flex-Fuel" Ethanol Cars

Almost any diesel vehicle—the norm in Europe, but still relatively rare in the United States—can run blends of standard diesel fuel and biodiesel made from soybeans. Biodiesel (which is 15 percent biofuel) is relatively easy to make in a garage, although some toxic chemicals are involved. To run 100 percent "grease"—basically, salad oil that could come from a local restaurant's fryers—you will need to convert a standard diesel through a kit available from firms such as Massachusetts-based

Greasecar (which will also do the work for you on premises for a higher fee). Check in with Greasecar at www.greasecar.com. A biodiesel production tax credit may be available.

European carmakers Volkswagen, Mercedes, and others are selling diesels in the United States, which (along with Europe) has recently mandated very clean low-sulfur diesel fuel. Every European automaker builds diesels, and thanks to tax incentives, more than half of the cars on the road there are diesel-powered. European demand for diesel is growing at an annual rate of 4.4 percent, according to Andrew Reed of Boston's Energy Security Analysis.

In Europe, some diesels—such as Volkswagen's BlueMotion Polo—routinely get as much as 60 mpg, better than the new version of the Toyota Prius. Volkswagen and partner Audi field a range of TDI (Turbocharged Direct Injection) diesels in the United States.

All of the Big Three manufacturers sell "flex-fuel" vehicles capable of running on E85 ethanol (which offers some emissions advantages), but because of the relative lack of ethanol stations around the country—most are in the Midwest—these cars run on gasoline most of the time.

### Economical Gasoline Cars

Most of the fleet cars in the country fit into the category of economical gasoline cars, and there are some very good options. Until the market success of the Smart and the Mini Cooper, it was generally believed that cars that small would not sell in the United States. But now a whole new generation of very economical vehicles, some of which use space very creatively, is on the road.

Some good choices include the Honda Fit (28/35 mpg, automatic); the Toyota Yaris (29/35, automatic); the Chevrolet Cruze, which replaces the Cobalt for 2011 and is a "global" car that will also be sold in Europe); the Mazda3 (22/30, automatic); and many more. The Smart Fortwo coupe may be small for some uses, but it does achieve 33/41 mpg fuel economy.

## How to Buy a Fleet Car

Let us start with this: You are not going to pay full price for this fleet car! It helps to know what you want before setting foot in the dealership, including not only the model but also the color and options. There is good advice on all this at www.wikihow.com/Buy-a-New-Car-Through-Fleet-Sales.

Dealerships and fleet companies work with bonuses that kick in when volume targets are met. So even if they sell you cars at cost, they will get the money back at the end of the year in the form of bonus/rebates (which can total several million dollars). And they especially like big purchases. With that in mind, you should go into the dealership knowing the car's invoice price (what they paid) and the manufacturer's suggested retail price (MSRP), which is what they want you to pay. Even if the dealer sells you cars at cost, the volume bonus makes it worthwhile.

When you have test-driven the car you are interested in, and the experience did not deter you, it is on to deciding all the specifications of your fleet vehicles and lining up financing. The next step is to contact the fleet departments of several dealers with your specs, let them know you are going to make a decision soon, and ask for a request for bids. Make the contacts on weekdays, because fleet managers may not be working on the weekend. Good timing is a week before the end of the month, because that is when dealers are trying to get cars off their lots. Cast your net wide: The dealership does not have to be next door—you can still get the car serviced locally if you buy it in the next state.

If a bid emerges that you like, it is negotiating time. Do not be afraid to offer a price that is somewhat lower, but make sure they know it is a firm offer. Your negotiating position is stronger if you are bidding on an unpopular model. The long waits for hybrid cars are a thing of the past—just about everything is available. In some cases, cars will have to be delivered from another state, so you should be prepared to wait. Fleet sales departments are actually easier to deal with than the retail operations because they handle both the financing and selling of vehicles.

The car industry may never regain the heady 16 and 17 million annual U.S. sales volumes it enjoyed in the early 2000s, so it will be a buyer's market for a long time to come. They want to sell you those fleet cars.

## How to Use Incentives for Green Transportation

The federal tax incentives for hybrids and clean diesel cars that went into place in 2005 were based on volume: After a certain number of cars were sold, the incentives got smaller and eventually disappeared. The credits (phased out in early 2010) were structured that way to encourage the sale of domestic hybrids.

That was then. Now we have a new federal tax credit designed to sell battery and plug-in hybrid cars. In fact, the bigger the battery, the bigger the subsidy, up to a cutoff of $7,500. The bill was designed to accommodate the Chevy Volt, which has a very big battery pack, but it may not be the best way to arrange tax breaks—the biggest battery is not always in the best car, after all. Vehicles with smaller packs get a smaller credit, even if the car has superior performance and range.

"The credit is welcome, but basing it on battery size disadvantages smart designs that substitute light, strong materials and better aerodynamics for costly batteries," said Amory Lovins, chairman and chief scientist of the Rocky Mountain Institute, a Colorado-based think tank. "A credit based instead on driving range would correctly reward automakers for saving the most gasoline."[6]

The law calls for a base credit of $2,500 for plug-in hybrid purchases, which increases by $417 for each kilowatt-hour of battery capacity over 4 kilowatt-hours, to a maximum of $7,500.

The tax credit was estimated to cost $1 billion over 10 years and begins to phase out after automakers collectively sell 250,000 plug-ins. The credit will be phased out to 50 percent for the following two quarters and 25 percent for the two quarters after that before expiring.

According to Felix Kramer of CalCars.org, "Tax credits for plug-ins now mean that carmakers' business plans have to take into account that any plug-in car can be up to $7,500 cheaper."[7]

A second, 10 percent federal tax credit applies to NEVs (the Wheego Whip) or to two- and three-wheel electric vehicles (such as the Aptera 2e) purchased before January 1, 2012. The maximum credit is $2,500, and the minimum battery size for four-wheeled NEVs is 4 kilowatt-hours. For two- and three-wheelers, the requirement is that they be propelled "to a significant extent" by a rechargeable battery of at least 2.5 kilowatt-hours.

Some vehicles will qualify for both forms of federal tax credit, but the rules do not allow claiming both on the same vehicle. If the vehicle is intended primarily for off-road use, a category that includes golf carts and all-terrain vehicles, it does not qualify for either credit.

The Honda Civic GX also qualifies for a $4,000 federal tax credit. And hybrid owners who buy a qualified plug-in hybrid conversion kit are eligible for a 10 percent credit, capped at $4,000, through 2011.

For green car enthusiasts who get really ambitious, a $1-a-gallon biodiesel production tax credit was available through the end of 2009, and may have been renewed. Diesel fuel made from biomass (an increasingly viable option that is also enshrined in the renewable energy portfolio standard) is also eligible for a $1-a-gallon credit. Through the end of 2010, there is a 30 percent tax credit for EV recharging stations as well as E85 ethanol and natural gas refueling. Check with the Energy Department at www.energy.gov/additionaltaxbreaks.htm.

There are numerous state and local tax incentives for alternative-fueled cars and trucks. For a rundown in your state or municipality, visit the federal Department of Energy database at www.afdc.energy.gov/afdc/incentives_laws.html. There is a clickable U.S. map. Sacramento, California, for instance, offers free parking to owned or leased EVs with a special parking pass at downtown lots (which are also equipped with free charging stations).

These tax incentives should be figured into any calculations about the costs of any fleet vehicle. People tend to miss some of the many ancillary costs involved in owning a car. If your estimates are based on what you are going to pay for your vehicle, plus the cost of gas, oil, and repairs, you are forgetting about insurance, depreciation, parking fees, tolls, and registration, among other things.

Cars cost more than most of us think, for families as well as businesses. According to the Bureau of Labor Statistics, American "consumer units" (similar to a household) spent an average of $8,758 on all forms of transportation in 2007 (up 2.9 percent from 2006).[8] We are a car-owning country, so only $537.81 of our average spending went to public transit, including taxis and air travel. The latter expenses would appear to skew the statistics because the lowest-income fifth of the population spent an average of $171.30 annually on transit and the richest fifth $1,406.45.

In 2007, a statistically average household, with an annual pretax family income of $63,091 and 1.9 vehicles, spent more on transportation than it did on clothing, healthcare, and entertainment combined ($7,432). The average outlay for new cars and trucks was $1,571.80.

Big cars and SUVs are (like some fast food) fairly cheap to buy, but the low price of entry is offset by high fuel bills. A Dodge Ram 1500 pickup, for instance, will use 22.8 barrels of oil in a year, and a Honda Civic only about half as much, 11.8 barrels.

# Driving Green

Even if your nonprofit's finances do not allow replacing your transportation with something greener, there are still ways to reduce both fuel costs and your carbon footprint.

- Reducing the clutter in vehicles (the junk in the trunk) improves fuel economy and greenhouse gas emissions. Carrying around an extra 100 pounds will affect fuel economy by 2 miles per gallon.
- Slowing down and observing speed limits bears the same dividends. According to the EPA (at Fueleconomy.gov), fuel economy deteriorates rapidly at speeds above 60 mph, and each 5 mph over that speed is like paying an extra 24 cents a gallon for gas.
- Leadfoots pay for the privilege. Aggressive driving, which includes rapid acceleration and braking, wastes gas and can reduce your fuel economy by 33 percent at highway speeds (and 5 percent around town).
- Use cruise control. It smoothes out choppy driving and saves you money.

# Fleet Management

Greening your company's transportation fleet is a great goal, but you do not have to do it yourself. Companies like Enterprise Fleet Management (www.enterprise. com/fleets/Home.action) have comprehensive environmental programs in place that include optimizing the vehicle mix, tapping into alternative fuels, and helping companies purchase offsets so their vehicles can be effectively carbon neutral.

Services like this are needed, because company fleet operations—from oil companies to the greenest nonprofit—are not living up to expectations. The same PHH Arval study that found that 80 percent of fleet managers had been asked about environmental impact also revealed that 15 percent of private sector fleet managers said that the environmental impact of their cars and trucks "is not a priority" at their organizations.

According to PHH Arval, one way to make the environment a priority is for fleets to set greenhouse gas reduction goals. That allows companies to track improvements in fuel efficiency (the only effective way to cut climate emissions), account for the impact of business changes on emissions, and assess the impact of driver behavior programs. But, the survey said, only 25 percent of companies studied had greenhouse goals and only 28 percent measured greenhouse emissions from their fleets at all.

Where reasons were cited for not taking action, cost was often seen as an obstacle. But as we have seen in this chapter, improving the environmental performance of auto fleets also saves companies money. In the survey, a savvy third of managers (37 percent in private companies and 39 percent in the public sector) was working to reduce emissions—and lower costs.

A lack of good green information is one obstacle, cited by 21 percent of private companies. But 68 percent of fleet managers say they have started to educate the people who drive their vehicles about their environmental impact.

## Conclusion

The good news is that, with a host of commercially available hybrid, plug-in hybrid, battery, and biodiesel-ready cars on the near horizon, it should soon be possible for green nonprofits to set an example with some of the cleanest transportation on the planet. It is time to lead the way, not trail a cloud of smoke.

### About the Author

**Jim Motavalli** is author or editor of six books, including *Forward Drive: The Race to Build "Clean" Cars for the Future* and *Breaking Gridlock: Moving Toward Transportation That Works* (both Sierra Club Books). He is a senior writer at *E/The Environmental Magazine* and a contributor to the *New York Times*, BNet.com, The Daily Green, and Mother Nature Network.

## CHAPTER 10

# Green Office Practices

## Lára Jóhannsdóttir

## Introduction

Why are "green office practices" important, and what do they entail?

The world's population is growing exponentially. Since 1960, it has increased from around 3 billion to just fewer than 7 billion in 2009; it is expected to reach 9 billion in 2040.[1] This means that Earth's biological and physical systems are under enormous strain to provide for people and absorb the waste generated by their activities. So far we have treated the environment as a boundless source of natural resources and a limitless sink for waste.[2] However, this has to change.

Greenhouse gas emissions steaming from human activities, such as deforestation and the burning of fossil fuels, are changing the climate, which may have a huge impact on our lives and the lives of our descendants. Greenhouse gas emissions have increased significantly in the past two centuries due to changes in sectors such as agriculture, manufacturing, mining, and transportation.

Today, "[c]limate change is one of our greatest environmental, social and economic threats,"[3] posing a threat to the economy and our way of living. "Even if all global emissions stopped today, our climate would continue to change for at least the rest of this century due to historic emissions already in the atmosphere."[4] Carbon footprint calculation allows us to estimate how many tons of carbon dioxide and other greenhouse gases we create each year with our current way of living.

A growing world population and increased consumption means that there is significant increase in the demand for natural resources. "Many resources are being extracted at levels that will inhibit future generations from satisfying their own needs."[5] Sustainable development, where there is a balance between economic, environmental, and social activities, can help reduce people's vulnerability to the consequences of climate changes and other environmental issues.

When striving for sustainability, there has to be coherent cooperation between domestic and international environmental governance, policy makers, the business environment, nongovernmental and nonprofit organizations, and civil society (see Figure 10.1). Organizations, whether they are nonprofit or for-profit, will have to find ways to fulfill their financial goals at the same time they improve their social and environmental performance. We might be inclined to think that as

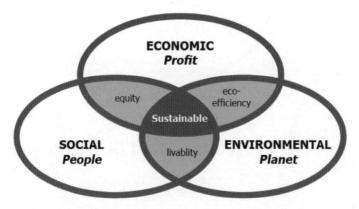

FIGURE 10.1   Dimensions of sustainability.

*Source:* A. Remmen, A. A. Jensen, and J. Frydendal, *Life Cycle Management: A Business Guide to Sustainability* (Paris: United Nations Environmental Programme, 2007), 10.

individuals we have little to say or do in solving environmental problems. That is not the case. Becoming aware of environmental problems and changing consumption behavior, both as individuals and staff members, means a great deal collectively.

Many environmental problems we are facing do not respect manmade boundaries, so we all have to share the burden and find solutions to these difficulties jointly. This is not just a question of other countries, other governments, other companies, or the next-door neighbor. We will have to reduce our ecological footprint, in both our private and professional lives. One way to make the necessary changes in our daily lives is to learn from nature. Nature works in cycles; we have spring, summer, autumn, and winter. Another cycle is the water cycle, where the sun's energy causes water to evaporate from oceans and lakes into the atmosphere. When the atmosphere cools, water vapor condenses, making clouds that produce rain or snow. In the spring, flowers start to bloom and trees grow leaves. In the autumn, when the vegetation starts to wither and perish, it breaks down, nourishing the ground and preparing it for a new life cycle. Those are just a few examples of how nature works in cycles.

Our way of production and consumption is linear, not cyclical. To produce the products we use, raw materials are extracted from nature; they are run through production systems, sold, used, and disposed of. For each product we buy, many more resources have been used upstream in the production process. When products have been disposed of, they go through an incineration process and/or get transported to landfill sites. This may lead to air, water, and land pollution. Applying a life cycle model means that the material loops are closed, and material is recycled as it continues to circulate through a recovery process (see Figure 10.2).

Greening your nonprofit office practices means improving the workplace and processes for the benefit of the environment. This also leads to improved working conditions for yourself and cost reduction for your nonprofit organization. This triple benefit, triple bottom line (TBL) is made up of economic, social, and environmental factors, also called people, profit, and planet. The planet will benefit from carbon footprint reduction, reduction in resource usage, increased recycling, less waste

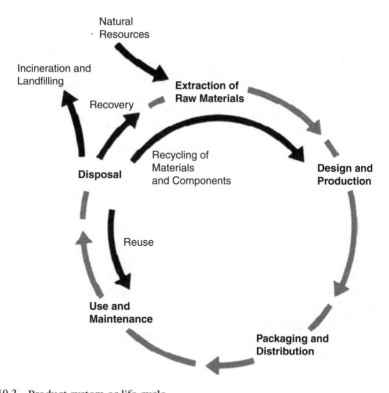

FIGURE 10.2    Product system or life cycle.

*Source:* A. Remmen, A. A. Jensen, and J. Frydendal, *Life Cycle Management: A Business Guide to Sustainability* (Paris: United Nations Environmental Programme, 2007), 12.

generation, and so on. In addition to cost reduction, your nonprofit organization might benefit from new fundraising opportunities and easier recruitment of volunteers as well as an enhanced image. Employees and volunteers can benefit from a healthier working environment, increased environmental awareness, shared commitment, and greater job satisfaction. The greening of your office practices means a lighter ecological footprint of your nonprofit organization for the benefit of the wider community.

The following chapter is organized into sections that address the main office practices of a nonprofit organization. By applying the solutions offered in the text, your nonprofit organization will lay the foundation for a healthier office, one with a lower environmental impact. In addition to the ideas provided, it is recommended that you brainstorm with your employees and board of directors about how your nonprofit organization can minimize its environmental impact and make the office a better workplace.

Each section starts with a short introduction and/or example(s) linked to the section heading followed by a list of ideas you can apply to your nonprofit organization. The lists provided are by no means complete but will offer your nonprofit organization a starting kit for greening your office practices. The final part of the chapter offers additional resources that can help with the transition to a greener office.

## Green Strategy for the Office

A green strategy for the office is the framework for greening office practices. It is not just a matter of economic, technical, and environmental issues. More important, it has to do with the cultural and behavioral aspects of the organization. To make behavioral and cultural transformations, the structure, job responsibilities, communication, and training have to be aligned to support the intended changes, from a nonenvironmental stage (or a passive one) to a proactive one.

The environmental policy is to be the beacon toward environmentally sound office practices of your nonprofit organization. The first step is to diagnose the current situation and see where improvements must be made. If possible, the nonprofit organization should measure its environmental impact by calculating its carbon footprint. Leaders of the organization then need to create a sense of urgency. The key question is: Why is it important that behavioral changes take place? The next step is to form a powerful alliance among those involved in the office activities. One way to start involving the employees is to survey them about the environmental issues foremost in their minds and where and how to prioritize those activities.

The next step is to create a vision and share it with all stakeholders. How far is the nonprofit organization willing to go? Will implementation of formal environmental management system and environmental reporting be a part of the vision? In the transition of the organization, there has to be a clear focus on communication. The nonprofit organization might also have to train its employees and volunteers so they can be empowered to act in accordance with the new strategy. Greening your nonprofit organization means behavioral changes and a change in consumption habits. Try to involve everyone, and keep in mind that both patience and persuasion are needed. Engagement and support of key suppliers might be needed in order to meet targets.

Leaders of the nonprofit organization should think about how to celebrate success in implementing the green strategy and how to maintain and surpass previous performance. Bear in mind that this is a long-distance race, not a sprint. Small, incremental steps are what will move your nonprofit organization in the right direction. After determining the priorities of the organization, start with one or two items listed in each section, and add new items as your organization becomes confident in implementing the previous one. If you are a part of a small nonprofit organization, keep in mind that it can still do a great deal to improve the working environment by greening its office practices and at the same time minimizing the environmental impact of its operation.

Purchasing strategy should be a part of your green strategy. For example, your nonprofit organization might emphasize selection of goods and services that offer the best value for money at the same time that they meet high-quality standards and have a low environmental impact. Green purchasing for your organization will set an example and influence the marketplace, which can lead to an increased product range of environmentally friendly products. You may then ask: What makes products green? No doubt there are many definitions of "green products," but one is that green products contain recycled content, are biodegradable or compostable with their chemical content having been reduced, and have been certified by a third party.[6]

## Eco-Friendly Furniture

When choosing eco-friendly furniture for the office, keep two things in mind: (1) the health of the employees and (2) the health of the environment. Furniture should work well and be effective for its purpose. It should also be strong so it lasts for a long time, and be affordable for your nonprofit organization. Buy only what you need, and buy secondhand furniture if possible. That will reduce the amount of energy, raw materials, and chemicals used in the manufacturing process of new items. It will also reduce waste in the landfills.

To produce cheap furniture, too much unsustainably harvested wood is shipped around the world. Enormous amounts of fossil fuels are used in the transportation process. Glue, varnish, and other carcinogenic chemicals are used in the manufacturing process. This is not good for our health or for the health of the environment. Furniture can be produced in a more sustainable manner. Wood from sustainably harvested forests, sustainably harvested tree farms, and reclaimed wood are the main sources. The Forest Stewardship Council and its largest forest certifier, the Rainforest Alliance, is the most widely used standard for sustainable forestry.[7] Eco-friendly alternatives to toxic chemicals are also available, such as beeswax, linseed oil, and walnut oil.

When eco-friendly furniture is produced, cradle-to-grave thinking is applied. This means that a full life cycle assessment is made from the "cradle," when the materials are extracted, throughout the production and use phases, all the way to the disposal, or "grave," phase. Choosing recycled furniture reduces the need for virgin materials. This checklist can help your nonprofit organization choose furniture needed for office activities wisely.

- ☐ Buy only what you need.
- ☐ Buy refurbished or secondhand furniture.
- ☐ Buy furniture that is durable and restorable.
- ☐ Buy furniture made from certified sustainable wood or reclaimed materials.
- ☐ When buying new furniture, buy eco-friendly furniture that can be easily repaired, disassembled, and recycled.
- ☐ Buy locally produced furniture.
- ☐ Buy furniture with Greenguard certification, which ensures that the furniture has low toxicity.
- ☐ Donate furniture you no longer need.

## Office Supplies

"Careless use and disposal of office paper and office supplies is rapidly clogging landfills, contributing to greenhouse gas emissions, depleting natural resources, contributing to air and water pollution, and wasting energy."[8] It is important to reduce the purchase of office supplies, such as binders, envelopes, paper, pens, folders, and stationery, as much as possible to minimize the negative environmental impact of the production and consumption of those items.

Paper is widely used in offices. Pulp and paper production has substantial negative impact on the environment. The production of paper threatens natural forests, flora and fauna, and livelihood of people depending on the forests. The paper production process consumes an immense amount of water and energy, in addition to the chemicals used, such as bleach. By changing consumption habits, your nonprofit organization can save a lot of money by using supplies wisely and at the same time reducing its environmental impact.

When supplies are delivered to your nonprofit organization, request that they are delivered in returnable or reusable packaging. This will send a message to sellers and producers, but it will also reduce the need for raw materials to produce new packaging, in addition to cutting down your recycling work and waste disposal cost. This list provides you with ideas on how your nonprofit organization can reduce consumption of office supplies and reduce its environmental impact at the same time. Start by taking inventory of all the office supplies. Have some items been sitting around unused for a long time? Rearrange them so that employees can find them, share them, or donate them to others who can use them.

☐ When buying office supplies, look for those containing a high percentage of recovered or recycled material.
☐ Create a "secondhand" corner to place used office supplies, such as binders and folders, for others to use.
☐ Reuse or salvage binders, folders, and notepads.
☐ Share office supplies such as staplers, punchers, glue, staple removers, stamps, scissors, highlighters, and the like.
☐ Send interoffice e-mails instead of paper memos.
☐ Use multiuse envelopes for internal correspondence, if needed.
☐ Create scratch pads from used paper.
☐ Buy recycled paper.
☐ Buy ink refills instead of new pens.
☐ Ask for paperless bills.
☐ When you need to buy new supplies, make purchases in bulk if cheaper.

## Electricity

There are many ways to reduce electricity consumption in your nonprofit organization immediately. Doing so will cut your energy bills without the need to invest in new equipment. However, when your nonprofit organization needs new appliances and electronics, look for the EnergyGuide and ENERGY STAR® labels, as doing so will help protect the environment and save money.

*ENERGY STAR labeled office equipment is widely available: it provides users with dramatic savings, as much as 90 percent savings for some products. Overall, ENERGY STAR–labeled office products use about half the electricity of standard equipment. Along with saving energy directly, this equipment can reduce air-conditioning loads, noise from fans and transformers, and electromagnetic field emissions from monitors.[9]*

According to PC Energy Report 2009:

*Each and every day many US workers are unknowingly wasting their organizations' money through one single act: leaving their PCs on when they are not being used, especially overnight and during the weekends. Collectively, US organizations waste $2.8 billion every year powering 108 million unused PCs. In 2009, these unused PCs are expected to emit approximately 20 million tons of carbon dioxide emissions—roughly equivalent to the impact of 4 million cars.*[10]

Buying "green" equipment will lower the electricity consumption of your organization, and it is easier to recycle or reuse the equipment at the end of its life cycle. Therefore, it has a longer lifetime, reduces needs for resources, and fewer materials end up as electronic waste (e-waste).

"Phantom energy" is a term used for the energy consumption of equipment plugged in but not being used. When reading the list, keep in mind that some ideas can be implemented immediately, while others are more of a long-term solution for your nonprofit organization.

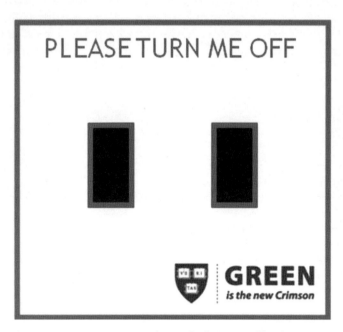

*Source:* www.greencampus.harvard.edu/green-office/energy

☐ Incorporate more natural lighting into your office.
☐ Turn off lights not in use during the day and at night, including common areas such as kitchens, storage closets, and bathrooms.
☐ Post prompts on light switches if needed.
☐ Lower your thermostat; use sweaters.
☐ Turn monitors and computers off at night.

☐ Unplug appliances in the evenings or use power strips that you can switch off to cut all power to the appliances.

☐ Create an energy-saving checklist that you can use while training new employees and volunteers.

☐ If using batteries, use rechargeable batteries and unplug battery chargers when batteries are fully charged.

☐ During cold weather, shut all the windows tightly, if possible.

☐ Purchase compact fluorescent light bulbs (CFLs) with the ENERGY STAR label.

☐ Use automatic shutdown of equipment if possible. If not, shut off monitors and put the computers into energy-saving modes (standby or hibernate) when they are not being used.

☐ If possible, enable a sleep mode on copiers and printers after a few minutes of inactivity.

## Office Equipment and Operation of Equipment

Behavioral changes can take some time to incorporate, but with the right training, motivation, incentives, and peer pressure, behavioral changes can be made quickly. Updating or replacing equipment is, however, more of a long-term strategy. When buying equipment, keep in mind that accessories for office equipment should feature an energy-efficient design as well. The checklist is split between operation of the equipment and the replacement of equipment.

### Operation of Equipment
☐ Train employees to use the equipment properly.
☐ Go paperless whenever possible.
☐ Use Internet and intranet for information flow, such as employee communication, press releases, and news sheets.
☐ Print several pages on one sheet of paper and/or use duplex printing.
☐ Share copies of printed material.
☐ Use scanners to digitalize documents.
☐ Buy remanufactured toner cartridges.
☐ Repair equipment if possible.
☐ Program fax machines so they do not automatically print out confirmation reports for each fax.

### Updating or Replacing Equipment
☐ Buy refurbished or used equipment.
☐ Purchase energy-efficient equipment and operate it efficiently.
☐ Install and use detectors for turning on lights in different areas (e.g., in restrooms).
☐ Choose printers that have double-sided printing and ink-saving options.
☐ Choose photocopiers that can copy double-sided and have energy- and ink-saving options.
☐ Choose laptops over desktops; they use less energy.

## Kitchen and Break Rooms

There are many ways to reduce the environmental impact of kitchens and break rooms. In September 2008, the city of Gothenburg, Sweden, banned the purchase of bottled water due to environmental concerns.[11] The production of the bottles, transportation of the water over long distances, and disposal of the used bottles all cause negative environmental problems. If your nonprofit organization stops buying bottled water, it can use its money more efficiently, since tap water or filtered water is much cheaper.

Most offices use many plastic and/or paper bags for wastebaskets or cleaning the office. Results of an environmental impact study made by the Scottish government in 2005 revealed that paper bags have a more adverse impact on nature than plastic bags for most of the environmental issues considered.

*Areas where paper bags score particularly badly include water consumption, atmospheric acidification (which can have effects on human health, sensitive ecosystems, forest decline and acidification of lakes) and eutrophication of water bodies (which can lead to growth of algae and depletion of oxygen).[12] Using paper sacks generates almost five times more solid waste than using plastic bags. After four or more uses, reusable plastic bags are superior to all types of disposable bags—paper, polyethylene and compostable plastic—across all significant environmental indicators.[13]*

| Indicator of Environmental Impact | Plastic Bag HDPE Lightweight | Paper Bag |
| --- | --- | --- |
| Consumption of nonrenewable primary energy | 1.0 | 1.1 |
| Consumption of water | 1.0 | 4.0 |
| Climate change (emission of greenhouse gases) | 1.0 | 3.3 |
| Acid rain (atmospheric acidification) | 1.0 | 1.9 |
| Air quality (ground level ozone formation) | 1.0 | 1.3 |
| Eutrophication of water bodies | 1.0 | 14.0 |
| Solid waste production | 1.0 | 2.7 |
| Risk of litter | 1.0 | 0.2 |

*Source:* SaveThePlasticBag.com.

Use ideas from this list to green your kitchen and break rooms.

- ☐ Use high-quality tap water or install water filters.
- ☐ Use washable kitchenware, such as plates, mugs, glasses, and silverware.
- ☐ Avoid disposable kitchenware.
- ☐ Use dishcloths and cleaning cloths in the kitchen.
- ☐ If necessary, use recycled and paper towels and napkins made without chlorine bleach.
- ☐ Use phosphate-free dishwashing liquid.
- ☐ Buy milk, sugar, and similar products in bulk.
- ☐ Buy fair trade organic coffee.
- ☐ Buy locally grown food.
- ☐ Use reusable shopping bags instead of plastic or paper bags.

☐ If necessary, use plastic bags rather than paper bags, and reuse them.
☐ Bring your lunch in reusable containers.
☐ Support restaurants and catering services that use locally grown food.

## Bathrooms

Cutting down on water, energy, and toxic detergents use is a great way to green your nonprofit organization's bathroom(s). At the same time, it will cut down on usage of natural resources, sewage use, and greenhouse gas production. Low-flow toilets save energy and water without compromising comfort and performance. The next list provides some ideas on how to green your bathrooms.

☐ Use energy-efficient air-dryers or hand towels in bathrooms.
☐ Buy hand towels made from organic cotton or bamboo.
☐ Use recycled and toilet paper made without chlorine bleach.
☐ Use biodegradable soaps made without chemicals such as paraben. (Parabens are widely used in the pharmaceutical industry as preservatives and to combat bacteria and fungi.)
☐ Clean the air with baking soda, vinegar, or a slice of lemon in a bowl of water.
☐ Install dual-flush retrofit on your current toilet(s).
☐ Do not leave the water running.
☐ Fix dripping taps immediately.
☐ Buy low-flush (dual-flush) toilet(s) when replacing old ones.
☐ Use greener cleaners for the bathroom or make your own cleaning mixture (see Figure 10.3).[14]

## Cleaning of the Office

Cleaning the office is a way to get rid of dirt and germs and to make the work environment more pleasant. This means keeping the furniture, floors, windows, bathrooms, and kitchen clean in most cases with formulated chemicals. Toxic substances float in the air, and we inhale them. In some cases, indoor air is more toxic than outside air and can lead to work-related asthma. Therefore, we should get rid of toxic cleaning products. Eco-friendly cleaning products are nontoxic, biodegradable, and made from nonpetroleum resources, preferably from renewable resources. Open windows helps clean the office air.

All-purpose home-mixed cleaners, which are both environmentally and economically feasible, are made by mixing either vinegar or baking soda with warm water. Slices of lemon or herbs in a bowl of water are great air fresheners. If your nonprofit organization prefers to purchase its cleaning products, look for eco-labeled products.

*An "ecolabel" is a label which identifies overall environmental impact of a product or service within a specific product/service category based on life cycle considerations. In contrast to "green" symbols or claim statements developed by manufacturers and service providers, an ecolabel is awarded by an impartial third-party in relation to certain products or services that are independently determined to meet environmental leadership criteria.*[15]

## A Basic Bathroom-Cleaning Mixture

Here are the ingredients for a cleaning solution that should work throughout your bathroom:

Mix 3 tablespoons baking soda, 1/2 cup ammonia, and 2 cups warm water.
Use for everyday cleaning.
Be sure to wear rubber gloves and use in a well-ventilated area.
For a bathroom cleaner without the ammonia, mix 2 cups baking soda,
1/4 cup dishwashing liquid, and 1 cup warm water.

## Bathroom Mirrors

Mix 1/3 cup clear ammonia in 1 gallon warm water. Apply it with a sponge or pour the solution into a spray container, and spray it directly on the mirror. Buff with a lint-free cloth, chamois, or paper towel. Vinegar may be substituted for ammonia.

FIGURE 10.3   Homemade cleaning mixtures.

*Source:* www.howstuffworks.com

This list provides you with ideas on how to clean the office in an environmentally friendly way.

☐ Buy reusable rags or microfiber towels for cleaning mirrors, sinks, and the like.
☐ Make your own cleaning mixtures or buy eco-labeled cleansers in refillable containers.
☐ If buying cleaning products, buy nontoxic, plant-based formula cleaners. They should be biodegradable and free of phosphates.
☐ Reuse spray bottles.
☐ Use two-sided scrubbing pads with fiber on one side and a sponge on the other to get rid of stains in kitchen or bathrooms. Use baking soda as needed.
☐ If you use plastic bags in the office trashcans, use the same bag several times before replacing it.
☐ Green your office with plants.

# Waste

Between 1960 and 2007, the amount of waste each person creates has almost doubled, from 2.7 to 4.6 pounds per day.[16] The growing heaps of garbage create environmental problems. Valuable lands close to urban areas are used as landfill sites, and there is a finite amount of land available in which to pile up the garbage. To reduce the enormity of waste, some of it is incinerated, which causes air pollution that risks our health. Toxic ash then needs to be disposed of. Hazardous substances from waste at landfills can leak out and contaminate soil, groundwater, rivers, and lakes. The best way to solve the problem is to eliminate waste upstream, which means to reduce the need for raw materials for production. Reusing what we have purchased is the next best solution to reducing. Recycling what we can no longer use moderates the problem as well.

Older generations were more austere and frugal than we are today. They made quilts from worn-out clothes and soup from meat bones, fixed what was broken, and so on. By embracing this kind of thinking, the nonprofit organization can become more economical, and the environment will benefit as well.

## Reduce

The most effective way to stop the above-mentioned trend is to prevent waste in the first place.

"Reducing" means that the amount of resources used when extracting raw material in the designing, production, and consumption phases is cut down, as well as the amount and toxicity of the garbage produced. The best way to reduce waste is to stop its generation rather than deal with it later. A large proportion of garbage comes from wrappers, containers, boxes, bags, and so on. In addition to reducing consumption, consumers can influence producers by sending a message about excessive packaging.

- ☐ Avoid disposable, single-use products.
- ☐ Rent or borrow equipment for temporary use.
- ☐ Choose durable goods that are built to last.
- ☐ Avoid overpackaged products.
- ☐ Think twice before you purchase: Do you really need what you are about to buy?
- ☐ Buy only what you need in order to avoid ending up with redundant equipment.
- ☐ Share office supplies and equipment with your coworkers.

## Reuse

"Reuse" means repairing what is broken and finding a new use for things. It also means donating to others what you do not need anymore. This will delay the time when the goods end up in the garbage or prevent items from ending up in your waste bin. Reusing items can help your nonprofit organization reduce waste disposal costs. It will also save handling costs for the community, such as composting, landfills, and incineration. It will also reduce pollution and emission of greenhouse gases that contribute to global warming. If you cannot reuse office supplies yourself, be creative about who *can* use them. The list provides you with ideas on how to reuse items at your office.

- ☐ Rinse and reuse jars, bottles, and other containers.
- ☐ Reuse folders by placing a new label over the old one.
- ☐ Refill toners for reuse.
- ☐ Reuse printed paper for other purposes, such as memos.

☐ Reuse packaging, such as cardboard boxes and bubble wrap, or donate it to others.

☐ Donate old furniture and equipment.

☐ Be creative when it comes to reusing items; donate unneeded paper, outdated stationery, jars, boxes, and the like to a local nursery school or day care center.

## Recycle

Production of items made from recycled materials saves virgin material and energy as it takes less energy to produce goods from used items than from new materials. It saves natural resources such as timber, water, minerals, and metals. It also decreases greenhouse gas emissions and helps sustain the environment. To make products from recycled material, the first step is to collect the recyclable, sorted materials. The recyclables are then processed into raw materials, such as fibers. Then they are reused in the manufacturing process of new items.

When starting or reforming the recycling program at your nonprofit organization, start by conducting a waste audit at your office. You can make an event out of it by collecting waste for a day or two and asking employees to examine the waste. How much did it weigh? How many categories were there? Which categories are you already recycling, and which ones can possibly be added? You can use results from the waste audit to set recycling goals. Repeat the audit on a regular basis. After the waste audit has been completed, you can create the office-recycling program.[17]

☐ Choose a recycling coordinator and green team.

☐ Decide on your collection methods.

☐ Select the waste categories you are going to recycle.

☐ Start with a few categories and keep adding until you recycle all the waste that is recyclable at your office.

☐ Purchase necessary containers and boxes.

☐ Label the bins, containers, and boxes.

☐ Place recycling bins and guidelines near fax machines and copiers and in the office, kitchen, and break rooms.

☐ Educate employees about recycling and waste management.

☐ Determine how recyclables will be hauled away.

☐ Monitor the progress of the program.

Recycling is a way to close the material loop. By closing the loop, the waste will be turned into new products. Among the categories that can be easily recycled are paper, cardboard, beverage containers, milk packages, plastics, glass, metals, batteries, and organic waste. Other things that can be recycled are used oil and paint. Construction and demolition waste created when renovating the office, for example, can also be recycled. To make your recycling efforts easy, familiarize yourself with the recycling services offered close to your nonprofit organization.

## Composting

Compost is organic material, such as food and garden waste, that is transformed through a decomposition process into a soil-like material. Composting is an inexpensive way to make valuables out of the waste and save diminishing land-fill space while reducing negative environmental impact.

The city of Portland, Oregon, recommends the formation of a "green" office team. These teams are responsible for collecting food waste and moving it to the central waste area. Team members can keep an eye on what goes into the waste container. Green team(s) share the workload and build support for the effort. The five main steps in forming such teams are to:

1. Obtain managerial support.
2. Form the team(s).
3. Get things started.
4. Communicate.
5. Clarify roles and objectives in addition to reviewing the process on a regular basis.[18]

When deciding what kind of food scrap collection containers you need and where to place them, consider the space you have and when food waste is collected from your office building. Most likely you will place the containers in the kitchen or in lunchrooms. Label the containers clearly. If you use bags to keep the container clean, you cannot use regular plastic bags; special compostable bags have to be used. Examples of office waste that can be composted are:

☐ Coffee grounds, filters, and tea bags.
☐ Food scraps.
☐ Vegetable trimmings.
☐ Paper towels and napkins.
☐ Paper coffee cups.
☐ Paper plates.

## E-Waste

"E-waste" is a popular, informal name for electronic products nearing the end of their "useful life." Computers, televisions, video cassette recorders, stereos, copiers, and fax machines are common electronic products. Many of these products can be reused, refurbished, or recycled. Unfortunately, electronic waste is one of the fastest-growing segments of the waste stream.[19] Another term used for such waste is "waste electrical and electronic equipment" (WEEE). Some components of e-waste are considered hazardous, such as lead and cadmium. Processing and disposing e-waste can cause both health and pollution problems.

*One problem related to e-waste is export of toxic wastes from rich to poorer countries, despite of the Basel Ban decision which effectively banned as of 1 January 1998, all forms of hazardous waste exports from the 29 wealthiest most industrialized countries of the Organization of Economic Cooperation and Development (OECD) to all non-OECD countries. The Basel Ban is still under serious attack and needs to be vigilantly protected against further efforts at sabotage ... primarily by the United States, Australia, Canada and such industrial lobby groups as the United States Chamber of Commerce, and the International Chamber of Commerce.*[20]

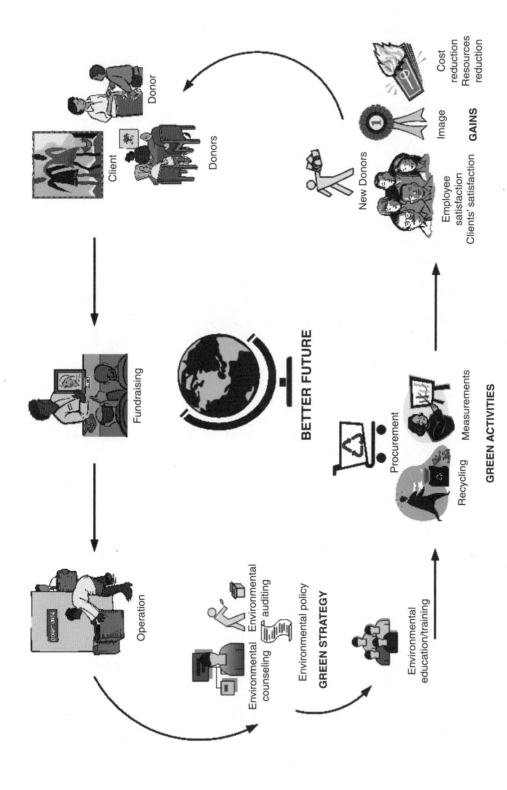

FIGURE 10.4  Value stream map.

*Source:* Adapted from Alvör Ráðgjöf ehf.

171

When getting rid of your nonprofit organization's e-waste, examine the background of the companies you use for recycling and refurbishment of the waste.

☐ Collect and recycle batteries.
☐ Donate old cell phones.
☐ Recycle toner and inkjet cartridges when it is no longer possible to refill them.
☐ When disposing of CFLs, place them in a plastic bag and deliver them to a trustworthy e-waste collection site.
☐ Donate used computers to other nonprofit organizations or a dependable firm that can refurbish them.

## Conclusion

Whether your nonprofit organization is large or small, it can make meaningful steps toward sustainability. A value stream map shown in Figure 10.4 is a useful tool to look at your operation. It starts in the upper right-hand corner, and you read it from right to left following the arrows. The map starts with the value your nonprofit organization is offering the client and also ends with the client. It describes the main activities of a nonprofit organization, the main "green activities," and possible benefits. Successful implemention of your green strategy results in better usage of resources that allows your organization to apportion a larger share of resources to its clients. Finally, yet importantly, the ultimate goal "better future" is placed in the middle.

In this transformation, the key message is to move away from linear thinking to life-cycle thinking where material loops are closed and materials used are reduced, reused, or recycled. Small, incremental steps are what will move your organization in the right direction. Remember, this is a long-distance race, not a sprint. The environment will benefit from this transformation, as will your nonprofit organization and various other stakeholders, including yourself. Perhaps most important, sustainability means that we are safeguarding the living condition of future generations.

### About the Author

**Lára Jóhannsdóttir** is a PhD student within the Faculty of Business Administration at the University of Iceland and the owner and chief executive officer of Alvör, a startup consulting company in the field of environmental management. She holds a BS degree in Business Administration and an MBA degree from Thunderbird School of Global Management. She previously worked in the Icelandic insurance sector for 14 years. Among other duties, she has worked as a quality manager, office manager, and specialist. Lára has key skills in project and operational management as well as quality and safety methodologies. She was in charge of the application process when her company received the Icelandic Quality Award in 2003. Lára has recently published a working paper and an article titled "The Environmental Literacy of Business Students."

## CHAPTER 11

# Green Technology Solutions

## Alex Shan and Joseph L. Khunaysir

## Introduction

When it comes to going green, most information technology (IT) departments—in fact, people in general—become lost in the hype. As a nonprofit, you are trusted with donor dollars to make smart, ethical, moral, and conscious decisions as to where and how you spend those dollars. At times you may find yourself at an interesting decision crossroad, trying to make that dollar go further. However, in the area of IT, making that dollar go further can be detrimental to the environment compared to more costly solutions. In the past, if less expensive products and services were generally lacking in the "green" category, we simply accepted it. It is safe to say that times have changed and the excuses as to whether to go green are a thing of the past. Rising costs of inefficiencies have caught up to us and the forces are aligned: Going green is not just the right thing to do, it is also the most cost effective. This chapter breaks apart a few of the many choices and initiatives a nonprofit can make to go green from an IT perspective.

Many topics can be discussed when it comes to green IT in the nonprofit sector. A recent report from the research firm Gartner, Inc. identified eight areas that can benefit organizations over the short term.[1] These are:

1. Improved design concepts for greener data centers
2. Advanced cooling technologies
3. Use of infrastructure management modeling and monitoring software
4. Virtualization technologies for server consolidation
5. More energy-efficient servers
6. Energy management for the office environment
7. Integrated energy management for the software environment
8. Cogeneration, or combined heat and power generation for data centers

Within this list, the most productive areas being identified are virtualization technologies and energy management in offices. The rationale and focus on these two areas is based on the simple premise that by virtualizing and consolidating more applications on fewer servers and thus decommissioning old servers, organizations will begin to realize savings in space, energy, money, and operational costs.

Whichever pieces of information presented in this chapter that you decide to adopt or digest, one thing holds true: As a nonprofit, you are responsible for making a positive impact on society. Although this impact is usually through programs and agencies, it is important to your donors, your stakeholders, and future generations that it is done in a green way.

# Energy Management

"Energy management" is a term used quite frequently in today's high-tech space. Hardware and software manufacturers are dedicating more and more of their research and development as well as marketing efforts to get the word out. There is a lot of emphasis on carbon footprint, and organizations are mobilizing to ensure that they do their part in reducing their respective contributions. Private sector organizations are going down this path primarily due to pressure from the government and the general public. Nonprofits should follow suit in order to maintain positive public sentiment and subsequently a leadership role in securing available donor funding. Reduced power consumption has a direct impact on energy costs to organizations. More important, from a cumulative point of view, reduced power consumption has a direct impact on energy requirements from unclean energy sources such as coal. According to the U.S. Department of Energy, more than half of the energy consumed by Americans is produced by coal.[2] By aligning the nonprofit movement with energy-conscious best practices in all areas of business—domestically, in the field, and by encouraging such practices by our staff and volunteers at home—we have the ability to effect global change.

## Energy-Efficient Products and Services

The selection of energy-efficient products and services from a technology standpoint is an integral step in aligning an organization with the global green movement. Energy-efficient products on the market have proliferated through into personal computing, servers/mainframe and network computing, handheld devices (mobile computing), printing, and various other technology components.

The term "personal computing" encompasses laptops and desktops for the most part. In purchasing these devices, an organization has the choice to select equipment that utilizes components that are optimized for low power consumption. Most major central processing unit (CPU), hard drive, and motherboard manufacturers offer a comprehensive line of more efficient/green products that desktop and laptop manufacturers can take advantage of. Look for the ENERGY STAR–compliant logo (see Figure 11.1). Also look for manufacturers that are EPEAT members (see the "Waste Management" section of this chapter for more details).

The term "server/mainframe and network computing" relates to enterprise or workgroup servers from manufacturers such as Dell, IBM, and Hewlett Packard/Compaq, and switches and routers from manufacturers like Cisco, Nortel, and Juniper. Server and network computing devices historically have been notorious for high power consumption due to the fact that they are always on, and often have multiple CPUs, hard drives, and power supplies in order to provide redundancy in service availability. This fact has also led to increased cooling requirements

FIGURE 11.1    ENERGY STAR® logo.


in corporate data centers and small-business server rooms. The U.S. Environmental Protection Agency (EPA) estimated that data centers and servers consumed 61 billion kilowatt-hours in 2006.[3]

As public and corporate demand has driven manufacturers to adopt an environmentally responsible mantra, the past several years have seen plenty of progress in the production of this equipment using environmentally conscious techniques to use less power and produce less heat. It is important to note that heat handling is an important aspect of energy management as it is directly related to cooling requirements and thus air conditioning energy consumption (see the section titled "Energy Efficient Data Centers"). In order to reduce the power usage and heat generation of enterprise servers, *virtualization* technology has developed into a fast-growing industry.


## How Virtualization Makes Sense

Until recently, the concept of "virtual" simply meant that something was in representation rather than the real thing. Some advertising would use the word "virtual" to describe "almost" or "there all around you" concepts (see Figure 11.2). However, in computing, "virtual" has taken on a new meaning that needs to be shared and explained in a simple manner; in IT terms and as defined in this chapter, "virtual" can be a major step toward greening your organization.

It has been almost five decades since IBM introduced virtualization as a way to leverage its powerful and expensive mainframes. What IBM did was to partition its large mainframes into separate logical "mini-mainframes" (see Figure 11.3). Splitting them up meant that each mini-mainframe could run multiple applications

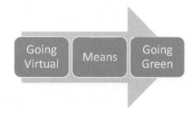

FIGURE 11.2    Going virtual means going green.

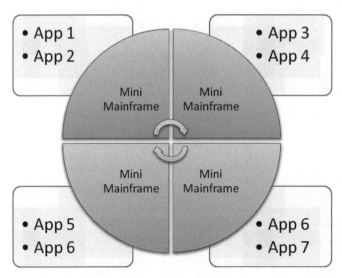

FIGURE 11.3   Mini-mainframe schema.

and processes at the same time, increasing efficiency and taking advantage of the supercomputer's capabilities. Having the applications and processes run in separate isolated mini-mainframes meant that there would be fewer conflicts among the applications, thus ensuring high availability of the services being provided and removing any large single points of failure.

Although virtualization faded in the 1980s and 1990s, it did lead the way to the distributed client-server computing that we know today. In essence, the ever-popular and cost-effective x86 platform consists of many isolated mini-servers and desktop computers working independently and residing on separate physical pieces of hardware—no expensive supercomputers necessary.

## Technology and Numbers

As we entered the twenty-first century, computing was becoming a mainstream must-have. For a long time, hardware capacity was seen as the bottleneck of processing (computing) capacity. Many new manufacturers sprouted to force forward the envelope of innovation, and the paradigm started to shift as the cost of hardware began to plunge. Suddenly many of these independent x86 servers were being underutilized by the applications and processes being run on them. Most industry experts estimate that a standard x86 server is using only approximately 10 percent of its capacity. As with the IBM supercomputer mainframes of the 1960s, this underutilization provides a great opportunity for partitioning and consolidation, and virtualization is now coming back to the forefront of server technology. Suddenly the advantages of virtualization have made it stand out as one of the top three priorities for many IT departments. What exactly is the technology of virtualization, and how do the numbers add up to make it such a hot priority now?

As seen in Figure 11.4, there are four separate components to a virtual machine: the hardware (processor), the hypervisor, the operating system, and the applications.

FIGURE 11.4   Virtualization components.

Each component serves a special and unique purpose. The critical key to a virtual machine is its hypervisor component. This layer of software serves as the crucial partitioning mechanism that allocates certain partitions of hardware into an interdependent silo where the virtual machine can exist. The hypervisor will read and write to the hardware resources allocted. These resources include things like memory, hard drive space, and processing power. The hypervisor will ensure the virtual machines resource allocation in turn making every attempt for high performance and availability. There are a few options for hypervisors in the industry; some are made by VMWare® (VSphere®), Citrix® (XenServer®), and Microsoft® (Hyper-V®).

According to studies done by many information labs and vendors, there seems to be consensus that virtualization can be a great way to go green while saving money, energy, and time, and reducing management headaches while easily accelerating business growth and mitigating risks. Save money and energy while reducing costs by maximizing your investments in hardware, cooling, and hosting footprint. Whether your environment consists of one or multiple servers, there are many cost-saving strategies involved when looking at virtualization, and multiple physical servers can be consolidated into one large machine.

Essentially, organizations can save time, accelerate growth, mitigate risks, and reduce management headaches using virtualization. On average, it will take an IT department three times as long to deploy a comparable virtual infrastructure as a separate server-housed infrastructure. Using virtualization technologies, the provisioning and decommissioning of servers is as easy as a few clicks. Backup strategies for virtual environments are plentiful, allowing the complete quick-restore of your entire server image to another available platform. Virtualization allows for easy replication and redundancy design between different virtual environments. If time means money, then going virtual makes a lot of sense.

Even though virtualization sounds like a silver bullet, it is not for everyone. In and of itself, virtualization can introduce new challenges to your computer infrastructure. Some applications and processes are very intensive and will likely run better on a physical server. Virtualization can have high up-front costs that will involve large investments in capital and resource hours for planning and deployment. Before adopting virtualization as one of your key initiatives, do your internal due diligence and make the business case work for you.

## Nonprofit Angle

As any nonprofit IT representative will tell you, installing new technologies usually has a barrier of cost and people resources associated with implementation and ongoing maintenance. As we have discussed, taking advantage of virtualization technology to save you on many fronts in the long run is very critical. Create your business case, and recognize whether your organization is a good candidate for the technology. Do your research and take full advantage of vendor pricing of software and hardware for nonprofits. There are great opportunities in this area. While numbers are crucial for making your virtual infrastructure business case, there is an ethical and moral obligation to helping our planet move toward sustainability; going virtual is one step to going green.

## Energy-Efficient Data Centers

**HISTORY** The Data Center Management Guide[4] defines a "data center" as the repository for the mission-critical data required for the optimal operation of an organization. The ability of the data center to perform properly relates directly to the organization's performance. According to statistics published by the U.S. Department of Energy, data center power consumption has more than doubled since 2001.[5] Although power consumption may be rising, it actually takes more energy to remove the heat generated by the servers than to power them. According to studies done by Cisco, powering and cooling your servers represent more than half the energy consumption in a data center.[6] Power consumption is of huge concern for our green movement. A data center plagued with cooling and power issues usually means that servers residing in the data center will have a shorter life span and will underperform or cease to operate in certain conditions, thus affecting the end-of-life cycle for these large capital investments.

As a nonprofit, whether you run your own data center or are outsourcing the hosting of your infrastructure, it is imperative that you decide with your dollars. Go with data center environments that are willing to go green. Examine how effective their initiatives are currently and their plans for future efficiencies. Then flaunt your partnership with a green data center initiative. This will help your stakeholders, donors, and peers to see the trends in the marketplace toward green IT and help them to recognize the efficacy and importance of these strategies.

**DATA CENTER** Whether your data center is comprised of one or a multitude of servers, a Cisco study found one thing holds true: A 1U server running 365 days a year delivers as many emissions as a Toyota Camry running 15,000 kilometers per year.[7] These numbers are staggering; most people do not realize the immense effect data centers have on our environment. According to an April 2008 study by McKinsey & Co., data centers emit more global warming gases than Argentina and the Netherlands combined.[8] The reasons to go green in your data center can range from moral to financial and legal directives. Whatever the specific driving factor may be, there is some confusion as to what the best strategy may be. In recent months, manufacturers have recognized that producing energy-efficient systems is a way to have an edge over their competition. Reducing the footprint is usually a good sell to anyone operating a data center, where power is by far the largest cost. In a data center, typically 45 percent of the power goes to the IT load (power equipment) and 55 percent goes to overhead, including cooling.[9]

The tactics involved in data center green initiatives vary widely. Some data center operators are simply looking at their existing data centers and attempting to build in efficiencies with the existing equipment, not waiting for the replacement life cycles. Options include the placement of servers to circulate hot and cool air more efficiently within the environment. By simply aligning data center aisles with hot- and cold-facing cabinets, data centers stand to save considerable resources in the large cooling pool.

Other methods include high-utilization models that attempt to achieve high energy efficiency through simple means and may run contrary to how data centers have operated for years. In most server environments, organizations are not taking advantage of the full capacity available to them. These idle processors are there to handle possible peak workloads or back up existing machines in case of a failover or disaster. Organizations should consider shutting down or sleeping these idle processors to conserve huge amounts of power. Virtualization and power management technologies hold tremendous potential in assisting with these types of situations as they can idle processors that are not being fully utilized. Virtualization environments can also swing resources between servers during varying peak or load times. As seen in our virtualization discussions, the cost savings just from a power perspective can be quite considerable when replacing a single server environment with large virtualized hubs.

Along the lines of high-utilization designs, many data centers are pushing the concept of high-density computing. Overall, this is the consolidation of discrete and unique servers into large single units that are then virtualized. In terms of power consumption alone, it is estimated that each single unit server will consume 70 percent less power when placed into a high-density configuration. As one of the largest costs of operating a data center is powering the IT infrastructure, the savings can really add up. It is estimated that of the power load used to operate the IT infrastructure (45 percent), 30 percent is used by the CPUs, while the remaining 70 percent is used by the accessory components found in servers (fans, memory, drives, and power supplies). After finalizing the calculations, a single CPU in a server utilizes 3 percent of the data center's power. Virtualization and high-utilization computing focus on the processors; there are plenty of cost-saving opportunities in other key areas of the data center environment.

When going green you can start with the basics: First ask that all unused monitors are turned off, printing is kept to a minimum, and power turned off on unused CPUs. Look to decommission old or unused systems, substituting to new power-saving systems. Make the business case for virtualization of a high-density computer with high-utilization computing, keeping in mind that a higher-density computing infrastructure needs a proper cooling model as well.

As time passes, all data centers will face large challenges of aligning their objectives with the business requirements of cutting costs and going green. The win-win situation for everyone seems to be that as organizations look to make these reductions in power consumption, carbon emissions, and their overall footprint, their need to be more efficient will naturally correlate to a greener IT initiative, a great coincidence for both people and the planet. As a nonprofit looking to select a data center to host your infrastructure, make the right choice: Go green in your decision and support the movement of efficiency.

# Waste Management

Waste problems exist wherever there is a human population, and many places are affected by the distribution of waste in waterways and landfills. The characteristics of these problems vary from one location to another, and although they may first appear to be local issues, their scope and magnitude are increasing as population density and standards of living rise. The boom of the middle class in developing nations such as India and China magnifies the problems of responsible waste management. The time is past when waste management could be considered in isolation; its impacts are being felt already in the global ecosystems. Environmental, technological, and financial factors all have some bearing, and the need to conserve resources also demands attention.

The concept of integrated waste management (IWM) has evolved over the past 10 years and is now becoming more broadly accepted. In such a system, the technical solution to waste disposal is not the only focal point. Instead, IWM relies on a number of different approaches to manage waste, focusing on all aspects, from generation to disposal and all stages in between. All stakeholders participating in and affected by the waste management system are considered to be cultural, social, economic and environmental factors.

## EPEAT and You

The Electronic Product Environmental Assessment Tool (EPEAT) was created by the EPA and the nonprofit Greener Electronics Council. The EPEAT rates computer and peripheral electronic devices based on their environmental attributes, evaluating them on 51 specific criteria into the grades of environmental performance—Bronze, Silver, and Gold. Responsible manufacturers register their products with EPEAT and are rated accordingly. The EPEAT is a significant first step toward responsible electronic procurement, but there are some limitations in its framework, particularly shortfalls in addressing the issues of labor conditions, production, and end-of-life management. Only limited requirements to eliminate certain hazardous materials exist; there are no requirements to enact policies that safely deal with e-waste, no requirements to enact occupational health and safety to protect workers, and weak requirements for responsible recycling and packaging.

Several other resources are available through various nongovernmental organizations, such as the Computer TakeBack Campaign, Health Care Without Harm, and Hospitals for a Healthy Environment; these groups have put together a short list of criteria to use with the EPEAT list to help in bridging the gap (www.epeat.net/Criteria.aspx).

## Responsible Hardware Purchasing

Electronic technology has become a very big part of life and business over the past several decades. It seems likely that this trend will only accelerate with the passing of time. Transportation, healthcare, education, manufacturing, agriculture, and even entertainment industries are powered by the marvels of technology, and at the most basic level—computers. Thousands of chemicals are used in the production of these computers and associated electronics, and they remain a relevant source of concern throughout the life cycle of the product. Eventually the vast majority of these components end up in solid waste landfill sites and release their harmful toxins (polyvinyl chloride, mercury, lead, etc.) into the environment through air and groundwater contamination. In addition, incinerated plastics release dioxins and furans into the air, substances known to have negative impacts on developmental and reproductive systems as they become concentrated in the environment and work their way up the food chain. There is not much we can do to stop the use of technology, nor is it the solution to the problem. However, purchasing this technology in a responsible manner helps us take a step in the right direction.

Concern for the environment has pushed many municipalities to ban the dumping of retired computer and related materials in the trash. Often organizations are forced to pay third-party companies for "safe disposal" of their discarded technology. These costs can be quite high, both financially and to the environment. Not all disposal companies are regulated or follow thorough environmental practices in divesting their inventory. When making your purchase decisions, make sure to consider the total cost of ownership inclusive of disposal costs. Many leading manufacturers have take-back programs in place, pricing for which is often included in the up-front cost of the machine. By investing in take-back programs when capitalizing the assets, manufacturers have incentives and are financed to design and implement recycling programs in order to effectively divest old equipment. Although sometimes there may be a small additional cost to use these programs, these costs are much lower than the cost to public health and the environment otherwise realized at the end of the life cycle. These inflated costs are usually shouldered by local governments and, indirectly, taxpayers.

Go to Epeat.net and follow the list of guidelines outlined by the EPEAT as well as some further recommendations made by Health Care Without Harm (www.noharm. org), Hospitals for a Healthy Environment (www.practicegreenhealth.org/), and the Computer TakeBack Campaign (www.computertakeback.com/index.htm) on how to best manage electronic procurement. Being a responsible green nonprofit can involve some difficult decisions regarding your hardware purchasing and retention policies—make the right decisions and be properly informed.

## New Age of Network Backups

Magnetic tape has been the backup medium of choice for a long time. The advantage of tape is cost, as it is less expensive than other storage options. However, the operational trade-off is performance. The information age has driven an explosion of content and subsequently data over the past 10 years. The amount of time it takes to back up all that data to tape has become increasingly inconvenient. Likewise, finding data on tape is a time-consuming process, making recovery of files an arduous process for IT departments. Consider music recorded to a cassette or reel-to-reel tape. In order to get to a song that is at the end of the tape, you have to fast forward through the entire tape. Compare this to a compact disc (CD), where you can start playing the disc at the place where the desired song is located.

A hard disk is read as a CD is read; the drive heads can move immediately to the location on the disk where the desired data are stored. Writing to disk is also significantly faster than writing to a tape, not to mention much more reliable. Transfer speeds for fiber channel disks are at least three times faster than tape. And hard disk space has been getting less and less expensive, making it feasible to back up from disk to disk and do away with tape backups altogether. In fact, when you factor in the initial investment in the tape drive along with the tapes themselves and the life span of each type of media, as well as administrative overhead, you might find that disk-to-disk backup is more cost effective than tape.

There is an ongoing debate about the power consumption of disks versus tape drives. However, advances in low-power drives and energy-saving arrays are fast bridging the gap. Besides, the life cycle of the average tape is between six and nine months; then tapes often are disposed of in the garbage to end up in a landfill.

**ADVANTAGES OF DISK-BASED BACKUP**    Faster performance is one good reason to consider moving from tape to disk for your backups, but it is not the only reason. Tapes break, as they are vulnerable to environmental factors, such as humidity and heat, and the loss of tension over time and use. Tape drive heads get dirty and have to be cleaned, and data are not always restored perfectly due to these and other factors. Some experts estimate that from 25 to 50 percent of tape restorations fail at least partially due to the wear and tear of the drive and media.

Disks are more durable than tape; they last longer, and they hold up under more frequent overwriting. Because they are contained inside sealed cases, there is less chance of the media being affected by the external environment. Of course, they never require retensioning or head cleaning.

Finally, disk backups are easier to manage. Keeping up with a collection of tape cartridges can become a logistical nightmare. Disk backup systems typically include management tools, often browser based, so you can easily configure settings and check status from anywhere.

**OFF-SITE DISK BACKUPS**    Another way of backing up disk to disk is to back up your data to someone else's disk, that is, to use an Internet-based backup service and store your backed-up data on that provider's remote server. These services provide for easy off-site storage of your backup data, while they remain easily available when you need them. Companies that provide online backup services generally build multiple redundancies into their systems and often provide 24/7 staffing and monitoring. They often use data vaults, so that your backed up information is physically secured within windowless rooms with reinforced concrete walls and redundant power supplies backed up by generators, to withstand natural disasters. Facilities are guarded and access is restricted, and the computer hardware is fault tolerant for minimal downtime. The better enterprise-level services provide service-level agreements that guarantee access availability.

**TRANSITION FROM TAPE TO DISK**    You already have an investment in your current backup system—most people use tape—and it may not be feasible or desirable to retire it and replace it with all disk-based backup. In fact, the two can be used together for a more effective backup solution. For example, you can use disk-based software to back up data from your workstations and servers to a central repository, and then use the tape system on that server to provide a backup of the backup. Additionally, if you have large amounts of data that need to be backed up, off-site storage of everything might be expensive (usually charged by gigabyte or in blocks of gigabytes). You can choose to back up non–mission-critical data on the tape volume and use the off-site system for the rest.

For even more redundancy, you could also back up the repository data to an on-line service. Now you have on-site disk backup, a tape backup, and off-site backup in a hardened location. This might seem like overkill, but if your business depends on your data, multiple backups could be a lifesaver in the event of a catastrophe.

## Green Printer Management

If someone told you that the nonprofit you were giving your hard-earned dollars to was causing more harm to the environment than your caring donation, how would that make you feel? There are many ways to state your claim as a green organization. Nothing is as profound as the ability to use responsible printer management and make sure you are communicating this strategy to your stakeholders. Being a green nonprofit is something you should be proud of and something you should flaunt to all channels. Driving toward responsible printer management can be one of your largest and easiest impacts. Green printing is guaranteed to conserve energy, save trees, reduce greenhouse gases, decrease waste, save time, and save money.

The more times in the day we print, the more trees we cut down, and the greater the environmental impact. With fewer trees, there is greater chance of ozone depletion, enlarging the ozone gap through which Earth is sprayed with harmful ultraviolet rays. Skin diseases, cancer, and even certain respiratory problems are a result of this dangerous ozone depletion. Dealing with these environmental challenges through green responsible printing will allow us to seek a greener Earth today and for future generations.

Most nonprofits produce myriad printed documents to send out promotions, collaborate with stakeholders, communicate with the board, or update donors. Although all these pieces are part of the general branding and communication strategy, put in place to generate positive feedback while advancing the cause, they involve printing internally or by a professional print vendor. Print vendors are one of the many contributors of the volatile organic compounds (VOCs) that are detrimental to the health of our planet. VOCs are known to cause cancers, birth defects, and even certain forms of cardiovascular disease. VOCs tend to be found most commonly in natural gas, cleaning solvents, gasoline, and paint thinners. When VOCs enter our air, they occur as methane and nonmethane. Methane is the greenhouse gas that is mostly responsible for ozone depletion and all the associated harmful effects. The double-edged sword here is that the common marketing and information brochure is most likely doing more harm to the environment than it is actually reaching for the positive call-to-action feedback that it was intended to accomplish.

Paper production decimates our forests while consuming inordinate amounts of water and energy. In estimates from the Environmental Defense Fund Web site,[10] production of 1 ton of virgin uncoated paper requires 3 tons of wood, 19,075 gallons of water, and can generate up to 2,278 pounds of solid waste. Add to those staggering numbers the fact that 90 percent of our printing and writing is done on this type of paper, which is also bleached through a chlorination process that releases harmful chemicals and pollutants into our water system. Many industry experts claim that the printing industry is the single largest air polluter and the third-largest consumer of fossil fuels behind automobiles and steel manufacturing. Although many may believe that everything printed is recyclable, this could not be further from the truth. Adhesives, certain bindings, and metal inserts such as foils are used in printing and packaging. These additions often can render the finished product completely unrecyclable, guaranteeing that it will end up in the garbage and eventually a landfill.

Do not fret. Like all the issues that have been discussed in this chapter, there are green solutions that will give you a more efficient outcome while making your organization look good. Better yet, it has never been easier to practice responsible green printing both internally and with the printing shops you select.

The ideal strategy for the environment would be the complete adoption of a paperless office, but this is not necessarily practical or feasible for many organizations. Your first real option will mostly likely include a change to your mail campaigns. Try reducing the number of mailshots (mailshots are bulk mail advertising sent through the mail) (reference: http://en.wikipedia.org/wiki/Mailshot) and look to make them as green and eco-friendly as possible. Consolidate your mailing messages into bundles rather than separate campaigns. Ensure that your designs are environmentally friendly *and* effective. Encourage your designers to create eco-friendly mailers using one or two colors and avoiding fancy add-on items like foils. Let your constituents know that you have taken a green approach to your mailers; you may find that this will have an even further impact on your campaigns.

Selection of your internal and external printers and supplies is essential to a green initiative. As an alternative to petroleum-based inks, try to use vegetable- or soy-based supplies. Not only are these inks low in VOCs, they are not outlandishly priced and can be easily part of your overall initiative to achieve green, responsible printing. When selecting an external printer, look for ones that make an attempt to go green by using waterless printing methods. In your final product, try to avoid using bindings and non–eco-friendly adhesives, and stay away from foils. Another plausible option is to bring all the printing in-house so you can keep control of your green efforts by selecting the printing methods, products, and accessories used.

Many still see green printing as expensive or of poorer quality, but technological advancements have made it very competitive and comparable to traditional printing. Today it is very hard to distinguish between recycled and virgin-fiber paper. Further, the finished product is typically very close in quality and not distinguishable by nonprinting professionals. Keep in mind that it is cheaper to make recycled paper, using much less energy than to make virgin paper. As more organizations use recycled paper, technology advances will further enhance the product while slowly reducing its cost as economies of scale start to take effect.

Remember to vote with your dollar. Keeping your printing initiatives as green as possible plays a huge role in having a positive impact on the environment. It also showcases to the world that you have everyone's interest at heart even when fighting for your own cause. Flaunt your green printing initiatives, sharing your stories with all your stakeholders. Let everyone know your efforts and the positive impact they are making on your organization and the world. Use the environment calculator at Neenah Paper[11] to calculate and detail your efforts. Not only is your nonprofit promoting its cause, but it is doing so in a green fashion.

## Paperless Office and Content Management Systems

One of the most elusive holy grail terms bandied about since the advent of the personal computer is the "paperless office." Meant to describe the world of the future, the paperless office was a vision that many had with introduction of the PC. Nevertheless, the advent of the computer has *increased* paper use with worldwide consumption doubling between 1998 and 2000.[12] Some statistics from Canada report that between 1983 and 2003, the consumption of paper rose 93.6 percent to 91.4 kilograms—about 20,000 pages per person.[13] As a team that runs a successful IT practice, we understand that a completely paperless office is a utopia that most of us will not achieve anytime soon. However, there is much progress that can be made in the short term to at least help bring the levels back in line with 1998 as soon as possible.

Consider your current position. As a nonprofit, your goal should be to provide the most impact per donation dollar and to keep operating costs to a minimum. A tremendous amount of dollars are wasted in printing and filing unnecessary paperwork. Cost savings aside, going green with your paper has many advantages, such as quicker access to information, better ability to collaborate, an outstanding moral obligation, great environmental responsibility, and a mind-set for the future. The technology to go paperless is readily available and quite cost effective. The challenge becomes your mind-set because going to a paperless office will affect your work processes and the flow of information among your peers, vendors, and clients.

As a nonprofit, you are probably very keen to make this transition but find that many within your organization are stuck in old habits; in some places, printing e-mails as a method of record filing is still the norm. Having done the math internally, we are confident there going paperless has a huge cost saving potential. Imagine getting rid of the expensive filing space that your cabinets take up. The cost of a standard office is about $45/square foot per year. A filing cabinet and space needed to navigate around it take up approximately 30 square feet, for a total cost of approximately $1,350 per year in addition to the cost of the filing cabinet ($1,000/year) and printer lease or management ($1,750/year). Add these numbers together and you have a cumulative cost of $4,100. While many might see this cost as something that would simply need to be factored into operations, we see it as an opportunity to position your paperless office and increase your environmental profile.

The business case may be quite obvious, but the solutions and strategies may not be. A standard information worker within your organization will interface with so many different pieces of content in different media that it can be challenging to understand where all those pieces should be stored—preferably in an easy-to-understand format, quickly accessible, secure, backed up, and available to archive for legal purposes. For the longest time, organizations have based their content filing and worker processes on individuals, allowing for freedom of habits and process. The more organizations leave it to their information workers to be green, the less uniformity there is across the office and the less efficient everyone will be. If you establish organization-wide initiatives vying for the ultimate goal of a paperless office, you will see sweeping changes that will not only make you more successful but ensure that you are doing it in a green way.

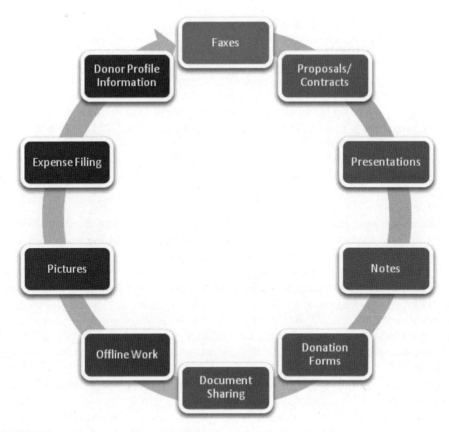

FIGURE 11.5   Organizational content map.

There are a few key steps to a paperless office strategy. Your first strategy might be to map out all the different types of content people use and interface with on a regular working basis. With these pieces of information mapped out (see Figure 11.5), you can start to build a comprehensive information worker strategy pushing toward a paperless environment.

You can employ many different strategies to address your information workers' needs on a case-by-case basis. However, your largest impact will come when you not only look to take all these potential processes and make them paperless but build them into your overall content management strategy. Using a content management platform such as Microsoft Sharepoint® services will ensure that your data are presented, organized, and available as demonstrated in Figure 11.6.

Each of the unique potential activities that your information worker is involved in has a specific technology solution that will get your offices one step closer to a paperless reality. There are many different approaches to organizing your information in a content management solution (CMS). One area of Web-based CMS that you will definitely use will be the team workspace areas. Workspaces tend to be focused on areas such as departments, projects, and donor groups. That way, every piece of information that is created and needs storing has a place to live within your new

FIGURE 11.6   Content management strategy.

office CMS. Examples of how this might apply to our information worker cycle are presented next.

- **Faxes.** Receive faxes electronically. Many printers have the option of receiving faxes and converting them into pdf files. These files can be easily stored in a document library on your network environment or in the team workspace of your CMS. You can also outsource this function as there are many third-party electronic fax solutions.
- **Proposals/contracts.** While sharing proposals is an easy task in a CMS, storing the signed proposals or contracts is key here. Using scanners and optical character recognition technology, you can easily convert any executed contract into a file that can live within your CMS.
- **Presentations.** Try not to print your presentations as handouts. Use a projector to share with your colleagues and send a link to your presentation for people to have a point of reference. You can also post your presentations online via free services such as SlideShare.
- **Notes.** Using written notebooks is a thing of the past. Try migrating to a note-taking application, such as OneNote® from Microsoft. OneNote looks and feels like a notebook but it is electronic, easily searchable, and can be easily shared or stored for others to review.
- **Donation forms.** Paper is out and the Web is in. Rather than use paper-based forms, encourage people to build forms in InfoPath®. InfoPath is from Microsoft and is included in some versions of Microsoft Office Suite. Building forms online is easy. With a bit of training, you can even add your complex business rules to save you the time of checking over everyone's work.
- **Document sharing.** Although you may be very tempted to give or use handouts at a meeting for everyone's reference, there is no need to do so. Simply send them a link to where documents are stored and have them review and reference them at their own leisure.
- **Offline work.** Thinking of taking that huge document home to work on? No need to print it. Placing things in electronic format will give you real-time access to the latest version.
- **Pictures.** Need a place to store all your incredible images or folders? There is no need to print and file them. By using a CMS, you can place them in organized bins in relation to the project with which they are associated.

- **Expense filing.** Filing expenses can be a paper-intensive process. You may require copies of the receipts for your organization and self. Use online forms and scanning technology to submit and attach the necessary documents.
- **Donor profile information.** All nonprofits require information about their donors. Make the best use of technology and invest in a CRM (Customer Relationship Management) that integrates with your CMS to help join this information to your master storehouse.

There are plenty of available technology solutions to going paperless. Make your name as a green nonprofit. Set up a committee that will help push through positive change. This change is guaranteed to improve efficiency and help you on your mission to becoming a true green nonprofit from the inside out.

## Future of Biodegradable Peripherals

The world's first biodegradable computer, iameco was produced by MicroPro, a company based in Dublin, Ireland, which produces eco-friendly computers, keyboards, mice, and flat-panel monitors.

Founder Paul Meher and 17 engineers started this endeavor 15 years ago with the objective of ending the era of computers with short life cycles and disposable nature. Meher was not happy with the common use of hazardous materials in most computers.

iameco computers have effectively cut this waste out. They are high-specification computers without any of the toxins traditionally used in computer manufacture. The computers are also powerful enough for everything from three-dimensional gaming and design, to simple e-mail and word processing. One of the amazing features of this new eco-computer is that implanted within the wood panels are seeds from native tree species, so that when the components are buried in a landfill, the wood breaks down and new trees begin to grow.

It is important to note, however, that these units are as much as 50 to 100 percent more pricey than their traditional counterparts. Fujitsu has also recently launched a laptop with a biodegradable chassis made from cornstarch. As this industry is in its infancy, progress in making this technology affordable and more available is likely.

Biodegradable plastics used in computer manufacture, although expensive compared to traditional plastics, decompose in a few months, whereas traditional plastic takes decades to decompose. Traditional plastics are manufactured from numerous nonrenewable resources, such as natural gas, coal, and oil; biodegradable plastics are made with plant-based materials and result in 15 percent less carbon emissions.

Starch, which is a natural polymer, can be processed into a "bioplastic." When the starch is harvested from corn, potatoes, or wheat, a microorganism transforms it into lactic acid. It is then chemically treated to cause the molecules of lactic acid to link up into long chains or polymers, which bond together to form a plastic called polylactide.

Companies such as Fujitsu Limited and Fujitsu Laboratories Limited use biodegradable plant-based material as a substitute for polystyrene in the manufacture of embossed carrier tape. This tape is used for packing large-scale integrated circuit chips when shipping them on reels. Biodegradable plant-based embossed carrier tape acts as protection against electrostatic discharge and product durability. It is eco-friendly and does not produce toxic emissions when incinerated.

## Conclusion

There are many options to make your nonprofit greener through the different facets of IT management. Working for an organization that has a positive cause and mission statement holds with it the responsibility of spending dollars in a moral and ethical manner. With the advancements in technology and ease of implementation, it has never made more sense to kick-start your green IT initiative. If you are already down this path or are going there soon, make sure to spread the message to all those who connect with you; with the competition for donor dollars increasing day by day, there has never been a better time to be green and give yourself and our planet the edge.

## About the Authors

**Alex Shan** is currently the chief executive officer of Jolera Inc., a leading information technology consulting company ranked in the top 50 of *Profit 100*'s fastest-growing companies in Canada. Alex brings a unique business acumen coupled with an extensive background in technology innovation and solutions delivery to Jolera. He is an insightful and strong leader, with the ability to motivate teams and consistently deliver results. He has appeared on television as an expert in the area of business computing trends on multiple occasions and has been published by *PROFIT* magazine on the topic of business management.

**Joseph Khunaysir** is the founder, chief information officer, and chief technology officer of Jolera Inc. Joseph is responsible for the research, development, and implementation of Jolera's technical service and product offerings. After successfully developing an award-winning network services and sales model in 2007, Joseph launched and continues to lead the Jolera SharePoint™ division. This team provides SharePoint and Web application design, development, and maintenance to several of North America's largest and most recognized organizations. A passionate and enthusiastic leader, Joseph believes strongly in corporate and personal social responsibility, regularly volunteering his time and expertise to several important causes.

# PART III

# Environmentally Friendly

## CHAPTER 12

# Being Green

## *Managing Chemical Use*

### Michael Goodsite, Esbern Warncke, Lars Moseholm, and Christian Monies

## Chemical Management Systems: Roles and Responsibilities

The term "chemicals" is defined, according to the U.S. Occupational Safety and Health Administration, as "any element, chemical compound or mixture of elements and/or compounds."[1] They are found either in natural occurrences—that is, in substances not being synthesized by humans—as well as in substances having been synthesized by humans. They are ubiquitous; they can be found all around us. From our medicines to our materials, our world is filled with products that require chemicals. Therefore, wherever you are reading this book, they are very likely on and around you, in the manmade as well as the natural environments. "Chemical management" deals with how we acquire, store, employ, and dispose of the chemicals that we require for ensuring success in our organization. It also includes setting and adhering to broader guiding principles throughout our value chain.

Properly managed chemicals enhance prosperity and quality of life. Improperly managed chemicals may ultimately have negative consequences for health, safety, and the environment (HSE). Chemicals and their use and associated risks must be responsibly managed. It is especially important for organizations that consider themselves as "green" to take a leading role in this effort.

The American Chemistry Council (ACC) published a set of five principles that outline the "basic elements upon which effective chemical management policy should be based":

1. A chemical management system must be risk based.
2. The system should screen all chemicals (new and existing) to determine further information needs in a tiered, risk-based approach.
3. The system should leverage available information.
4. The system should recognize the responsibilities of each party throughout the chain of commerce.
5. The system must promote quality and transparency.[2]

Although the principles are intended for "management systems for both government and individual chemical companies," the nonprofit organization can and should consider these principles when establishing a chemical management system. By applying the principles, the ACC states that effects will:

> *(a) Assure that public health and the environment are protected from unreasonable risk resulting from exposure to chemicals through the application of appropriate risk management measures.*
>
> *(b) Assure that the risks of chemical manufacture, distribution, use, disposal, and recycling are adequately characterized and managed.*
>
> *(c) Apply chemical control management systems that sustain a global competitive chemical industry by enabling innovation and that balance social, economic, and environmental needs.*
>
> *(d) Increase public confidence about the safety of chemicals.*
>
> *(e) Provide timely responses to public concerns about chemical risks.*

As shown from the quotations and inferred from the principles, effective chemical management is always consistent with good business practice, whether the business is nonprofit or for profit.

## The Nonprofit Organization as an Intentional (Professional) or Accidental Manager of Chemicals

**NOTE: A handbook cannot and should not replace effective on-site guidance.** In many countries, this guidance must come from individuals certified to provide such guidance. If you *think* that your organization needs this guidance, find out for certain from the appropriate regulatory agency and seek its advice as to whom you may turn to as a consultant.

If you are reading this chapter to find specific expertise because your nonprofit organization is dealing with chemicals as a core competency, especially so-called hazardous chemicals (those that are a physical hazard or a health hazard), this chapter is *not* written for you. It may, however, provide you with useful background information and resources.

This chapter is written primarily with "accidental" chemical managers in mind, that is, those who cannot avoid having chemicals around them but do not deal with chemicals as part of their core business or fall under regulations specifically dealing with chemicals, their use, or their disposal. Seek the advice of a professional consultant and governmental regulatory organizations if you are intentionally managing chemicals or planning on doing so. Consider hiring a professional as part of your organization or hire an expert as a consultant. This is important, since laws may vary locally. Many issues need to be dealt with and can be prudently dealt with only on-site.

This chapter is intended for the senior managers and directors who should be familiar with chemical management systems and ultimately have the responsibility for ensuring that safe and sustainable systems are in place in the organization. If you have any doubts as to whether this is the case in your organization, it is always better to *proactively* lay them to rest through the efforts of an expert rather than

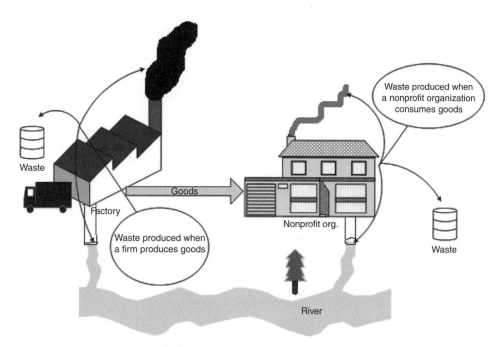

**FIGURE 12.1** A nonprofit organization's activities introduce chemicals into the surrounding environment throughout the life cycle of the chemical.

*Source:* Drawn by Christian Monies based on information and sources from Esbern Warncke.

*react* to an incident or accident. A company may be required by law to set up the internal system to monitor the HSE requirements. In Denmark, an executive order deals with the Health and Safety Activities of an Enterprise;[3] most countries have similar regulations.

### Your Organization as a Source of Chemicals to Your Employees, Your Environment, and Perhaps Your Customers

Your organization is likely a source of chemicals to your employees and the environment. It might even be to your customers, as can be the case with any new product that emits chemicals to the atmosphere (see Figure 12.1). Even the greenest buildings and organizations will have some emissions of chemicals to their ecosystem, that is, the environment that they are a part of.

The question then becomes: How do we manage this fact? We mitigate hazards from chemical use by managing risk (see Figure 12.2). Doing this involves ensuring that the firm takes into account engineering and technical solutions and advice to mitigate risk; trains employees and relevant stakeholders about these risks through an educational program; and continuously ensures enforcement internally of rules and regulations.

Chemicals have a life cycle (see Figure 12.3). From the time you choose to use them in your process or business, you should ensure prudent and safe management

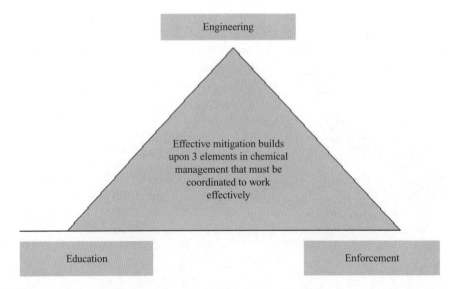

**FIGURE 12.2** Effective mitigation in a chemical management system.

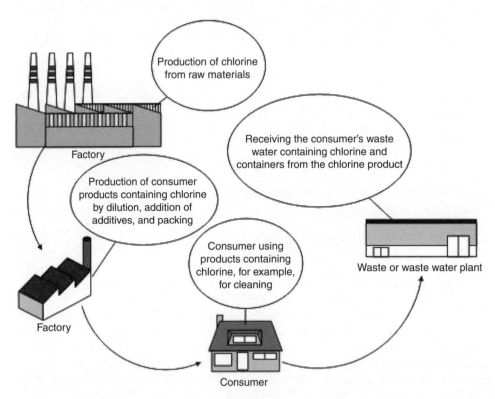

**FIGURE 12.3** Life cycle of a chemical from acquisition to disposal.
*Source:* Christian Monies.

for health and the environment through the portions of the process that you control.

Once you have made the decision to use chemicals, either intentionally or through "accidental" usage, you must manage the chemicals throughout the parts of the life cycle that you can influence based on principles of good chemical management.

## Principles of Good Chemical Management

On its chemical management homepage, the University of Arizona concisely summarizes the possibilities of effective chemical management, both for mishap and for economic gain:

> *Effective chemical management is consciously considering all aspects of safe, responsible and economical chemical handling from the beginning, during work planning and chemical acquisition, through final chemical disposal. It can be broken down into a number of definable elements—acquisition, identification, inventory, storage, distribution and disposal. Each step provides opportunity for misadventure but each step also offers opportunity for economic gain, environmental protection, and to drastically improve workplace safety and reduce workplace accidents and illnesses and minimize the severity of those that might occur.*[4]

Chemical management is just one aspect of an integrated safety management plan as part of the organization's overall HSE strategy. Even at a service-based office, such as a consulting agency, there are chemicals in cupboards and cleaners being used. Some chemicals are so common that they are perhaps taken for granted. All of these chemicals should be appropriately managed. Doing so will improve not only the HSE aspects of the organization but the business itself.

### Organizational Roles in Chemical Management

The roles that individuals and firms play may be defined by local laws, but, in general: The owner or administrative director along with the board of directors is responsible for everything that happens or fails to happen with respect to meeting HSE regulations and concerns in the organization. They may delegate the authority to handle and address these issues to either line leaders or an HSE manager, but in most instances, the legal responsibility may not be delegated. Along with rights at each level come responsibilities. Typical responsibilities for line managers and employees are listed next.

#### Line Managers
- Line managers are responsible for implementing HSE policies and procedures and holding their employees trained and accountable for their proper use.
- They must identify hazards and analyze associated risks to be managed and ensure that the associated risks are managed (or *controlled*) to whatever standard

of compliance there is, whether it is organizational or other law- or policy-making organizations.

- They must then implement this risk management through a system that meets legal requirements together with their available staff.

**Employees**

- Employees are responsible for ensuring that they take no actions directed or on their own initiative that place themselves or others at risk.
- They must use appropriate reporting procedures to bring to the attention of management or authorities, as appropriate, hazards and risks that might not be recognized.
- They must be active participants in continuously improving the chemical management system and its place within integrated safety management. This means that they must always utilize the appropriate and assigned control measures put in place when managing chemicals (e.g., updating the chemical register; explained later). They should inform managers of the opportunity to move up the control hierarchy or the need to adjust down the hierarchy, depending on the specific needs of the organization and requirements of the product.

The control hierarchy is a principle for managing hazards. According to the hierarchy, it is always best to eliminate a hazard (priority 1) rather than be intentionally exposed to it (though with protective devices). It is management's responsibility to ensure that all hazards are properly identified, risk is managed, and controls are in place.

Although the control hierarchy is to be implemented in chemical management, in good practice, a range of controls often is employed. For every substance, ask: Do we need it? If you do not, do not use the chemical. If you do need it, is there a better substitute (substitution principle)? Use safer and greener substances wherever possible. If the chemical is hazardous, lock it up and control it in accordance with laws or just good sense. Is there something you can do to make it less hazardous? If so, enact it. Employees accomplish routine processes all the time. Ask yourself: Where they have learned to employ the chemical? Develop safe procedures, make them standard, and train and supervise on their use. When needed or required, use personal protective measures. Supervise legal requirements and your standards. Generally legislative guidelines detail these principles. In Denmark, for example, they are electronically available.[5] Such guidelines may be reviewed at www.unisa.edu.au/ohsw/procedures/hazard.asp.

## Define Your Organization's Needs and Uses of Chemicals

Walk around your establishment and building. Where are you using chemicals or substances? Which of them are hazardous? Are any classified by law or by common sense as possible immediate dangers (such as radioactive isotopes in some machines) and therefore "dangerous"? What control measures do you have in place for them? What risks are involved? As a green nonprofit organization, you are sending a powerful signal through the chemicals you utilize in your organization. Those around you will assume that you are the local experts and may look to you as to how to effectively manage chemicals. You should establish a chemical register—a record of all nonhazardous, hazardous, and dangerous substances that you are using or services that you are employing. Many examples of registers may be found online, or contact one of the chapter authors. The forms may be color-coded based on the various hazard level associated with the chemical. Management should extend these thoughts to what is being used by businesses in the chain of commerce and should require suppliers to live up to the same standards as the business itself. It also should choose customers that also live up to the organization's standards.

## Integrating Chemical Management with Your Other Safety Issues

In many countries, legislation requires a workplace assessment to ensure that aspects related to work are planned, organized, and implemented so as to ensure safe and healthy working conditions. The Danish guidelines are a comprehensive example of the process of conducting a workplace assessment.[6] In the absence of any other regulatory guidelines, they may be used to assess the workplace. The workplace assessment should include an assessment of the chemicals employees are exposed to. Thus, the assessment is a prerequisite for an outstanding chemical management system. Once the chemical management system is established, employees dealing with chemicals have two external guidelines and one internal guideline: The external guidelines are the manufacturer's instructions for use and the material safety data sheet (MSDS), both of which are available from the manufacturer by law. In many countries, organizations also are required to produce an internal work safety data sheet (WSDA) that details how the product is to be used in the course of work. An example from the authors' workplace for chlorine, a common cleaning chemical, is shown in Table 12.1. This guidance forms the basis of an employee's use and training and should be in a language that the employee understands. The original copy of this document was in Danish. Some important data were presented in two languages, as it is important, and may be required, that the WSDA for your employees is available in their mother tongue. (Note that this example is based on Danish legal requirements. It has been annotated and is for illustration purposes only. It should *not* be used or construed as valid for chlorine.)

## A Basic Tenet of Chemical Management Is Managing Risk, Not Hazard

Many substances are inherently hazardous (i.e., have the potential to cause damage or injury to health or the environment), but when judged necessary for a process and properly managed, they have an acceptable risk to health and the environment. "Risk" is generally defined as the likelihood or statistical probability of harm or damage occurring from exposure to the substance. The risk is dependent on many factors and may not depend just on the substance used; typically it is related to the concentration and form of the substance and what it is used with. Some substances have not yet been documented to *not* have a negative impact on health and the environment. These should be excluded under the precautionary principle. The hazards of a substance or chemical must therefore be recognized and often are declared by the manufacturer in accordance with law.

For example, regarding chlorine: Using it in a cleaning product is generally much less hazardous than using it in great concentrations in an industrial process.

TABLE 12.1   Work Safety Data Sheet: Chlorine

**Product identification:**

Name: Chlorine (Klorin)              Producer:                     Xxxxxxxxxx
                                     Xxxxxxx xxx Xxxxxxx

Active Chemical Ingredients:

Sodium hypochlorite solution 5% active chlorine

**Hazard identification:**

Local irritation, eye and skin irritant.
A hazardous gas (chlorine gas) may develop when this comes into contact with other chemicals or surfaces.

**First aid: immediate action:**

In case of skin contact, rinse continuously with water and soap. Seek medical attention if the irritation exists after washing. If in eyes, rinse continuously with water and seek medical attention.
*Refer to the exact physical location of the nearest eyewash.*

**In case of fire:**

This product is not easily ignited. In case of fire, remain away from the fire's smoke and notify the fire brigade of the presence of the products.

**In case of spill:**

Wash with water and dry. Ensure area is ventilated and waste is properly disposed of.

**Storage:**

Stored in accordance with laboratory rules, in original container, closed, and away from children and food sources.
*Note exactly where product is stored and where product register is.*

**Personal protection guidelines:**

Do not blend with other products. Use approved safety glasses and gloves. Wash hands with soap and water after use.
*Note exactly where safety glasses and gloves may be found.*

**Disposal:**

Any remaining product and container is disposed of in accordance with local regulation.
*Refer to the regulation and any points to be followed.*

Therefore, in both cases, the chlorine ultimately can be managed so that it does not present an unreasonable risk to employees, the public, and the environment.

To understand the risk of utilizing a substance, you must systematically analyze it so that decisions made regarding the substance are based on an objective scientific evaluation of risk. Risk assessment decisions must be made prior to product utilization but may be adjusted after new knowledge is gained. Therefore, risk assessments can and should be monitored and adjusted to reflect the latest knowledge. This is the responsibility of the person who decides that the product should be used. Benefits and costs need to be considered in the decision since there is a very simple conclusion: Either your organization has the financial means to utilize the substance at an acceptable risk level, or it should not use it.

The University of South Australia's guidelines provide an excellent form for investigating and assigning risk.[7] Managers must remember that examples in this chapter and ones they find online are for illustrative purposes only; organizations must develop their own risk assessments based on local requirements and expertise.

## A Key to Excellent Implementation

Management needs to actively promote a culture of safety. Initially it can do so via a chemical management implementation plan. The plan may include training as mandated by law or through new employee orientation or as new substances are introduced. The implementation process is best monitored with involvement from employees; such involvement might be mandated. Once established, the plan must be reviewed and monitored regularly by leadership. It might also be subject to monitoring or investigation by local authorities. Enforcement mechanisms must be in place and part of personnel handbooks. What are the consequences for an employee or division that does not live up to the requirements? What are the rewards for those that exceed requirements? These types of policies should be clear not only to employees but to any stakeholder who asks. It is the authors' firm belief that in accordance with the fifth principle of chemical management discussed at the start of this chapter—"The system must promote quality and transparency"—all hazard, exposure, and risk characterization and risk management information should be made publicly available.

## What If There Is an Accident?

Despite all the best analysis, training, and controls, accidents will happen and they will come as a surprise. How to react to accidents should not be a surprise: Plan and rehearse what to do when accidents occur, and coordinate with local officials if the potential for a major accident is a possibility. For certain businesses and sectors, this type of collaboration is compulsory. The chemical management organization must establish a way to capture lessons learned and continuously learn from them. Based on its chemical management risk analysis, the organization must plan to limit damage to health and environment when accidents occur for the hazardous situations that might arise. Such plans should comprise evacuation plans that include responses to accidents or incidents, internal and external communication plans, and incident recovery plans to clean the environment or rebuild lost assets. These plans do no good sitting in a file; they must be used for training, practiced, rehearsed, and updated appropriately.

Many of these organizational mechanisms are mandated by law. An accident or near-accident reporting system should always be followed up at safety board meetings. The goal of the organization is to continuously improve, so that the risks for incidents or accidents that negatively impact health or the environment are always minimized. It is beyond the scope of this chapter to give examples of good crisis or evacuation plans as these are necessarily dependent on the local circumstances. The main point to remember is that the plans should be easy to remember and execute; it is too late to try to remember what to do or how to react as an accident or incident develops. The International Organization for Standardization (www.iso.org) and others publish international guidelines and standards for expert use.

As a manager or leader of this process for your organization, the best you can do is to ensure that experts are utilizing accepted standards with respect to both the local authorities and the international community. Your organization should always strive to set the local example via internationally accepted standards, regardless of the actual local conditions.

## Limiting and Controlling Chemical Hazards

Effective limitation and control of chemical hazards on a broad scale can be made by applying the fourth principle of the ACC: "The system should recognize the responsibilities of each party throughout the chain of commerce." Users and manufacturers should communicate with each other to ensure that they provide feedback to improve chemical products with respect to health and the environment. Local distributors should be used where feasible and in cooperation with the organization helping to ensure that they live up to the expectations of the nonprofit organization's chemical management system. Incentives should be developed to encourage voluntary compliance, as this compliance will lead to lasting change. If a practice involving a chemical product is identified as presenting an unreasonable risk to human health or the environment, collaborative efforts should be made to reduce the risk. The independent actions of the organization should be to minimize or eliminate the risk as quickly as possible, and buyers should be afforded the opportunity to stop purchasing from firms that do not take all reasonable measures to mitigate risk once discovered. Such risks might be found in all areas of the supply chain, from receipt of active ingredients, to production, to shipping.

On the local scale or organizational level, the aim of limiting and controlling hazards is to ensure effective chemical management: acquisition, identification, inventory, storage, distribution, and disposal. The University of Arizona's standards are a good guide for any organization, as they reflect good chemical management practice.

### Chemical Acquisition

When ordering chemicals, order the smallest practical quantity for the application and within safe storage limitations. Order from local vendors when possible. This helps limit the effects of transport on the environment, and improves your relationship with the society within which your organization is operating. Collaborate with the local vendors to ensure that they live up to your organization's values.

Use recyclable packaging when possible. Ensure that distributors properly dispose of any nonrecyclable elements and properly recycle elements that can be.

Centralize purchase and delivery of chemicals, in an area of your firm away from the general public. Chemicals should be delivered to a knowledgeable person and immediately stocked and entered into the chemical register. If for some reason a knowledgeable person cannot take the delivery, then the order delivery should be delayed.

Properly and legally label the substances and products at all times, from receipt to disposal. Do not accept any chemical without a proper, complete label and guidance as to how to use the product and MSDS if applicable. As a rule, store products in their original containers in approved chemical storage areas following guidelines noted on the package. Remember to date and check chemicals once they are opened. Abide by any considerations as to "use before" dates or "use within so many days after opening."

Specialists employing hazardous chemicals should use good laboratory practice, the principles of which are beyond the scope of this chapter. Take steps to segregate and easily identify nonhazardous substances, such as water, from substances that can be mistaken for chemicals.

Ensure that damaged labels are replaced at the time of damage. If need be, create a supplemental label with information in the language the employee is proficient in, but do not cover or replace the original label.

## Your Organization's Chemical Inventory and Stock

At all times, all work and stock areas that utilize chemicals must maintain an easily accessible inventory of the hazardous chemicals in an area. Physically examine the inventory periodically to ensure that the registers and inventory match. Properly dispose of any chemicals that have any type of problem. For most firms, the chemical stocks will be so small that if the principle of stocking only the minimum possible amount is used, relatively fresh stocks will always be on hand. Still, a physical inventory, even if not mandated by law, is a must for effective chemical management.

Use a standardized chemical registry form for the organization. Many examples can be found online, or contact one of this chapter's authors for the register used in their laboratories. Some inspecting organizations may have their own compulsory form or format for a chemical registry; if so, it must be used. Ensure that the document is kept up to date and with the other documents, especially the MSDSs. Many chemical purchasing systems also offer inventory management.

## Storing Your Organization's Chemicals

Hazardous chemicals must be stored in a manner that is in full compliance with all local laws and ordinances and otherwise reasonable measures. The method of storage should minimize safety and health hazards to personnel, equipment, buildings, and the environment. To minimize the need for an appropriate storage facility, as well as to minimize the risk associated with chemical storage, always purchase the smallest amount necessary for your work and dispense the correct amount needed at the time it is needed for the job. Proper storage therefore generally requires advice from an expert.

Develop special rules and procedures for ordering hazardous substances. Abide by local rules when storing fuels and gasoline. Keep these and other volatile chemicals at a bare minimum for your needs. Do not tap multiple containers prior to emptying the first.

Ensure that chemicals that can react with each other with hazardous consequences do not come into contact with each other during storage. Design work areas so that employees do not bring chemicals out of the assigned work areas or work unnecessarily near them. If need be, ensure that employees change shoes and clothing when working with chemicals. These work clothes should not be brought outside of the working areas and should never be near food or drinking water stocks.

Have spill kits ready, and ensure that secondary containment systems are utilized in your storage areas. Ensure that disposal procedures are followed.

## Transporting or Distributing Your Chemicals

In general, chemicals should be transported via the shortest and safest possible route from their storage facility to where they are to be used. Then they should be transported directly back to the storage facility following legal guidelines for transport internal to the work area and outside of it. Many agencies regulate storage and transport. It is compulsory to find, follow, and enforce local regulations, at a minimum.

## Disposing of Your Chemicals

The cost of disposing of chemical waste may exceed the actual cost of the chemicals. Therefore, use is always preferred to disposal. This use may be optimized through methodology such as LEAN.[8] For most common products, disposal information is included in the user's instructions. For more hazardous products, special methods of disposal are likely required, and a disposal routine must be formalized. A special consideration, even for chemicals that otherwise seem nonhazardous, is not to mix chemicals with others that then create a hazardous mixture or toxic emission. Special disposal regulations exist for biological materials, sharp instruments, broken glass, and even something as mundane as batteries. It is important to appropriately segregate waste. Use color coding in the disposal area, and ensure that only a few trained personnel are in charge of disposal.

## Applying LEAN Principles: Moving Toward a Culture of Continuous Improvement in Your Chemical Management

James P. Womack and Daniel T. Jones in their 1996 book *Lean Thinking*[9] defined a set of five basic principles that characterize a lean enterprise. Within these principles are found not only keys to improving production but also how to eliminate waste, or *muda*.[10] LEAN emphasizes that waste should be eliminated. We extend these thoughts to a chemical management system, with the intended result that an organization that considers elimination of *muda* and focuses on its chemical management system will also have a system that has the basis for efficient operation. We illustrate our example with seven forms of waste, noted below:

1. **Overproduction.** Do not produce more than you need. Production requires chemicals. Minimize risk by minimizing the chemicals your firm uses in whatever production or service segment it serves.
2. **Waiting.** The more you are around chemicals, the more time there is for something to go wrong.
3. **Conveyance.** All of the parts of your chemical management system should work when they are designed to work, for the purpose that they are designed to work, and in concert with the rest of your safety management system.
4. **Processing.** All of your chemicals processed should be managed at the highest possible level of the control hierarchy, as previously discussed.

5. **Inventory.** Unless your organization deals with chemical storage, keeping chemicals in storage is costly and wasteful to your operations. It also increases the potential for an incident.
6. **Motion.** Chemicals should be moved physically or between processes as infrequently as possible. Storage and work areas need to be designed carefully to meet the appropriate safety ordinances but also to minimize movement of chemicals used by the organization. When movement is necessary, it must be safe and efficient as well as in accordance with the law.
7. **Correction.** Work for continuous improvement. Ensure that suggestions can be received, reviewed, and implemented on a regular basis, if they show potential. Ensure that incidents or accidents are learned from and improvements made so that similar incidents never will occur again. Never accept "It was a freak accident" as an explanation that nothing should be changed. Something can always be improved. Find out what it is and improve it.

It may prove useful to pay proper attention to the adage "One person's waste can be another person's valued resource." In its purest and most evident form, items such as solvents, concentrated acids, oils, and wastes having high concentrations of metals (e.g., batteries) may be a goldmine to others. The transferring of waste to a location where it is viewed as a resource may go through a so-called waste information clearinghouse. Look for such houses or institutions and ask for advice. One major focus is to keep data and transactions confidential so that trade secrets are not compromised. More waste may be recovered economically than previously perceived. Disposal practices may continue to change according to the technological and economic development toward an overall greener economy. In general, society's interest in reuse, recycling, and recovery of materials (paper, glass, used electronics, etc.) has grown significantly. Any green management should develop a clear strategy with actions implemented in this area.

# Conclusion

## Nonprofit Organizations Setting the Example for Good and "Green" Chemical Management

This chapter presented basic tenets and principles of chemical management and how to employ them from a strategic perspective to an operational perspective. Numerous nonprofit organizations and funds practice excellent "green" chemical management; a review of cases of green chemical management in nonprofits is beyond the scope of this chapter.

In all cases, the material in this chapter is meant as a guide and foundation for further discussion with appropriate experts. Organizations should contact local experts or the authors for further specific guidance or strategic considerations. The term "green chemistry" normally is mentioned in connection with the substitution of chemicals that have lesser effects on the environment. This is important; substitution is the second priority in our control hierarchy. It is not within the scope of this chapter to recommend "green" substitutes for your organization; new innovations are being recommended for different chemical substances almost on a daily basis.

It is our contention that a reasonably planned and analyzed chemical management system, with focus and oversight from leadership on achieving the highest possible levels of control, will result in the most green and efficient structure for the organization. In any case, at the time of this writing, certain international agreements are being enacted of which those in charge of chemical management at a green nonprofit organization should be aware.

## Resources Especially for Chemical Management and Important Agreements, Classifications, and Guidelines

Universities are often excellent resources for information and expertise relating to chemical management. One of the authors attended the University of Arizona, which, like many organizations practicing chemical management on a routine basis, has excellent online resources with respect to chemical management best practices (http://risk.arizona.edu/healthandsafety/chemicalmgmtbestpractices/index .shtml). Organizations may be well served by asking their local university for advice or support, as they should be experts in application of the local rules and regulations. However, rules and regulations as applied to research, development, and education might be different from industrial rules and regulations, so the reader is cautioned not to just "cut and paste." The starting step should be the regulatory agency.

Many excellent industrial handbooks for chemical management are available online.[11] Most focus on intentional uses of chemicals in production; however, some of the basic tenets apply to accidental managers of chemicals. The online resources nearly always need to be adapted to the on-site situation and modified to meet local requirements. Therefore, it is not normally adequate or recommended to cut and paste from online handbooks.

There are certain contemporary reference documents that chemical management system managers should be familiar with.

### UNEP SAICM (Strategic Approach to International Chemical Management)

The SAICM is a policy framework adopted in 2002 to promote chemical safety worldwide.[12] Its overall objective is the sound management of chemicals throughout their life cycle so that by 2020, chemicals are produced and used in ways that "minimize significant adverse impacts on human health and the environment." For most organizations, the strategies and goals are much higher than where they currently operate. For the chemical manager in organizations working with developing nations or internationally, the SAICM is a policy document warranting general familiarity.

### Chemical (Hazard Information and Packaging) Regulations (CHIP)

CHIP is a U.K. law, mandated in 2002 and last updated in 2004, that applies to suppliers of most dangerous chemicals.[13] Its purpose is to protect people and the environment from the effects of the chemicals supplied by requiring suppliers to package the chemical safely and provide information about the dangers.

Chemical managers of organizations dealing with U.K. suppliers or organizations operating in the United Kingdom should be familiar with CHIP.

### Registration Evaluation Authorization and Restriction of Chemicals (REACH)

REACH is the European Community Regulation from June 1, 2007, on chemicals and their safe use (EC 1907/2006).[14] It deals with the *r*egistration, *e*valuation, *a*uthorization, and restriction of *ch*emical substances. REACH aims to improve the protection of human health and the environment through "the better and earlier identification of the intrinsic properties of chemical substances." It also aims to enhance the innovative capability and competitiveness of the EU chemicals industry. The REACH provisions will be phased in over 11 years, and benefits are expected to increase as more phases in the REACH program are reached.

In contrast to the U.K. CHIP requirements, greater responsibility is given to industry by REACH to manage the risks from chemicals and to provide safety information on the substances. A compulsory database will be established and maintained. REACH calls for the substitution of the most dangerous chemicals.

REACH is important for managers operating within the European Union or dealing with producers, suppliers and manufacturers within the EU and should be harmonized with CHIPS.

### Globally Harmonized System of Classification and Labeling of Chemicals (GHS)

This system addresses classification of chemicals by types of hazard and harmonized hazard communication elements, including labels and safety data sheets. The GHS provides a basis for harmonization of rules and regulations on chemicals at the national, regional, and worldwide level. The current edition of the GHS is the second revised edition of the GHS (published in July 2007) and countries are encouraged to have a fully operational system by 2008, but many countries are yet to be fully operational. The GHS Web site (www.unece.org/trans/danger/publi/ghs/ghs_welcome_e.html) may be visited to see status reports for each reporting country. GHS familiarization is recommended for chemical managers in any sector.

### Prior Informed Consent (PIC) for the Export and Import of Dangerous Chemicals

PIC is a provision from the Rotterdam Convention[15] and applies to the export of some of the most hazardous substances known. Therefore, it is only of interest to managers dealing with very hazardous substances such as pesticides. A list of these substances and other useful background information are found at the homepage as well as the status of countries with respect to adopting the provisions.

## About the Authors

**Michael Goodsite,** MBA, PhD, is the National Environmental Research Institute Professor of Atmospheric Chemistry, Climate, and Global Processes at Aarhus University. He has served as chairman of the University of Southern Denmark's chemical registration and inventory system and for its Department of Physics and

Chemistry, where its chemical management systems were positively noted in an international evaluation of laboratories. He advises the University of Delhi on rebuilding and renovation of its labs. His scientific background is supplemented with an MBA in global management, and he serves on the board of directors and board of advisors of for-profit and nonprofit organizations in the United States, Denmark, Iceland, and Canada. His research focus is climate mitigation and strategy, coupling local and corporate-level climate mitigation and strategy with national and global processes.

**Esbern Warncke,** M.Sc., D.Sc., is associate professor of Botany at the Department of Biology, Aarhus University. Esbern has extensive field experience in European as well as remote locations and has written the practical and extensive handbook for field biologists, a resource for organizations that might be conducting basic scientific studies. His research interests are the reproductive ecology of flowering plants emphasizing pollination, dispersal, and establishment, as well as cytology, determination of plants, in bryology and in plant reproductive ecology.

**Lars Moseholm,** PhD, is director of the Research Department, National Environmental Research Institute, Aarhus University, and head of 75 researchers and support staff and head Koordineringsenhed for Forskning i klimaTilpasning (*KFT*), the National Coordination Unit for Research in Climate Change Adaptation in Denmark. His research and professional environmental engineering, planning, and public administration experience spans more than 30 years of work on environmental problems, in particular in air pollution monitoring, management, and modeling.

**Christian Monies,** M.Sc., is a chemist at the Department of Atmospheric Environment, National Environmental Research Institute, Aarhus University, and manages the department's chemical management system. The department routinely operates at locations all over the world and has certified environmental monitoring and analysis of many contaminants. The system has proven to be safely employed throughout the scientific range of fieldwork where it has been implemented. Christian has practical experience with as well as expert knowledge of certified environmental monitoring.

## CHAPTER 13

# Closing the Loop

## *Reducing, Reusing, and Recycling*

### Kelley Dean-Crowley

## Introduction

> Anyone who believes exponential growth can go on forever in a finite world
> is either a madman or an economist.
>
> —Kenneth Boulding

We hurtle through space using every resource as if there is an endless supply to draw on as time stretches infinitely before us. Until suddenly, from the darkness, we emerge to see not a lovely blue marble but a ball covered with trash. Those key resources are becoming more expensive, scarcer, or polluted by any number of toxins that are incompatible with life. As a result, we find ourselves searching for ways to preserve those resources and reduce our resource consumption to stretch them a bit further for a bit longer before it is too late. Reduction, reuse, and recycling of waste or products are simple methods to maximize our finite resources in an environment that has many people to support, but where resources are distributed in an inequitable fashion. Within the simplicity of these methods lies their strength and the power to change limited resources into limitless resources through a paradigm shift from disposal of used materials to extending the usable life of our limited resources. You will learn about these methods, including an introduction to the life cycle of waste, how you can use the methods in your agency to identify opportunities for changes, as well as some real examples and checklists that you can use in the field to drive real social and environmental change.

## Dealing with Waste

There are many resources used in modern and even in not-so-modern life. These resources include:

- Raw materials such as wood to make lumber, paper, or even textiles and to build houses and other structures that are desired for civilized life

- Metal to produce tools, containers, or any number of vessels to transport people across land, or water, or into space
- Energy produced from coal, solar, wood, hydroelectric, animal power, or any number of other methods to process raw materials, provide heat and light, or move people, materials, or manufactured goods from one place to another
- Water, which all life on Earth needs to survive and is easily contaminated, used, and wasted

As a nonprofit agency, you may already use your resources conservatively as the result of an environment where every dollar is hard won from grants, fundraising activities, and donations. You may have thought about reducing waste or had staff or volunteers make suggestions for changes but feel overwhelmed by the depth and breadth of the problem. You may have already started to make changes but know that there is even more to be done to minimize waste within your agency, which will extend what resources you already have as well as extend those hard-won dollars for other purposes. You might be thinking that your agency does not have time to do more with its waste. Recycling, reusing, and reducing does not have to take a lot of time. One change can have a huge impact when others make the same change. One change also leads to another, and another, leading to big impacts from small changes and small decisions made on a daily basis.

## Waste Life Cycles

The minimization of waste through careful use, reuse, and return to the raw material state does not have to be overwhelming, time consuming, or difficult. Let us start with what the waste life cycle looks like without efforts to minimize waste, then with some efforts to minimize waste, and finally a waste life cycle that uses all the techniques heavily.

The typical waste cycle for the developed world, where recycling and the other methods are not considered, would look like Figure 13.1. In this particular example, the materials that enter the system invariably exit the system into a disposal method, requiring a constant supply of new materials, energy, and other resources in order to make and distribute new products for use. This is probably the most wasteful way to consume resources. You may be pleased to know that this dynamic rarely occurs in the developed and much of the underdeveloped world today. Fortunately, the economic systems of the world produce intense pressure to reuse materials and products repeatedly. You can see this pressure in action on farms, ranches, and small homesteads all over the world where the farmers and ranchers use materials repeatedly. You also see this in the landfills of the developing world, such as the Philippines or Honduras where large communities of people

FIGURE 13.1   Waste cycle for the developed world without waste reduction.

FIGURE 13.2   Waste life cycle for the developed world with some waste reduction.

subsist entirely on their ability to comb the dumps for food, clothing, and objects to sell.[1]

Once attention to the rates of consumption and disposal increases, the waste life cycle changes as well, and could look more like Figure 13.2. Notice that the life cycle is now longer with more steps along the way, but it is still an open-loop process, with materials entering the system and then being disposed of at the end. This process has the effect of starting to reduce the sheer volume of materials needed to meet the needs of the people in the system through the reuse and repurposing of materials.

In this particular example, the waste cycle makes better use of the materials through the reuse and repurposing of materials and continues to eke additional life cycle out of an object, perhaps as lowly as a milk carton or aluminum soda can. The life cycle for any particular consumer item becomes much longer and more creative, where even something as small as the tab from a soda might see continued life as anything the human mind and hand can conceive.

By adding recycling to the system, the waste cycle changes again to be something like Figure 13.3. This cycle is the ultimate waste cycle, where very few new raw materials enter the system because all materials are reclaimed and recycled, and products are reused as long as possible and repurposed as much as possible. Why is recycling so important in this picture?

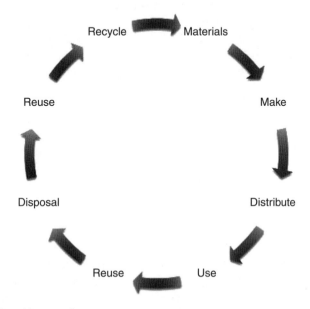

FIGURE 13.3   Closed-loop cycle.

Recycling is key to the process because recycling:

- Allows us to reclaim material in some cases infinitely, thereby reducing the raw materials needed to sustain us.
- Reduces the amount of energy required to manufacture new products. According to the National Recycling Coalition, recycling a single aluminum can saves enough energy to power a television for three hours.[2] By comparison, production of aluminum cans from recycled materials saves 95 percent of the energy required to manufacture from new materials.[3]
- Reduces the amount of water needed to manufacture products from new materials.

Closing the loop is the gold standard of waste reduction, but closing the loop is not always possible with all materials. Aluminum is one of the true success stories of recycling, but other materials have limitations that prevent them from being a closed-loop system, such as paper fiber, which weakens with each use and reuse. Therefore, you can strive to close the loop in only some instances. Nevertheless, in striving, your changes make great gains when combined with millions of other people.

The rest of the chapter focuses on providing both a method for looking at your agency and its operations to find opportunities to reduce waste and a checklist of the most common changes to make.

# Reduce

The most important of the methods you will use is the reduction of waste that reaches the landfills. If we can reduce the amount of waste that we produce, we can keep resources out of the waste cycle entirely. Reduction should always be your first goal, the foundation in your goal of eliminating waste, with reuse and recycling following reduction in priority in the waste cycle. Reuse and recycling address only the materials already in the system, as opposed to reduction, which addresses both materials and products already in the product and waste life cycle as well as preventing raw materials from entering the product and waste life cycle. After we reduce our use and consumption of a natural resource, we then look to reuse and recycling to extend the life cycle of the materials and products in the system. So then reducing our consumption becomes the foundation on which you will build your effort to green your agency, with reuse and recycling coming in thereafter. (See Figure 13.4.)

## Energy

Of course, your agency consumes energy for daily operations. The goal is to reduce the use of energy incrementally or to reduce the amount of energy used that comes from sources that produce energy in an unclean manner. The next questions will help you to identify opportunities to reduce waste in your unique environment.

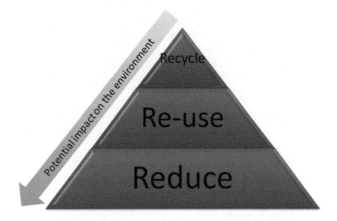

FIGURE 13.4   Impact of waste reduction.

**Do I really need to use this energy in this way?** An excellent example of this is in our heating and cooling methods for a building. Frequently and typically, buildings are kept at a temperature that is excessive. A good indication that the temperature is excessive is seeing women or men who keep sweaters at their desks in the summer to stay warm while inside or dress very lightly in the winter while indoors. Decreasing the climate control temperature just a few degrees will save a substantial amount of energy over time, which can translate into a financial savings over time. The best part is that people may actually be more comfortable as well.

**Can I do without this usage entirely?** There will be instances of obvious waste, such as having climate control on during the spring and fall when temperatures are milder and the climate control is not as necessary.

**Is there an obvious way to reduce the usage?** Sometimes there are instances where a total reduction is not possible, but there are other inexpensive ways to reduce usage or consumption. A perfect example would be the lights in bathrooms or storerooms, which in office buildings frequently are left in the on position. A simple and inexpensive solution is to install a light switch with a motion detector that will turn the lights on when someone enters the rooms and off when no motion is detected after a short time.

**Is there a less obvious way to reduce the usage?** At this point, you have decreased the obvious areas of energy waste, and now you will be looking at the less obvious ways to reduce energy consumption. One of the areas that can be looked at is the supply chain for materials or other products. As a customer, you have a choice with whom you do business, and you can assess their location and transportation and environmental impact through an environmental lens. This will have the immediate impact of reducing transportation overhead in the supply chain and will drive social change over time. Of course, there are instances where using a local supplier will not be possible or cost effective. In those instances, a vendor or supplier assessment can be made on the strength of the company's own environmental policies, starting with its recycling program, energy usage, purchase of carbon offsets, and so forth.

**Energy Checklists**

☐ Reduce climate control temperatures by heating to a lower temperature and cooling to a warmer temperature.

☐ Install electronic or "smart" thermostats for climate control systems and program them for optimum usage, including minimal temperatures during off hours. Turning a thermostat off entirely is not recommended, as the energy required to get to optimum temperature again is excessive. Minimal temperatures are more efficient.

☐ Use passive temperature control methods as much as possible to manage environmental temperatures, including keeping blinds closed in seasonally warm periods and opening blinds in winter and keeping doors and windows closed to keep temperatures steady.

☐ Use compact fluorescent or other low-energy lighting where possible or natural lighting rather than artificial light.

☐ Install motion detectors on light switches in areas that have little or no traffic.

☐ Get an energy audit to find other opportunities to save energy. Your local power company can make excellent recommendations specific to the region, transmission methods, and other factors and provide additional suggestions for conserving energy.

☐ Seek out green Web hosting options, including hosts that use only renewable energy or that offset energy consumption with carbon offsets.

☐ Identify and eliminate phantom loads related to equipment by installing surge protectors with on/off switches that prevent phantom loads.

☐ Reduce consumption of gasoline in the agency fleet by grouping destinations together by location wherever possible.

☐ Use local vendors and suppliers to reduce consumption of fuel in transportation costs.

☐ Create carpooling programs for agency staff or identify carpooling programs that staff can use in the area.

☐ Provide bike racks that are anchored securely to buildings, concrete, or other immovable objects.

☐ Allow alternative work arrangements for employees where possible to reduce transportation and climate control costs.

## Water

Water is one of the keys to all life on our planet. The Pacific Institute is working on the problem of water scarcity, which has the potential to be the source of conflict and violence in the world as it becomes more scarce.[4] Much can be done to conserve water with a bit of care and thereby to reduce our overall waste and consumption of this most valuable resource.

These questions may help identify opportunities to conserve water:

**Can I do this without water?** This particular scenario probably is unlikely in most instances, but it should be mentioned, regardless. One instance where this might be valid would be a situation where there is a choice between washing surfaces down with water as opposed to using a broom, brush, or soft cloth.

**Can I do this with less water?** Many tasks can be done with less water. A big one is landscaping, where the choice of plants can significantly reduce the water needed to maintain the landscaping.

**Can I do this in a different way to conserve water?** This is an excellent question, because frequently there is another way to do a task to conserve water or get more from the water. An excellent example of this is watering landscaping. Frequently, landscaping is watered in the morning or during the day. In areas with high evaporation, watering after sundown may be better, as it allows the water to soak into the ground well. Also longer, less frequent watering will encourage the roots of plants to grow deeper, making the plants less vulnerable to drought or excess heat.

**Can I do this in a way to avoid contaminating water or waterways?** What you put in water is at least as important as the use. To that end, your agency can make choices about chemical use in water.

**Water Checklist**

☐ Install low-flow toilets. Funding assistance may be available from the local water district, particularly in dry or drought conditions.

☐ Install motion detectors on faucets, soap dispensers, and toilets.

☐ Favor native, low-water-use or drought-resistant plants in the landscaping.

☐ Adjust watering of landscaping to minimize evaporation and lower water usage.

☐ Sweep landscaping and avoid using water to wash sidewalks.

☐ Use biodegradable soaps and cleaning products.

☐ Use excess water to irrigate landscaping instead of allowing it to go down storm drains or run off.

☐ Consult the local water district for additional measures that can be taken or are available in your area.

## Material Resources

Next are raw materials, which are where most agencies or people start when they are first considering going green, because these materials are quite simply some of the most obvious starting points. We will touch on a number of raw materials that are the most common. This list is not intended to be exhaustive but will provide some insight into approaching other areas that may be related to an agency's specialty. The materials we discuss specifically are: wood/paper, clothing/textiles, metals, glass, plastics, manufactured goods such as electronics and batteries, and finally food or biodegradable waste.

## Wood/Paper

Wood and paper is used for so many consumer products in the developed world, as well as some other purposes in the developing world, that we cannot ignore its usage. It is used to build houses, bridges, barns, and fences; to make paper, cardboard, insulation, boxes, furniture, transportation, and other products. In fact, it is difficult to think of a purpose that wood or paper is not used for, making this a wonderful opportunity to reduce waste. When looking at processes, products, and the way that your agency does its work, consider these questions:

**Can I reduce or eliminate the amount of wood, paper, or waste for this purpose?** The use of wood and paper products is so pervasive now that often the use is not even noticed or considered. Some of the obvious examples are packaging of products in many layers of paper and cardboard and excessive printing of documents in office spaces.

**Can I source the wood or paper from a more sustainable or conservative source?** We live in exciting times where a broad range of products are available to us, including products designed and manufactured with sustainability at the forefront. Therefore, it is becoming easy to find wood or paper products that are sourced from more sustainable crops, such as bamboo, hemp, rice, soy, and even corn. Wood can be sourced from plantation forests of fast-growing timber instead of wild old-growth forests where clear cutting has real environmental impacts, such as soil erosion, ecological disruption, and loss of wildlife habitat. By far, one of the most exciting sourcing opportunities is in products made with both postconsumer and manufacturing waste. This method allows agencies to source their paper and other supplies with materials that have already entered the product life cycle, thereby reducing the materials in the system. Later in this chapter we discuss how to assess vendors and suppliers.

**Is there a full alternative to using wood for this purpose?** In the developing world, wood still is burned for light, heat, and cooking. There are many drawbacks to this use, and it is such an easy thing to address with solar or wind energy or even just a solar oven easily constructed from materials readily available even in the developing world. Addressing this use also has additional benefits of reducing air pollution, reducing deforestation, and improving the health of the human beings who need the light, heat, and food to survive. Other opportunities to use a full alternative to wood or paper products include transitioning newsletters and other communications to donors, clients, and other agencies to be fully electronic, which will substantially reduce paper and printing costs. Of course, it is exceedingly difficult to eliminate paper and printing altogether, since there is a large segment of the global population that is not connected to the Internet. Still, paper and printing costs can be substantially reduced with a simple opt-in for nonpaper communications.

### Wood and Paper Checklist

☐ Reduce the use of paper products in the office by replacing disposable cups and plates with reusable supplies. An effective way to do this is to encourage everyone in the agency to bring their own containers with extras on hand for guests.

☐ Purchase products that have significant recycled paper content. In the United States, recycled paper costs about the same and can include up to 100 percent recycled paper fiber.

☐ Seek out wood products made from alternative fibers, such as bamboo and recycled wood chips.

- Review the suppliers and vendors for all wood and paper products for opportunities to use recycled or sustainable sources of the raw materials.
- Buy wood and paper products in bulk to reduce packaging waste if you have consistent usage or sufficient storage.
- Reduce the printing of documents and reports within the agency. Circulate documents and reports electronically via e-mail, shared network drives, or other methods. This has the added advantage of allowing for easy and fast collaboration on materials as well as easy circulation.
- Consider alternatives to print reports and documents outside the agency. Many new methods to circulate information may also increase donors' donation opportunities while reducing expense, including electronic newsletters, Web publishing, and social networking. These methods can be quite effective in increasing contact with donors, clients, and other agencies using readily available and inexpensive tools. Not only can this decrease paper and printing costs, it can increase contacts and donation opportunities in areas where there are large populations of people who are connected through these channels. The power of an electronic network was demonstrated most recently in the U.S. presidential election cycle, where texting, e-mail, and electronic newsletters drove election results in an unprecedented manner.
- Purchase printers that have duplexing capability to reduce paper. The additional cost for the duplexing will be easily justified by the savings on paper.
- Print documents double sided on a duplexing printer. Most printers with this capability can be set to duplex as a default.
- When building or doing building repairs, use materials from sustainable or recycled sources.

## Metals

Reducing the amount of metal that we use is fairly easy in common applications, as metal is much more durable in products or as a material than wood or paper. The best ways to reduce metal are through recycling and reuse, which will extend the useful life cycle of the metal and also reduce the need to mine and smelt metals from ores. Mining and smelting are much more expensive in terms of energy and water usage than using metals from recycled sources. Refer to the recycling and reuse sections for more information.

## Glass and Plastics

Any number of plastics can be used to manufacture products for the consumer markets. Most plastic items are labeled with numbers. Plastic types 1, 2, and 3 are easily recycled and accepted by most recycling centers. Plastic types 4 to 7 are not generally accepted by recycling centers and should be avoided in purchasing wherever possible. This does not mean that we should not use plastics, but we should ask ourselves these questions as part of our decisions to do so.

**Does the glass or plastic produce contaminants in the course of usage or disposal?** Our knowledge of plastics—in particular, their components and their impact on the ecosystem—is constantly evolving and growing. Recent developments have highlighted an issue with plastic compounds in baby bottles that are now being phased out of production.

**Can the glass or plastic be recycled using existing local recycling programs?** This question is phrased this way because the extent and effectiveness of local and municipal recycling programs and facilities vary considerably. The local recycling facility should have published the types of plastics that it can accept, using established plastic symbols that should correspond to the symbol on the plastic to be recycled. There are generally not the same recycling restrictions on the material components in glass.

**Are there alternatives to plastic products that are either more reusable or recyclable?** By making choices that are more reusable or recyclable, you can remove or substantially reduce the amount of plastics in the system. These alternatives may be metal or glass but will have a much longer usable lifetime.

**Are the plastics single use or reusable?** So much of our plastics use is oriented to packaging, such as bubble packages, single-use bottles for beverages, and containers for food. A good waste reduction program will discourage single-use or convenience packaging while encouraging use of reusable products. All of these actions will reduce the amount of plastic in the system.

### Plastic Checklist

- ☐ Choose refillable containers over single-use or convenience packs that are made from plastic.
- ☐ Choose kitchenware that is reusable or made from other recyclable materials. There is excellent work being done to produce kitchenware from various starches, including potatoes and corn, which can then be composted.
- ☐ Choose products made from materials other than plastic, such as glass, wherever possible.
- ☐ Reuse glass until it breaks and no longer can be used for the purpose.

## Manufactured Goods Such as Electronics, Batteries

Manufactured goods are the key to reducing waste in landfills, which are full of appliances, electronics, and other equipment or products that may be beyond their usable life span. It is essential to keep electronic waste, in particular, out of landfills, as circuit boards contain a heavy metal cocktail that can leach into groundwater or contaminate people directly. There is also a large upside in reducing the amount of manufactured goods that we use on an ongoing basis with reduced costs and energy consumption.

When considering our use of manufactured goods, the next questions will guide the process.

**How critical is it to replace/own/upgrade this piece of equipment?** This is probably the most critical part of the process, since a piece of equipment can make processes and procedures much faster, easier, and more efficient. The most important consideration is need relative to product life span. It is nice to replace a computer every 18 months, but over 10 years, that means that 5.5 computers will be built and purchased to meet computing needs. Replacing computers every 2 years reduces the number to 5. If you replace every 3 years, that number drops to 3.3 computers over 10 years, for a net reduction of 2 computers to be disposed of, not to mention the associated cost savings.

**How often would I use this piece of equipment?** The amount of usage a particular piece of equipment sees can be critical, since some equipment has a usable life span related not to time but to mileage, pages, use-hours, or other measures. Usage should be tailored to the equipment as this can change the equipment choices as well. Occasionally the answer to this question will negate the need for the equipment. For instance, electric staplers that can staple 100 pages easily are not really needed if you only ever staple 12 sheets together, unless you staple 12 sheets together all day long; then you want to reduce the wear and tear on the human who does this work. Purchasing an electric stapler that staples only 20 sheets at a time might be a better solution.

**Do I have other equipment or options that will suit the purpose?** Going back to our stapler example, it might be better to have a local copy shop do the stapling for you, both in terms of equipment cost and people costs.

**How often will this equipment have to be serviced and/or replaced?** Servicing needs may affect your equipment choices, since servicing equipment can have real environmental impact.

**Does this equipment have specific disposal needs?** This has a direct tie-in to the environmental goals that you are trying to meet. Disposal needs that emphasize correct disposal of hazardous materials should be considered more carefully, as the environmental costs and impact will be higher.

## Manufactured Goods Checklist

☐ Extend the amount of time between replacing manufactured goods such as phones, computers, appliances, and others.

☐ Lease or rent equipment for use in the agency, wherever possible. Leases typically come with maintenance and replacement provisions to keep equipment up and running optimally.

☐ Purchase manufactured goods only when the existing piece is broken or has severe limitations on its use.

☐ Replace components of equipment instead of the entire piece of equipment.

☐ Purchase equipment that is certified to consume less energy and has the relevant local certifications, such as ENERGY STAR in the United States. In some instances, some types of equipment are overall better environmentally than others; for example, laptops are now believed to be a better environmental choice for computers as they are compact and have sophisticated power management routines.

☐ Use rechargeable batteries in equipment as much as possible.

☐ Dispose of all manufactured goods appropriately and according to relevant hazardous materials guidelines.

☐ Contact other nonprofit agencies through www.recycles.org to find ones that can reuse electronic equipment that you have replaced.

## Biodegradable Waste

Why does it matter what we do with food and other biodegradable waste? It matters because if we can reduce this kind of waste, we also reduce the amount of energy and water that gets wasted and reduce the material that ends up in landfills.

### Biodegradable Waste Checklist
☐ Use low-maintenance plants in landscaping.
☐ Use appropriate storage methods for all foods and other biodegradable products to avoid waste due to spoilage.
☐ Compost all food or biodegradable waste in a compost heap for the agency. Many options for composting can be used, even in an office setting.
☐ Use green waste disposal programs for landscaping waste as provided by local or municipal waste programs.
☐ In the field or in landscaping, use keyhole gardens to complete the cycle. A keyhole garden uses green waste to grow vegetables in a very small space, although they can be used to grow anything that is of use, including demonstration gardens of low-maintenance plants and drought-resistant plants.

# Reuse

Now that we have reduced our use of energy, water, wood and paper, and other raw materials, we can consider reuse of those same resources. Reuse comes in a couple of different flavors, including:

- Reuse a product or materials for what it was intended, as in energy or water.
- Refit it for a similar use, such as one might do with wood building materials, which may have been damaged somewhat during the reclamation process.
- Repurpose materials for a new use.
- Remanufacture or refurbish the materials or products, such as car parts that are remanufactured with new gaskets to be reused, or refurbishing furniture for reuse.
- Reuse scrap or identify users of scrap materials.
- Refills are also another type of reuse.

All of these methods are part of reuse, which allows us to take something that is already in the use life cycle and keep it in the use life cycle.

## The Case for Reuse

The cost benefits of reuse are staggering. Let us take a humble glass juice bottle as an example. This bottle for our example is 1 quart with a resealable lid and was chosen over a plastic bottle. Once the juice has been consumed, the bottle can be disposed of in a landfill, but you decide to reuse it to store water, which you drink throughout the day. The bottle lasts over a year being refilled at least once a day before breaking in an accident. At the end of its useful life cycle as a bottle, the bottle has been refilled conservatively 365 times, meaning that it may have eliminated 365 plastic water bottles over the course of its life as a bottle.

## Water

These questions may help identify opportunities to further conserve water by reusing it wherever possible:

**Is this water clean enough to be reused in some way?** It is possible to reuse water in some instances, either by reserving the water from one purpose, or through the use of a gray water system according to local regulations. We are all familiar with watering plants with water left over from other uses. There are more options for reusing water if chemical use is also being reduced and managed effectively.

**Can I do this in a different way to reuse the water?** Doing something differently allows us the opportunity to reuse water. This can be as simple as capturing wash water to water plants, where soaps and chemicals are either biodegradable or used very sparingly. In fact, soapy water can also be an effective pest-control technique for certain types of pests. It can also be reused for cleaning other surfaces.

### Water Checklist

☐ Use relatively clean water for watering landscaping or office plants as opposed to putting it down a drain.

☐ Use wash water for pest control or for dirtier cleaning jobs.

## Reuse of Materials and Consumer Products

Wood and paper present some opportunity for reuse, but that opportunity will diminish over time, as wood is cut and processed, and paper fibers will weaken over time. So when looking at processes, products, and the way that your agency does its work, consider this question:

**Can I or someone else reuse this for something?** It is quite common to have materials or products that no longer suit for whatever reason. That does not mean that the item no longer has value, because there may be someone in the community who would be able to find use.

### Reuse Checklist

☐ Reuse paper for scrap paper or pass the paper on to other agencies that may be able to reuse it, such as schools, preschools, day care centers, art schools, and others, depending on the nature of the materials.

☐ Wood and metal products and materials can be salvaged out to the community easily. If someone is not immediately identified to salvage the material, the material can be listed on sites such as Craigslist, FreeCycle, and others.

☐ Reuse furniture by both purchasing and selling used furniture. Even after furniture is beyond the useful life of its intended purpose, it may have life repurposed for something else. Furniture may also be listed on the Internet if it is not in sufficient condition for resale.

☐ Office supplies that are no longer appropriate for use in your agency may be passed on to other agencies, schools, and educational and craft centers. These organizations will be happy to take supplies as it reduces their costs for the same materials.

☐ Check with equipment manufacturers to determine if they have programs to recycle or remanufacture their old equipment to conserve the materials.

☐ Send materials no longer appropriate for use in your agency to a local creative reuse center or similar.

☐ Local waste disposal facilities may have reuse centers for paint and other products; dispose of paint there or find some to use to paint your own agency.

# Recycle

Your agency has reduced the overall use of the raw materials and consumer products at your agency and identified opportunities for reuse. However, your agency still has a pile of products and materials that are beyond their useful life. This is where recycling becomes useful. Recycling is really the reclamation of raw materials to be used in the manufacturing process again. In the developed world, this is not always clear, because municipal recycling programs often pick up recyclables and whisk them away to large recycling centers that then process the recyclables into raw materials out of sight of the consumer. This reclamation of materials can involve melting of aluminum and other metals down to create new aluminum products, such as cans or building materials. Aluminum is an amazing success story, and comes the closest to being a closed-loop cycle than any other material.

Recycling also can occur as part of the manufacturing process, where manufacturing waste is returned to the beginning of the process. Finally, recycling raw materials, such as aluminum, glass, wood, and paper, saves energy and water that would be used in manufacturing. In the case of aluminum, the energy savings are substantial.

As easy and efficient as recycling is, there are limitations to recycling. Not everything actually can be recycled due to technical and material limitations, or even due to the hazards of the materials themselves. Paper fiber, for example, weakens over time and use and eventually can no longer be recycled.

## Cost Benefit Analysis for Recycling

Generally, the cost benefit analysis for recycling can be tricky. The cost of recycling in your agency will mostly be minimal after people become accustomed to the new process. The agency will incur a cost associated with adding recycle bins, unless the local sanitation department supplies these. But realistically, any container can be used for recycling, including the box the printer paper comes in. The good news is that with the sea change that is happening around climate change (as a political issue), few employees complain about recycling. More frequently, employees are asking when the recycling program will begin and suggesting other ways to recycle. A paper recycling program can make a huge difference. For instance, according to the National Recycling Coalition: "Americans throw away enough office paper each year to build a 12 foot high (~4 m) wall of paper from New York to Seattle" and a "stack of newspapers just 3 ft (1 m) high saves one tree."[5] Every foot of that wall recycled will save four trees, and the entire wall will spare over 50 million trees from being harvested for paper. In addition to the trees not being cut down, there are substantial water and energy savings associated with recycling paper, plastic, glass, and metals.

## Establish a Recycling Program in Your Agency

The benefits of recycling are clear, but the next question is how to start a recycling program in your agency. The key is to start a chain of small changes in your agency. Here are some ideas:

- Start with recycling just one material and add more as time goes on.
- Provide recycling bins for paper, cans, bottles, and other items anywhere there is a trash bin, but especially in conference rooms, by desks, and in kitchens.
- Place a paper-recycling bin next to the printers and faxes.
- Labeling trash bins as going to the landfill will drive home the impact of putting something into it.
- Establish a large recycling bin near the main Dumpster for the recycling to be put into.
- Establish a container for disposable batteries to ensure that they are disposed off in a manner consistent with the local hazardous materials guidelines.
- Communicate the program to everyone in the agency.
- Solicit suggestions for inclusion to the program from everyone in the agency, as some individuals may have ideas and actions unique to your agency.
- Recycle all e-waste appropriately and according to hazardous material disposal regulations for your area.
- Use a shredder or engage secure recycling services for confidential or sensitive materials.

# Vendor and Source Assessment

Part of increasing your environmental position is reviewing your sources for materials and products that are used for any purpose. This may sound ominous and time consuming, but there is no need for that to be the case. This section assists with terms that are used in the mainstream to convey the environmental value that a particular product has.

## Use of Terms

**Local.** Refers to materials and products that are sourced, manufactured, or otherwise produced locally. The goal of local sources is to reduce hidden transportation costs associated with manufacturing, packaging, and distribution as well as contribute to the local economy. It is an excellent green approach but can have limitations, particularly where the source is not otherwise working to reduce waste through the methods we mentioned. A local source of coal is still an unsustainable fuel source, regardless of being local. A local source of organic food is an excellent choice.

**Fair trade.** Refers to products that are produced frequently as a result of economic development projects around local arts and crafts, agriculture, or other vocations in developing countries or regions. Fair trade practice can require fair labor practices, including a shorter workweek, not using child labor, adequate pay, and so on. The artisans gain employment opportunity that is local, usually centered around using local materials to create products that are then distributed either to local sales centers with high tourism rates or around the developed world. The focus on fair trade tends to be centered around social problems but is perfectly valid as an environmental approach. Healthy economies produce healthier communities that may focus more on educating women, which has been proven to result in smaller families—families that ultimately will be easier to support on available resources.

**Sustainable.** Refers to materials that are coming from sources selected for their ability to renew themselves. Examples of sustainable materials would be wood coming from a plantation of fast-growing trees planted only for harvest as timber for building; textiles made from easily grown plants, such as hemp or bamboo, which grow quickly and easily in most climate zones and allow for a continuing harvest that uses fewer resources. The term "renewable" may be used in the same way. In the United States and Europe, there are emerging standards of certification and labeling for sustainably sourced materials.

**Organic.** Refers specifically to processes, crops, and other resources that come from pesticide- and fertilizer-free sources. Organic certification can be quite involved and covers only certain circumstances. Because the certification is so involved, in some instances organic practice is in use but certification has not been completed. The U.S. Department of Agriculture sets organic standards for certification in the United States.

**Carbon offsets.** Financial commitments by an agency or supplier to contribute financially to causes that work to reduce negative environmental impact. Carbon offsets are calculated based on estimates of the carbon dioxide ($CO_2$) that human activities are contributing to the atmosphere. This $CO_2$ will be offset by charitable contributions to environmental agencies that are actively working to mitigate $CO_2$ through a number of methods. Some carbon offsets are focused on planting trees to absorb $CO_2$; others are focused on renewable energy projects, such as solar or wind installations. Carbon offsets can be another opportunity to support social change aligned with your agency's service goals.

**(Post-Consumer) Recycled content.** The amount of material that comes from consumer waste or other recycled content; the higher the number, the more material that comes from recycled sources.

## Avoid Greenwashing

Your agency will want to use caution and skepticism for organizations that use the term "green" in certain ways because of "greenwashing." which is the increasing practice of making unsubstantiated claims of a product or service's environmentalism to capture market share. The basic assumption underlying greenwashing is that since green is popular now, calling a product green will entice people to purchase the product and save the planet. The degradation of our planet can be reversed only through careful consideration of the impact of a particular product on the environment and the planet and by applying environmental practice to minimize that impact. When assessing products, services, and other vendor or supplier offerings, your agency should be very cautious about believing claims of being green. Your agency should consider these questions to assess whether products and services are green, or just painted that color.

**Does the vendor back up its green claims with real examples or explanations using the terms just defined?** Vendors and suppliers that are concerned about their carbon footprint will happily expand on their claims and usually will be able to back them up with facts, process descriptions, green certifications, and other data to demonstrate that they are green.

**Does the vendor claim that its product is greener than other products manufactured in the same way?** A good example is a major chemical manufacturer that recently claimed that its new, less dangerous cleaning product is green, while ignoring the fact that the bulk of its product line produces huge amounts of dangerous chemicals marketed to sterilize even the cleanest office or agency.

**Does the vendor balk at answering questions with real examples, descriptions, and data to justify its claims or provide only marketing materials with no substance?** This is a big indication that the claims are greenwashing. Beware any organization that claims to be green and cannot substantiate this in real terms.

## Other Vendor Considerations

In working with vendors and other providers, there will be instances where there may be opportunity to improve, but they have taken no action and they are the only source for a particular service. At this point, your agency can start a dialog about what the vendor can do to make its operation more environmentally friendly. Often the vendor's organization simply has not considered environmental concerns or issues, or has not realized that through small incremental changes over time, significant impact and cost savings can accrue to the bottom line.

This situation can prove to be an opportunity to educate other companies and agencies about environmentalism and going green. To help this process get off the ground, listed next are some references that, even though they are aimed at for-profit organizations, can be helpful in formulating your strategy.

Jonathan Estes, *Smart Green: How to Implement Sustainable Business Practices in Any Industry—and Make Money*

Rich Mintzer, *101 Ways to Turn Your Business Green: The Business Guide to Eco-Friendly Profits*

Bruce Piasecki, *The Green Advantage: How Today's Best Businesses Profit by Going Green and Solving Global Problems*

## Conclusion

We have reviewed a number of ways to reduce, reuse, and recycle waste in our daily lives and work. It is hoped that this discussion leads to changes within your agency and helps you to find opportunities specific to your agency to reduce waste, recycle, and reuse things that would otherwise go to landfills or dumps. When you first start to look at the way that things are used around you, it can be overwhelming. There is really so much waste and so many opportunities for change. The good news is that the best way to address these opportunities is with small changes made over a period of time, adding more changes as time goes on. In this way, you can change your agency, the organizations that you work with, and even the world.

### About the Author

**Kelley Dean-Crowley** was first exposed to a municipal recycling program while earning her degree at the University of California at Davis. As an artist, dyer, and small green business owner, Kelley is passionate about her materials even as she employs eco-friendly business and studio practices and traditional yet modern techniques. When not dyeing in the studio, Kelley can be found managing enterprise projects in the financial industry, where she continues to refine her "reduce, recycle, and reuse" philosophy.

## Bibliography

Debrouwer, T. (2008, October 8). *Working the Landfills a Dangerous Occupation.* Retrieved April 2009, from Honduras This Week: www.hondurasthisweek.com/component/content/article/412-dangerous-occupation.

## CHAPTER 14

# Water-Wise Actions in a Warming World

## Green Solutions to Help the Planet and Your Bottom Line

### Juliet Lamont

## Introduction

Water is our lifeblood; it is the fundamental natural resource on which we all depend. In developed countries, we turn on the tap for drinking, washing, irrigation, cooking, and numerous other tasks each day without giving a second thought to the amount we use or where it comes from. We have assumed it is abundant and virtually infinite in supply. But the reality is quite different. Of Earth's water supplies (including oceans), fresh water accounts for just under 3 percent of the total. Of that, roughly 69 percent is currently captured in icecaps and glaciers, about 30 percent in groundwater, and a mere 0.3 percent in surface water[1] (see Figure 14.1).

By contrast, in most developing countries, water is viewed as precious and difficult to access, and often is very scarce. For example, according to the Dutch-based Water Footprint Network, a comparison of the national water footprints of the United States and Zambia highlights this disparity: roughly 2500 $m^3$/capita/yr versus 750 $m^3$/capita/yr, respectively.[2] This footprint calculation includes all types of water uses, from daily visible uses (e.g., toilet flushing, drinking water, clothes washing, etc.), to "hidden" (or "embedded") uses, such as product manufacturing, electricity delivery, and the like.

Americans, in particular, use an astonishing amount of water. The United States Geological Survey (USGS) cites the average American's daily domestic water use at roughly 80 to 100 gallons per day.[3] Europeans tend to use less water than Americans, averaging around 50 gallons per day per person.[4] The average Zambian resident, by comparison, uses only about 17 gallons per day.[5] Access to, and availability of, water in rural and poor communities in developing nations is even more limited. Rural domestic water use in some developing African nations is a mere 4 to 5 gallons per day.[6]

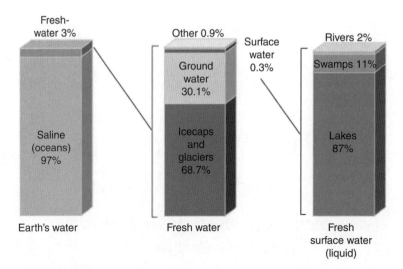

FIGURE 14.1   Distribution of water on Earth.
*Source:* Diagram courtesy of U.S. Geological Survey.
http://ga.water.usgs.gov/edu/waterdistribution.html

Climate change has added a critical and potentially devastating factor to both the supply and the distribution of the world's fresh water, changing a range of historical ecological processes: where precipitation falls, how much, and changes in the ability to store fresh water in mountain snowpack (see Figure 14.2). As developing nations grow, as industrialized countries continue their high-consumption water habits, and as manufacturing and development continue to generate higher water pollution loads, the global water future is grim. Water experts all agree: Water resources are in a crisis, across industrialized nations and emerging economies alike. Political leaders, regulatory agencies, environmental organizations, many elected officials, and even water managers now acknowledge the tremendous challenges of future water supply in the face of climate change impacts, growing global population, and sprawling, rampant development.

Changes in climate are already leading to changes in water distribution patterns, both in terms of total amounts of water and in the severity of precipitation events. Some geographic areas—such as Africa—are experiencing less total precipitation each year, leading to devastating droughts, while other areas are experiencing dramatic shifts in when precipitation occurs, and how severe the storm events are. For example, in the California Sierra Nevada mountains, precipitation is now predicted to occur in much more severe storm events, leading to extensive flooding. Moreover, with increasing overall temperatures due to climate change, that precipitation is no longer held on the mountains as snowpack that slowly melts over the spring and summer, delivering a steady supply of water to the lowland rivers, the Bay Delta, and coastal areas. Instead, the precipitation is now starting to arrive in large, immediate pulses with no retention through snowpack. If current trends continue, water supplies from the mountains will literally dry up by late spring, leaving the California freshwater drinking supply system—and a whole host of critical ecosystems—in complete collapse. Increasing global temperatures can

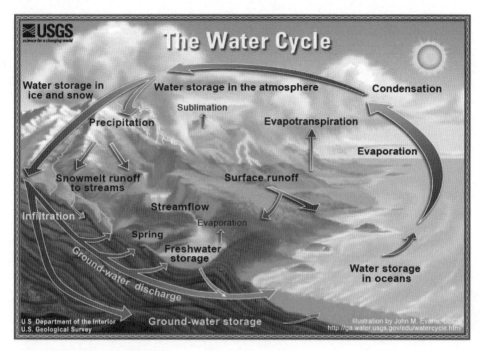

FIGURE 14.2 Earth's water cycle.

*Source:* Diagram courtesy of U.S. Geological Survey (http://ga.water.usgs.gov/edu/
watercycle.html). Illustration by John M. Evans, USGS, Colorado District.

accelerate water quality degradation by raising temperatures in streams and rivers,
which promotes microbial growth (often called algal blooms) and depletes dissolved
oxygen levels. In addition to these blooms, the lower dissolved oxygen levels slow
processes of biodegradation, the natural self-cleaning mechanism for water bodies
in which all kinds of inputs (leaves, organisms, and chemicals) break down over
time.[7] Increased demands on dwindling supplies exacerbate these effects further:
Rapidly growing populations worldwide—along with the requirements of greater
industrialization—are demanding more water resources at every step while the provision of clean, safe drinking water is a major concern for developing nations.
Concurrently, this growth and demand destroys the lakes, river corridors, stream
tributaries, and wetlands that provide and filter the water that we need and use.

Beyond human needs, wildlife habitat and biodiversity are suffering catastroph-
ically from water overdrafting (i.e., when water withdrawals exceed the natural rate
at which water is replenished through the natural water cycle) and the same water
quality degradation is impacting humans. Critical wetlands for migratory birds are
shrinking, riverbeds and lakes are drying up, and the species that depend on these
natural areas are plummeting in numbers.[8] In sum, the impacts of our global population growth and rapidly expanding consumption of resources, coupled with climate
change impacts—both anticipated and under way—will have profound effects on
the sustainability and stability of our planet, not only ecologically but economically
and politically, as well.

## Positive Actions and Impacts

All doom and gloom? Absolutely not. The good news is that water conservation and water recycling can be among our best strategies for ensuring a sustainable energy and water future. It will reduce overall energy used—and concurrent greenhouse gas emissions—while also protecting against water shortages. Additionally, conservation and recycling provide multiple benefits for habitat, recreation, flood control, and water quality, which are essential components of adapting to and mitigating for such climate change impacts as greater flooding, loss of snowpack, and water quality degradation.

Water experts are weighing in heavily on this issue. Award-winning global water policy specialist Peter Gleick has published numerous reports and extensive data sets detailing the looming shortages and distribution concerns while highlighting the direct linkages between water use and climate change. In several recent publications, both Gleick and the Natural Resources Defense Council (NRDC) conclude that water conservation and recycling—and the concurrent restoration of watersheds and waterways—are the primary tools with which to actively and successfully address the global water crisis and provide real adaptation to climate change impacts. Although the reports focus on the western region of the United States, their conclusions and recommendations are applicable worldwide.

Many businesses and citizens simply do not realize how closely water use is linked to greenhouse gas emissions and to adaptation and mitigation for climate change impacts that we are already experiencing. For example, nearly 20 percent of California's electricity usage each year is for water, primarily for conveying water from its source to end users, for water treatment, and for heating the water.[9] Every time we turn on the tap, we add to the energy—and climate-change—burden of our planet. Conversely, when we reduce our use, save a drop, and recycle where we can, the positive repercussions are felt all the way to the watersheds from which that water flows.

Equally important, water conservation has substantial economic benefits to organizations, businesses, and residential homeowners through reduced costs for water utility bills, water delivery, drinking water treatment, and wastewater treatment cost. Nonprofit organizations are in a unique position to take leadership on this issue through their own actions; they can "walk the walk," not just "talk the talk." Such leadership will bring tangible benefits to these entities through water and energy cost savings as well as promoting the message of sustainability to the public—a message that can be a major factor in attracting new donors and supporters.

In sum, aggressive water conservation and water recycling are the only tools that can provide a reliable buffer against water shortages in the future while mitigating climate change impacts through reducing greenhouse gas emissions and providing multiple benefits for habitat, recreation, flood control, and water quality improvement.

## Water-Wise Planning and Actions

Can a nonprofit really implement effective water conservation and stewardship actions? Yes, and it is a lot easier than you may think. We have all heard the phrase

"Reduce, reuse, recycle!" But most of us think about packaging and material sup-plies when we hear this; how many of us apply it to water use? Yet reduce, reuse, and recycle are water conservation basics, too—we just do not know them as well. Adopting that mantra for *every* planning decision and action will set you on a course for positive, tangible changes toward a sustainable water future.

Every organization—small to large—can start by prioritizing water conservation in long-term business strategies and planning. Good strategy and planning leads to on-the-ground actions; some of these are short-term, immediate changes—others can be implemented over several years as a business plan unfolds, as capital upgrades occur, and as budgets allow. Nonprofits that own their property or buildings can implement many actions at and around these sites along with changing internal business practices and decisions. Smaller nonprofits that rent or lease may not have the full range of capital improvements available to them, but there are still many options for immediate, direct water conservation and stewardship actions that bring benefits both in-house and to the environment as a whole. In addition, nonprofits that rent or lease often can work with their landlords to encourage and implement substantial structural and site improvements by citing the reduced water bills and/or broader environmental contribution that these actions will generate.

## Reduce

*Reducing demand* (i.e., decreasing water use) is the most effective step you can take as an organization to help address global water supply problems. Less water coming out of the tap means less water needed from the watersheds, more water staying in the rivers and lakes for fish and endangered species, more water supplying our critical wetlands for pollutant filtration and habitat, and more water to percolate down to natural groundwater storage areas (called aquifers), which supply many cities and regions with their drinking water (see Figure 14.2). And of course, reducing demand means using less electricity and energy (and greenhouse gases!) to bring that water into your business.

Additionally, reducing your use outright means less water has to be treated for human consumption at your regional water treatment facility, before coming to your tap, as well as less wastewater and sewage treatment volume at the discharge end. These are far-reaching benefits that we do not often think about: Reducing treatment volumes is a cost-saving strategy for consumers, municipalities, and public utilities, and it is also a win for the environment. Every gallon of water we treat requires input of harsh chemicals (e.g., chlorine) that linger in our environment for years and years. Less water to treat translates into fewer chemicals used, fewer toxic materials contaminating our waterways, and significantly lower dollar outlays for chemical purchases and disposal.

Sewage and wastewater treatment puts additional stresses on water bodies and the environment as a whole. In industrialized countries, public works agencies and engineers are constantly challenged to develop additional, expensive infrastructure to convey, contain, filter, and chemically treat the many pollutants that are present in water discharges. Many of these infrastructure systems are old and decaying with sewage spills and overflows a constant occurrence in even the most advanced systems. In early 2009, a break in a pipe at a San Francisco Bay sanitation facility poured over 500,000 gallons of sewage directly into bay waters, contaminating a biologically diverse water body that is habitat for endangered whales, fish, and birds. In developing countries, sewage discharge is a critical issue for public health and welfare. Many countries do not have the resources or technology to treat wastewater and pollution; any inputs to water use are discharged directly into streams, rivers, and oceans, impacting habitat as well as spreading disease among human populations. Any reduction in wastewater produced is thus a gain for our water ecosystems overall, easing yet one more stressor in the cycle.

There are many ways to reduce water use, from adopting and using water-efficient products and processes, to changing individual behavior, to landscaping decisions that emphasize native plants and low-water-use species. *Sustainable office practices and purchasing* can make a significant impact as a start. Simple actions, such as changing drinking water supply from bottled water to using tap water, provide immediate bottom-line benefits for your business while saving the energy and environmental costs that are embedded in producing plastic bottles, trucking (or flying) bottled water to your organization, and handling the enormous plastic waste resulting from the bottles themselves. In addition, bottled water in industrialized nations is generally no safer than the water right from your tap, and the extraction of water for bottled water use has a significant—and negative—environmental impact overall, destroying wetlands supplied by critical groundwater aquifers, as well as depleting waterways that depend on underground springs and water sources.

Implementing tools that automatically regulate—and limit—water use in your organization is another simple way to reduce your demand. Installing motion detectors and automatic timers and/or low-flow units on your bathroom and office kitchen faucets limits the time that the water is flowing or the volume of that flow as it comes out of the tap. Motion sensors have gained widespread acceptance in many countries; you often see this feature used on faucets in airport restrooms and other facilities, which have high usage rates. But they can work equally well in smaller venues where there are many employees using water frequently. An even simpler (and cheaper) mechanism that any organization can implement is a retrofit aerator device screwed on to an existing faucet thread. These aerators mix air with the water coming out of the faucet to reduce water flow. While these may seem like small changes, these water savings add up, ecologically and economically.

Toilet technology is another simple target point with big paybacks. In the United States, toilets are the single largest daily user of water in residential homes, accounting for roughly 25 percent of total daily use. Nonprofit businesses may have several bathrooms in their building or share bathrooms with other tenants. In either case, the multiple daily flushes add up. One of the simplest and cheapest methods for reducing that water demand is simply to put a device in the toilet tank to reduce the amount of water used in each flush. Traditionally, bricks were the item of choice; unfortunately, they can disintegrate over time, damaging your plumbing. Instead, an effective, nondamaging solution is to put a large, water-filled plastic bottle into the tank, adding a few stones to the bottle to weight it down. The bottle will act as your "brick." Knowing the unfortunate longevity of plastics, you are in no danger of ruining your toilet mechanisms. Building owners can do this just as well as renters (make sure you speak with your landlord first), so whether you are a nonprofit that owns or leases, this is an easy fix, with real impacts.

A better long-term investment is to upgrade your toilets to new high-efficiency toilet (HET) designs: specifically, improved low-flow or "dual-flush" systems. Low-flow toilets automatically use less water per flush. Older toilet designs use around 3 gallons per flush (gpf), and any leaks or malfunctions can drastically increase this volume. In the United States, the U.S. Environmental Protection Agency (EPA) now requires that all toilets use 1.6 gpf or less. But many manufacturers—notably in Japan and Australia—have been much more aggressive in new toilet designs aiming for less than 1 gpf and even for "waterless" or "no-flush" urinals.

"Dual-flush" designs are a variant on the low-flow idea. The toilet unit has two buttons on the tank (or two handle positions), one of which is used for liquid-only use while the other is a full-flush design used when there is solid waste. The liquid-only flush (plus minimal toilet tissue) can be as low as 0.8 gpf, while the "full-flush" is around 1.6 gpf. These design improvements bring enormous water savings over the course of a year, along with associated water costs. The EPA estimates that replacing an older toilet with an HET system can save about 4,000 gallons of water per year, translating into water bill savings of close to $100 per year, just for that one plumbing unit.[10]

And it is getting easier and easier to find and purchase such products. For example, the EPA now oversees a mainstream "WaterSense" certification program to promote water-efficient products and supplies.[11] In the United States, many such products come with rebates and financial incentives from your local water supply utility, so you not only gain the benefits of long-term water conservation and lower water bills, but you may get some cash back right away. That is good business—as well as "eco"-sense.

One additional target area for water conservation—with big returns—is also one of the most neglected: leaks and drips. Those slow drips from the faucet, a slowly leaking toilet tank, or a break in your irrigation line all lead to hundreds of gallons per year in wasted water. To illustrate this point more clearly, using the USGS's "drip accumulator calculator,"[12] a *single* faucet leak of only 5 drips per minute leads to over 170 gallons of water wasted annually (water you pay for, no less). The solution to this waste? Regularly check your faucets, toilets, and irrigation lines for leaks and malfunctions, and when you find one, fix it. If you are a renter, show your landlord this example (or better yet, plug in your leak's figures on the USGS Web site); it will be a compelling argument for making that repair.

Indoor practices and actions are not the only way to reduce water demand. Landscape irrigation is another huge draw on water resources, accounting for up to 50 percent of total daily residential use in some climatic regions. *Sustainable site design and plant selection* is a key element in reducing this water demand at the outset; likewise, actual irrigation practices and products further impact water use. One of the biggest steps an organization can take in promoting sustainable water use is to replace lawn and turf, or nonnative water-loving plants, with native, water-efficient species. Lawns are water hogs and, worse, are often accompanied by heavy fertilizer and pesticide use. Native plants use their evolutionary design to succeed in a given region, without additional inputs and extraordinary water use. They are specifically adapted to the climate and soils in which they developed over time and are thus inherently resilient to the conditions of their region. This is particularly important in Mediterranean and desert climates, where the irrigation demands of even moderately water-loving, nonnative plants translate into rapid and severe depletion of water supplies.

The tools and techniques for providing irrigation water also impact demand. Drip irrigation (units that deliver water to a plant stem through slow drips), low-flow bubbler systems, soaker hoses, or any technique that allows for targeted water delivery to plants are huge improvements over conventional sprinklers. Installing timers on drip (or similar) irrigation systems is a practical and effective method for further controlling the volume of water used for irrigation; overwatering is a common gardening mistake, and a quick way to waste a precious resource. Finally, you can replace free-running hose ends with spray nozzles that have automatic shut-off valves and that allow for variable water flows, to ensure that water is used only when you want it and only in the amounts you really need.

## Recycle

*Recycling water* on-site can help to reduce your water demand overall, or at least stretch each drop a lot farther in terms of its functions. Recycling water includes sending slightly "used" water (e.g., rinse water) out to your garden or your site to irrigate plants; sending sink water (or similar) to your toilet tank; and recirculating water for ornamental features such as water fountains. These strategies are often referred to as gray water recycling systems with the associated plumbing linkages referred to as purple pipe systems.

In developing countries, recycling water is often a default strategy; water is too scarce *not* to reuse it whenever possible. By contrast, in developed countries, we have been slower to understand how important this strategy is. To their credit, some countries in Europe, such as Germany and the Netherlands, have been promoting water recycling for more than a decade. More recently, areas of the United States where desert conditions predominate—such as the state of Arizona—have already made it easier to adopt gray water recycling features into homes and businesses through streamlined permitting and model gray water ordinances. The increase in droughts throughout the nation has prompted other states to follow suit: New Mexico and Texas both passed new gray water legislation and code updates in 2003, while Montana adopted legislation allowing gray water reuse in homes in 2007.

Other states have been slower to adapt, but even in these locations, simple actions in your business and home are both feasible and legal. For example, the EPA has developed a set of guidelines for water reuse that can help you understand the options available.[13] One of the simplest recycling techniques—available to any organization—is to purchase several handheld buckets or dishpans, leave them near sinks (and showers, if you have them), and collect rinse water, shower water, and the like, which you then use to "flush" your toilet or to water indoor and outdoor plants. (This latter strategy emphasizes the importance of a related water stewardship practice: Use only biodegradable, nontoxic soaps and cleaners throughout your organization.)

More sophisticated systems are products that actually link your sink's drainage water directly to your toilet tank (e.g., WaterSaver Technologies' AQUS system[14]) or that create a small sink washing station on your toilet tank itself, with the water draining directly into the tank (e.g., Environmental Designworks' SinkPositive system[15]). These are more expensive retrofits, but are relatively easy to install and are low-maintenance. Full gray water systems, where separate pipes carry fresh (or "blue") water, gray (or "purple") water, and sewage (or "black") water, are more difficult to install, particularly in the United States. However, with increasing awareness of water supply issues worldwide, these technologies and systems are certain to improve in design as well as in availability. As a nonprofit, you can take some of the easier actions described right now while working more comprehensive water recycling strategies into your organization's future planning goals.

## Retain and Reuse

*Retaining water* on-site is yet another effective method for reducing demand and maximizing the use of water. Organizations can install both simple and more comprehensive features to capture and store rainwater as it falls and then use this water for landscape irrigation and/or to recharge depleted groundwater sources. Not only is this cost effective in providing an additional "free" source of irrigation water, but you are doing the environment a huge favor by capturing runoff, particularly in denser urban and suburban areas. The benefits are so widespread that many environmental nonprofits, regulatory agencies, and municipalities are promoting these strategies with public campaigns, such as Mississippi River Action's "Retain the Rain" program, and Utah's statewide water conservation program to "Slow the Flow—Save $H_2O$."

In brief, when it rains, soils become "saturated" (i.e., their capacity to hold more water maxes out), and any additional rainfall runs off the ground surface into nearby street gutters, storm drains, and local creeks and rivers. In developed areas, this runoff picks up pollution along the way, such as oil deposits from cars, pesticides on lawns, and so on. The polluted runoff enters creeks and rivers—polluting those waterways—and eventually ends up in lakes, wetlands, and bays as part of the water's movement downstream. That pollution is now considered one of the primary causes of fisheries loss, amphibian mutations and declines, and the concentration of toxics up through the food chain of marine mammals and other top marine predators.

Moreover, in developed areas, we have paved over so much surface area and added so many buildings with hard, impermeable roofs and features that we have severely compromised the natural process by which soils and vegetation absorb rainwater as it falls. Instead of the spongelike retention of water as it drips through trees, settles on bushes and leaves, and slowly infiltrates into the soil, the runoff rolls off the land surface in large, rapid pulses. Large volumes of water flow into our roads, creeks, buildings, and infrastructure as intense floods, causing costly ecological damage as well as damage to businesses and residences. Severe flooding also erodes creek and riverbanks, adding large sediment deposits to waterways, wetlands, and bays, deposits that ultimately suffocate fish hatcheries and other beneficial organisms.

In 1998 and again in 2006, the San Francisco Bay Area experienced some of the worst urban floods in recent history due to just such a phenomenon. Damage to businesses and residences amounted to hundreds of millions of dollars while the

ecological damage included destruction of fishery restoration projects, massive col-
lapses of streams and riverbanks, and deposition of garbage and debris throughout
the region's waterways. Climate change projections all indicate that severe flooding
and storm events will increase worldwide; thus, organizations that "slow the flow"
and "retain the rain" through water retention features on-site contribute to the greater
environmental whole by helping to mitigate for—and adapt to—these impacts.

One of the simplest on-site water retention solutions is the installation of rainwater catchment cisterns. Cisterns range in size from small, 60-gallon plastic barrels
or units that fit under decks or along the side of a building (e.g., Rainwater HOG[16]),
to larger, more sophisticated units that can be attached to building walls (e.g.,
BlueScope Water cisterns[17]). The cisterns capture water collected from rainwater
downspouts and store that water until it is needed, or desired, for irrigation purposes. Individual cisterns can be aggregated into groups to heighten the storage
capacity of the whole system. While individual units fill up quickly in storms and
may appear to have a minor impact in reducing floods, individual cisterns installed
on properties across an entire watershed add up to a tangible effect. And actions
like these go a long way to educate people about water use and to heighten their
awareness of the water cycle as a whole.

Green roofs are another effective water retention strategy that is now gaining momentum and visibility worldwide. The city of Chicago is promoting the
installation of green roofs on buildings as a method to capture rainwater, alle-
viate flooding, and cool local temperatures (i.e., "heat island" mitigation). These
green roofs—now cropping up in cities around the world—use previously ignored
available rooftop space in dense urban areas where every square foot of property is precious. Not only is Chicago seeing benefits in terms of reduced runoff,
but these green roofs actively combat the local warming effects of climate change
that we are already experiencing, act as carbon sinks (i.e., where vegetation ab-
sorbs carbon dioxide), and improve local air quality (vegetation acts as a natural air
pollution filter).

In a remarkable study, the city has been monitoring and comparing two publicly owned, neighboring buildings: City Hall, which has a green roof planted with
native, water-efficient vegetation, and the adjacent Cook County building, which
is covered with black tar. Data collected at both sites during the hottest days of
summer describe an amazing phenomenon: The green roof surface temperatures
have been recorded as up to 50 degrees lower than temperatures on the adjacent
black-tar roof.[18] Apart from the obvious climate change implications, the city has
estimated that such temperature differences will lead to the avoidance of direct
energy costs at that site of roughly $3,600 per year, in addition to indirect ecolog-
ical and economic benefits such as improved air quality and reduction of urban
runoff.

"Green walls" (sometimes called living walls) take this idea a step further with
vertical panels of vegetation applied to buildings' walls, providing similar benefits
to green roofs in terms of water retention, localized air temperature reductions, and
air quality improvement. One company based in Vancouver, British Columbia, has
now installed green walls on company buildings throughout North America, from
Starbucks to W Hotels.[19] Meanwhile, in countries such as Germany, Norway, and
the Netherlands, green roofs and walls are a rapidly expanding, profitable industry
sector.[20] Green wall panels are designed as relatively small, discrete units so that

they can be used on a variety of building structures and locations, irrespective of size.

On-site water retention can go hand in hand with another valuable water stewardship strategy: on-site water pollution treatment and filtration. While retaining that rain and runoff, why not improve it at the same time? Many cities, regulatory agencies, and even developers are beginning to see the immense value in finding ways to filter and treat water on-site, through natural features such as wetlands and swales (vegetated runoff ditches that allow water to percolate into the soil, where microorganisms break down pollutants). In the late 1980s, the city of Arcata, in northern California, implemented an award-winning project for treating its wastewater and storm water runoff, creating and managing a large natural wetlands area that filters and treats all of the city's wastewater. At $5 million, the construction of this wetlands area cost one-tenth of the $50 million that a new regional treatment facility was projected to cost ($10 million of which Arcata would have had to cover), with annual maintenance costs at about one-third of those of a traditional treatment plant.[21] Moreover, the wetlands now provide a local recreational benefit and serve as a major tourist draw (with its associated economic boost) for the many birdwatchers and naturalists coming to the region.

Natural systems such as these can be implemented on a small-site scale as well. Rather than paying high construction and materials prices to run concrete culverts along a business property to convey rainwater, vegetated swales serve the same conveyance purpose but allow water infiltration into the soil along the way so that some of the precipitation is redirected into the ground (that important sponge idea again), helping to minimize flooding and damage elsewhere. Likewise, the creation of small wetlands areas on-site allows for another opportunity for water retention and filtration of pollutants by aquatic plants, which are some of the best natural cleanup mechanisms around. The cities of Portland and Seattle have constructed "rain gardens" and water capture-and-treatment street curb designs on many of their streets. They have had tremendous success in minimizing flood pulses while addressing storm water runoff issues at the same time.[22] And citizens appreciate the aesthetic benefits of these designs. In fact, Seattle's model Street Edge Alternatives Project for storm water retention, which created wide vegetated swales along several street blocks in the northwest area of the city as well as adding extensive tree cover and bushes, is expected to increase neighborhood property values. Another win-win for the environment and the economy.

## Water Quality Stewardship

Beyond the water conservation mantra of reduce, reuse, and recycle, it is important to understand that actions to protect and improve water quality go hand in hand with sustainable water use. For example, recycling water on-site for irrigation means that any toxics in your water will end up on and in nearby soils and in runoff going to local creeks and bays. That is a strong argument to switch to fully biodegradable cleaning products and soaps. Likewise, fertilizers and pesticides that you apply to landscaping end up contaminating lakes and water bodies, harming wildlife and humans alike. Why not pledge to use only organic mulch and compost to coddle your plants, and make your site (and organization) a pesticide-free zone? You will save the escalating costs of artificial, chemically loaded products while encouraging beneficial natural processes, microorganisms, and bugs to thrive and manage the truly "bad" pests.

Several of the biggest sources of pollution in runoff center around cars. Replacing your motor oil or cleaning your car on a street or driveway leads to a very real—and very toxic—stream of pollutants entering the storm water system and its downstream water bodies and habitats. There are easy alternatives, but they require some changes in habits. Ideally, oil changes should occur at a commercial garage or gas station, where drainage and runoff are supposed to be directed to on-site systems that capture the oil for later disposal at a hazardous waste facility. If you are determined to change your own oil, always use a collection pan and large fabric underneath your car, to capture all the drips and any spills. Then take that oil waste to a licensed hazardous waste disposal facility. Likewise, try to clean your car at a local car wash; again, the drainage at these facilities is directed toward an on-site pollution filtration system (and water is often recycled, as an extra environmental benefit) or directed into the city sewage pipes. There is almost no good way to clean your car at your home—but if you must, make sure that the vehicle is on gravel or natural turf (or some other permeable surface), so at the very least, some of the pollutants will infiltrate into the soil, where a limited amount of pollutant filtration will occur.

Finally, one of the biggest changes you can make to protect global water quality is to switch to organic or pesticide-free—and preferably local—food and beverages. Organizations often forget that their own daily activities may include providing lunches and snacks for meetings, food and beverages for fundraising events, or even just a constant supply of the office coffee. Food produced with pesticides and synthetic fertilizers is the source of severe water contamination on a massive scale, with component chemicals making their way into waterways and oceans and then back into the food chain as plants and animals process or ingest the chemicals. Do not be a part of this global problem; instead, make a commitment to support your local organic food producers when able and aim to be pesticide-free in your food products as a whole. Not only will your food taste better, but you will know that you are helping the planet to maintain the healthy water cycle on which we all depend.

## Water-Wise Checklists for Your Organization

Figures 14.3 through 14.6 provide summary checklists of the many strategies, actions, and tools discussed in this chapter for organizations to reduce, reuse, and recycle water. These checklists are designed to be a quick visual reference for guiding your water-wise actions and suggesting where you may have gaps. The checklists include items that are part of the Green Nonprofits certification program, but they also include elements above and beyond that certification. Knowledge about our environment and natural resources is constantly changing, as is the concurrent ability to take effective action based on that knowledge; your actions should continue expand over time as you build your water awareness. Appendix A lists additional sources for understanding water conservation concepts overall as well as implementing water-wise strategies and finding specific products through Web site links, publications, and other informational sites.

| Conservation Strategy | Specific Targets | Options |
|---|---|---|
| Water-efficient Products | Toilets | Low-flow |
| | | Dual-flush |
| | | Plastic bottle in toilet tank |
| | | Waterless urinals |
| | Faucets & Showerheads | Retrofit aerators (low-flow units) |
| | | Motion sensors & timers |
| Water-efficient Landscaping | Irrigation Design | Drip irrigation |
| | | Irrigation timers |
| | | Soaker hoses; low-flow units |
| | | Automatic shut-off spray nozzles for hoses |
| | | Variable volume spray nozzles for hoses |
| | Plants | Native plants (no turf!) |
| | | Drought-tolerant or low water use plants |
| Sustainable Business Operations | Drinking Water | Tap water (not bottled) |
| | Leaks & Drips | Identify and fix all leaks (even small drips) |
| | Hot Water | Eliminate all nonessential hot water use |

FIGURE 14.3   Water conservation checklist.

| Recycling Strategy | Specific Targets | Options |
|---|---|---|
| Water Recycling | Internal Plumbing Landscaping/Irrigation | Shower/sink-to-toilet piping |
| | | Shower-to-garden piping |
| | | Hand-held buckets or basins for water capture |
| | Ornamental Water Features | Recirculated water for fountains (closed-loop) |
| | | Shower-to-fountain piping |

FIGURE 14.4   Water recycling checklist.

| Retention & Reuse Strategy | Specific Targets | Options |
|---|---|---|
| Water Retention | Landscaping | Rainwater cisterns |
| | | Vegetated swales |
| | | Rain gardens |
| | Water Infiltration/Absorption | Green roofs |
| | | Permeable pavers, concrete, & asphalt |
| | | Green/"living" walls |

FIGURE 14.5   Water retention and reuse checklist.

| Stewardship Strategy | Specific Targets | Options |
| --- | --- | --- |
| In-House Product Use | Indoor Chemical Use | Nontoxic cleaning products |
| | Outdoor Chemical Use | No car-washing on streets, driveways |
| | | No artificial fertilizers; organic compost, mulch instead |
| | | Eliminate pesticide use for landscaping |
| Broader Product Choices | Global Pesticide Reduction | Use local, sustainable organic food for parties, in-house meals/snacks, catering, etc. |
| | | Use organic cotton for all organization products, member gifts, etc. (e.g., T-shirts, etc.) |

FIGURE 14.6   Water quality stewardship checklist.

## Long-Term Planning, Education, and Outreach for a Greener, Water-Wise Organization

The checklists include both short-term, easy-to-implement actions (e.g., water-filled plastic bottle in the toilet tank; converting from bottled water to tap) as well as actions that organizations can implement over a longer timeframe, as a business undergoes structural upgrades, retrofits, and landscaping changes (e.g., replacing grass or turf with landscaping designs for native plants; installing green roofs and walls). Although your organization may not be able to make every change listed right now, *every* organization can put both short-term and long-term water efficiency goals and strategies into its business plan, setting timelines and benchmarks for achieving these actions.

Likewise, actively focusing on employee education and outreach programs for greening your organization will have excellent paybacks down the road. Implementation of in-house programs such as brown-bag lunches, weekly or monthly online "green newsletters" and water-saving tips, a "green corner" on your organization's Web site, and even friendly in-house and team competitions for reducing water use can build both camaraderie and a sense of goodwill among employees, while establishing an important—and constantly evolving—knowledge base about green business practices. And there is no need to stop in-house: Why not extend this participation into your local community? Organize and encourage employee participation in local water-saving charitable programs and activities, such as the annual Coastal Cleanup Day held every fall across the United States, creek restoration and urban reforestation planting events, and the like. Not only does this boost employee morale through tangible action in the environmental arena, but it acts as an effective, important, and welcome public relations tool for your organization.

Long-term strategic planning that focuses on prioritizing water-wise structures and operations is an excellent complement to—and component of—effective strategies for greening your organization overall. Virtually all of the strategies and actions for water conservation and stewardship listed in this chapter are also strategies that reduce greenhouse gas emissions, help to adapt to and mitigate for climate change impacts, improve habitat for wildlife, increase biodiversity, improve public health and well-being, and ultimately benefit the economy. Simply put, water-wise thinking and actions have multiple benefits across a whole range of environmental, social, and economic arenas.

Once your organization is thinking and acting green, you can consider even broader water-wise planning strategies to accelerate and heighten the positive environmental impact of your organization overall. Comprehensive green planning includes such elements as:

- Actively integrating green retrofits into existing operations and structures.
- Adaptively reusing existing structures wherever possible.
- Thinking small for new building and site design—small and compact is water-wise and attractive.
- Actively restoring your landscaping for water efficiency and wildlife habitat enhancement.
- Building organizational public relations programs based on water awareness.
- Leveraging your organization's environmental responsibility programs for positive company image and profits (e.g., market and publicize green practices to draw new donors, members, etc.).
- Developing public/private/nonprofit partnerships and coalitions for programs, grants, and the like that promote and implement water-wise behavior and green practices overall.

## Your Contribution to a Greener, Water-Wise Future

In this time of daunting, global environmental challenges, the world needs strong environmental leaders across all sectors and arenas. Nonprofit organizations are uniquely positioned to take the reins in delivering and promoting effective environmental action and leadership, both through their extensive outreach abilities and through their own internal choices and business practices. Water conservation and recycling are critical components in leading the way toward real, enduring global sustainability. Water-wise strategies have multiple benefits, provide the only reliable buffer against future water shortages, and directly and indirectly help to decrease greenhouse gas emissions.

Greening your nonprofit through water-wise actions and planning—and the many parallel green business practices and decisions discussed in this book—will leave a permanent, positive legacy for our environment, our economies, and our communities.

## About the Author

**Juliet Lamont** is an environmental consultant with her own practice, with substantial experience in water policy and management as well as ecosystem-based restoration of watersheds and natural infrastructure. She has over 20 years' experience in environmental planning, management, and research. She has an extensive background in environmental science, policy, and planning, with recent work focused on watershed planning and restoration and implementation of green infrastructure policies and techniques for water management. Juliet graduated from Harvard University (AB, History of Science, ecology emphasis) and the University of California at Berkeley, where she received an MS in Wildland Resource Science (water ecology and environmental policy) and a PhD in Environmental Planning and Urban Design, focusing on ecologically sensitive urban planning and design. She is the former chair of the Sierra Club's San Francisco Bay Chapter and of the Berkeley-based Urban Creeks Council, and was recently the mayor of Berkeley's appointee to the city's downtown revitalization commission.

## CHAPTER 15

# Green Energy for Your Nonprofit

## Gary Skulnik and Michael Goodsite

## Introduction to Clean Energy

One of the greatest ways organizations directly impact the environment, especially regarding climate change, is through their use of electricity. Electricity generation is the largest source of carbon dioxide ($CO_2$) emissions in the United States, accounting for approximately 40 percent of all $CO_2$ emissions.[1] The energy supply sector had an approximately 25 percent share in total anthropogenic (from human activity) greenhouse gas emissions in 2004 when calculated in terms of $CO_2$-equivalents. The climate system is dominated by greenhouse gases that remain in the atmosphere for decades, centuries, or even longer. These are called the long-lived greenhouse gases, and their emissions are covered by international agreements. Globally, greenhouse gas emissions due to anthropogenic activities have grown since the pre-industrial times, with an increase of 70 percent between 1970 and 2004. $CO_2$ is the most important greenhouse gas emitted by human activity. The Intergovernmental Panel on Climate Change, in its 2007 synthesis report, stated that together with the preceding data, the warming of the climate system is unequivocal.[2]

Impacts of a warming climate will depend on many factors and will vary from location to location, but they are already being observed and will continue to intensify. State-of-the-art science demonstrates that the state of the changing climate is worse than described in the report.

The time for talk is, therefore, over; action is required now. Business as usual is not an option, nor is building as usual.

Despite the impact of energy on the climate, energy is not the main problem for developing sustainable firms or societies. The problem is how we create, capture, distribute, and use the 10,000 times more energy Earth is hit by than we use. Therefore, nonprofit organizations together with scientists, engineers, architects, and designers should play a vital role in collecting this energy and using it responsibly in the choices that humankind needs to make for a sustainable future.[3] Energy use must be integrated into the long-term climate and operational strategy, regardless of whether energy is an intensive part of the business or service production needs. To use meaningful examples for readers, rather than using global values, we have chosen to base our chapter on examples and cases from the United States. Many countries have excellent governmental resources; readers who need more information are encouraged to seek out these resources where appropriate.

Before discussing measures to reduce your environmental impact, it is worthwhile to have an understanding of the various sources of energy that power the electricity grid of the United States and most developed countries.

## Coal

The United States relies heavily on electricity production from coal, as coal is the most abundant fossil fuel located within the nation's borders. While it is accessible and relatively inexpensive, its environmental impacts are numerous and widespread. Per unit of heat energy produced, coal releases the most carbon emissions in the atmosphere compared to other fossil fuels. In other words, it is extremely carbon intensive.

The United States is home to 25 percent of the world's known coal reserves. There is a long-established coal industry in many states. It should come as no surprise then that coal is used to produce half the electricity consumed by Americans.[4] Because energy production through coal fired power plants is so carbon intensive, 80 percent of carbon emissions related to electricity production are from the use of coal-fired power plants.[5] Burning coal to make electricity not only releases $CO_2$ but also produces nitrogen oxide, mercury, and sulfur dioxide. Nitrogen oxide and sulfur dioxide can degrade the quality of water in the area in which they settle. Mercury also can end up in water sources and potentially be ingested by fish and other marine life. It is a toxic substance that affects health and productivity.[6] In recent decades, often spurred by government regulation, the coal industry has reduced the amount of harmful emissions that are released into the atmosphere by using technology such as scrubbers and using coal with fewer emissions.[7]

In the mid-Atlantic region of the United States, mountaintop removal is increasingly used to access coal. The materials removed from the mountaintop are deposited in nearby valleys, which are referred to as valley fills. In surrounding areas, an increase in the minerals present in the water includes zinc, sodium, selenium, and sulfate—all of which could negatively impact fish and other aquatic life. In some cases, streams are completely filled by the materials. The compacted nature of the soil inhibits the regrowth of trees, so the area is difficult to return to an area of natural resources.[8]

Carbon sequestration has been offered as an option for reducing carbon emissions from power plants. After coal is burned to create energy, the carbon emissions are captured before being released into the atmosphere. Then the carbon is pumped underground into geologic reservoirs. This practice has yet to be implemented on a wide basis in the United States, mainly due to the high cost of implementation.[9]

## Oil

In the United States, oil is used to meet 40 percent of domestic energy demands.[10] Not only does the burning of oil itself adversely impact the environment, but the transport of oil to consumers also has environmental impacts. Oil generally is not produced in the same place where it is used. Oil usually is transported through pipelines and large trucks over very large areas. The emissions from the transport of oil are high in themselves. Additionally, it has long been argued that pipelines in rural areas put wildlife at risk, should there be a leak in a pipe. During transport, there is also the possibility of oil spills; most people have seen the images of marine life covered in oil as a result of an oil spill.

Drilling to reach oil reserves results in what is called produced water. Safely disposing of this water is a serious concern. Produced water has higher amounts of saline and nutrients that could alter the chemistry of the water and soil in the surrounding area.[11]

## Natural Gas

When natural gas is burned, it releases fewer emissions than other fossil fuels. This is partly due to the fact that natural gas contains fewer impurities than other fossil fuels. However, one of the main components of natural gas is methane, which has 21 times the effect of $CO_2$ on global warming.[12] Natural gas also contains $CO_2$, nitrogen, helium, and propane.[13]

Natural gas is extracted from gas wells or produced from the extraction of crude oil. When compared to the impact of other fossil fuels, it has a smaller negative impact on soil, surface water, or ground water.[14]

Natural gas is transported through pipelines throughout the United States. Many times the construction of these pipelines requires changes to the landscape, dredging, trenching, and the like. Further, the Environmental Protection Agency has stated that during the operation of the pipelines, there is the possibility of leakage, resulting in air pollutant emissions. The compressor stations also emit nitrogen oxide, volatile organic compounds, and methane.[15]

## Nuclear Energy

Nuclear energy provides stable base-load power: The minimum amount of electric power delivered or required over a given period of time at a steady rate, without emitting greenhouse gases. However, the costs to construct new nuclear facilities are high, and the construction period is quite long.

The main environmental concern regarding nuclear energy is how to dispose of the spent fuel produced as a by-product of the energy creation process. Spent nuclear fuel is highly radioactive. Spent fuel has been produced and stored since the 1940s; however, there is no method for its destruction or permanent disposal. It is stored throughout the country, not only in rural areas but also in urban and suburban areas, often located near large bodies of water.[16]

## Hydropower

Hydroelectric power is currently the largest form of renewable electricity production in the United States.[17] Hydropower facilities capture the kinetic energy produced from flowing water and convert that energy into electricity that can be used in homes and businesses. It is common for hydropower facilities to utilize dams in order to control the water flow. Building dams affects the surrounding landscape, flooding areas of natural habitat.[18]

Small or low-impact hydropower facilities can be an emissions-free form of electricity production, with minimal environmental impact compared to larger hydroelectric projects. Low-impact hydro projects often are marketed as green power options. However, hydropower projects are dependent on a stable water supply. In recent years, choices over allocation of water resources due to shortness of supply have brought many to question relying on hydropower for electricity production.[19]

## Biomass Energy

"Biomass energy" is a term used to describe the use of plants and plant-based materials to produce energy. The term also is sometimes used to describe the waste from agricultural crops as well as animal waste and municipal waste materials.

Biomass can be used to produce electricity as well as gas fuels and heat. In regard to renewable energy production, biomass is the second most common method of energy production in the United States, behind only hydropower. Biomass accounts for 3 percent of primary energy production in the United States.[20]

Using biomass for energy production is discussed frequently as a possibility for increasing the energy independence of the United States while also reducing greenhouse gas emissions by reducing the use of fossil fuels. However, the production process through which biomass is converted into energy for use does have environmental impacts. Simply producing the feedstock that is the main building block of biomass results in greenhouse gas emissions. When the natural landscape is altered in order to clear more land for the production of feedstock, greenhouse gas emissions increase in these areas as well.[21]

Carbon dioxide is still emitted when biomass is used for energy production. Biofuels are considered carbon neutral because when a new feedstock crop is produced, it removes carbon from the atmosphere. Photosynthetic plants absorb $CO_2$ and emit oxygen. However, using biofuels may not result in an exact energy equivalent to using fossil fuels; therefore, the reduction in emissions would be slightly less as well. As stated previously, the process to produce ethanol results in emissions. Soybean diesel is estimated to reduce carbon emissions by 78 percent compared to an equivalent use of fossil fuels.[22]

Emissions related to the production of feedstock include $CO_2$, methane, and nitrous oxide. When plants are removed from the land, carbon that was stored in them is emitted into the atmosphere. Much of the nitrous oxide emissions come from the use of fertilizers used in cultivating feedstock. Water is used throughout the production process, from irrigation, to transformation of the feedstock into biofuels. Therefore, availability of water can be a limiting factor when selecting sites at which biofuels can be produced. As with any change to land use, there is the potential to affect nearby waterways with runoff, sedimentation, and nutrient flow—all of which can potentially impact the quality of the nearby water supply.[23]

## Solar Energy

There are multiple ways in which the sun can be used for energy production as well as for heating and cooling systems. Solar energy systems generally come in three forms: photovoltaic arrays, solar thermal systems, and concentrating solar power.

Solar photovoltaic, or PV, converts light energy into heat energy. PV cells are made of semiconductor materials, and multiple cells combine to create larger PV modules or panels. PV panels are widely used in various sizes, from powering small calculators, to traffic signs, to homes and businesses.[24] Crystalline silicon is the mostly widely used material for creating PV cells.[25] PV systems do not consist of PV panels only. An inverter is also required, which converts the energy coming through the panels into electricity that is usable inside your building or home.

Solar thermal systems use light energy to heat water used in buildings and homes. There are two parts to a solar water heating system: solar collectors and a storage tank. Direct-circulation solar thermal systems use pumps to move potable water through the system. Indirect-circulation systems pump heat-transfer fluids through the collectors rather than actual water. Heat exchangers then transfer the heat from the heat-transfer fluids to the potable water.[26]

Solar concentrating power uses mirrors to reflect light onto receivers that convert solar energy into heat. The thermal energy from that heat can be used to produce electricity using either a stream turbine or a heat engine that drives a generator.[27]

Concentrating solar power systems are usually larger systems, most likely utility scale.[28]

The benefit of using solar is that the energy is produced in the same place in which it is consumed, whether the panels are placed on a rooftop or a ground-mount system.

## Wind Energy

Producing electricity from wind does not release emissions, and it prevents emissions from being released from the burning of fossil fuels.[29] For example, a 1.5-megawatt wind turbine can displace 2,700 metric tons of $CO_2$ per year, which is equivalent to planting 4 square kilometers of forest per year. Using wind energy will also reduce national water consumption, as 50 percent of all water use in the United States is for the purpose of electricity generation.[30]

In some places in the United States, wind has become the least expensive form of production for new utility-scale electricity generation.[31]

There has been some public discussion about the environmental impacts of large-scale wind farms. Specifically, there is concern over the impact of turbines on birds and bats. While there have been bat and bird fatalities related to wind turbines, the occurrence of such instances is decreasing. This is mainly due to improved methods of site selection—specifically avoiding the installation of wind turbines in areas with high bird or bat populations or areas that sit within the migratory path of birds.[32]

Wind energy facilities have a lower impact on birds than do many other human-related activities. Buildings have a much larger impact on bird deaths throughout the United States.[33] The case is similar for bats, with the impact of human activities from the spraying of pesticides that impact the diets of bats to the location of communities that disrupt their hibernating patterns.[34]

Wind plants are relatively quiet compared to manufacturing facilities or road traffic. The sound of the wind often is louder than the turbines. In hilly areas, the sound of the turbine may carry farther than it does in flat terrain. Most of the sound is a "whooshing sound" attributed to the aerodynamic nature of the wind spinning the turbines. The mechanical sounds of the turbine operation are negligible, as turbines have been designed with sound barriers to block the sound of the gearbox. The level of sound that is permitted at a given site is determined locally.[35]

## Geothermal Energy

Throughout the United States, the first 10 feet below the Earth's surface remains at a relatively constant temperature around 50 degrees Fahrenheit (10 degrees Celsius). Using geothermal heat pumps, which consist of pipes buried in shallow areas below the Earth's surface, accessing the temperature beneath the ground allows for the cooling of buildings during the summer and heating during the winter. A heat exchanger allows for the transfer of the warmer air into the house during the winter, and it pulls the relatively hotter air out of the house during the summer. In the summer, this heat can be used to heat hot water. These heating and cooling processes are emissions free.[36]

# Overview of Options for Purchasing Clean Energy in the United States

For options in other countries, readers should consult local energy councils and ministries.

## Federal Incentives

Incentives are at the heart of changing attitudes and behavior. What to make an incentive and what to use as a source of revenue and financing (e.g., a tax) is difficult.

There are now significant federal incentives for the installation of certain renewable energy systems. The Business Energy Investment Tax Credit gives a federal tax credit for a percentage of total installation costs for renewable energy technologies. For example, solar and small wind turbine operations are eligible for a 30 percent federal tax credit, while geothermal is eligible for a 10 percent tax credit. In its current form, federal tax credits are available for systems installed on or before December 31, 2016. No maximum dollar amount limits the amount that can be claimed for solar technologies. Eligible solar technologies include solar electric systems, heating or cooling systems, solar thermal systems for production of hot water, and hybrid solar lighting systems. Passive solar design and solar pool-heating systems are not eligible for the federal tax credit. There is also no maximum dollar amount that can be claimed for wind energy technologies that were installed after December 31, 2008. Eligible wind turbines include those that are up to 100 kilowatts of capacity.[37]

### Survey of U.S. State Incentives
- 21 states have grant programs for renewables.
- 27 states have loan programs for renewables.
- 42 states and DC have net metering programs.
- 37 states have property tax incentives for renewables.
- 14 states have a solar provision within their Renewable Portfolio Standard.[38]

## Purchasing On-Site Clean Energy

SOLAR ENERGY    There are multiple variables to consider when assessing whether installing solar on your site makes sense. Some of the variables are physical and others are financial.

The amount of electricity produced from a PV system depends on the amount of the sun's energy available at a given site. Within the United States, the southwestern states receive the most amount of solar energy.[39]

South-facing roofs and panels are the optimal orientation for PV panels in the northern hemisphere. Local weather conditions can change the orientation of your panels slightly, so you will want to take these into consideration when planning the installation of your PV system.[40]

You will want your roof to have unobstructed access to the sun. You will want to consider landscaping, such as trees that might shade the roof at certain times of the day or year. You will also want to consider any adjacent buildings that might shade your roof. Some states enable you to purchase easements in order to maintain access to the sun's energy for your system.[41]

If your roof does not prove to be an ideal place for a PV installation, the panels can also be installed on the ground, either on a fixed mount or by utilizing a tracking system that follows the sun throughout the day.[42]

You will need to consider the how many solar panels you can fit on your roof and the size of the system that you would need. Your roof may be too small or not have enough optimal area to install the size system that would have an impact on your electricity use.

When planning for the installation of your solar electric system, you will need to understand local covenants, permitting, and zoning regulations. Permits can be obtained through your local county or city building department. Applicable permits for solar installations can include both building and electrical permits. Usually these are obtained by the company that installs your PV system. Local covenants can include homeowners' associations and historical preservation requirements. Obtaining the appropriate permits can add additional costs to the total installation cost of your solar electric system.

Having an optimal site for solar is one of the first considerations. Next you will need to assess the financial variables related to solar. The cost of electricity at your site is important to use in your calculations. Areas where electricity prices are higher may make more sense for a solar installation than where electricity prices are lower. Your payback period generally will be quicker in areas where electricity prices are higher.

As discussed previously, federal incentives are offered throughout the United States. This tax incentive covers 30 percent of the total installation costs. Solar electric technologies also qualify for accelerated depreciation, classifying the systems as five-year systems, reducing the company's tax liability during that five-year term.[43] Additionally, there are also state incentives, including grants and tax credits. Some state incentives require documentation of an evaluation of your site for utilizing solar energy. It may require that your site be free from shading during certain hours of the day at certain times of the year.[44] There are also local incentives offered at the county or municipal level, including production tax credits.

Not only will a solar electric system save you money, but it can also make money for you. Net metering allows you to sell excess electricity that your solar electric system produces back to your utility company. This is increasingly becoming the preferable method for designing a system rather than utilizing a battery as backup. Net metering is set up differently in different states, based on legislation that requires utilities to compensate solar electric system owners in certain ways.

When a system produces excess electricity, that electricity can be put back into the grid to be used by others. A bidirectional meter will track the amount of electricity that is sent into the grid. Customers will then be credited for electricity that they use from the grid, assuming that their PV system does not produce enough electricity to meet all of their needs, which is safe to assume for systems without a battery for backup.

Electricity used when the sun is not shining will be pulled from the grid. In some states, any credit left on a customer's account will effectively be owned by the utility without compensation to the customer. In other states, the utility will actually write a check annually to the customer for excess electricity that is generated but not credited. Readers are referred to their local government to ascertain if their state requires utilities to write a check.

Selling solar renewable energy credits (SRECs) is also an option for some owners of solar electric systems. In states that have a Renewable Portfolio Standard (RPS), there may be a certain requirement that the utility companies and electric suppliers have to produce a certain percentage of their electricity from solar electric sources (see Figure 15.1). If the entity does not meet the requirements on an annual basis it

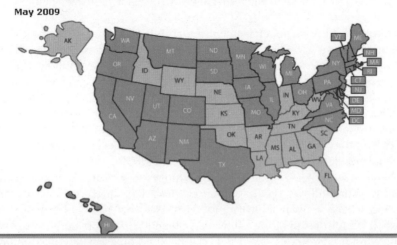

**U.S. Department of Energy – Energy Efficiency and Renewable Energy**
EERE State Activities and Partnerships
## States with Renewable Portfolio Standards
Select a state on the map below for a link to an explanation of the renewable portfolio standard (RPS) for that state published by the Database of State Incentives for Renewable Energy (DSIRE).

- Map Linking to Descriptions of State Renewable Portfolio Standards
- Chart Summarizing State Renewable Portfolio Standards

A renewable portfolio standard is a state policy that requires electricity providers to obtain a minimum percentage of their power from renewable energy resources by a certain date. Currently there are 24 states plus the District of Columbia that have RPS policies in place. Together these states account for more than half of the electricity sales in the United States.

Five other states, North Dakota, South Dakota, Utah, Virginia, and Vermont, have nonbinding goals for adoption of renewable energy instead of an RPS.

**May 2009**

FIGURE 15.1   States with RPSs.

is required to pay an alternative compliance payment (ACP). For many utilities, it is more cost effective to pay the ACP than to pay for the installation of solar electric systems. As a financing mechanism for solar electric systems, states allow electric entities to purchase SRECs from solar electric system owners. Utilities and electric suppliers can use these SRECs to satisfy their solar requirement.

There are presently 24 states plus the District of Columbia that have RPS policies in place. Together these states account for more than half of the electricity sales in the United States. Five other states, North Dakota, South Dakota, Utah, Virginia, and Vermont, have nonbinding goals for adoption of renewable energy instead of an RPS.[45] The RPS requires that load-serving entities, utility providers, and suppliers produce a certain percentage of their electricity from renewable sources. The minimum requirement for the RPS increases over time, and the standards are expected to be met on an annual basis.

There are ways to utilize on-site solar electricity production without the high up-front cost of installing a solar electric system. Some companies will install solar panels on-site while maintaining ownership of the panels. Through a Power Purchase Agreement (PPA), you can contract with one of these companies to purchase electricity produced from the solar electric systems at a set price for a certain number of years. These contracts are usually between 20- and 30-year agreements. You can lock in a rate with the company that might be a premium at the current electricity rates, but with the expectation of electricity rates rising in the future, it could be equivalent to a utility rate.

An alternative financing mechanism also allows you to forgo the high up-front cost of installing a solar electric system by leasing solar panels.

Nonprofits may have benefactors that are interested in financing a solar electric system at the nonprofit's site. The nonprofit can pay back the benefactor for the installation over time. These can be a periodic payment made to the benefactor or the nonprofit can pay a smaller rate per kilowatt-hour of electricity used than what its utility charges.

**STATE POLICIES AND THEIR IMPACT**  In Maryland, the Renewable Portfolio Standard is intended to encourage growth in the renewable energy industry. The standard for Maryland is 20 percent by 2022. The RPS is implemented by the Maryland Public Service Commission.

These standards can be met by purchasing Renewable Energy Credits (RECs) from renewable electricity generating facilities. In Maryland, the RPS also requires that a minimum amount of electricity be produced from solar electricity generation. Solar-specific requirements are meant to ensure that the RPS is not met solely by least-cost technologies, such as wind technologies and landfill gas capture technologies. Maryland is required to have 2 percent of its electricity production from solar electric systems by 2022.

Those who install PV systems in Maryland can sell their SRECs to load-serving entities required to comply with the renewable portfolio standard. As stated previously, annually these entities are required to meet their standards, or they will have to pay an ACP. It makes financial sense for these Load Serving Entities (LSEs) to purchase SRECs at prices lower than their ACP in order to comply with the RPS. Thus, as a result of the solar carveout, an additional financing mechanism has been given to solar photovoltaic system owners.[46]

In Maryland, additional financing from solar is available from grants administered by the Maryland Energy Administration. The Maryland Solar Energy Grant Program is funded by the Regional Greenhouse Gas Initiative and the American Recovery and Reinvestment Act. PV systems can qualify for $1.25 per watt for the first 1,000 watts (DC) of capacity, $1.00 per watt for 4,001 to 8,000 watts, and $0.50 per watt for 8,001 to 10,000 watts. The maximum grant amount is $10,000.[47]

**WIND ENERGY**   Multiple resources can be used to assess the wind resource at your site. Anemometers provide the most accurate representation of wind resources for electricity production. These devices can be utilized directly on the site at which you would like to install your wind turbine. National and state maps also can provide wind resource information, but they are not site specific. Further, it is important to note at which height this data is gathered. Many times the data are gathered at 50-foot levels; however, in many cases 75-foot or 100-foot levels are optimal for electricity production.

Zoning and permitting can restrict the height of your turbine, how many turbines you can install on your property, and in some cases if a turbine is even allowed to be installed on your property. In areas where utility-scale and residential wind turbines have yet to be utilized as a method for electricity production, the process for obtaining appropriate permits can be long and cumbersome. This is due in part to the fact that local governing bodies have yet to analyze and address how they would like to regulate and address the installation of wind turbines. Some local regulations may set the height limit for the wind turbine much lower than the optimal height for electricity production. Other local regulations may make height restrictions so that the entire turbine could fall on the property on which it is installed without falling onto a neighbor's property.

Pricing is also an important consideration in choosing whether to install a wind turbine for electricity production. As with solar, the utility price of electricity should be included in calculations to evaluate whether the price of electricity makes the installation more or less of a financially viable option. When choosing the capacity of your wind turbine, consider your electricity use when deciding on the size turbine that you would like to install.

State grants may also be available for the installation of small or residential wind turbines. Net metering is also available for systems that produce more electricity than necessary for consumption.

Community wind projects are those that are owned at least partially by residents and businesses using the energy that is generated from the wind turbines. The opposite of a community wind project is an "absentee" project, where ownership of the project is held by a utility or private investors. The local economic benefits are more limited in an absentee project.[48]

## Purchasing Clean Energy through the Grid

About 50 percent of electricity consumers have the option of purchasing green power from their electric supplier. Everyone has the option of purchasing Renewable Energy Certificates. There are numerous programs through which consumers can purchase green power. Green pricing allows customers to pay to have green electricity at a premium over their standard electricity supply rates. Customers also have the option in competitive markets to choose to purchase their electricity from an alternative supplier that offers green electricity. Green certificates allow customers to purchase the environmental attributes related to the production and use of green electricity.[49]

**U.S. ELECTRIC GRID** The U.S. electric grid covers the majority of the United States. Traditionally the grid connects large power generation facilities centrally located to where electricity consumers are located. The location of large power generation facilities resembles a hub; they are located near a large city to provide power to that city or are located in the middle of three cities in order to generate power for all three cities.

There are two components to the grid: high-voltage electricity lines, which transmit the power from the plants to locations miles away where it will be used, and lower-voltage transmission lines, which transmit the power directly to the end users.[50]

**REGIONAL TRANSMISSION ORGANIZATIONS** Regional transmission organizations (RTOs; see Figure 15.2) can be nonprofit or for-profit entities. They are independent organizations that operate transmission systems and provide wholesale transmission services throughout defined geographic regions. RTOs generally cover multiple states. RTOs typically do not own transmission facilities but operate them on behalf of the utilities that own the facilities. In addition to operating transmission service, RTOs may serve other functions, including facilitating or operating day-ahead energy markets, planning transmission, monitoring markets, managing the queue for generator

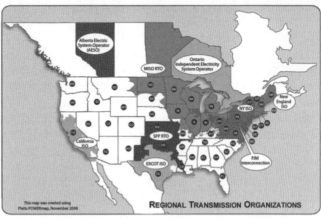

**FIGURE 15.2** Regional transmission organizations.

FERC: "Industries—RTO/ISO," Federal Energy Regulatory Commission, August 20, 2009, www.ferc.gov/industries/electric/indus-act/rto.asp.

interconnections, and administrating transmission tariffs for transmission service. According to the Federal Energy Regulatory Commission, RTOs are important in their ability to minimize transmission owners' favoring the use of their own generation facilities, to facilitate the development of market-based approaches to congestion management, and to enhance the reliability of electricity service through regional transmission planning and operation.

RTOs have the potential to both encourage the entrance of renewable technologies into the electricity market and create barriers to entry in some instances. RTOs broaden the market for selling renewable energy, allowing for transmission relatively far from where the electricity is produced. However, RTOs may place tough financial penalties on generators that cannot meet all scheduled power deliveries.[51]

### Deregulated versus Regulated States

There are four main types of electric utilities within the United States. Investor-owned utilities (IOUs) are for-profit companies that are owned by their shareholders. States allow IOUs to franchise certain areas of the states in which they serve. The states then regulate the IOU rates and distribution system. Public power utilities are not-for-profit entities that can be owned by cities, counties, or Native American tribes. These are generally not regulated at the state level but rather by the local governing body. Cooperatives are not-for-profit entities that are owned by their members. Federal utilities are generally wholesale utilities that provide electricity to private utilities.[52]

Many states throughout the United States are experimenting with deregulated electricity markets, with the goal of offering customers more choices in their electricity supply. The ideal result would be increased efficiency and reduced transaction costs, as companies in a competitive market will find innovative ways to provide products that their customers want at a lower cost. Deregulation also attracts new investment in many areas, increasing the funds that can be used to building infrastructure. Also, with additional supply companies acting in the same market, reliability of electric supply is expected to increase.

In deregulated states, customers have the option of choosing their electricity supplier. Many times the distribution of the electricity and ownership of the power lines will remain with the utility supplier.[53]

## What Is a Renewable Energy Credit?

Purchasing renewable energy certificates (RECs) allows you to contribute to the generation of renewable energy if you do not have the option of purchasing clean energy from a competitive supplier. RECs are also referred to as green certificates, green tags, or tradable renewable certificates. RECs allow for the separation of environmental attributes from the actual power that is produced. Renewable energy producers can sell their electricity at market value while selling the RECs, or environmental attributes, separately in order to make up for the higher cost of generating green power. The additional income encourages growth in the renewable energy market.[54]

Once an electron enters the grid, it is impossible to track exactly where that electron goes—no matter if it was produced from a wind turbine, coal-fired power plant, or solar electric system. For every 1 megawatt-hour (or 1,000 kilowatt-hours) of electricity that is produced from a renewable source, a REC is created.[55]

Certification and verification are both important considerations when purchasing RECs. Certification ensures that the product that you are purchasing meets a wide variety of environmental and consumer standards. The certification process validates the environmental attributes that you are purchasing when you buy RECs. Verification is provided by third-party auditors to ensure that the green power that produced the REC was in fact put into the grid and that the environmental benefits are available for purchase. Certification and verification protect consumers so that no two consumers purchase the same product. Two organizations that certify RECs are the Center for Resource Solutions through the Green-e Program and Environmental Resources Trust, Inc.[56]

RECs can be used by utilities and suppliers to meet mandatory generation requirements. In regions where there is a mandatory compliance for the use of renewables in electricity generation, RECs can command a higher price than in regions where there are no standards or compliance is voluntary.

In some regions, electric customers have the option to purchase RECs as a bundled product from green power marketers, utilities, and electric suppliers. The product bundles together traditional electricity used from the grid with RECs to match the customer's electricity use. The customer's electricity use is therefore effectively carbon neutral. Customers also have the option to purchase RECs without switching from their electricity supplier. In most cases, these RECs can be sold throughout the United States.

RECs are a valuable means of encouraging growth in the renewable energy market for multiple reasons. RECs allow for the monetization and separation of the environmental value of renewable electricity from simply power generation. The REC systems use efficient markets to distribute those environmental attributes to those that value them the most. The systems also provide a cost-effective means for compliance with renewable portfolio standards. Purchasing RECs also allows consumers to direct their funds toward renewable sources of energy rather than relying solely on what their utility or supplier provides.[57]

Purchasing carbon offsets has both similarities to and differences from RECs. The environmental and technological attributes of both are also divergent. A carbon offset is also a tradable financial unit, but it represents a certain quantity of greenhouse gas emissions reductions from implementing a project. Carbon offsets are usually measured in tons of $CO_2$ equivalent. In order to qualify as an offset, renewable energy projects cannot sell RECs, as this would be double counting.[58] The money involved in purchasing carbon offsets frequently goes to the funding of carbon sequestration projects. Some of the projects include reforestation projects and forest preservation projects, as trees are thought to be the best currently available means for sequestering carbon that has been released into the atmosphere as a result of human activities.

When comparing the purchase of carbon offsets versus the purchase of RECs, it is important to understand your organization's goal in making that purchase. If you are concerned with the emissions related to your use of electricity, purchasing RECs seems to be the more logical option. RECs directly benefit renewable, emission-free technologies, and encouraging growth in those technologies has a significant impact on the carbon emissions from electricity use going forward. Offsets simply sequester a portion of the carbon that has already been released. No funding is given to projects that plan for curbing future emissions.

## Empowering Your Community to Switch to Clean Energy

Once your organization has made the decision to switch to clean energy, there is a fantastic opportunity to expand the educational impact of the purchase through broader outreach to your community. In this case, your community means your members, supporters, employees, and other interested stakeholders. You can leverage the environmental impact of your clean energy purchase by getting your community to join you in this endeavor.

Depending on the market you are in, there are different options for affiliate programs that you can run. If you are in a deregulated market, you can strike a deal with a competitive energy supplier to promote its clean energy product in exchange for a member benefit or donation to your organization. For example, the energy supplier might offer a payment for each customer you help sign up. The payment could come in the form of a donation to your group, a free membership for a customer, a green "goody" (tote bag or something else environmentally friendly), or money toward a community project. This kind of situation is a win-win for both parties. For you, you are raising needed funds, or acquiring new members, or supporting a project in your community. For the energy supplier, it is getting new customers and associating with your organization. Before entering an arrangement such as this, be sure to research the supplier you are considering. You do not want to affiliate with a supplier that acts in a way that is detrimental to your community or that does not share your values.

## Communicating Your Clean Energy Message

Once you have made your switch to clean energy, communicating the message behind the switch is extremely important. The content of the message should include your commitment to environmental sustainability, the actual environmental impact of the purchase, any additional relevant details, and information on how your community can get more involved. Like all good messages, your green message should be clear, simple, and easily accessible to your target audience. It is also important to get stakeholder buy-in for your message. Senior staff and interested personnel should be included in any work done on crafting the message. The message must be followed up with action and leadership. It is not enough to manage and administer your energy use. The organization or firm's leader must lead it as any other essential element of the overall operating strategy.

## Conclusion

Making the switch to clean energy is an extremely important step to green up your organization and take responsibility for your carbon footprint. Given the impact global climate change has socially, economically, politically, and, of course, environmentally, it is incumbent on every organization wishing to make positive change to make an effort to solve this problem. Standing on the sidelines is not an option, no matter what your organization's specific mission is.

There are multiple incentives and benefits for switching to clean energy, depending on where your organization is located. It is important to do your homework and fully understand your options before making a decision. Once you make the switch, it is important to communicate to your stakeholders, employees, and supporters. You should craft a message about your clean energy commitment, and use that message in every aspect of your organization's communications. At the end of the day, the most important thing is to be taking a step forward toward a cleaner, better future.

## About the Authors

**Gary Skulnik** cofounded Clean Currents, LLC, after several years of working in the nonprofit environmental field as an advocate for clean energy solutions to global warming. He founded the Clean Energy Partnership in 2004, a nonprofit green business group based in Maryland, where, among other things, he led efforts to market global warming solutions to small businesses. Gary was the lead advocate for passage of the landmark 2004 Maryland Renewable Portfolio Standard and the 2006 Maryland Healthy Air Act. He has worked for groups such as Greenpeace, Sierra Club, and the Chesapeake Climate Action Network. Gary also has a background in public relations and marketing as well as television writing for CNN. He has a BA from Vassar College and an MA from the University of Miami, Florida. Gary is currently on the board of directors of the Maryland/DC/Virginia Solar Energy Industries Association.

**Michael Goodsite**, MBA, PhD, is the National Environmental Research Institute Professor of Atmospheric Chemistry, Climate, and Global Processes at Aarhus University. He has served as chairman of the University of Southern Denmark's chemical registration and inventory system and for its Department of Physics and Chemistry, where its chemical management systems were positively noted in an international evaluation of laboratories. He advises the University of Delhi on rebuilding and renovation of its labs. His scientific background is supplemented with an MBA in global management, and he serves on boards of directors and boards of advisors of for-profit and nonprofit organizations in the United States, Denmark, Iceland, and Canada. His research focus is climate mitigation and strategy, coupling local and corporate-level climate mitigation and strategy with national and global processes.

## CHAPTER 16

# Advocacy for Green Nonprofits

## Clinton O'Brien

Look up a definition of "advocacy" in the dictionary and you will see some variation on this theme: that advocacy is an activity aimed at influencing and changing society's established rules or behaviors, in order to directly change people's daily lives.

People who engage in advocacy—for kicks, let us call them "advocates"—are intentionally trying to upset the status quo and/or build on it with new ideas and rules that they think are better than existing ones. Advocates "want to change the world from what it is to what they believe it should be," said the great community organizer, Saul Alinsky, in his book *Rules for Radicals*.[1] Or to take liberties with Robert F. Kennedy's famous words, advocates either "look at things the way they are, and ask why" or else "dream of things that never were, and ask why not?" Or both.

Advocating credibly and effectively requires practicing what you preach, of course. Otherwise, it is hard to persuade others. Internally greening your organization and its practices is indisputably the most important initial step you can take, and this book is packed with concrete steps and resources to help you do just that. But suppose you and your colleagues have taken those steps to at least put your organization's house in order, and you are well on your way to becoming a green organization. Then advocacy becomes not only "possible" as a next step, it becomes the absolutely essential next step. Fortunately, there is an increasing supply of "green" methods to conduct successful advocacy, to boot.

Is advocacy for everyone? No, but some level of advocacy is worth doing for most nonprofits. Nonprofits that decide to become "green" must early on decide whether their mission—and human "bandwidth"—will extend far enough to include advocacy. That is, they face the choice of either focusing their energies primarily inward, on transforming their organization into a sustainable, environmentally and socially responsible nonprofit, or else they can also direct some of their energy outward, by evangelizing green practices to other nonprofits, businesses, governments and the public. In other words, will the organization become an advocate for the green movement? There are many reasons why your answer should be a resounding *yes*.

Why is engaging in advocacy so important? One way to think about this is in the religious framework, considering the different types of sins. We all know about sins of *commission*, which are the things we do that are bad, wrong, or otherwise in conflict with our conscience or some system of values. (Think murder, theft, cheating, lying, etc.) But many religions also tell us that we commit sins of *omission* when we fail to affirmatively, wholeheartedly devote ourselves to doing the things that are right and good, such as feeding the hungry, clothing the naked, comforting the sick, or defending those who cannot defend themselves. Using this kind of religiously inspired framework, or simply a secular framework to advance social justice, it is not sufficient for us only to clean up our own act and become conscious green practitioners of sustainable activities. We have got to do more. We have got to create a ripple effect and get other people to follow our green example—both in what we do and in the way we do it.

## Creating a Ripple Effect

This imperative to create a ripple effect, and influence other people, is a lesson that dawned 10 years ago on pioneering green entrepreneur Judy Wicks, whose popular White Dog Cafe for many years enjoyed the unique position of being the sole restaurant in the city of Philadelphia known for buying and serving only humanely raised animal products and sustainably grown produce from local family farmers. In addition, Wicks made sure that 100 percent of the White Dog Cafe's electricity was purchased from wind power generated in Pennsylvania, and she paid her more than 100 staff members a living wage. She was a social capitalist devoted to pursuing the triple bottom line of people, planet, and profit.

Word got around that the White Dog Cafe was a different kind of restaurant. It acquired a "do-gooder" status that gave Wicks a lock on the city's socially responsible patrons, including legions of green-minded college students from the adjacent University of Pennsylvania who to this day help ensure that it is hard to get a table at the cafe.

But in 2002, Wicks realized that if she was really serious about her mission of social responsibility and environmental sustainability, she could not be content with having differentiated herself so successfully from other restaurants in the city, no matter how financially rewarding her de facto monopoly status was. Instead, she felt a nagging duty that compelled her ultimately to take a sledgehammer to her cozy niche by persuading other city restaurants to copy what she had done and green their own practices, too. The vehicle for this was a 501(c)(3) nonprofit organization, called White Dog Community Enterprises (WDCE), which Wicks founded in 2002 to spread the gospel of sustainable, local food sourcing among restaurant chefs, grocers, and wholesale food buyers in Philadelphia and beyond.

Fast forward seven years, and WDCE has established itself as a green nonprofit that successfully advocates by using the marketplace as a vehicle for social change. Today, thanks to WDCE, dozens of restaurants in Philadelphia are trying to be green, following the White Dog Cafe model of buying ingredients from local, sustainable sources. WDCE's "Fair Food" program even builds wholesale markets for local farmers and improves distribution channels for locally grown food while educating shoppers and expanding their access to this food coming from farmers whose practices are people, animal, and earth friendly. In addition, WDCE recently spun off a second successful nonprofit, called Sustainable Business Network of Philadelphia, that fosters green practices among businesses across the city and region.

Judy Wicks's epiphany that it was her duty to evangelize through advocacy—that she could not just settle for having greened her own practices—is in fact a realization that comes to many successful green activists. In 1986, Rink Dickinson cofounded the highly successful fair trade coffee cooperative Equal Exchange. Then until the late 1990s, Dickinson basked in the knowledge that his organization enjoyed nearly 100 percent U.S. market share as the only source of fairly traded (and sustainably sourced) coffee, most of which in the early days came from the Sandinista-led nation of Nicaragua. But then as the message of Dickinson and other fair trade activists began to take root, more and more fair trade enterprises were launched, and Equal Exchange's share of the U.S. fair trade coffee market began to fall. Today Equal Exchange's coffee sales have never been higher, and yet its share of the U.S. market is only 7 percent. But Dickinson is happy. This is exactly what he says he wanted all along—to build up consumer demand for fair trade products and to entice new companies to enter the field.

Although green advocates like Judy Wicks and Rink Dickinson initially distinguish themselves as iconoclasts and pioneers, they achieve their greatest ultimate success when their green values become so widely adopted that they are no longer considered unique—when such values become mainstream. When this happens, so does real and lasting change.

## Advocacy = Fundraising

A nonprofit that commits to advocacy as part of its mission is not only doing a noble and useful thing for society. It is also doing something that can help the nonprofit immensely in its marketing activities and even generate major revenues.

This is because many nonprofits have learned to use advocacy activities as an effective vehicle for identifying and recruiting supporters, many of whom subsequently make donations to the organization.

For example, among green nonprofits, some of the greenest are environmental groups that advocate vigorously in favor of renewable energy and against pollution, especially against carbon emissions that cause global warming. The Sierra Club, Environmental Defense Fund, Natural Resources Defense Council, and the Wilderness Society, just to name a few, are all examples of environmental groups that use their advocacy programs partly as a way to recruit donor leads. Some percentage of these leads, even up to 15 percent or more, ultimately can be cultivated into becoming donors to the organization.

This tendency to use advocacy both for its own sake and as a fundraising tool has increased dramatically since the fast adoption of the Internet in the 1990s. As we will discuss, the Internet is proving to be a much greener means of conducting grassroots advocacy than direct mail was. But at the same time, the Internet also is proving to be a more effective means of acquiring, cultivating, and converting donors, too. Today there are nonprofits raising many millions of dollars online this way each year, and of course Barack Obama's historic 2008 presidential campaign dramatically illustrated the power of using online, cause-driven advocacy to raise a gargantuan volume of small-dollar donations from citizen supporters. How dramatically? Of the heart-stopping $745 million that Obama's campaign raised, it is estimated that more than

$500 million came from 3 million individual citizens donating online at an average gift level of only $80. In fact, 93 percent of Obama's campaign war chest came via donations of less than $100.

The Obama campaign's inspirational fundraising results cannot be chalked up to some kind of freakish anomaly, either, because nonprofits in a wide array of advocacy issue categories—especially green issues—have found a strong and unmistakable link between the propensity of citizens to take action on behalf of a cause and their propensity to make a financial contribution to nonprofits. In fact, fundraising experts say that a person is almost four times more likely to donate to a nonprofit if the organization first cultivates a relationship with the supporter by asking him or her to take action in an advocacy campaign, such as by signing a pledge or petition or making a phone call to an elected official.

Why is an advocacy supporter so much more likely to make a donation than someone who does not participate in advocacy?

A major part of the answer seems to be that advocacy is a medium of strong and binding engagement. By prompting citizens to take an advocacy action on behalf of your organization, you are giving them a relatively easy way to do something for your cause and helping them climb what fundraising professionals call the "ladder of engagement." You are also creating solidarity with the citizens, who then feel a part of the cause or movement. If they were not fired up about the cause when they started the process, your engaging them to join and help the cause over time may well bring out their passion, possibly leading to financial support.

There are many tools and techniques involved in successful fundraising using advocacy campaigns, but this topic is beyond the scope of this chapter. Here we focus primarily on how nonprofits can conduct advocacy in a greener and more sustainable manner. For more information, look at Appendix A.

## "501(c)...What?"

As nonprofits wade into the surging waters of advocacy, it is important for them to carefully consider what their goals will be and to make these goals as concrete and achievable as possible. Nonprofit leaders should ask: What is my organization advocating for? What problems are we seeking to address? How will we measure success? Is there a discrete result—such as the passage or defeat of a bill in Congress—that will signal either a victory or a defeat for our efforts? How will we engage our supporters to enlist their help in achieving our advocacy goals?

Along the way, it is also legally important for nonprofits to decide how deeply into advocacy, and particularly election-related advocacy, they want their organizations to go. Depending on the answer, they may need to create a separate, stand-alone legal entity, called a 501(c)(4), to engage in activities that constitute attempts to influence the outcome of a political election.

The U.S. Internal Revenue Service (IRS) dictates that the typical U.S. nonprofit organization, which is usually registered as a 501(c)(3), in order to preserve its special tax-exempt status, may not directly or indirectly participate in any political campaign for or against a candidate for elective public office. The IRS rules likewise bar a 501(c)(3) from making financial contributions to political campaign funds or public statements (verbal or written) for or against a candidate for political office.

There is a loophole of sorts in these rules that allows a 501(c)(3) to engage in "voter education" activities, including statements at public forums and by publishing voter education guides, as long as these educational activities are nonpartisan in nature. Many nonprofits take advantage of this loophole to do voter education on their key issues. Similarly, a nonprofit is free to engage in get-out-the-vote activities, including urging people to participate in elections instead of staying home, but only as long as these activities are unbiased and nonpartisan. (The IRS is actually pretty strict about these rules, having threatened to revoke even the tax-exempt status of the Roman Catholic Church, following election-year statements by some U.S. Catholic bishops who urged parishioners to vote for or against specific presidential candidates based on positions on such issues as abortion rights.)

But if a nonprofit does not want to limit its political activities to voter education, then it has another perfectly good option—one that many nonprofits have used. This is the option to set up a 501(c)(4) organization that is financially independent of the 501(c)(3) and viewed as a completely separate entity in the eyes of the law. Unlike a 501(c)(3), this other type of organization is allowed to lobby for legislation (e.g., in Congress or in state legislatures) and to participate in political campaigns and elections. However, the 501(c)(4)'s political purposes must be secondary to its social welfare purposes. Also, the money spent by the 501(c)(4) on trying to influence political elections may be a taxable expenditure. For more information, consult the information about social welfare organizations on the IRS Web site at www.irs.gov. For that matter, if you are thinking about setting up a 501(c)(3) or a 501(c)(4), you should always consult with an experienced lawyer who can advise you on the best ways to do it and the pitfalls to avoid.

## Getting Started with Green Advocacy

How does a nonprofit get started doing green advocacy? And isn't advocacy something that takes a lot of resources, so that only big nonprofits can do it well?

Actually—no. In the past, it was true that mostly only well-endowed organizations had the wherewithal to organize and mobilize supporters on a large scale and thereby to compel the attention of government and corporate officials. This was due partly to the costs of travel needed to organize supporters and obtain petition signatures and because one main advocacy recruitment and communications tool was direct mail, which is a comparatively expensive—as well as decidedly ungreen—undertaking.

But thanks to many recent technology advances, travel and direct mail are no longer as necessary as they once were. Most important, the Internet has served as a powerful leveling force for grassroots advocacy that, to a remarkable extent, puts smaller and larger nonprofit organizations on a more equal footing. The Internet enables even a small nonprofit to mount a significant grassroots advocacy program with very few actual staff members dedicated to the effort, although it definitely helps to have volunteers—at least remotely located ones—to help engage supporters with regular communications about the group's activities and goals.

Social media author Clay Shirky, who wrote *Here Comes Everybody: The Power of Organizing without Organizations*, notes that the Internet has changed the game for people seeking to accomplish great things. "We are living in the middle of a remarkable increase in our ability to share, to cooperate with one another, and to take collective action, all outside the framework of traditional institutions and organizations," Shirky says.[2] The result is that even people working outside of established nonprofit institutions can take powerful advocacy actions, just acting as informal and often ad hoc, collaborative groups. One key success factor that social media gurus like Shirky have identified is the principle of "pushing power to the edge" or "network-centric campaigning" in which a movement's leaders equip its supporters to take actions on their own, leveraging their own personal networks on behalf of a cause.

Perhaps the best-known champion of this new empower-your-supporters approach is author-entrepreneur Seth Godin, who uses the metaphor of a top-down "funnel" to describe the way that most companies, and nonprofit organizations, historically have marketed to the public.[3] Godin says organizations typically have worked hard to expose their brand and messages to the maximum number of people—the wide mouth at the top of the marketing funnel—in the hope that some of these people will travel all the way down and pop out through the narrow bottom of the funnel as strong, loyal supporters and donors. To boost success, marketers thought, just try to get the word out to the maximum number of people, pouring more of them into the top of your funnel.

But that is hard and inefficient, Godin says. The marketing environment has become so crowded that it is a huge challenge just to get noticed by the public, who increasingly tune out the barrage of messages they get every day. Instead, Godin urges organizations to "flip the funnel" and turn it into a "megaphone" instead, to leverage the power of word-of-mouth and peer-to-peer marketing. Invest most of your attention and resources into cultivating relationships with those strong, loyal supporters and donors who are popping out through the bottom of your funnel, Godin says. If you properly motivate and equip them with content and tools about your organization's work and mission (i.e., give them a megaphone), then these supporters will spread word of your cause and recruit more supporters for you, with more credibility and influence, than you ever could do on your own. In recent years, more and more nonprofits have applied these principles with more and more success for their advocacy efforts.

## Greener Advocacy Tools

The Internet and other telecommunications tools also enable nonprofits to conduct advocacy in a much greener way than previously was possible. One of the most important advances is the ability to stop using direct mail, which is perhaps the most ungreen practice that most nonprofits have depended on for decades.

What is so bad about direct mail? For starters, it mostly uses heavy stock paper to boost weight and perceived quality. Unfortunately, the long fibers needed to produce heavier stock paper preclude using much recycled paper content. Direct mail also must be delivered by the U.S. Postal Service or some other means, using up more fossil fuels and increasing pollution and greenhouse gas emissions. But the most ecologically damaging aspect of direct mail is its relative wastefulness. Roughly 44 percent of all direct mail is thrown in the trash without ever being opened— leading critics to call these solicitations "junk mail." In fact, the U.S. Environmental Protection Agency (EPA) estimates that 4 million pounds of direct mail is thrown away annually, with less than one-third of it recaptured through recycling. All told, an average of only 2.8 percent of direct mail sent to consumers each year succeeds at producing a response, so direct mailers have to send out about 36 pieces of mail for every 1 response that they get back. From a conservationist point of view, such waste is unconscionable. It is not surprising that by the end of 2008, 12 state legislatures had "Do Not Mail" bills under consideration, and as of this writing, in 2009, two more bills had been introduced—plus an anti–direct mail resolution was near adoption in one major U.S. city.

Travel is another costly but critically important tool that nonprofits historically depended on to mobilize advocacy supporters. Yet air travel, especially, is a huge source of greenhouse gas emissions. Fortunately, many successful advocates have shifted away from travel and instead are using widely available, low-cost or no-cost phone and video conferencing services as a means of holding meetings with field representatives, supporters, and coalition colleagues. Some of the new tools, such as video conferencing software from provider iLinc, even provide nifty "green meter" features to track how much carbon you are avoiding releasing into the atmosphere by not traveling to meet in person. (You can also track the money you are saving.) Using similar principles, travel providers from Amtrak to Travelocity and the major airlines now enable consumers actually to purchase carbon offset credits online when they buy their tickets, thereby offsetting the damage of their travel on the environment. Nonprofits can use such features to reduce their own net contributions to global warming.

Yet another key advance in the world of greener advocacy is the online petition, which has propelled the once-laborious task of gathering expressions of public support and moved it light-years ahead. The great Quaker abolitionist Thomas Clarkson, whose heroic eighteenth-century journeys by horseback through England obtained hundreds of thousands of signatures on antislavery petitions to present to Parliament, never could have dreamed that one day an online petition could gather 10,000 signatures per day, or 100,000 signatures in just a few weeks, without anyone's having to saddle up to travel anywhere. As only one of many such examples, Care2's petition site (www.thepetitionsite.com) in 2008 alone collected more than 15 million signatures on thousands of petitions created by both nonprofit organizations and legions of ordinary citizens determined to win advocacy victories large and small, global and local. (See Figure 16.1 for an example of a petition on Care2.com, created by nonprofit advocacy group Environmental Defense Fund to garner support for a bill in Congress to reduce global warming.)

Advocates certainly should try hard to reduce or eliminate direct mail and unnecessary travel, and to avoid buying newspaper and magazine ads for similar reasons. But it is also important for nonprofits not to lose sight of the forest for the trees. That is, major environmental advocacy groups routinely fight battles that, if successful, might preserve or protect an entire forest, or millions of square miles of ocean, or save an entire endangered species. With so much at stake, it sometimes is justifiable—or even advisable!—to put less emphasis on "ecological correctness" than on winning the battle, even at the cost of creating some direct mail waste or emitting some carbon due to airplane travel. In other words, green advocates should not slavishly adhere to green principles to the extent that it prevents them from achieving much more important and far-reaching benefits for our environment. At the same time, though, it is always more credible, and less risky from a public relations perspective, for an advocacy group to not just talk the talk, but also walk

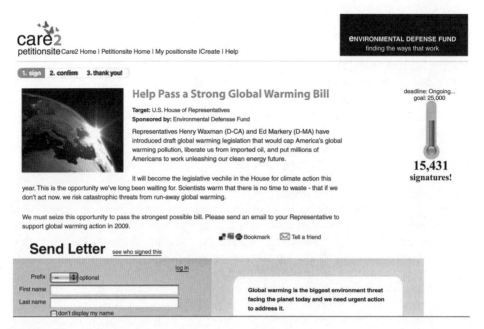

**FIGURE 16.1    CARE2 petitionsite.**

*Source:* www.thepetitionsite.com/takeaction/792682449

the walk. For an example of how not to behave, consider the universally bad impression made by the chief executive officers of Ford, Chrysler, and General Motors in 2008 when they each flew separate private jets to Washington to testify before Congress about why the U.S. government needed to bail out the auto industry. This unwise decision severely undermined the corporate leaders' credibility, just at the time when lawmakers were demanding that they rein in their companies' expenses and start building greener, more fuel-efficient cars.

The bottom-line message for conducting green advocacy is to deemphasize as much as possible travel, direct mail, faxes, and other paper-based means of conducting advocacy and marketing and instead focus on e-mail, online petitions, conference call meetings, videoconferencing, and other electronic tools to get the job done without depleting resources or emitting carbon.

## Putting Together a Green Advocacy Team

What does a high-functioning, green advocacy operation look like? Typically, an advocacy team at a national nonprofit will have a field director to organize on-the-ground operations, and this field director will interact with contacts with supporters nationwide at local chapters or affiliates. These supporters may be staffers or they may just be volunteers. A large advocacy department may also have a government relations director who is responsible for lobbying activities on Capitol Hill to serve as the nonprofit's liaison to members of the U.S. Congress, their staffers, and the staff of various congressional committees with influence over policies. The government relations director may also be responsible for keeping track of key policies and rulemakings at certain federal agencies of interest to the nonprofit, such as the EPA if the organization's mission is focused on the environment.

Increasingly the advocacy operations of national nonprofits have another star player, the online advocacy director, whose role has become very important in recent years. The online advocacy director is the person in charge of adapting the organization's overall policy positions and messaging for communication via the nonprofit's Web site and e-mail communications, such as e-newsletters and e-alerts. This online advocacy director is, by necessity, part editor-in-chief, part copy writer and part Webmaster, equally comfortable with writing up articles about various aspects of the nonprofit's cause as with filling out spreadsheets to track the in-box deliverability, open rates, click-through rates, and action rates of the nonprofit's online grassroots e-mail campaigns.

If the online advocacy director is lucky, he or she might also have access to some good online tools, including a robust e-mail marketing tool, such as Constant Contact (or one of many competing products) that is capable of tracking the open, click-through, and action rates of the nonprofit's online grassroots e-mail campaigns. If really lucky, he or she might have access to a full-featured online constituent relationship management (CRM) tool—some examples include Convio, Blackbaud, Democracy in Action, and Capitol Advantage. This kind of CRM tool can provide built-in measurement of key metrics of an e-mail campaign, allowing for tactical changes to be made in real time, to optimize the campaign's results. In addition, a CRM tool enables the nonprofit to provide conditional content to users that is tailored to specific subsets of the organization's user base. For example, a sustainable agriculture nonprofit might maintain two separate lists of supporters, one that is meat eating and another one that is strictly vegetarian, and tailor the content of each group's e-mail messages accordingly.

Nonprofits thinking about hiring an online advocacy director might find useful this sample job description for an online advocacy director at a statewide nonprofit organization. To some extent, the job combines advocacy, public relations, and marketing—and the person who is hired will be uniquely able to set green policies to guide the way that the organization pursues its advocacy goals.

### Director of Advocacy and Communications

Washington State Nonprofit X Headquarters Office (Elmwood, Washington)

The Washington State Nonprofit X Association is seeking applicants for the position listed below. To be considered for this position the following documents are required:

- Cover letter
- Updated resume reflecting qualifications for this position
- Signed application form
- Five (5) professional references
- A writing sample provided at the time of the interview. Prior research is not required.

Washington State Nonprofit X application forms are required. If not attached, applications may be obtained at the Washington State Nonprofit X office located at 32032 Tractor Way South, Elmwood, WA 98001 or by calling Human Resources at 253-766-0000 or 1-800-3383 extension 7002.

**Responsibilities**
- Direct the statewide operation of the Washington State Nonprofit X. Manage the day-to-day functions of our progressive, action-oriented and member-driven advocacy team. Develop and help manage the department's $2.5 million budget.
- Develop and implement internal and external communications plans and programs for our 80,000 members and education stakeholders around our state. Your work encompasses member communications, marketing, public relations, advertising, media relations, online and new media/social networking.
- Serve as a management team member and participate in overall management of the Association.
- Advise governance leaders and management on communications and public relations strategies including collective bargaining.
- Work with communications staff to develop both earned and paid media campaigns and strategies, integrate online and offline strategies into all plans, and oversee media relations.
- Develop and execute broad-based communications plans that include benchmarks and measurements for success.
- Work collaboratively with public policy team in developing communication plans, setting strategy and crafting messages around ballot initiatives, legislative sessions, political campaigns, policy development, and other mission-related actions.
- Direct work of outside consultants including but not limited to pollsters, media firms, ad agencies and graphic designers.
- Write plans, speeches, white papers, messaging, presentations, member communications, and other materials as needed.
- Conduct training sessions and/or provide appropriate counsel to Association leaders on communications, media, and PR issues.
- Manage staff to include hiring, evaluating, mentoring, and coaching.

**Minimum requirements**
- Bachelor's degree in journalism, communications, public relations, public affairs, marketing, or related field.
- At least five years' experience in communications, public relations, or related field in positions of increasing responsibility including positions guiding strategic planning and/or directing other team members.
- Proven experience in developing communications plans, setting strategy, and executing plans with measurable successes.
- Experience with local and large-scale organizing campaigns.
- Experience in developing integrated online strategies and advancing organizational goals through the use of new media.
- Excellent presentation skills and experience in speaking/presenting in front of groups larger than 50.
- Excellent written and verbal skills.
- The ability to think strategically and translate organizational goals into integrated communications strategies and tactics.
- The ability to think creatively to translate organizational goals into eye-catching, off-the-wall, or guerrilla strategies that could generate buzz, spread virally, and/or generate earned media.

- Ability to work well in a team environment, juggle multiple priorities under pressure, respond to tight deadlines, and answer to numerous stakeholders with competing needs.
- Strong working knowledge of Microsoft Office, including PowerPoint and/or Adobe Creative Suite products.
- Strong understanding of audience identification and analysis, including experience in using polling and research to craft messages.
- Ability to work collaboratively with a six-person communications team, and to foster and encourage a fertile, creative work climate.

**Preferred job requirements**

- Experience developing a vision for new or expanded communications strategies and programs.
- Experience in and knowledge of sustainability issues.
- Graphic design skills and knowledge.
- Experience with paid advertising campaigns including work with ad agencies on creative development and media placement of TV, radio, and newspaper ads.
- Experience in a union environment, government agency, public sector organization, or nonprofit.
- Experience in and/or knowledge of the political process and political strategy planning.
- Experience in working in a progressive, member-driven environment.
- Experience in developing and conducting communications/media/public relations training.

## Online Social Media as a Green Advocacy Tool

Yet another potentially powerful resource for nonprofits to use in conducting green advocacy is the new breed of online social networks, including Facebook, MySpace, LinkedIn, YouTube, Flickr, Digg.com, StumbleUpon, and Care2.com. Facebook alone has more than 200 million members worldwide, and roughly 25 million of these members (as of this writing) have downloaded a software application called Facebook Causes, indicating that they have at least some basic level of interest in supporting causes. The presence in these social networks, involving so many people who might be willing to take advocacy actions to benefit a cause, is obviously very attractive to nonprofit organizers. However, it is also true that reliable tools and models for driving social network users back to nonprofits' own Web sites or for persuading these social network users to sign up for the nonprofits' e-mail lists are still only emerging, and bona fide success stories are few. For this reason, many nonprofits so far are justifiably reluctant to assign staff members to work full-time on so-called social media activities to cultivate supporters in the online social networks. What is clear, however, is that hundreds of thousands, and in some cases millions, of social network users have "friended" many of the nonprofit organizations that have established a presence on these networks. Whereas these linkages have not translated so far into fundraising successes for most of the nonprofits, they have opened up a new channel of communication—for example via Facebook's so-called news feed—that potentially could be utilized to recruit advocacy supporters for causes.

They are also undoubtedly useful for creating buzz about new initiatives, which sometimes is useful in achieving public relations objectives, such as attracting the attention of members of the mainstream media or other influential people.

Nonprofits seeking to drive social network members back to their organizations' own Web sites would do well to think broadly about which online communities to target in their efforts. The relevant set may extend far beyond just Facebook and MySpace. For example, The Nature Conservancy (TNC) has been a pioneer in recent years at actively cultivating relationships with environmentalist-minded supporters in MySpace, Facebook, and other online communities. Until recently, this role fell to Jonathon Colman, who led TNC's social media efforts. But Colman reported that, even though he spent a great deal of time trying to engage with TNC's supporters on Facebook and MySpace, he actually got more results—as measured by visits back to TNC's Web site at www.nature.org—by cultivating users of people-powered news network Digg.com and social bookmarking Web sites StumbleUpon and Del.icio.us, as well as to a lesser extent the TNC discussion group participants on do-gooder community Web sites such as Care2.com. Colman also said that he invested considerable time in building out a presence on photo-sharing site Flickr.com and video-sharing site YouTube.com with some good results.

As of this writing, another online social network that is starting to become a significant source of Web traffic and new supporters is the microblogging network Twitter, which limits its users to posting short status updates of no more than 140 characters at a time. Many nonprofits have reported success in using Twitter to spread the word quickly about their campaign initiatives, including advocacy campaigns.

A sample job description for a social media intern, a position that is popping up more and more often at many nonprofits these days, is presented next.

### Social Media Intern

[Nonprofit X] is looking for an intern to support its online outreach efforts and advocacy campaigns. We're looking for someone who knows about social networking and blogs but, more important, wants to learn how to crack these sites' potential in getting people involved to protect the environment and curb global warming. You'll learn about our existing presence on these sites as well as research and implement ways to improve it. Work hours are flexible and can be determined on a per-candidate basis. Telecommuting arrangements are possible. This is a great opportunity to use the skills that you have gained by doing things you do every day for fun (watching videos on YouTube, updating your MySpace profile, etc.) all while making a difference to preserve the environment and curb global warming.

*Specific duties include:*

- Help manage our organization's social networking profiles (MySpace, YouTube, Facebook, Flickr, Care2).
- Expand our network of friends and supporters online by actively participating in the blogosphere and on social networks.
- Research potential social networking and advertising opportunities and partnerships.
- Respond to reader comments in the blogosphere.
- Monitor buzz on environmental topics and mentions of our organization online.
- Explore new Web 2.0 technologies like Twitter and Digg.com.
- Stay abreast of nonprofit technology and Web 2.0 trends.

- Learn organizational priorities and policies and ensure they are reflected accurately in online correspondence.
  *Skills needed include:*
- Familiarity with social networking sites and blogs
- Basic HTML/Cascading Style Sheets knowledge
- Familiarity with Web 2.0 technologies such as widgets and RSS (Really Simple Syndication)
- Proficient with Microsoft Office
- Basic knowledge of environmental and global warming issues
- Solid communication and organization skills
- Exhibit good judgment when communicating online
- Quick learner

## Types of Advocacy: Everyday, Grassroots, and Grasstops

Nonprofits can choose from three main types of advocacy in which they can engage: everyday, grassroots, and grasstops. Some experts divvy up advocacy into many more types than this, including ideological, bureaucratic, budget, and media advocacy, just to name a few. But for most purposes, these three main types are helpful ways to consider how your nonprofit can become an effective and green advocacy organization. Of course, these three approaches are not mutually exclusive, and many organizations combine two or even all three types to maximize their opportunity to create lasting change.

### Everyday Advocacy

Everyday advocacy is the most basic form, and in many ways the most profound. Everyday advocacy is based on the idea of setting a powerful example and then ensuring that as many people as possible know about it. Everyday activists model the behavior that they want others to follow and educate the public about the value of this behavior.

In many ways, the carbon-neutral movement, in which people and organizations pledge to reduce carbon emissions and/or support projects to offset their carbon emissions, exemplifies everyday advocacy. The more that organizations (both for-profit and nonprofit) publicly pledge to become carbon neutral and take concrete steps to achieving carbon neutrality in their operations, the more peer pressure is brought to bear on every other organization to follow suit. These organizations are leading by example in order to bring about change on a massive scale.

Similarly, social pressures are growing for nonprofit organizations to green their workplaces through recycling programs and energy-conscious remodeling projects. In a growing number of cases, nonprofits are investing significant resources into such projects and attempting to obtain recognition for their efforts by meeting the U.S. Green Building Council's Leadership in Energy and Environmental Design (LEED) standards for energy savings, water efficiency, reduced carbon emissions, improved indoor environmental quality, and stewardship of resources and sensitivity to their impacts.

The Chesapeake Bay Foundation (CBF), which is dedicated to saving the Chesapeake Bay from pollution and protecting its fish and wildlife, earned the first-ever

"Platinum" LEED rating for its headquarters building—the Philip Merrill Environmental Center—which opened in 2001 on the banks of the bay. The visually striking building—which in some ways resembles a modern ski lodge on stilts—was designed and built according to Earth-friendly principles with recycled materials and processes that did not damage the environment. CBF's building needs very little energy for its cooling and heating—achieving an estimated annual savings of at least $33,000 in utility bills—because of smart placement of windows and skylights that maximize sunlight in winter and breezes in summer. The building also boasts special composting toilets that use very little water and make no negative impacts on the environment. CBF welcomes the public to take tours of the facility, which is considered a model of green architecture and construction. CBF calls it "one of the world's greenest office buildings."[4]

An hour's drive to the west in downtown Washington, DC, another very green-minded nonprofit—the Union of Concerned Scientists (UCS)—in 2008 opened its new office, for which the group earned the Green Building Council's "Gold" LEED rating, a rating that is second only to platinum. UCS's achieving the gold rating was no small feat; it is difficult to obtain such a rating for an urban building that was erected long before the LEED standards were created.

Both the Chesapeake Bay Foundation and the Union of Concerned Scientists have used their green office conversions as everyday advocacy opportunities, essentially by treating them as teachable moments for the public and other organizations. Both CBF and UCS provide extensive resources on their Web sites (CBF: www.cbf.org/Page.aspx?pid=389), painstakingly explaining, with photos and diagrams, the thinking that went into the greening of the office spaces. The UCS Web site even provides a virtual tour (www.ucsusa.org/about/our-sustainability-efforts) in the form of an online slide show of its environment-friendly offices in Washington and in several other cities. In this way, these nonprofits are not so subtly advocating to the public and their peer nonprofits how to green your workplace, as well as what the costs and benefits are.

Nonprofits that practice everyday advocacy have found Web sites to be terrific channels for reaching the public about all kinds of greening efforts, but there are many other excellent channels, too. Many nonprofits hold open houses and community forums to publicize their activities. Many organizations send speakers to address audiences at conferences, schools, and churches, leaving behind brochures, K–12 lesson plans, and other materials. Still other nonprofits hold awareness days—think "River Cleanup Day"—that both attract volunteers and earn media attention for the nonprofit's mission and activities.

## Grassroots Advocacy

The type of advocacy that grabs the most headlines and attention is grassroots, or mass, advocacy, in which a large group of citizens come together around a cause and then unite through holding massive demonstrations or by otherwise collectively demanding some kind of change. It is a centuries-old form of advocacy that in the United States is an enshrined right in the First Amendment of our Constitution, which protects the right of citizens "to petition the Government for a redress of grievances."

Some would say the first important example of grassroots advocacy was actually the signing in 1215 of the Magna Carta, the great charter that British citizens supposedly forced King John to sign guaranteeing certain individual rights. In actuality it was a group of British barons who forced the king to sign, so arguably that was more a case of "grasstops" advocacy (we cover that one next). But there is no doubt that by the eighteenth century, at least, the British were in the vanguard of using grassroots advocacy effectively. Citizen petitions to Parliament were common, and sometimes even effective.

In fact, one of the greatest early grassroots advocacy campaigns was led by British citizens, including the previously mentioned Thomas Clarkson. Over a period of more than 50 years, they tirelessly built a movement to force their Parliament to ban slavery throughout the British Empire, an action that ultimately fatally weakened American slavery, too, although the latter was not ended until after the U.S. Civil War. The antislavery movement in Britain was an especially major development for activists because it introduced many organizing techniques—from mass petitions to campaign posters and buttons, to logos, direct mail fundraising letters, and muckraking journalism—that are now familiar tools for grassroots organizers everywhere, including to the green activists of today. (For a riveting account of the British antislavery movement, read *Bury the Chains* by Adam Hochschild.

In the modern era, nonprofits large and small are using grassroots advocacy to advance the green cause on a national level—and they are doing so increasingly by using green tools.

**UNION OF CONCERNED SCIENTISTS**   One good example of a nonprofit's skillful use of green advocacy at the national level was a campaign conducted several years ago by the Union of Concerned Scientists, the same group we described as practicing everyday advocacy by greening its downtown Washington, DC, office space. The UCS campaign was in response to a proposal from officials at the EPA under then-President George W. Bush to greatly weaken the reporting requirements that for almost two decades had forced U.S. companies to report the type and quantity of toxic chemicals that they were releasing into the air, water, and land. These rules had been established under the Right-to-Know law enacted by Congress after the tragic 1984 chemical disaster in Bhopal, India. In that tragedy, an industrial plant owned by U.S.-owned Union Carbide released toxic methyl isocyanate gas into the air, killing about 2,300 people within the first two weeks and many thousands more gradually over the next few years. Green activists celebrated the Right-to-Know reporting rules as a prime example of successful pollution regulation that informed citizens about toxic pollution in their own backyards while also helping first responders prepare for chemical spills and other accidents.

Scientists and campaigners at UCS, outraged that the Bush administration would even contemplate rolling back the toxic chemical reporting rules, determined to mount grassroots opposition. The EPA had invited the public to comment on the proposal via the agency's Web site for a period of several months; thereafter, the EPA would decide whether to move ahead with weakening the reporting rules. In response, UCS sent out e-mail messages urging its thousands of supporters to write comments opposing the EPA's proposed rollback and then delivered those comments to the EPA's Web site. To ratchet up the pressure, UCS also sponsored a four-week petition campaign on online social network Care2.com, to recruit some of Care2's millions of member activists to join in opposing the EPA proposal, too.

By the time the EPA's comment period ended in January 2006, the agency had received more than 110,000 messages—almost all of which were from green-minded activists who fiercely opposed the notion of weakening the rules for toxic chemical polluters. Fully 31,265 of the comments—more than one out of every four—had been generated by UCS's efforts, including 18,368 gathered via the four-week UCS-sponsored petition campaign on Care2.com. In response to this public outcry, EPA backed down on its proposal, and a few months later a bipartisan group of members of the U.S House of Representatives voted 231 to 187 in favor of an amendment to protect the Right-to-Know rules against future attempted rollbacks.

In true green fashion, the UCS victory was won without requiring the use of travel, direct mail, newspaper advertising, or other methods that create negative impacts on the environment. Instead, the entire campaign was conducted online, mobilizing tens of thousands of citizen activists through e-mail and online petitions.

One by-product of the episode for UCS was that the organization greatly expanded its base of green e-activist supporters who were willing to take action on behalf of UCS causes. In addition to the more than 18,000 new UCS supporters recruited from the Care2 community, UCS recruited thousands of additional activists simply by urging their own incumbent subscribers on the group's e-mail list to forward UCS's appeals to their friends and families. This so-called viral growth, which does not incur any direct costs for the nonprofit organization, is one main benefit of engaging in online green advocacy. One reason such advocacy campaigns often deliver viral benefits is because they have a built-in sense of urgency—especially if there is a deadline, as was the case in the EPA struggle—and this urgency provides a handy justification for supporters to spread the word and become evangelists for the organization's cause.

**ILOVEMOUNTAINS.ORG**   Still another grassroots advocacy success that illustrates similar green techniques and principles is the remarkable "iLoveMountains.org" online campaign, led by a small green nonprofit called Appalachian Voices, based in North Carolina. This recent campaign gained justifiable praise because it combined the best of online peer-to-peer marketing techniques with an extremely interactive, so-called Web 2.0 approach that personally engages members of the public in a powerful and effective way.

The mission of Appalachian Voices is to empower people to defend the natural and cultural heritage of the Appalachian Mountains by providing them with tools and strategies for their own successful grassroots campaigning. In particular, the group has worked hard to stop a destructive form of coal mining—called "mountaintop removal"—in which entire mountains are literally blown up to obtain coal. Mining companies in this way have devastated hundreds of square miles of Appalachia, endangering wildlife and polluting the headwaters of rivers used for drinking water by millions of Americans, as well as harming the quality of life for people living in the mountains.

Appalachian Voices' small Web team in 2007 created their innovative iLoveMountains.org Web site, which uses Google's mapping software to show site visitors the tragic impact of mountaintop removals as well as ways to help stop this tragedy. For example, the site provides a tool enabling users to type in their zip code and find out if the electricity provided by their local power company is actually being supplied (as much public power is) by the same mining companies that are blowing up mountains to extract coal. This allows people to understand the direct personal connection between their roles as electricity consumers in creating the demand that prompts coal-mining companies to despoil Appalachian Mountains to meet that demand. It also creates a sense of responsibility among conscious consumers to do something about the problem. Then the Web site provides tools to do just that—for example, by signing petitions urging lawmakers to put a stop to mountaintop removals. Appalachian Voices also has conducted campaigns to promote the iLoveMountains.org Web site on Care2.com and other online communities that attract activist-minded citizens.

As part of helping users to "flip the funnel" and turn it into a megaphone—to use Seth Godin's concept—the iLoveMountains.org site incorporates software enabling users to keep track of how many people they get to sign up, how many people those people get to sign up, and so on, and shows how the campaign is spreading across the country in real time. The site also makes it easy for supporters to share links to powerful videos, photos, and audio clips on personal blogs and social networking sites such as Facebook, MySpace, YouTube, and Flickr.

The great news is that Appalachian Voices' innovative, green advocacy efforts appear to be paying off. As of this writing, the EPA under President Barack Obama has so far blocked five different mountaintop removal mining permit applications, raising concerns about the threat to water quality and asking the Army Corps of Engineers to place holds on the projects. In addition, legislation has been introduced in the U.S. Congress that would place major restrictions on mountaintop-removal coal mining.

This example shows yet again how a nonprofit can achieve advocacy success by leveraging low-cost Internet-based tools—and without resorting to costly direct mail, travel, and other less sustainable practices that in any case were financially beyond the means of Appalachian Voices to utilize.

## Grasstops Advocacy

Professional nonprofit advocacy organizers often use grassroots advocacy to get the government's attention—as in the UCS toxic chemical campaign example—and this is certainly true of the many grassroots advocacy campaigns that target members of the U.S. Congress. After all, members of the U.S. Senate or House of Representatives must be concerned about satisfying the voters back in their home district, if they want to be reelected. Any time a substantial number of these constituents collectively contact their elected representatives, those lawmakers usually pay attention. But professional advocates also know that getting a lawmaker's attention is usually only half the battle; you still have to convince him or her to do what you are asking.

In these situations, successful organizers often employ what is called grasstops advocacy, mostly as a way to distinguish it from the more widely known grassroots advocacy. In grasstops advocacy, sometimes called lobbying, the focus is not on the quantity of people calling for change but on the "quality" of those people, as measured by the strength of their influence with the authorities in charge. For example, a classic form of grasstops advocacy on Capitol Hill is to pay a visit to a lawmaker or member of his or her policy staff and to bring along an influential person whose opinion will compel respect. This may be an award-winning scientist who is a recognized medical authority and can speak credibly about the need for a proposed piece of health legislation. Or it may be a major employer in the senator's district, or the head of a labor union, or a wealthy donor to the senator's campaign—or someone else whom the lawmaker will perceive as being influential.

In each case, chances are the lawmaker or staffer will at least give the advocates a fair hearing, which significantly boosts their chances of success.

One intriguing example of modern grasstops advocacy was accomplished by the famous musician turned activist Bono of the Irish rock band U2, who spent many years persuading authorities in the United Kingdom, the United States, and other wealthy nations to forgive the debts of the much poorer developing nations of Africa and to provide aid to help them fight HIV-AIDS. Bono recognized early on that in order to get an aid bill through the U.S. Senate to forgive African debts, he would need to somehow win over Jesse Helms, the longtime Republican senator from North Carolina and notoriously conservative chairman of the Senate Foreign Relations Committee. Bono managed to get introduced to Jesse Helms's wife at a social event, which led to a private meeting in 2000 with the senator. As Helms described the encounter later, he was entirely won over by Bono's sincerity, knowledge, and persuasive powers. Helms ultimately threw his support behind a $200 million package that Congress enacted to provide U.S. assistance for African nations in the fight against HIV-AIDS.

The most successful nonprofit advocacy groups combine grassroots and grasstops advocacy in their campaigning to give themselves the best possible chance of success. For example, a recent campaign by the Marine Fish Conservation Network (MFCN) included visits to key congressional lawmakers by influential experts on the subjects of the fishing industry as well as the protection of endangered ocean fisheries. The purpose of these visits to the lawmakers, who chaired key House and Senate committees with jurisdiction over ocean-related legislation, was to advocate in favor of certain amendments to the Magnuson-Stevens Act, which is the main law governing the protection of endangered fish species in U.S. coastal waters. But at the same time, MFCN added a powerful grassroots component by delivering to the same lawmakers hundreds (and in some cases thousands) of signed letters and e-mail messages from the lawmakers' own constituents. The citizens' messages, which had been collected through old-fashioned door-to-door canvassing as well as via online petition campaigns that Care2.com conducted on MFCN's behalf, all supported MFCN's amendments and urged the lawmakers to do the same. In the end, the legislation was successfully reauthorized with most of MFCN's amendments included.

In this example, MFCN's online recruitment campaigns through Care2.com, which targeted only those congressional districts whose lawmakers wielded major influence over the fishing legislation, enabled MFCN to avoid using direct mail and travel and yet to show a very high level of public support in the American hinterlands (where it most counted) for the bill.

## Green Online Advocacy: Some Dos and Don'ts

There are hundreds of good practices that experienced online campaigners agree will enhance a nonprofit's chance of success at green online advocacy while employing advocacy tools that are green and sustainable. Here are a few major dos and don'ts.

**DO...**
- Engage with your supporters often and make it as interactive as possible. Consider running polls and surveys to invite their input, or ask them to "vote" on what your organization should do next to advance your cause.

■ Give your supporters concrete actions they can take for you, including making a donation. They will expect you to ask, at least occasionally, and some of them actually want to support you this way.

■ Positively reinforce your supporters' actions by reporting back to them when their efforts have resulted in a victory. It is okay to report back occasional defeats, too, as these can galvanize support.

■ Track each e-mail supporter's performance over time. In this way, you can determine which issues and sources are most effective at attracting your best supporters to the cause and which issues are best at retaining and engaging your supporters.

■ Give your supporters prominent, easy opportunities to unsubscribe from your e-mail to avoid being perceived as a spammer—which could result in your e-mails getting blocked by AOL, Google, Yahoo, HotMail, and other Internet service providers.

■ Set goals to continuously grow your e-mail list of supporters. You can do this by posting boxes on every page of your Web site for visitors to sign up for your e-newsletter as well as by taking advantage of the free-to-nonprofits "Google Grants" program to attract supporters by bidding on search keywords. You should also try to buy permission marketing campaigns from targeted, reputable online sources, especially those willing to guarantee you a specific number of e-mail sign-ups at a pre-agreed price (as opposed to traditional online advertising campaigns that come with no guarantee of lasting results).

## DON'T . . .

■ Pay supporters to take actions for you. This would leave you open to charges of astro-turfing—creating artificial grassroots support—and weaken your credibility.

■ Let too much time go by between communications to your supporters. One message per month is typically the minimum frequency, but once a week may be even more effective if you have enough news and meaningful actions for your supporters to take.

■ Send so much e-mail that your supporters start to unsubscribe or stop opening your messages. This is why it is so important to monitor the rate at which people are unsubscribing or ceasing to respond to your messages, as measured by e-mail open rates and click-through rates.

■ Send too little e-mail—this may be an even bigger mistake than sending too much! You do not want your supporters to forget about you or your cause.

■ Fail to segment your base of supporters—treating them all as generic. Over time, you should have a strategy for identifying clear differences among your supporters, at least for the "super-activists" who take the most actions, and vary your messaging to these segments accordingly.

■ Fail to be topical, by capitalizing on news that is in today's headlines. When the mainstream media is reporting on an issue that relates to your cause, you have a golden opportunity to recruit many new supporters—and/or raise money—by asking supporters to forward your petitions and messages to friends, family, neighbors, coworkers, and others. Be ready to pounce on such opportunities.

## Conclusion

This is an exciting time for nonprofits to use advocacy, and to do it in a thoughtful and green manner, in order to spread their mission.

The Internet revolution has given nonprofits a large toolbox of inexpensive and widely available tools, including open source software that can be used for free, to conduct green advocacy campaigns. These innovations have leveled the playing field for even the humblest organizations, which increasingly are being started by civic-minded individual citizens. Make no mistake: Money, resources, and know-how are still extremely valuable for any nonprofit, but peer-to-peer mobilization of activists via the Internet now makes it possible for every nonprofit to flip the funnel and enlist the aid of its staunchest supporters to spread the organization's mission far and wide, with exponentially greater impact than was possible in the past. This impact can be achieved at very little financial cost and at surprising speed. Zip-code driven search engines and mapping, as well as software to track the ripple effect of activists' efforts, have created ways to highly personalize a cause and help people as never before to "think globally and act locally."

Appendix A contains some resources that nonprofit professionals might want to check out to learn more about strategies and tactics for successful advocacy, particularly online advocacy, which will both save money and reduce negative impacts on the environment.

### About the Author

**Clinton O'Brien** helps nonprofit organizations win grassroots advocacy victories in his role as Vice President of Business Development for Care2 (www.Care2.com), the 12-million-member online social network founded in 1998 with a mission to enable its members to "make a difference." On behalf of its more than 500 nonprofit clients, Care2 mobilizes its army of "e-activists" to support good causes, such as by signing petitions that target government and corporate leaders, by phoning members of the U.S. Congress, by writing letters to newspapers, by filing public comments with federal agencies, and by volunteering, boycotting, making donations, and generally exercising their rights as engaged citizens.

Prior to Care2, O'Brien worked for nonprofit TV network PBS, first leading business development for the interactive division and then company-wide. For three years he led the PBS Adult Learning Service, a business supplying online courseware to colleges. In a past life, Clint spent seven years working as a news reporter in Washington, DC and overseas. In 1988, he won the National Press Club Outstanding Washington Correspondent award for investigative reporting on toxic chemical polluters. He later reported from Moscow, from 1991 to 1993, on the Kremlin coup and USSR collapse, for *Newsweek* magazine and the Associated Press. He is a contributing author to the book *Seven Days that Shook the World*, about the breakup of the Soviet Union. He holds an MBA in Marketing from Wharton and a BA in History from Brown University. He lives in northern Virginia with his wife and four children.

# Green Nonprofit Office Audit

# Green Audit

## *Green Nonprofit Office Audit*

### Ted Hart

With the assistance of Friends of the Earth Scotland, we offer this Green Non-profit Office Audit (nine questions with supporting information). It will help those putting a green office policy into practice and those who want to protect the environment but may not have the time or the money to overhaul the workplace immediately.

As you prepare to develop a green office environment (and to seek GreenNon-profits Certification; see Appendix B for application sample), it is important to review the resources your organization uses and to reduce the waste and pollution that is created each day. This audit will provide guidance in creating your greener office.

## Green Nonprofit Office Audit

This audit is designed so you can find out how green your office is. The audit includes basic information on identifying environmental impacts and will help instruct your planning process. Most of the questions will apply to all nonprofit offices. This audit will help you gather some important basic information about your office, take action, and track your progress.

Performing this audit is a good way to start gathering information and to determine if you are ready to start thinking about GreenNonprofits Certification.

Use the audit to look at each aspect of your office. Determine how your activities affect the environment, assess the significance of the impacts, and look at options to make low-cost and no-cost improvements.

Your group may decide to use outside consultants for a more formal audit or simply gather the information yourself.

### Nonprofit Green Audit Question #1 (Staff)

How many full-time equivalent staff members are there in your office? (Add up the hours of part-time staff/volunteers to calculate equivalent full-time staff numbers.)

### Nonprofit Green Audit Question #2 (Management)

(See Chapters 3, 4, and 16 for more green management and marketing tips.)

Is there currently a person or team responsible for greening the office? (This may be a voluntary or paid position.)

## COMMITMENT

**Management Commitment.**   The first step for a charity wanting to move toward becoming greener is to take the GreenNonprofits.org pledge. (This should be adopted by the board of directors and administration. It is also advisable to ask all staff to review and understand the pledge.)

---

### Green Nonprofit Pledge

I/We Pledge:

1. To become more aware, to practice, and to promote a healthy environment within our organization and community.
2. To learn about the effect of our nonprofit on the environment and to take responsibility for that impact.
3. To actively adopt environmentally friendly practices within our organization and community.
4. To take steps in advocating environmentally friendly practices to other nonprofit/NGO organizations.
5. To seriously consider moving toward seeking GreenNonprofits certification.

www.greennonprofits.org

---

The second step for any office wanting to improve its green credentials is to establish an environmental policy. This policy should explain to staff, suppliers, and customers where you stand on green or environmental issues.

It is imperative that the organization's chief executive, senior management, or equivalent adopt, authorize, and commit to this policy. It will be harder to maintain enthusiasm for greening the office without this real support and application of staff resources.

The organization should establish an environmental policy that states its aim to:

- Minimize the use of natural resources and lessen the impact on the environment.
- Meet or exceed all applicable regulations on the environment at all locations.
- Purchase nonpolluting and energy-efficient technologies wherever possible.
- Set its own standards and targets where no relevant government regulation exists.
- Establish an action plan with a regular review of progress.
- Measure progress against set targets for resource efficiency and pollution reduction.
- Assist suppliers and customers to promote greener products and services.
- Report fully the environmental performance of the organization to stakeholders and communities in a clear and concise annual report.

Once drafted, the policy should be accepted by the executive, trustees, board members, or equivalent. This will be your public policy on the environment. To implement your policy, staff time and resources will be required to take the next step in drafting an action plan: defining responsibilities and reviewing the progress of any actions taken.

**Coordinating Responsibilities.**   The next step is to appoint a coordinator (for a small organization) or committee (for the larger organization) to take special responsibility for implementing the initiative. Your committee should contain staff representatives, the building manager, purchasing officer, and senior managers. It is important that this team has adequate time and resources to sustain the green initiative. For some offices, one person may be sufficient. The coordinator should have access to all heads of departments.

Staff involvement in this work is crucial. People who are involved in thinking about why and how you are going green are more likely to support any actions your organization decides to take on. Going green can be a positive, team-building experience for your office.

**Action Plan.**   After the environmental audit and discussions with staff, your committee or coordinator should draft an action plan. This will spell out the actions you will take in areas such as paper buying, recycling, energy, finance, general office supplies, and transport.

Make sure your action plan is specific and realistic. *Starting small is always best—*you can always revise and update your plan when you have achieved some of your early objectives. Your plan should say how you are going to achieve each action, who will be responsible for carrying it out, and how the results will be measured.

An example appears in the next table.

| Office Activity | Environmental Impact | Product Source Quantities/Cost | Responsibility | Action/Time Scale |
|---|---|---|---|---|
| Paper buying. Purchase of chlorine-bleached, nonrecycled multifunction paper. | Resource use potential. Unsustainable use of forests and destruction of habitats. Pulp source unknown. Emissions. Energy use and carbon dioxide production. Persistent pollutants. Chlorine for bleaching and paper mill discharge of wastes. | Un-Green Paper Ltd. 200 reams per year $ ?.?? each. Green Supplies Inc. FSC-Certified 100% recycled post-consumer waste, totally chlorine free. $?.?? each. | Head of Procurement | Carry out paper use audit. *1st week of next month*. Employ paper-saving techniques. *Review 2nd month*. Discuss sourcing 100% recycled paper from Un-Green Paper. *Next purchase of paper supplies*. |

The action plan can be presented to the chief executive and senior management for approval and adoption. It is also important to let staff know that the action plan is a key part of workplace policy and that everyone is expected to play their part.

**Monitoring and Communication.**    Adopting an action plan is not the end of the process. The coordinator or committee should talk to staff and be prepared to listen to their comments. You need to know how these new policies are affecting their work habits. They may have come up with more ideas now that they are starting to think green.

Let staff know what results have been achieved. Produce charts and notices to display on staff comment boards or at the reception area so customers can see your efforts in protecting the environment.

## Nonprofit Green Audit Question #3 (Paper)

(See Chapter 8 for more green purchasing tips.)

  a. How many reams of office printing paper did your office purchase last year? (Include copier paper in this, too. A standard ream of paper equals 500 A4 sheets, and a carton or box contains five reams.)
  b. Of this, how many reams where made from virgin pulp or recycled post-consumer waste? (Look for approved eco-labels and standards accredited by an independent and verifiable body.)
     ☐ Virgin pulp
     ☐ Recycled post-consumer
  c. Of the office paper purchased, how much is recycled? (Include all paper, including newspapers and magazines. Majority is greater than 80 percent.)
     ☐ None
     ☐ Some
     ☐ Majority
  d. Are any paper-saving initiatives carried out in your office (e.g., desktop paper-saving trays or double-sided printing)? (Include initiatives that are carried out by the majority of the office.)
     ☐ Yes
     ☐ No

**PAPER**    The use of paper within the office is increasing despite the idea that technology would bring about the paperless office. It is important that the current use of paper within the office changes.

The use of virgin and old-growth forests for office paper is destroying habitats and communities in many parts of the world. The majority of these trees are used for low-grade timber and office paper. Added to this impact is the pulp and paper manufacturing process, which is energy intensive and a producer of considerable volumes of polluting waste.

To reduce these significant impacts, every office can take the next steps.

**Purchase paper:**
  ▪ That has a high-recycled content with a post-consumer waste content greater than 70 percent.
  ▪ That is totally chlorine-free during production.
  ▪ Sold with an accredited environmental or green label that details emission standards and post-consumer waste content.

## Paper-Saving Techniques

**Employ:**
- The most efficient possible use of paper with mandatory double-sided photocopying and printing.
- The use of e-mail and voicemail to minimize paper use.
- Green printing standards, printing paper documents that are as short as possible and only when necessary.

## Equipment Use and Paper Saving

**Learn how to:**
- Set the photocopier to print both sides as standard.
- Use the revision marking function available in most word processing software. Not only will this save paper, it will also save you time, because the changes have to be made only once rather than twice.
- Use once-used paper for draft copies in all desktop printers.
- Scan your letterhead into the computer to produce an electronic template copy.
- Reuse paper used on one side for fax cover sheets and notepaper.
- Retain documents on your computer (or using online storage services such as http://carbonite.com) rather than in hard copy. This saves paper, saves on file storage space, and keeps documents right at your fingertips.

## Paper Use Policy into Practice

**Establish:**
- Green printing standards with regular training and advice for staff and new employees. (A simple bookmark placed occasionally on each desk detailing basic paper-saving techniques will help to remind people.)
- Regular paper audits prior to the collection of recycled paper. Have a careful look through waste bins and estimate reused paper against once-used paper.
- Recycle points near workstations, and ensure that staff are clear which paper products are recyclable.
- Simple codes/guidelines for all staff so they can operate the photocopier correctly, that it is well maintained, and that mistakes that waste paper are avoided.
- Policy to purchase photocopiers and laser printers that give priority to those with duplex (copying on both sides) capability and to plain-paper fax machines. Give preference to equipment capable of using unbleached paper with up to 100 percent post-consumer recycled content.
- A space for publications on your Web site so reports and documents can be downloaded and viewed on-screen.
- E-mail lists to distribute the e-version of your latest reports. Urge those on your list to forward your reports to others, thereby multiplying the effect of your work.

**What Else Can You Do?**   Where reports or newsletters must be published in hard copy, there are many ways to reduce paper use:

- Print on both sides of the paper.
- Use line spacing of no more than 1.5.
- Lay out your publication with the minimum necessary white space.
- Avoid using varnishes during printing.
- If adhesive binding is necessary, do not use those containing chlorinated organic compounds.
- If you send out free reports, mail a postcard first, notifying recipients that the report is available if they want it and providing the means for them to order a copy.
- Label your publications with relevant environmental information about how it was produced.

The more readers know about the paper you use and how a document was printed, the more likely it is that they will consider using similar practices.

## Nonprofit Green Audit Question #4 (Energy)

(See Chapters 10 and 15 for more green energy information.)

  a. Does your office pay a green (renewable) energy tariff? Green Energy Tariffs are available in various parts of the world (China, Europe and the UK, Ukraine, Vermont). Typically they come in one of two types:
  *Renewable tariffs*
  On these tariffs, every unit of electricity bought by the supply company on behalf of the charity is generated by a renewable energy source.
  *Eco-fund tariffs*
  These tariffs involve the customer paying an additional premium which is invested in funds used to finance new renewable energy projects, often based in developing communities.
     ☐ Yes
     ☐ No
  b. Has an energy-efficiency survey been carried out at your offices? (Answer yes only if a survey has been conducted in the last 12 months.)
     ☐ Yes
     ☐ No
  c. Is nonessential office electrical equipment switched off overnight when not in use? (This includes computer monitors and copiers but not servers, fax machines, safety, or emergency equipment.)
     ☐ None
     ☐ Some
     ☐ Majority
     ☐ All

**ENERGY**   Scientific opinion is now united that the planet is facing an unprecedented period of climate change: a warming of the atmosphere leading to storms, rising sea levels, and unpredictable weather patterns. Our offices are contributors to this problem.

**Saving Energy in the Office.** Have an energy audit conducted. This will tell you where your greatest losses are and where you could make the greatest savings. These audits should look at all aspects of office energy including insulation, heating, lighting, and equipment use.

## Energy-Saving Tips

- Encourage staff to switch off lights, computers, photocopiers, and other electrical equipment at night. Enable energy-saving features on all computers and copiers.
- Ensure that lights and nonessential equipment is turned off when not in use.
- Replace normal filament bulbs with energy-efficient alternatives.
- Put the monitor to sleep rather than use screen savers; they often consume more energy.
- Consider energy efficiency when purchasing new equipment. Give preference to equipment with low-power standby or sleep features. Check with your supplier.
- Printers spend lots of their time idling. Compare the energy consumption of different makes.
- Keep a regular account of how much energy is used by the office, and set targets for reducing consumption to a practical level.
- Make sure external doors and windows are draft proofed.
- Regular maintenance of your heating system can improve efficiency.
- Insulate pipes and hot water tanks.

## Nonprofit Green Audit Question #5 (Recycling)

(See Chapter 13 for more recycling tips.)

Does this office recycle any of the following materials or products? (Answer yes only if there is a regular collection and recycling of these materials or products.)

**Plastic Bottles or Vending Machine Cups**
☐ Yes
☐ No

**Plastic Magazine Wrapping (low-density polyethylene [LDPE])**
☐ Yes
☐ No

**Aluminum and Steel Cans**
☐ Yes
☐ No

**Printer and Fax Cartridges**
☐ Yes
☐ No

**Office Electrical Equipment**
- ☐ Yes
- ☐ No

**Packaging**
- ☐ Yes
- ☐ No

**Fluorescent Lighting Tubes**
- ☐ Yes
- ☐ No

**RECYCLING**   The economic advantages of commercial recycling are clear. Commercial recycling programs can reduce waste volumes and disposal costs, provide revenue from the sale of recyclable material, and reduce operating costs. Recycling provides raw material to make new products and creates jobs in collection, processing, and manufacturing. Over time, recycling saves energy and natural resources and can enhance a company's public image.

Waste composition will vary from office to office, but most waste bins contain:

| | |
|---|---|
| Computer printouts | 29% |
| Mixed papers | 23% |
| Corrugated containers | 8% |
| Newspapers | 10% |
| **Total Paper** | **70%** |
| Other wastes: glass, metals, plastics, food, etc. | 30% |
| **Total Office Wastes** | **100%** |

*Source:* www.green-office.org.uk/audit.php?goingto=factsheet4.

**Setting Up a Recycling System.**   The basic rule is for recycling collection boxes to be situated in visible areas close to workstations, printers, copiers, or where staff often pass by.

- Maximize the convenience of use and collection. This will minimize the effort and contamination by nonrecyclable material.
- Provide clear notices for what is and what is not recyclable.
- If you collect ink jet and toner cartridges, put the old cartridge in the box of the new product. This protects the ink jet heads and avoids toner powder being spilled. If damaged, these products will not be recycled.
- For hazardous products, such as fluorescent tubes, store unbroken tubes in protective containers prior to collection by authorized recyclers.
- Ensure that there is a central area where colleagues can bring unwanted office supplies. These may include pens, staples, folders, and other general office materials. Put these back in the stationery cupboard for future use.

**Options for Small Organizations.**   If the amount of recyclables produced by your business is not enough for recycling collection service, you may wish to consider these options.

- Speak to your current waste carrier to see if it offers a recycling service. Ask if diverting recyclables from your current waste stream will reduce your collection costs, freeing up funds to pay for the recycling scheme.
- Check with recycling vendors to see if they will accept material that you deliver to their facility.
- Check with your local town or city recycling office to see if commercial recyclables are accepted at public recycling drop-off centers.
- Store materials for less frequent collection. Ensure that storage adheres to relevant health, safety, and environmental regulations (i.e., fluorescent tubes, waste oils, etc.).
- Contact other businesses in your area to set up a cooperative recycling program.
- Contact property managers of multitenant buildings or business parks; talk to local chambers of commerce and network with your own business contacts.
- Contact local charities, schools, and other groups that may be interested in picking up certain materials as a fundraiser or service project.

**Hard-to-Recycle Products.**   Most products are now recyclable. However, a few products prove more difficult. This may be due to the numbers of items, hazardous components, or lack of facilities to reprocess the material. This situation is common with certain plastics and packaging, batteries, televisions, and videocassette recorders.

- If possible, speak to the original supplier to find out if it has a take-back policy or recycling scheme.
- Contact a state or local waste exchange program to see if someone else can use your product. Do a Google Search for "Waste Exchange" and the name of your city, state or country for details.
- Specialist companies collect white goods, computers, and other information technology equipment. Often there is a nominal charge. If equipment is in working order, contact local groups and charities to see if they can reuse it or refurbish it for resale.
- Reduce the amount of hard-to-recycle products that you buy. This will ultimately reduce your waste costs.
- As commercial recycling improves and as the amount of landfill space diminishes and becomes more expensive, it will be financially viable to recycle rather than dump.

It is important to recycle or dispose of products and components in an environmentally responsible manner. Always ask for written documentation on any service being offered.

### Keep Publicity Up

- Make sure your recycling schemes get as much publicity as possible.
- Produce posters and flyers and use internal e-mails to remind everyone of how and what to recycle and how well it is going.

- Special events, debates, talks, and visits to other organizations can maintain the enthusiasm.
- Ensure there is a commitment from top management and that they take part in office recycling. Put a bin by their desk/area.

Experience shows that individual resistance from colleagues will diminish as the system gets under way and everyone sees how simple it is.

**Monitoring and Communication.**   Keep a record of how much the office recycles each week or month. By recording how much you recycle, the office can achieve a number of outcomes. Chart the number of:

- Ink jet cartridges recycled and the volume of oil saved in using remanufactured products.
- Reams of paper per person recycled and equivalent energy or carbon dioxide saved in production.
- Equivalent numbers of trees with habitats saved. (Seventeen trees are needed to produce 1 ton of paper—enough for around 7,000 copies of a national newspaper (*source:* http://www.earthgreetings.com.au).)

**Long-term Success.**   To ensure long-term success of your recycling program, it is important to establish a contract or agreement with a reputable recycler. Recycling service fees and/or payments tend to vary according to fluctuating commodities markets. Get further information from your supplier.

**Questions to Ask a Recycler**
- What authorization or licenses does the company hold to collect, transfer, and send to disposal the products in question? Ensure that you receive written confirmation of competency and conformity with relevant regulations.
- Will the company be able to accept the amount of recyclables that you produce?
- How should materials be prepared (separated or mixed)?
- Who pays for the cost of the program?
- What conditions are associated with the costs/charges associated with the program?
- Will there be a rebate for any of the recyclables? If so, under what conditions?
- How will the pricing structure work (fixed price or price tied to market index)?
- Will assistance be provided for collection containers, promotional materials, or training?
- Will recyclables be collected on a scheduled or on-call basis?
- If confidentiality is a concern, are document destruction or confidentiality assurances available?
- How must materials be prepared (consolidation in a central location or for pickup from a pickup point)?

Do not let recycling hide the priority aim of reducing the amount that you consume in the first place.

## Sample Recycling Memo

Scan your letterhead and use it here.
TO: All Employees
FROM: [Chief Executive]
SUBJECT: Office Recycling
Program On (DATE), (OFFICE NAME) will begin an office recycling program. The objective of this program is to recycle (LIST PRODUCTS) that we generate in the (OFFICE/FACILITY).

The recycling program is simple and will require few changes in our daily habits. Each (DEPARTMENT/DESK) will receive a special recycling box in which you should place uncrumpled acceptable types of paper instead of throwing it in the waste bin. A list of the types of paper we are trying to recover is attached to this memo and is printed on the recycling boxes.

At your convenience, please take the accumulated paper to one of the nearby central collection containers. These containers are located _____ (enter locations staff can find collection containers).

The material that we currently shred will continue to be shredded as usual and will be recycled. If you feel more comfortable tearing a document before placing it in the recycling container, please feel free to do so. The size of the paper does not matter.

There are also white boxes with lids and two holes for your used drinks cans. They are located in (LOCATIONS). Please make sure that the cans are completely empty. We are only recycling used beverage cans, so do not place food containers in the boxes. Please do not use the recycling containers for other waste. Soon we hope to have composting facilities for kitchen/catering waste. (GREEN OFFICE TEAM NAME) is currently looking at other environmental impacts as a result of office practice. Your (GREEN OFFICE TEAM NAME) will be circulating an e-mail on important forthcoming initiatives soon.

On (DATE), there will be a 15- to 20-minute training program for all employees. Training sessions will be scheduled every half hour during the day, so that all employees can attend without disrupting business. We will distribute a schedule so that you can attend this important meeting.

The success of this program depends on you. (COMPANY) is doing its part to reduce the amount of waste sent to landfill or incineration facilities and protecting our environment.
**Please join us and recycle!**

### Nonprofit Green Audit Question #6 (Catering)

Is office kitchen or catering waste collected for composting? (This includes regular collection and composting carried out by a staff member or composted in an office wormery.)

☐ Yes
☐ No

## Nonprofit Green Audit Question #7 (Water)

(See Chapters 12 and 14 for more tips on managing chemical use and green water practices.)

Are water-saving devices fitted within office toilets and washrooms (e.g., variable flush handles, flush sensors, or low-flow taps)? (Answer yes only if the majority of areas are fitted with water-saving devices.)

☐ Yes
☐ No

WATER   According to the World Health Organization, less than 1 percent of the world's fresh water, or 0.007 percent of all the water on Earth, is readily available for human consumption.[1] Fortunately, there is still enough for our needs, if we use it wisely and avoid contaminating a precious resource with harmful pollutants.

There are many ways in which both water use and costs can be reduced.

Calculate Water Consumption.   The first step in reducing water use is to calculate the amount of water used in your office or building. Look at you water bills for the last year (longer if you can), to see if there have been any significant increases in usage. Note that usage increases also may be due to significant increases in staff numbers.

Reduce Consumption.   Install a water meter. This will enable you to monitor how much water you use. There are various types. Ask your current water supplier for information.

### Find and Fix Leaks

- If you have a water meter, you can check for leaks by turning off the water and taking two meter readings several minutes apart. If the reading is different, there may be a leak.
- Leaks occur more often in supply pipe work below or adjacent to your premises.
- Contact your supplier if you are unsure where the source of increased water use is.
- Some water areas provide free water audits.
- Check cisterns, overflows, and pipe work to and from heating and cooling systems.
- Check all areas where water is used in your office/building. A dripping tap could waste as much as 24 gallons (90 liters) a week. Check for leaking taps.

### Simple Water-Saving Techniques

- Install a special water-saving device in your toilet, such as the inexpensive Hog Bag or *Hippo* Water Saver. Less water is wasted when you flush the toilet. Note that these do not work with all toilet types.

### New Fittings

- Fit spray inserts in often-used taps. These reduce the amount of water from the faucet but do not reduce washing efficiency.
- Fit new percussion taps, which turn off after a set period.

- Fit variable flush handles to all applicable toilet cisterns. Standard toilets use between 1.5 and 2.5 gallons (6 and 9 liters) of water every time they are flushed.
- If you are replacing automatic-flush urinals, consider proximity flush control systems, or use waterless and air flush systems where possible.
- Fit supply restrictor valves in supply pipes. These maintain a steady water flow, whatever the change in water pressure, and can reduce water flow by up to 50 percent.
- If your business uses washing machines and dishwashers (or other appliances), make sure they are the most water and energy efficient. Ask the supplier for resource saving features or look for ENERGY STAR–rated products.
- If your office has a large canteen, fit extended trigger handles to tap points. These reduce water use during food preparation and cleaning.

**Consider Gray Water Reuse**
- Gray water is wastewater from washbasins, showers, baths, and cooling processes. It can be partially treated on-site and reused, for example, for toilet flushing and garden irrigation. This is often more appropriate if carrying out new building work or extensive overhaul of water services. A number of specialists can advise you.

**Consider Rainwater Use**
- Rainwater can be collected in butts and used for various processes. This water is used principally for washing of vehicles, for example. With the use of a more sophisticated collection and treatment system, rainwater may also be used for flushing toilets and for office landscaping.

**Efficient Water Use within the Office**
- Ensure that everyone in your organization is aware of the need to be water efficient. Communicate the measures you are taking and the results of any changes made.
- The simplest measures are the easiest to adopt.
- Fill kettles with enough water for your needs but not to the brim. This will reduce your fuel bills, too.
- Use a plug in the sink and a bowl of water to wash cups and plates rather than washing them under a tap with an open drain.

**Water Pollution.** It is also important to reduce the volume and concentration of pollutants that end up in our water treatment works, rivers, and beaches. Many of these pollutants come from everyday items that we wash down the sink or flush down the toilet.

*Chemicals and Detergents*
The disposal of persistent and harmful chemicals into the water system is adding to increasing levels of persistent organic pollutants in the food chain. Chemicals increasingly found as pollutants in wildlife include hormone-disrupting compounds such as phthalates, alkylphenolic compounds, and bisphenol A.

- Use environmentally preferable products where possible. Many products now have a green alternative.
- Do not wash oils, solvent, paints, or thinners down sinks or drains. Store them in a safe container and take them to an authorized collection center or community paint store for reuse.
- Use accredited biodegradable detergents in washrooms, kitchens, and toilets. Many are available and are now comparable in quality and price to conventional products.

### Sanitary Products

Flushing nonbiodegradable sanitary products down the toilet can have a direct impact on the quality of our environment. Depending on the adequacy of sewage treatment facilities, many of these products end up on coastal beaches and riverbanks.

- Provide sanitary collection bins in women's office toilets.
- Inform staff that other nonbiodegradable products, including medicines, should not go down the drain.
- Do not buy feminine hygiene or sanitary protection products that are marketed as flushable. Choose those that feature the Bag It Bin It logo.
- Make sure all staff know that only paper tissue and human waste go down the toilet.

## Nonprofit Green Audit Question #8 (Purchasing)

Do you select suppliers based on environmental criteria (e..g., their green policy or products with accreditation to recognized environmental standards)? (Senior management should adopt and sign a policy to this effect.)

☐ Yes
☐ Some
☐ None

### SUPPLIERS AND PURCHASING

**Green Purchasing.**   More and more organizations are establishing environmental or green purchasing policies and strategies. Such policies and strategies are important for these reasons:

- Green procurement of products and services raises environmental awareness, which in turn moves more people to buy more environmentally sound products.
- Green procurement has potentially direct environmental benefits: fewer emissions, less waste, and more efficient resources use.
- An increase in demand for greener products and services improves the market position of suppliers.
- Demand for green products acts as an incentive for technological development toward greener products.

Greener purchasing aims to avoid unnecessary purchasing by:

- Reviewing the actual need for the product.
- Seeking alternative goods and services.
- Purchasing a greener variant with comparable if not better performance than a conventional choice.

**Green Claims: Sustainable Forests, Recyclable, Earth Friendly.**  An increasing number of products falsely claim that they are environmentally friendly. It is important to verify claims made by manufacturers and suppliers.

- Ensure you have written documentation that backs up the claims of suppliers and manufacturers.
- Ask when their documentation and process was last reviewed and to what standard or accreditation.
- Ask for a copy of their environmental report or technical data.

Establish environmental purchasing policy and criteria for products and services in contracts or in tender documents. Doing so ensures that staff, customers, and suppliers know what your minimum environmental requirements are. (See Appendix B for another green purchasing policy option.)

## Purchasing Criteria

### Environmental Purchasing Criteria for Products and Services
☐ Is it essential to buy the product, or can it be leased or rented?

### Resource Use and Recycling
☐ Does production/extraction of the product cause ecological damage, such as loss of habitats or damage to threatened species? Are there alternatives?
☐ Is this a remanufactured product?
☐ Can the product be reused, refilled, recharged, or reconditioned to extend its life?
☐ Can the item be easily upgraded by adding or replacing a part?
☐ Does the product have a recycled content? What percentage?
☐ Is the product accredited with a recognized environmental standard?
☐ Can the product be recycled easily (in the workplace and/or local community)?

### Hazardous Content
☐ Is the product or are its components hazardous to humans and/or the wider environment? If yes, what are the health and safety implications and disposal requirements? Are there any nonhazardous alternatives available?
☐ Are technical data sheets available?

### Energy
☐ Does the item use energy (e.g., electrical appliances, equipment, machinery, space heating, or vehicles)?
☐ If so, is the item as energy efficient as the alternatives?
☐ Does the item have energy consumption data for all operation modes?

## Packaging

☐ Can product packaging be reduced or eliminated?
☐ Is packaging made of recycled material(s)?
☐ Can packaging be reused, recycled, or returned?

## Food

☐ Can organically grown produce be purchased?
☐ Has the food been genetically modified?

## Transportation

☐ Is the product locally manufactured and/or locally supplied?
☐ Does the supplier have a green transport plan for its operations?

## Supplier Environmental Reporting

☐ Does the supplier have a company environmental management system?
☐ Does the supplier report on its environmental performance against set targets?

**Purchasing: Decision Making.**   To implement an effective environmental purchasing policy, use a step-by-step approach to increase your purchase of greener goods and services. It is important to raise awareness with both current and new suppliers and to link with other organizations in the same sector.

Here are some options:

- Focus on products or services within your company that have the greatest environmental impact.
- Examine products that would be highly visible within your company, for example, stationery or office electrical equipment.
- Integrate reused, refurbished, remanufactured, and recycled-content products into your operations wherever possible.
- Use greener products available through your existing suppliers, such as energy-saving office equipment and biodegradable cleaning products.
- Support local manufacturing efforts by purchasing at least a portion of your recycled products from local manufacturers, where they exist.
- Actively encourage suppliers to provide products and services that have a minimum adverse environmental impact. Request that suppliers identify harmful processes and materials in their manufacturing processes. Seek suppliers that are working toward the phase-out of such practices.
- Remember it will not be possible to purchase a green alternative for every product or service. Compromise will be required. It is therefore important to address the significant environmental impacts of your current purchasing policy.
- Set targets and dates to achieve changes in purchasing practice (i.e., all paper to be of recycled content throughout the office by next financial quarter).
- Work cooperatively with other organizations to purchase environmentally. Network with departments and neighboring businesses. It is often possible to buy cheaper in bulk. This can also reduce packaging and transport impacts.

## Nonprofit Green Audit Question #9 (Transportation)

(See Chapters 6 and 9 for more green travel and transportation tips.)

Does your office operate a green transport plan (e.g., support and promote public transport, walking, cycling, car sharing in travel to and at work to reduce local and global environmental impacts)? (This should be an adopted policy signed by senior management.)

☐ Yes
☐ No

**TRANSPORT**  A green transport plan is a way by which organizations and businesses manage the transport needs of their staff and visitors. The aim of any plan should be to reduce the environmental impact of travel associated with work, whether by plane or car. The plan should not be seen as anticar. In certain situations, the use of the car is required, as no other means of transport is feasible.

The green transport plan includes a range of measures to address different transport needs of the office:

- Staff commuter journeys
- Customers and visitors to your office or events
- Staff travel while at work
- Management and purchase of company vehicles

**Aims of a Green Transport Plan.**  It is important that you communicate the aims of your plan and stress the benefits both to business and to the environment.

Your aims should include:

- Reducing reliance on the car through the reduction in the length and number of motorized journeys (in particular, those journeys carried out in single-occupancy vehicles).
- Promoting the use of alternative means of travel that are more sustainable and environmentally friendly.
- Reducing emissions and encouraging the purchase of energy-efficient vehicles.
- Encouraging work practices that reduce the need to travel.

The adoption of a green transport plan for the office will serve as an example for other organizations. In addition, the work can be used to encourage the wider adoption of plans throughout the community.

**Benefits.**  The introduction of a green transport plan can:

- Make local communities less congested and more accessible.
- Reduce local pollution levels of carbon dioxide, hydrocarbons, nitrogen monoxide; ozone, and particulates (PM5 and PM10s).
- Reduce climate change gas emissions.
- Provide equal opportunities by providing travel incentives to all in the organization and supporting those employees without access to a car.

- Offer wider travel choices to staff.
- Provide long-term savings in reduced business travel costs.
- Help employees to be healthier, fitter, and more productive. Thirty minutes a day of moderate exercise, such as cycling or brisk walking, protects many against ill health.
- Improve the environmental image of your office.

## Promoting Alternatives

### Public Transport
- Prepare a public transport pack with prices and times of routes taken to work and on work business.
- Make a policy to use public transport for business purposes.
- Be understanding of people arriving late because of bus or train delays.
- Arrange a taxi for staff using the bus for times when they may work late.
- Provide salary advances to pay for season tickets.

### Bikes
- Distribute free cycle helmets.
- Provide free bicycle proficiency training.
- Set up an equipment pool of lights, reflective clothing, and accessories.
- Make battery or light chargers available in the office to charge up batteries during the day.
- Put up a cycling notice board for routes, bike repair shops, and organizations. This will encourage staff in using bikes, making it easier for them to find assistance and fellow bikers.
- Provide incentive schemes and salary advances to buy bikes on installments.
- Buy an office bike and link up with a local bike store for regular maintenance.
- Install shower and changing facilities during office refurbishment.
- Provide a mileage allowance for cyclists.
- Provide a secure place at work to store bikes.

### Pedestrians
- Promote the benefits of walking to work for those who live nearby, without targeting specific people. Provide posters and leaflets from relevant organizations.

### Cars
- If your office uses a car for regular essential journeys, promote good driving techniques. Simple techniques can reduce fuel consumption by as much as 25 percent.
- Ensure regular maintenance to maintain fuel efficiency and vehicle longevity.
- If you buy new, buy small, fuel-efficient models.
- Consider pooling car use with other organizations or joining a local car club.
- Consider converting existing vehicles to use liquid petroleum gas.

### Couriers
- Use bicycle couriers for delivering small items within the town or city.
- Some couriers also have gas-powered vehicles for longer journeys.

**Audio and Video Conferencing**
- If office staff members have to meet regularly with other regional/national offices, consider using Web-based or audio/teleconferencing as an alternative to travel by plane. Long-term financial savings can offset initial equipment and training costs. By reducing business air travel, your office can avoid adding to the several negative impacts of the increasing use of cheap short-haul flights. Air travel is a significant contributor to greenhouse gases being released into the atmosphere.

**Targets.** Establish targets for your office and monitor their success over a set period. For example:

- A 15 to 20 percent reduction in car-borne commuting in the initial year of the plan, thus increasing the proportion of employee commuter trips by modes of transport other than single-occupancy cars.
- A zero short-haul flight policy within three months.
- No increase in the number of parking permits/spaces for employees; in the future, an annual reduction in permits/parking spaces.

**Monitoring.** Identify current staff transport patterns by conducting a sample survey. After you have formed your travel plan, identify actions that can be put into effect immediately. Repeat the survey annually to monitor the success or hurdles of your green transport plan.

**Keys to Success.** There are several keys to the successful development and implementation of a green transport plan. These include:

**Commitment from Management**
- Green transport plans involve changing established habits and working practices. To achieve staff cooperation, it is essential for senior management to promote the wider objectives and benefits of the plan. Senior management should lead by example. This commitment includes the provision of the necessary resources to develop and implement the plan, beginning with the introduction of the "carrots," or incentives, for changing travel modes.

**Communications**
- Good communications are an essential part of any green transport plan. It will be necessary to explain the reason for adopting a plan, promote the benefits available to staff, and provide plenty of information about the alternatives.

**Building Consensus**
- It will be necessary to obtain broad support from staff for the introduction of the green transport plan.
- Allow time for staff to get used to a change in travel patterns, then gather comments and monitor changes. Some changes will require more planning than others. Try not to do everything at once.

## Conclusion

This nine-question Green Nonprofit Office Audit is a terrific way to start preparing your organization for Green Nonprofit Certification. The tips contained in this audit will help you organize your effort and establish policies/procedures that will serve your organization well as it seeks certification.

## About the Author

**Ted Hart** is founder and chief executive of the international nonprofit environmental movement called GreenNonprofits (http://greennonprofits.org), dedicated to helping nonprofits and nongovernmental organizations (NGOs) around the world to learn how to become part of the much-needed global environmental solution. He is considered one of the foremost experts in ePhilanthropy around the world, having founded the ePhilanthropy Foundation and P2PFundraising.org.

Ted is sought after internationally as an inspirational and practical speaker and consultant on topics related to nonprofit strategy, both online and offline. He serves as CEO of Hart Philanthropic Services (http://tedhart.com), an international consultancy to nonprofits/NGOs. He has served as CEO of the University of Maryland Medical System Foundation and before that as chief development officer for Johns Hopkins Bayview Medical Center. He has been certified as an advanced certified fundraising executive by the Association of Fundraising Professionals. Ted is author to several published articles, an editor, and author of the books *Major Donors—Finding Big Gifts in Your Database and Online (2006)*; *Nonprofit Internet Strategies Best Practices for Marketing, Communications and Fundraising Success (2005)*; and *Fundraising on the Internet: The ePhilanthropyFoundation.Org's Guide to Success Online (2001)*, and a contributing author to *Achieving Excellence in Fund Raising*, 2nd ed. (2003) and to *People to People Fundraising: Social Networking and Web 2.0 for Charities (2007)*. Hart is a graduate of the University of Rochester and the State University of New York at Brockport, where he received his Master's degree in Public Administration (MPA). He has also served as an adjunct faculty member to the Master of Science in Fundraising Management program at Columbia University. He resides in the Washington, DC, and New York City areas with his daughter, Sarah Grace, and son, Alexander Michael.

# PART V

# Case Studies

## CHAPTER 18

# IFAW's Green Initiative Case Study[*]

## Cindy Milburn

## Introduction

The International Fund for Animal Welfare (IFAW) has its headquarters in Massachusetts, with 16 country and regional offices over six continents. While staff sizes range greatly from 2 to 40 employees, all IFAW offices are staffed almost exclusively by nationals of the country or region in which the office is located. Most office space is leased.

IFAW headquarters are housed in a green building on Cape Cod, Massachusetts. Country office locations include suburban towns and major metropolitan centers, in both developed and developing countries, with great variation in the sophistication of energy, telecommunications, and transportation infrastructures. This case study describes the rationale and focus on the process that IFAW has gone through to reduce its environmental footprint, highlighting some challenges and lessons learned.

## Background

IFAW's Green Initiative was started in 2000 when the organization began the planning of a new headquarters to be built to meet energy-efficient green building standards. After September 11, 2001, the project was put on hold and was reactivated in 2005 with the purchase of a former industrial brownfield site. Groundbreaking for the new building occurred in October 2006, and the building was completed in January 2008.

---

[*]This case study has been prepared by Cindy Milburn drawing on original material produced by members of IFAW's core green team: Miriam Salerno (Advisor), James Kinney (Programs Communications and Reporting Editor/Writer), Katie Miller (Special Assistant to Executive Vice President), Jan Hannah (Senior Education and Research Specialist), and Sue Wallace (Senior Education and Research Specialist). In addition, every IFAW Country Office and HQ Department has contributed to the material in this case study. The information contained within this case study was correct at the time of submission. As the organization evolves to meet new challenges, IFAW will be revising implementation of the Green Initiative.

304

The official launch of IFAW's Global Green Initiative in 2006 was preceded by several green business practice initiatives at country office level. Through their appointed headquarters and country office representatives, IFAW's Global Leadership team oversees the initiative under the guidance of the Green Initiative director.

## Rationale

As an animal welfare organization concerned about the protection of wild animals and wild spaces, IFAW is working to ensure that the organization embodies a practical application of animal welfare and environmentalism.

The choices policy makers, organizations, and individuals make regarding the use of natural resources, especially fossil fuels, as well as the production and consumption of commodities and food, have major consequences for the biosphere and for the welfare of animals.

For these reasons, IFAW's Green Initiative combines:

- Appeals to governments and policy makers to provide adequate protection for wildlife and wild spaces.
- Collaboration at a community level to introduce innovative animal protection projects as part of wider "sustainability" programs.
- Organizational investment in IFAW Green Headquarters.
- Development of an IFAW-wide Green Initiative to encourage IFAW's headquarters departments, country office directors, and individual staff to learn about and contribute to IFAW's Green Initiative.

## Animal Welfare and Climate Change

There are now many scientific studies, including some by IFAW, affirming that global warming is already affecting animal welfare. If current trends continue, disruptions in climate will have increasingly catastrophic effects on a global scale before the end of this century.

Some possible effects on animal welfare:

- More droughts in some areas create shifts in water availability for animal populations.
- More flooding in other areas can mean a loss of habitat and food supplies as well as contamination of remaining water sources for both human and nonhuman animals.
- More severe weather events—heat waves, hurricanes, rainstorms, and tornadoes—can displace and harm both domestic and wild animals.
- Rising sea levels will inundate coastal cities and farmlands, causing coastal erosion and, again, loss of important animal habitat.
- Rising temperatures in the oceans and in the atmosphere will alter ecosystems, causing shifts in prey availability that could lead to die-offs of dependent species.
- Changes will occur in the distribution and prevalence of infectious diseases.

# Key Components to the IFAW Green Initiative

The key components to the IFAW Green Initiative include:

- Staff
- Awareness and challenges
- Green headquarters
- Audits
- Green business practices

## Staff

The development and supervision of IFAW's Green Building was overseen by IFAW's Facilities Group parallel to, and independent of, the establishment of IFAW's Green Team.

IFAW's Green Team comprises staff representatives from headquarters and country offices.

## Awareness and Challenges

**Awareness.** A key component to IFAW's Green Initiative is an ongoing organization-wide education and awareness campaign.

IFAW's global Green Initiative was launched with an online survey of IFAW employees entitled "Checklist for Change" to establish baseline attitudes on green and environmental issues. The "Checklist for Change" provided important baseline information establishing that IFAW employees overwhelmingly supported the idea of a green initiative, but this was not always reflected in actions (i.e., always turning off lights and computers).

The development of an electronic IFAW Green Newsletter was an important tool within IFAW for educating employees about climate change and its impacts on animals as well as no-cost and low-cost ways of reducing carbon emissions, at an office and an individual level.

**Challenges.** IFAW is a global nonprofit with offices in 16 countries around the world. Each of the countries has different regulatory standards (on such things as lighting, recycling, products) and different opportunities. Recycling facilities are not always available. Surveys, audits, and feedback from the international green teams confirmed attitudinal differences among the offices, leading to a range of expectations on what should be standard within an office. Most IFAW offices are located in leased or rented spaces. This greatly limits the types of structural changes and improvements that can be made to the space. These offices worked to comply within these constraints, often using creativity (e.g., putting a brick in a toilet to limit water use) to compensate. For example, IFAW's rented office in Washington, DC, is located in a historic building in the Dupont Circle neighborhood. As with many older buildings, energy efficiency is poor; however, this is not the result of negligence on the part of IFAW staff.

Geographic considerations also play a large part in energy consumption. IFAW's office in Dubai is situated in a climate zone where temperatures can routinely exceed 110 F and humidity can be very high. Conversely IFAW's office in Russia experiences long, cold winters with snow cover for an average of three to five months.

## IFAW's Green Headquarters

IFAW's headquarters was completed in January 2008. It comprises three, two-story, barnlike structures totaling 40,000 square feet.

The combination of restoration of a brownfield site, advanced architecture, efficient energy systems, and high percentage of recycled construction materials makes the new international headquarters a model of contemporary green building.

IFAW's headquarters achieved a "Gold" rating in the Leadership in Energy and Environmental Design (LEED) Green Building Rating System™. LEED is the nationally accepted benchmark for high-performance green buildings, based on five key areas of achievement: sustainable site development, water savings, energy efficiency, materials selection, and indoor environmental quality.

## IFAW Headquarters Key Features

■ **Habitat reclamation.** IFAW voluntarily cleaned up a former industrial (or "brownfield") site that was covered with contaminated soil and littered with tires, metal scraps, and other debris. The months-long reclamation involved removing 9,000 cubic yards of soil polluted with lead, toxins, and trash, then restoring the site with native plants. The site now meets the unrestricted use requirements of the Massachusetts Department of Environmental Protection. And because we built on previously used land, other parcels of pristine local habitat were left undisturbed.

■ **Advanced water treatment.** IFAW headquarters minimizes contributions to water problems in several ways. Bioswales (shallow ditches) and rain gardens collect and cleanse rainwater that runs off the parking lot. This system mimics nature's own: As water moves through the landscape, native vegetation filters it and breaks down pollutants, such as motor oil. Retention ponds help collect rainwater after large storms. Dual-flush toilets and low-flow aerator faucets reduce water consumption within the building.

One hundred percent of the wastewater we generate is treated on-site with a state-of-the-art septic system that uses a number of biological nutrient removal processes (the Amphidrome® Process) to remove ammonia and suspended solids and significantly reduce nitrogen-loading into the groundwater.

*(continued)*

*(Continued)*

- **Passive solar technology.** The full-height glass curtain wall that wraps around the building courtyard harnesses the sun's light and warmth. The use of wooden louvers and frit glass—glass with a shading pattern silk-screened onto it—protects against solar heat gain in summer, allows sunlight to warm the building in winter, and reduces the need for artificial lighting and gas heating all year long. Overhead fabric "sails" bounce light onto interior work surfaces. IFAW headquarters is designed to consume 32 percent less energy than a typical office building.

- **Energy efficiency.** The building's energy-efficient mechanical systems include an evaporative-cooled air-conditioning system with ozone-friendly refrigerant; high-efficiency gas heating condensing boilers; and modern fluorescent lighting. Overall, the building is designed to use 45 percent less energy for heating and air conditioning, and 22 percent less energy for lighting, compared to similar buildings that meet the latest energy standards.

- **Responsible resources.** Overall, 91 percent of the wood used in the building was harvested from sustainably managed forests, and 53 percent meets the stringent requirements of the Forest Stewardship Council. The exterior decks and window louvers are constructed of fast-growing jarrah wood from Australia. Jarrah is naturally fire and rot resistant and requires no chemical treatment. The interior floors and walls are made from eucalyptus wood.

- **Recycled material.** Many of the materials used in the building's construction were chosen for their high recycled content:
  - Structural steel: 31% postconsumer, 26% postindustrial.
  - Window framing: 49% postconsumer, 21% postindustrial.
  - Ceramic wall tile: 36% postconsumer.
  - Ceramic floor tile: 70% postindustrial.
  - Carpeting: 35% postindustrial.
  - Rubber flooring: 44% postconsumer, 9% postindustrial.
  - Foundation insulation: 100% recycled closed-cell foam.
  - Workstations: aggregate recycled content of 76% by weight, one of the highest tested percentages for any office systems product in the industry.
  - More than 75% of the construction materials used in our new building was recycled.

## Audits: Energy, Travel, Commuting

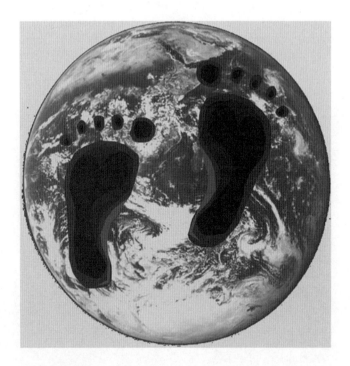

   A variety of audits have been a key component of IFAW's Green Initiative. As assessments of quantifiable data based on current business practices, the audits provide important baseline information on which to base policy recommendations and guidelines.

   A comprehensive energy audit was conducted to determine the amount of direct energy use by the organization as a whole and by individual country offices, including calculating carbon footprints for office energy use, commuting, and, to some extent, business travel.

   The resulting data were published internally as baseline data to help measure progress toward reducing energy consumption and ultimately reducing our organization's contribution to greenhouse gas (GHG) emissions and climate change.

**SCOPE OF AUDIT: ENERGY, TRAVEL, COMMUTING**    The scope of audit included these facilities in the inventory:

- All headquarters facilities located in Yarmouth Port, Massachusetts (including storage facilities)
- All country offices

   The IFAW-owned vessel, *Song of the Whale*, was included in the audit. However, due to the unique nature of the vessel, separate guidelines were established.

ACTIVITIES   The initial energy audit was conducted in two phases, spanning two fiscal years. These emissions-causing activities were included in the audit:

> **Phase 1** was IFAW's fiscal year 2008 and included two categories of data: office energy use and employee commuting.
> **Phase 2** was to begin July 1, 2008 and include a third category of emissions data: business travel.

### Phase 1: Fiscal Year 2008 (July 1, 2007–June 30, 2008)
1. Office energy use: electricity use and heating/cooling
2. Travel—daily commuting of IFAW employees:
   - Distance of daily commute
   - Method of daily commute

### Phase 2: Fiscal Year 2009 (July 1, 2008–June 30, 2009)
1. Office energy use
2. Travel—daily commuting of IFAW employees
3. Travel—business travel: IFAW employees and non-IFAW employees traveling for IFAW events:
   - Business travel—commercial flights
   - Business travel—automobile
   - Business travel—other (rail, bus, fixed wing and helicopter charters, etc.)

Providing data on office energy use and business travel was compulsory. Data on employee commuting were requested.

DATA COLLECTION   **In the office,** successful completion of this audit required cooperation from all IFAW employees. Office electricity and heating/cooling data were relatively easy for most offices to collect information based on historical data with special instructions for those not metered separately.

Utility bills from past months were accessed by office managers or obtained directly from the utility company by the office manager. In order to account for fluctuations in energy use due to seasonal weather variability, in most offices we requested data for the entire year. For the headquarters building, we had to use data from the old facilities for June 30, 2007, until January 21, 2008, when the office moved to the new facility. For January 22, 2008, through June 2008, we used data from the new facility, understanding that the data for the first couple of months would show some irregularities as the new heating systems were being tested and balanced.

**For business travel,** we recognized we would run into problems retroactively collecting this information from individuals due to variations in individual record keeping. To date, this information is based on best estimates.

**Data on employee commuting** was based on a weekly average since these practices vary only slightly with months and seasons.

For each category, these data were collected:

- **Office electricity use.** Facility/office managers to find these data on bills from the electricity company. They were asked to provide:
  - Kilowatt-hours of electricity per month

Where an IFAW office was not separately metered (such as a leased space where utilities are included), please provide:

- Total area of the building
- Total area occupied by IFAW
- Total kilowatt-hours for the entire building

- **Office heating.** These data also are found on utility bills. Staff were asked to provide data in one of these units:
  - Therms or cubic meters of natural gas used per month
  - Liters or U.S. gallons, for U.S. offices, of heating oil used per month

  As with electricity use, if an office is not separately metered, staff were asked provide:
  - Total area of the building
  - Total area occupied by IFAW
  - Total oil or natural gas consumed per month

- **Travel—daily commuting.** Due to the GHG intensity of these activities, information on daily commuting is important to the success of understanding the wider impact of IFAW on global emissions. We recognize that several factors play into commuting options, many of which are beyond the control of individuals. Some IFAW offices clearly benefit from being in locations where public transport is easy and abundant; others do not.

  Each IFAW employee was asked to provide this information:
  - Round-trip kilometers or miles commuted to and from work
  - Number of days per week the employee commutes
  - Method of transportation—bus, car, rail, or a combination
  - For personal vehicle: average mpg (km/liter or m/gal) of vehicle or make/model/year and number of occupants—IFAW and non-IFAW

- **Travel—business travel (Phase 2 *only* beginning July 1, 2008).** This information was collected for IFAW employees as well as non-IFAW employees traveling for certain IFAW events. We used the protocol established by the "IFAW's Carbon Neutral Travel Plan 2007."
  - For air travel: dates of travel, departure, and arrival.
  - For rail and bus travel: dates of travel, departure and arrival.
  - Automobile data: dates of travel, make, model, and distance traveled.
  - Chartered fixed-wing and helicopter flight data: In very rare instances when these forms of travel are used, information gathered included total fuel consumed or estimated total fuel consumed based on total flight hours and the average fuel consumption of the aircraft flown. This information was obtained from the charter company.

The green representatives, with help from their office managers, were responsible for the collection of the necessary data for each office. The green representative from IFAW's Web team created an electronic survey to assist in collecting information about individual employee commuting habits.

Following the initial audit, the data collected were used to calculate the greenhouse gas emissions of the entire organization. Table 18.1 presents summary data for the audit.

TABLE 18.1    Summary of Data for Energy Audit

| Category | Data Required | Units | Time Span |
|---|---|---|---|
| Office energy | Electricity | Kilowatt-hours/month | July 1, 2007–June 30, 2008 |
| | Oil | U.S. gallons or liters per month | July 1, 2007–June 30, 2008 |
| | Natural gas | Therms or cubic meters per month | July 1, 2007–June 30, 2008 |
| Travel—daily commute | Method of commute (car, bus, rail, or combo) | Total miles | Average week |
| | For CAR ONLY | Make/model or average mpg, number of occupants | N/A |
| Travel—business travel | Air travel | Arrival and departure | PHASE 2 ONLY |
| | Rail or bus travel | Arrival and departure | PHASE 2 ONLY |
| | Automobile | Make/model, distance traveled | PHASE 2 ONLY |
| | Chartered fixed-wing and helicopter flight data | Total fuel use or estimated fuel use | PHASE 2 ONLY |

## Green Business Practices

## ENERGY USE AND EFFICIENCY

**Energy Conservation.**   Within geographic and office constraints, IFAW staff are encouraged to make a personal commitment to the organization's green initiative through changes in personal behavior. Behavior changes offer low-cost, no-cost, or cost-saving returns.

IFAW's energy efficiency program was approached as an awareness-raising exercise with these recommendations given to office managers:

- Share office equipment as much as practicable.
- When replacing equipment, buy energy-efficient models.
- Activate equipment standby mode, which can use as little as 10 percent of normal operational electricity. Switch off all office equipment at night.
- Shut down PC monitors if not in use for more than 20 minutes; shut down both the CPU and monitor if not in use for more than 2 hours.
- Make sure all staff members have monitors, printers, and other accessories on a power strip/surge protector that can be switched off.
- Post signs near all light switches reminding employees to turn them off at the end of the day. If possible, install automatic timers or occupancy sensor so that lights accidentally left on are turned off in the evening.
- Replace all existing incandescent bulbs with compact fluorescent bulbs.
- Encourage staff members to turn off overhead lights and use a small desk lamp instead.
- Adjust thermostats to save energy used in heating and cooling. Try setting the thermostat a few degrees cooler in winter, a few degrees warmer in summer.
- Use a programmable thermostat to set the temperature lower/higher during nonworking hours.

**Green Energy Procurement.** Electricity generation is one of the leading causes of industrial air pollution in the world. However, in many cases, customers can choose to support clean and sustainable electricity suppliers. IFAW offices are encouraged to consider green energy options.

**Paper Efficiency.** According to the Web site of Lawrence Berkeley Labs,[1] the typical office worker in the United States uses about 10,000 sheets (20 reams) of paper per year.

### Recommendations
- Purchase recycled paper.
- Employ double-sided printing and copying.
- Minimize handouts at meetings.
- Reuse paper products.
- Add this tagline to e-mails: Please consider the environment before printing this e-mail.

**"Green" Procurement.** IFAW's approach was to minimize purchasing of new products, encourage staff to reuse or share whenever possible, and provide guidelines for green procurement.

## Recommendations

- Reuse materials whenever possible, and set aside an area in each office for materials that can be reused by other employees.
- Purchase chlorine-free paper with the highest percentage possible of postconsumer recycled content.
- Whenever possible, purchase other office products made from recycled or biodegradable materials.
- Purchase nontoxic cleaning and bathroom/kitchen supplies.
- Purchase "green" option in all cases if the price premium is 15 percent or less. If the premium is greater than 15 percent, consider each item on a case-by-case basis.

**Recycling.** Recycling is a key part of any green office strategy. Most IFAW offices recycle cans, bottles, and paper, but not all have access to recycling facilities.

## Recommendations

- All products that can be recycled should be recycled.
- Products that contain toxins, such as batteries and compact fluorescent bulbs, should be properly disposed of.

**Responsible Water Use.** IFAW offices were asked to calculate and take measures to reduce water use.

## Recommendations

- Install a water meter to better monitor how much your office uses.
- Find and fix leaks promptly.
- When replacing toilets or appliances, look for water-efficient models.
- Attach low-flow aerators to sink faucets.
- Consider reusing gray water, if possible.

**Air Quality.** Depending on geographic location, some IFAW offices have cooling and heating systems; some have windows that open, and others do not. Many air-quality issues cannot be altered by office managers. However, proposals were made for improvement.

## Recommendations

- Purchase indoor plants that naturally remove toxins from the air.
- Use low- or no-VOC (volatile organic compound) products whenever possible.

**Catering and Events.** Hosting events is an important part of IFAW operations. Guidelines are given to improve the sustainability of these events.

## Recommendations

- Choose a city that minimizes travel for participants.
- Choose a venue that is connected to the airport by mass transit and within walking distance to hotels, restaurants, and the like.

- Choose a venue that is interested in doing more to become green—a willingness to cooperate will make the task at hand much easier.
- Include a statement of preference in your venue request for proposals (RFPs) especially regarding catering.

**Hotels.**   Where the option is available, staff members are encouraged to choose hotels based on their commitment to corporate environmental responsibility, such as hotels that are a member of the Green Hotels Association. In addition, IFAW has language in its RFPs when choosing hotels for IFAW events that includes a request to see the hotel's environmental policy.

### Recommendations

- Always turn off the lights and minimize heating/cooling of the room.
- Unplug electronics when not in use.
- Participate, if available, in towel and linen reuse options.
- Limit the use of disposable plates, cups, and so on.

**Catering.**   As global demand for meat has increased, so has the intensive farming of animals. Intensive farming presents serious animal welfare issues. Raising animals for food on an industrial scale is also one of the leading causes of both environmental pollution and resource depletion today.

### Recommendations

> IFAW catered events and meetings should serve only vegetarian dishes and/or fish from nonendangered species

**Travel.**   Travel can be a major contributor to an organization's carbon footprint, but it is often a necessary part of doing business, particularly for an international organization like IFAW. IFAW has invested in many technologies that allow employees to communicate and run meetings without actually leaving their office. Such programs as video conferencing, net meetings, and telephone conferencing systems allow staff to maintain close working relationships across oceans and continents.

### Recommendations

- Make the most use of technology such as Web meetings to limit travel.
- Replace air travel with train travel if feasible.
- Rent smaller cars with high mpg.
- Choose hotel locations close to public transit.
- Be environmentally conscious when staying in a hotel (lights, etc.).

**Commuting.**   How employees get to and from work is often calculated in an organization's ecological footprint.

> IFAW encourages green commuting habits—public transportation if possible, otherwise carpooling or biking (when safe).

### Recommendations

- Encourage the use of public transportation, carpooling, or ride sharing.
- Provide preferred parking or discounted parking (where applicable).

- Provide increased flexibility regarding work hours in order to accommodate multiple schedules and one driver.
- Provide a safe place for employees to lock their bikes.
- Provide shower facilities in the office or local fitness club.
- Look into local government programs that provide incentives for commuting to work.

**Carbon Offsetting.**    There are serious concerns about the impact of air travel on climate change. IFAW uses various forms of air transportation during the course of its regional and international work, from disaster response, to monitoring the Canadian seal hunt, to internal strategy meetings and campaigner training.

No organization or company can eliminate carbon dioxide emissions completely. However, an organization can try to minimize the impact of those carbon emissions through offsetting.

IFAW purchases offsets from two providers offering two different project portfolios: carbon sequestration offsets provided by the World Land Trust and renewable energy/energy efficiency offsets provided by Atmosfair.

Protecting and restoring forest habitat complements IFAW's mission while addressing the impacts of climate change. Renewable energy/energy efficiency projects address the root cause of climate change. Both types of offsets are important components of IFAW's overall plan to reduce emissions.

However, not all offset providers or offset projects are created equal, and early on in our research, we decided that we would need to look for vendors with credibility, transparency, and robust project criteria. In particular, IFAW's carbon sequestration provider must meet the Climate, Community and Biodiversity Project Design Standards (CCB Standards).

CCB Standards and our renewable energy provider must meet the Gold standard. The World Land Trust (WLT) is a registered charity in the United Kingdom that was established over 15 years ago. IFAW donations were earmarked for a restoration ecology project that secures new forest corridors for Asian elephants in southern India by purchasing new land, securing legal protection, planting trees, and providing ongoing monitoring. WLT's projects are developed with ethical conservation principles (local involvement, promoting biodiversity, and conserving in perpetuity) and meet their own robust project criteria (sustainable development, additionality, leakage, monitoring, and permanence).

Of the Gold standard renewable energy providers available, IFAW chose Atmosfair because it appears to have the most easily accessible and transparent verification process and the most comprehensive online calculator supported by a well-researched background paper.

## What Is Carbon Offsetting?

Carbon offsetting is a way to neutralize, or cancel out, our carbon dioxide ($CO_2$) and other greenhouse gas (GHG) emissions when we engage in fossil fuel–burning activities for work, such as travel. The global warming effect of a given amount of GHGs emitted by an activity (such as flying) can be canceled out by another activity elsewhere that saves, reduces, or stores an equivalent amount of GHG emissions, such as solar power generation, the use of compact fluorescent lights, or the uptake of $CO_2$ by a growing tropical forest.

IFAW calculates how many tons of $CO_2$ are produced by a given activity and then buys an equivalent amount of offsets. In other words, IFAW donates money to be invested in the development of projects that cancel out our GHG emissions.

In order to achieve IFAW's primary goal of offsetting approximately 99 percent of carbon emissions from transportation associated with identified major travel events, a protocol was developed and refined over the course of the pilot phase for capturing and compiling staff travel data and calculating and offsetting $CO_2$e (*carbon dioxide equivalent*). A carbon dioxide equivalent is "A metric measure used to compare the emissions from various greenhouse gases based upon their global warming potential" (California Energy Commission, 2005) produced from five different modes of transportation: commercial flights; bus and rail trips; car and van rentals; fixed-wing charters, and helicopter charters.

## About the Author

**Cindy Milburn** is senior advisor, research and development, at IFAW Headquarters. She has worked in senior positions in the field of animal welfare since 1979. She has worked for the International Fund for Animal Welfare since 1996, as the U.K. country director and then the program director of IFAW's Animals in Crisis and Distress.

## CHAPTER 19

# Connect the Dots for Conard House Case Study

## Greening Community Mental Health

### Maikhanh Nguyen

## Overview

Conard House opened its doors as San Francisco's first mental health halfway house in 1960. It later developed "supportive housing" in single-room-occupancy hotels and apartment buildings to meet the needs of those graduating from their residential treatment program. This marked the beginning of supportive housing—that is, affordable housing with on-site support services to meet the needs of a complex, multicultural community.

Every year, Conard House serves over 1,500 clients, 600 of who are residents in its housing facilities. In keeping with its mission to develop sufficient resources to meet present-day and future challenges, Conard House pursues cost-effective, environmentally responsible practices in its operations. Mark Bennett, Director of Real Estate at Conard House, writes:

> *Each year, the cost of resources goes up while our funding sources become more competitive. This impacts our clients who, incidentally, are already challenged to make ends meet on limited incomes. Clients rely on our services. When the cost of resources goes up, this affects the quality of our services and, therefore, the quality of life for clients. We at Conard House have a responsibility to operate a lot more efficiently.*

With this in mind, Conard House contacted Connect the Dots, a nonprofit effort dedicated exclusively to helping nonprofit organizations reduce their environmental footprints. Connect the Dots has designed a program to help nonprofit organizations realize immediate reductions in water usage, energy consumption, and waste production. This program, called Green Start, reduces operating costs for its clients, which in turn encourages them to pursue other greening projects beyond Green Start. Connect the Dots consolidates disparate services and programs into a powerful portfolio for nonprofits to leverage without expending precious research time.

Connect the Dots emphasizes practical solutions and regular reporting to track tangible results so that good intentions can be harnessed for real change. It had implemented its Green Start program at nonprofit organizations with multifaceted residential programs (e.g., the Hamilton Family Center, which provides transitional housing and emergency shelter for homeless individuals and families). Subsequently, the Green Start program had already been adapted to facilities with any combination of housing, recreational, and administrative spaces.

Conard House was initially hesitant to adopt programs like Green Start because it wanted to avoid "greenwashing"—that is, making disingenuous claims about being environmentally friendly in order to curry public approval. It had found that too many groups were "going green" without tangible results. Consequently, Conard House approached Connect the Dots with tremendous skepticism. After learning about the potentials of Green Start, Conard House decided to try the program at one of its eight resident properties, the Jordan Apartments.

Between September and December 2008, Connect the Dots implemented its Green Start program at the Jordan Apartments, and the results were extremely positive for both organizations. The latter saw tangible reductions in energy and water consumption as well as the amount of waste going to landfill. Such reductions amounted to significant cost savings. Meanwhile, Connect the Dots was pleased to further its mission of involving evermore communities in the movement toward sustainability. It found great reward in helping conserve water and energy usage while redirecting purchasing power to businesses whose operations are aligned with the environment. In February 2009, Conard House extended its environmental commitment by contracting with Connect the Dots to look at its other residential properties.

## Key Challenges

Located in the Tenderloin district, the Jordan Apartments offers 54 studio apartments with private bathrooms and kitchens to formerly homeless individuals diagnosed with mental illness (Figure 19.1). Residents share a living room, an outdoor patio, and a laundry room. Two case managers provide support services on-site along with 24/7 coverage by the property management staff.

The Jordan Apartments faced challenges that commonly plague nonprofit agencies:

- **Competing priorities.** Although sustainability is recognized as important and staff members are eager to change their work environments, it remains a low priority because of the time and resources needed to conduct proper research. As Frank Hidalgo, the assistant building manager, puts it, "It's easy to say 'be energy efficient!' but in implementing, it raises questions that branch to more: what lights are better, how much will they cost, who offers the best price, and so on. I want to be energy efficient, but the devil really is in the *details*! It's always more complex than you'd think."

   Most organizations find themselves stuck in the research stage. Unlike their for-profit counterparts, nonprofit agencies typically do not have the resources to form their own sustainability department or hire outside assistance. Instead, they often rely on motivated staff with limited "free" time. Subsequently, intentions often remain unrealized.

FIGURE 19.1   Jordan Apartments, home to 55 residents with psychiatric disabilities.

- **Financing.** The Jordan Apartments lacked the up-front capital funding to invest in facility upgrades that would lower expenses. With little or no knowledge about the existing incentive programs, its management assumed that facility upgrades were too costly to fund out of pocket. Moreover, like most nonprofit organizations with overworked development teams, Conard House was unable to conduct fundraising for projects that were not directly related to its core services. Unable to bootstrap itself toward the facility upgrades that would result in substantial cost reductions, the Jordan Apartments found itself locked into high monthly utilities expenditures. Its management felt trapped.
- **Skepticism/Morale.** The Jordan Apartments was overwhelmed by the amount of changes that would be necessary for the facility to operate in accordance with environmental sustainability. Typically, it questioned whether such efforts were really making significant gains for the organization, the population it serves, or the environment as a whole. This skepticism persisted as Connect the Dots began to implement Green Start.

## Solutions

Connect the Dots and the Jordan Apartments teamed up for three months to implement the Green Start program. This program establishes an effective plan to immediately lower an organization's environmental footprint, reduce its operating cost, and provide a supportive structure to promote ongoing action. It focuses on energy and water conservation, waste reduction, responsible purchasing, and education. The common thread across these areas is the discipline to monitor and evaluate the effectiveness of these actions.

Connect the Dots has extracted the fundamental conservation practices found in most green certification programs, resource lists, and handbooks to guide nonprofit organizations toward gaining immediate, measurable savings. Nonprofit organizations that have completed the Green Start program can pursue any certification program, knowing that their initial efforts will be applicable. The Jordan Apartments received this assistance:

- A comprehensive approach to leverage incentive programs to conserve water and energy
- Support to deepen its waste reduction and diversion
- An environmentally preferred purchasing policy that was immediately put into practice
- Planning and tracking tools to document the economic and environmental benefits

## Summary of Results

Connect the Dots worked with the Jordan Apartments staff to establish an internal Green Team that, in addition to fulfilling their primary job responsibilities, also implemented the sustainability practices outlined by the Green Start program. Table 19.1 summarizes the financial savings and environmental benefits realized by their efforts.

TABLE 19.1   Jordan Apartments Savings[a]

| Area | Immediate Actual Savings (incentives/rebates) | Annual Projected ($) | Annual Projected Metric Ton of $CO_2e$ (carbon dioxide equivalent) |
|---|---|---|---|
| Waste[b] | $    0.00 | $    0.00 | 0.00 |
| Electricity | $3,496.82 | $  6,273.68[c] | 30.00[d] |
| Water | $4,754.60 | $  1,648.88[e] | 0.40[f] |
| Total savings | $8,251.42 | $  7,922.55 | 30.40 |
| **Savings in Year 1 (including incentives)** | | | **30.40** |
| **Savings in 5 years** | | **$ 47,864.19[g]** | **152.00** |

[a]Projection assumes no additional conservation steps to be made.
[b]Implemented by the Recycling Internship Program offered by the Community Housing Partnership—Supportive Housing Employment Collaborative (CHP-SHEC).
[c]Projection provided by the San Francisco Department of Environment—SF Energy Watch program.
[d]Conversion based on the US Environmental Protection Agency Greenhouse Gas Equivalencies Calculator at www.epa.gov/cleanenergy/energy-resources/calculator.html.
[e]Calculations based on the first two-month billing cycle and projected for the remainder of the year.
[f]Conversion provided by the San Francisco Green Business Program.
[g]Projection is based on the current water and electricity rates and does not account for the rising costs of resources.

## Summary of Savings at the Jordan Apartments

The Jordan Apartments leveraged existing incentive programs from local government (San Francisco Department of Environment) and utilities (San Francisco Public Utilities Commission and Pacific Gas and Electric Company) to gain immediate savings of $8,250. These incentives covered for 90 percent of the energy-efficiency upgrades and 50 percent of the water-related upgrades, making it financially feasible for the Jordan Apartments without any additional fundraising effort. By investing in these upgrades, the Jordan Apartments is projected to reduce electricity cost by $6,270 each year and water expenses by $1,650 each year.

Overall, it is projected to save approximately $16,170 in its first year and $47,865 in five years, based on current rates. However, considering that California is investing in renewable energy and faces a long-term drought, making water an even scarcer resource, these costs for resources (and therefore the savings) are expected to increase over time.

From just three months of actions, the Jordan Apartments is projected to have lowered its environmental impact by 30.4 metric tons of $CO_2$ equivalents per year, comparable to removing 5.6 passenger vehicles from the road for a year.[1]

## Steps Taken toward Energy Efficiency

One of the main pillars to greening is energy efficiency. The Jordan Apartments participated in the San Francisco Energy Watch (SFEW) program, a local energy-efficiency program providing businesses with free energy audits along with incentives and rebates.

The audit revealed close to $3,500 in incentives that paid for 90 percent of the implementation cost. The Jordan Apartments paid only $350 out of pocket for upgrades that are projected to save $6,300 (26 percent) each year in electricity costs.

Electricity savings were gained by upgrading light fixtures, removing unnecessary bulbs, and adding occupancy sensors and timers in strategic common areas. With the help of Connect the Dots in submitting the incentive application, the Jordan Apartments received payment in full from SFEW two months after commencing the Green Start program.

## Steps Taken toward Water Conservation

California is facing its third consecutive year of drought weather with some cities imposing water rationing. San Francisco requires a system overhaul to deliver the same quality and quantity to an ever-increasing population. With the cost of water expected to double within five years, the rising cost of water reemphasizes the need to be especially prudent with water usage. (See Figure 19.2.)

Connect the Dots introduced the Jordan Apartments to the San Francisco Public Utilities Commission (SFPUC) Water-Wise Evaluation program to help lower its water consumption. SFPUC provides free water audits and helps customers identify leaks at facilities. It also provides free water-saving devices, such as showerheads, aerators, and basic parts for toilets. Through the program, the Jordan Apartments received $2,254 in free equipment and became more vigilant in repairing leaks, encouraging the residents who are typically shy to interact with others to report water leaks.

FIGURE 19.2   Kitchen faucet aerator given to reduce flow to 1.5 gallons per minute (gpm).

It upgraded its 3.5-gallon-per-flush (gpf) toilets to those consuming only 1.28 gpf. The program's rebates paid for 50 percent of the project cost, which saved $2,500 to replace 20 toilets.

Connect the Dots helped the Jordan Apartments analyze its water bills to calculate annual projected savings of $1,649, a 12 percent reduction in water expenses.

Encouraged by these savings, the Jordan Apartments increased replacements of 45 high-efficiency toilets by June 2009, raising annual projected savings to $4,095. More important, it projects to save over 534,000 gallons of water each year. (See Figure 19.3.)

FIGURE 19.3   New high-efficiency toilet replaced throughout the residential building.

## Steps Taken toward Waste Reduction

Prior to the Green Start program, the Jordan Apartments had successfully implemented the Recycling Internship Program (www.chp-sf.org/housing_employ.html) offered by the Community Housing Partnership (CHP). To further divert waste, Connect the Dots encouraged composting and introduced alternative hauling services and additional steps to reduce waste generation at the source.

Connect the Dots convinced the Jordan Apartments to take on the challenges of composting. San Francisco's waste service provider offers pickup service of organic refuse, similar to waste and recycling, to be converted to fertilizer at its facilities. The Jordan Apartments provided each resident with a kitchen compost pail along with free compostable bags for food waste. The Jordan Apartments solicited CHP's assistance to educate the residents on proper waste disposal.

Connect the Dots also referred the Jordan Apartments to affordable hauling services that incorporate proper recycling and disposal. Similar to most nonprofit organizations in the social services sector, the Jordan Apartments often becomes the last stop for material goods before going to the landfill. With good intentions, donors occasionally give furniture, electronic equipment, and other goods that may not be usable by the nonprofit agencies. Combined with possessions frequently abandoned by exiting residents, these rejected goods become a costly monthly hauling expense. For example, Connect the Dots connected with a local nonprofit, ELMARS, that offers free hauling services and ensures that electronic parts are safely recycled domestically rather than shipped overseas to unregulated markets.

Other steps the Jordan Apartments took to significantly reduce its waste generation were to encourage double-sided printing by its staff, transition its accounts to receive online billing notifications, and adjust the number of catalogs and phone books to match the residents' needs.

## Steps Taken toward Responsible Purchasing

Eliah Bornstein, property manager at the Jordan Apartments, expressed the frustrating realities of competing priorities best when he commented, "We all want to do the *right* thing. But when it comes to deciding between fixing an overflowing sink or researching what type of paper to purchase and from where, guess which choice will matter more to our residents."

Connect the Dots understands such sentiments and assists well-intentioned nonprofits in these purchasing decisions. It does the vetting and relationship building with green-certified vendors to help organizations shift their supplies to safe and environmentally sustainable products.

The Green Start program focuses on commonly consumed products to reinforce the principle of responsible purchasing such as office supplies, toner cartridge, and compostable food ware.

The Jordan Apartments successfully changed its purchasing to support environmentally preferred products and businesses in these areas. It even began demanding environmentally preferred products from its service providers. For example, it renegotiated the lease with its laundry-supply vendor to obtain energy-efficient and water-saving washing machines. (See Figure 19.4.)

## Measurements and Evaluation

The Green Start program stresses the necessity to track and routinely evaluate the consumption of natural resources as a framework to sustain future actions. The tracking tools provided in the Green Start program enabled the staff to be more resource conscious as caretakers of the facility.

With careful attention to the utility bills, Connect the Dots discovered an additional $6,000 annual savings by changing the electricity rate schedule on key accounts. These savings are not included in the savings summary shown here as they were not from reduced consumption. (See Figures 19.5 and 19.6.)

FIGURE 19.4  The Jordan Apartments demanded resource-efficient washing machines from its service provider.

FIGURE 19.5  Collection of energy-efficient bulbs installed at the facility.

**FIGURE 19.6**   Electric meters for the apartment units.

Eliah Bornstein remarks that such valuable reporting would not be possible without outside assistance like Connect the Dots. He notes, "It's difficult to imagine any staff working in a nonprofit agency whose core services are not environmentally related to be disciplined enough to track and calculate these metrics effectively during their 'spare' time."

## Key Success Factors

Several factors contributed to the successful collaboration:

- The Jordan Apartments benefited from the full support at all levels of the organization.
- Team members from both organizations met regularly to hold each other accountable and, more important, kept each other motivated.
- The Jordan Apartments benefited from the strong ecosystem of services and incentive programs made possible by dedicated advocacy groups and policy makers.
- The ability to track progress encouraged the team to stay engaged and take further action.

## Conclusion

Conard House finds itself in agreement with the core philosophy of Connect the Dots: The critical junction in environmentalism has moved beyond awareness building and policy setting and now requires sustained action to evolve to the next level. Fortunately for nonprofit organizations, incentive programs already exist to encourage actions toward efficiency and sustainability. Toward this purpose, Conard House and Connect the Dots observe:

- **Environmental sustainability is an investment that feeds itself.** Organizations, whether for-profit or nonprofit, enjoy significantly lowered expenses after adopting sustainable practices. This can give them the financial wherewithal to invest in other greening efforts. According to Eliah Bornstein, "What makes this particularly exciting are the economic benefits. The Jordan Apartments is now on track to reinvest its savings back to the residents' community in the form of ENERGY STAR appliances to realize *additional* environmental and economic benefits. Resident satisfaction has increased as well leading to higher retention rates, less vandalism, lower maintenance costs, and most significantly a more positive and engaged community."
- **Green is action.** Success at the Jordan Apartments has inspired Conard House to look at the rest of its facilities. Success has come from action. The hardest part is *starting*. Once an organization starts taking concrete steps, the results naturally encourage more action. In no time, an organization begins operating along green lines even though it has not adopted new missions or altered its ideals. Action creates the fertile ground that gives ideas opportunities to grow.
- **Beyond Green Start.** Operating more efficiently, Jordan Apartments is now working with Connect the Dots to investigate solar energy for its building. Connect the Dots is once again leveraging existing programs in helping organizations obtain alternative energy solutions. The Jordan Apartments is also working with Connect the Dots to design compelling educational sessions for its residents and staff to deepen their commitment to sustainability.

## Sustainability through Community

By forming a network of nonprofits using a methodical approach to resource efficiency, Connect the Dots seeks to leverage the knowledge gained at one facility to distribute to the rest of the community. On the value of such knowledge networks, Mark Bennett remarked:

> *Imagine the time and energy expended by each nonprofit to go through this on its own, learning the same lessons and trying to keep up with the latest incentives and best practices. Conversely, imagine the amount of energy it takes for these incentive programs and green vendors to reach each organization. Talk about energy inefficiency! There needs to be an affordable alternative to help us access what we need to be environmentally sustainable.*

Connect the Dots aims to move the nonprofit community more efficiently and expediently down the path toward environmental sustainability. Its vision includes all nonprofit organizations, regardless of their specific focus—health and human services, education, arts and culture, and so on. Environmental sustainability can be a formidable challenge, requiring many changes that can seem daunting for organizations to undertake by themselves. The good news is that we nonprofits are savvy at reinforcing one another so that our strengths overlap. We are quick to form communities, often for survival's sake. Connect the Dots represents one such community. The strategy of Connect the Dots is in its name. When one organization learns, we all learn. In this way, each individual nonprofit organization can continue to make progress toward its unique social mission within an overall framework that ensures the sustainability of our world.

## About the Author

**Maikhanh Nguyen,** executive director and cofounder of Connect the Dots, has over 15 years of experience in matching information technologies to mission statements. She has overseen the development of technology programs for enterprises in the financial, service, and manufacturing sectors. In 2004, she established her own consultancy to offer technology implementation to organizations whose mission statements are aligned with social progress. Among her clients were Hamilton Family Center, Grid Alternatives, and the United Nations Environment Program in Switzerland. Maikhanh draws on her upbringing as a refugee immigrant from Vietnam, having experienced the severe shortages of basics (water, sanitation, etc.). Like most immigrants, she learned from her parents' unconscious teaching to make do with less. She also relies on her career in technology to help understand the critical factors for success in implementing organization-wide change. In her experience, the best programs incite subtle and daily action from all levels of organization.

## CHAPTER 20

# Motivation for the Schizophrenia Society of Canada to Become Green

## *Case Study*

### Betty Penny

In 2006, a client—the Schizophrenia Society of Canada (SSC)—experienced a significant need for change. Funds generated exceeded $1 million, but the organization was showing a deficit position of $32,000 at its year-end and the reserves remaining were at $93,000, which meant the organization could survive for only a little over a month if no further donations/funding dollars were received in the next fiscal year. The SSC had no fixed funding; all monies received were based on programs, annual fundraising activities, and direct mail campaign efforts.

Penny & Associates Inc., which provides outsourced accounting and management services for nonprofits, had managed the accounting functions of the organization since 1999. It had not seen a deficit position in any of those years. Costs were tightly controlled and monitored with monthly statements. Fundraising income, program dollars, and donations were not always predictable and were based on best estimates from the executive director and historical data.

There was more bad news in 2007 when the executive director resigned. This was a turning point for the organization, which was run by a volunteer board of directors and paid administrative staff. Before going into detail on how the organization changed and the processes it went through, it is best to provide an organizational outline. Additional information is available on the SSC Web site: www.schizophrenia.ca.

## Organization

SSC is a national registered charity that has operated since 1979. Its mission is to improve the quality of life for those affected by schizophrenia and psychosis through education, support programs, public policy, and research.

Using a federation model, the society works with 10 provincial societies and more than 100 chapters and branches to help individuals with schizophrenia and their families have a better quality of life, while searching for a cure. (See Figure 20.1.)

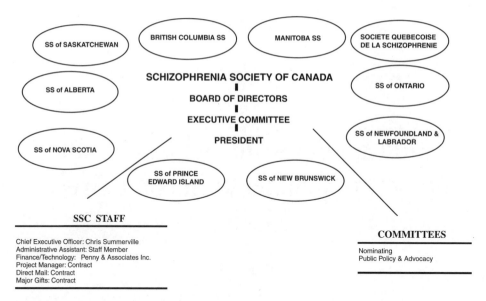

**FIGURE 20.1**    Schizophrenia Societies of Canada Federation members.

Each province under the federated model is responsible for its own fundraising efforts and has an executive director and board. The 10 societies meet annually in a designated province. During the annual meeting, the national body shares information with the distribution of financial statements, materials, lobbying efforts, and updates provided by the executive director and the board.

### Challenges Faced

Numerous challenges faced the SSC after the executive director resigned. The funding base was being depleted, and administrative costs, such as rent, wages, and salaries, were starting to exceed what was being brought in from fundraising and direct marketing efforts. The organization was depleting its reserves and was running almost on empty. (Figure 20.2.)

## Schizophrenia Society of Canada Rising Costs

### Change

Since there were 10 other provincial societies, it seemed the best idea was to draw from the society's current resources, from someone with whom the board was familiar and who could best do the job on a temporary basis. Chris Summerville, the executive director of the Manitoba Schizophrenia Society, was brought in as interim executive director in the Markham, Ontario, head office until a replacement could be found.

### Reduce, Recycle, Reuse, and Realign Resources

Chris Summerville, the new interim chief executive officer (CEO), Betty Penny of Penny & Associates Inc., and Dr. Pam Forsythe, president of SSC, developed strategic groundwork enabling the organization to become sustainable.

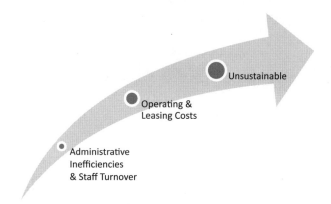

FIGURE 20.2    Challenges faced 2003 to 2007: Rising costs of administration, turnover, and fixed costs forced SSC to be unsustainable.

Through e-mails, teleconferences, and personal visits using recyclable cups for coffee, management and board members brainstormed and decided to use a green philosophy model using the three *R*s: reduce, recycle, and reuse.

Since the SSC already practiced recycling, it needed to look at what could be done to reduce costs, reuse items, and build on. A fourth *R*—realignment—was added:

- Reduce
- Recycle
- Reuse
- Realign

With limited funding, the 4R strategy made perfect sense. The green aspect was very appealing and gave the organization a best green model from which to work. It would work toward making SSC a virtual operation.

When the Markham office was closed, all office furniture was sold or donated to other charities.

The main telephone and toll-free line were redirected to the Manitoba office (Chris Summerville's office). Mail was forwarded to Penny & Associates in Port Perry, Ontario, to be redirected, and all staff e-mails were redirected to the interim CEO's e-mail address. Notification of these changes was sent to all vendors and supporters.

Files needed for immediate use were sent to Summerville's office in Manitoba. Files not needed for immediate use were put in storage and labeled with access only by Penny & Associates and the interim CEO. A master list of files was made and shared between the CEO and Penny & Associates, while banking arrangements were set up to handle deposits.

Human capital resources were made available through the different provincial societies. As a green virtual model, however, resources were not fully aligned to allow the SSC to take advantage of that expertise and position it properly. Those resources were spread across Canada. In order to make it work, the organization would have to fly those people to the main office, which did not make economic sense.

Four key components needed to be protected during the transition: (1) the key relationships with funders, (2) project management for existing projects, (3) the financial management and auditing process, and (4) the direct mail fundraising campaign.

The move had to be seamless. There was a need to coordinate and work collaboratively with the provincial societies and professionals who had the expertise and resources that the SSC could tap into.

## Components of SSC's Green Initiative

The SSC Green Initiative is a multifaceted program with several components. In addition to cutting costs to help the organization survive in a lean economy, funds saved can be redirected as needed into community outreach programs that further perpetuate the company's mission statement. The Green Initiative proposal will cut unnecessary supplies and usage not only to save money but to be more environmentally friendly.

REUSING AVAILABLE RESOURCES   When the office and staff were reduced, it made sense to look within the SSC's provincial societies for who best could handle adding some of the national functions within their own organization.

It was not going to be an easy transition. There were many considerations—the sharing of information, such as mailing lists, and handling of funds and resources. A template for the groundwork had to be completed. Trust had to be placed with the professionals who could provide the services without having everyone in the same location.

Expertise was drawn from the known talent pool of the society. Providers were asked to submit bids for fixed-priced contracts.

Alberta was known for having a strong direct marketing manager. Why not reuse the resources and knowledge of direct mail experience that was available in that office?

Manitoba had a strong mental health advocate, so why not reuse this expertise as a voice for the national office?

The national office had a contract in place for accounting, which was already managed remotely.

A contract was developed for each service with fixed monthly pricing; it was a win-win situation, as SSC funds were reinvested into some of the other provincial societies.

SSC now needed to build a capacity framework within the national organization with different departments spread thousands of miles apart.

Processes were carefully developed regarding how the mail and deposits were to be handled by Penny & Associates in Ontario and Alberta. Documentation of procedures was vital to everyone understanding the process.

The organization basically operated through the Internet by e-mails, and mail was being forwarded to a virtual address at Penny & Associates (PA) in Port Perry. It was necessary to set up an audit trail as well as a plan to control the flow of information.

LEVERAGING ONLINE TECHNOLOGY   With 10 different branch locations in 10 provinces, it is essential to ensure that information and business applications are accessible as needed.

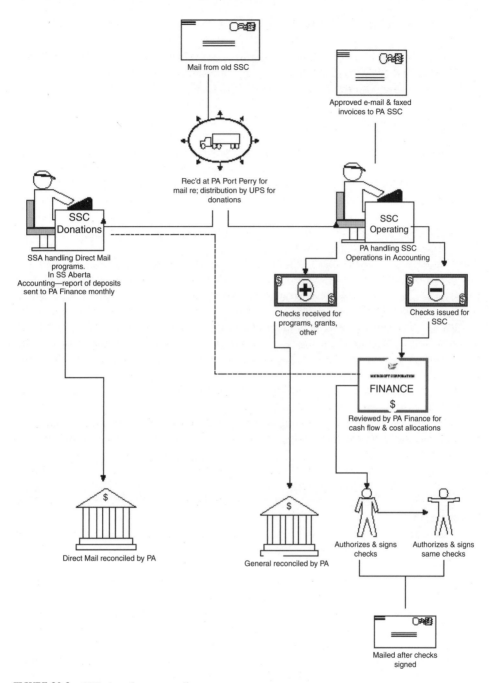

FIGURE 20.3   SSC virtual setup mail process.

To this point, information was scattered across people's computers or locked in poorly managed servers without adequate access and security. This greatly slowed access to critical information and business applications, reducing productivity. Furthermore, it put the integrity of company-critical data at risk.

Two options face any nonprofit operation:

1.  Invest in deploying and maintaining your own technical infrastructure—
    information technology (IT) personnel, servers, backup devices, communica-
    tion equipment, and various software applications.
2.  Take advantage of a new model for using technology that does not require any
    IT infrastructure in the company or any up-front capital expense or IT expertise
    on the company's part. This model is referred to as Software as a Service (SaaS),
    where one can access information and business applications online from any
    browser anytime, anywhere. This leverages the existing IT infrastructure of the
    SaaS provider, which guarantees system uptime and data integrity. It is paid on
    a monthly basis without any long-term commitment.

SaaS is one of the fastest-growing sectors of technology and is being adopted by
businesses of all sizes. Small- and medium-size businesses in particular are adopting
SaaS solutions at a rapid pace and realigning resources with their business objectives.

Considering these options, it was clear that operating a successful virtual green
business model would require an SaaS solution, a cost-effective online portal where
everyone could access and share information in a secure system.

Through months of research in a due diligence process, Hyperoffice was evaluated and determined to fit the needs of the organization. The price point was
attractive, training was interactive, and the system is easy to learn, especially for
users familiar with Outlook.

Penny & Associates designed the infrastructure to have the document information scanned and put into file folders that can be accessed by anyone with
secure password information. Necessary files can be placed in a centralized location
for company-wide access. This streamlines processes and allows companies to save
time and resources that would be spent finding files, printing, mailing, or couriering.

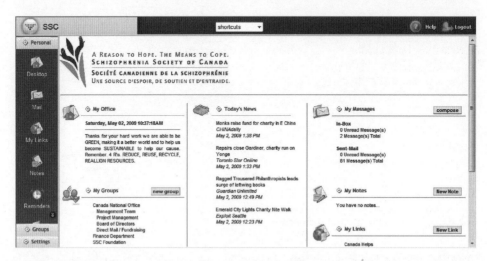

As mentioned, Hyperoffice has similarities to Outlook and has many features. It
is an organizational system with an interactive to-do list, where the you can enter
tasks that need to be completed and check them off as they are finished. You can
keep a calendar of upcoming events.

Another benefit is that documents and information are kept on a host server and can therefore be accessed securely from any computer or mobile phone with Internet access. Hyperoffice also manages contacts, meaning there is no more need to call central office in order to find an important phone number or address. You can also keep track of notes and information that need to be kept at your fingertips as well as reminders that pop up when scheduled.

In addition to its organizational capabilities, Hyperoffice is a communications tool. First, there is an e-mail system for interorganizational communications that provides a common e-mail address for company branding. It also allows you to create groups within the organization for separate committees and projects. This gives you the ability to share certain files and information with specific coworkers as part of a common workspace. Furthermore, these groups can be password-protected to keep information confidential.

Within these groups, you can set up announcement messages, assign tasks, and have a shared calendar, shared contacts and documents, as well as discussion forums. SSC utilizes this to announce updates, messages of the day, or good news shared when accessing the desktop.

A discussion forum is a synchronized method of communication in which management or board members can post questions and comments to which other members can respond. You can even set up voting within the group when trying to decide on issues.

The best thing about the Hyperoffice portal is that it creates one virtual office for workers all over the country or around the world if necessary. You can communicate, share ideas, assign tasks, share documents and resources, and schedule appointments. Company forms can be standardized without printing a single sheet of paper.

**UTILIZING HOME OFFICES TO REDUCE EMISSIONS** In a traditional business model, an employee wakes up, dresses, and drives to work. While there, he or she utilizes resources. Aside from the water, beans, and cardboard cup in that morning cup of coffee, the employee uses electricity, water, air conditioning, gasoline, paper, and ink. A person at work tends to keep his or her computer on all day. It may not seem like much, but multiplied by hundreds and thousands of employees, it truly adds up.

With the implementation of an online server such as Hyperoffice, work can be accessed from anywhere. By having employees telecommute, or work from home via an Internet connection, the company can save large amounts of money and waste. Companies tend to pay for electricity and heating/air conditioning in large spaces that are used only a percentage of the time. Leasing an office building to house many employees is expensive. Cutting back by utilizing the home office not only saves money but reduces the company's carbon footprint.

When considering telecommuting as a viable option, it is necessary to consider which jobs can be done from home. Writing a press release or preparing a report does not require sitting in the office. Even cutting back to a weekly meeting rather than having workers come to the office every day can cause major savings. Groups and committees can use office portal software, such as Hyperoffice, to meet virtually rather than spending the gas and money to be in the same place.

SSC has successfully used telecommuting for several years. Staff have the option of working at home when weather conditions are not ideal or when there is need to do so.

## Developing Policies and Control Methods

Many employers are leery of the virtual workplace and of telecommuting. After all, with employees scattered to the wind, how does a boss ensure that work will be completed? Certainly many people would take advantage of such a situation in counterproductive ways. Although telecommuting can be a way to save money and resources, guidelines and rules must be in place to keep the system productive.

Not all employees are cut out for working from home or self-motivated enough to do so. It is wise to offer this option only to workers who have been with the company beyond a probation period or who have worked there long enough for work habits to be observed and evaluated. A psychological profile is also a good idea to determine which personalities are best suited to these working conditions. Proper monitoring, through various reports due on a scheduled basis, provides a level of accountability.

It should also be made clear that in a productive telecommuting environment, working from home should not be a substitute for child care. Unless arranged in advance for special situations, an employee who is also taking care of a child will not be as productive as at the office. When dealing with employees who are also parents, it is necessary to impress the importance of this fact on them. Employees should be encouraged to share with their managers when a situation arises (such as an illness) that requires the child to be at home while the parent is telecommuting.

It is also essential for the worker to be in contact with the office. He or she should be available via phone or computer for telemeetings and client calls during scheduled hours. Contact information should be included on the employee's voicemail, and it should be made clear that he or she is working away from the office. Employees are also responsible for keeping hardware and software up to date, with office assistance provided where necessary.

In order to make sure that the telecommuting program is successful rather than counterproductive, it is important to reassess employees and their level of productivity consistently. In their alternative work situation, there should be a defined workspace. This means that working from home should not mean working from the kitchen table, where confidential information is open for all to see. If an employee's productivity level dips, then this means that he or she may not be a good fit for telecommuting and should return to the traditional office setting. With precautions and checks, telecommuting can greatly reduce costs and waste.

## Implementing the Green Process

Creating new habits and bringing in new ideas can be a tricky and complicated process. There may be resistance. Some may think that the new methods using technology are too difficult and require too much training; therefore they avoid it. Some who have been with the company for a long time may be very comfortable with the current way of doing things and find the transition too difficult. In order to deal with these issues, it is important to make sure that your employees understand why change is necessary and how the company will benefit as a whole. After all, saved money can mean saved jobs and fewer cutbacks. If your workers can see how they will benefit, the transition will be much smoother.

As much as possible, the message must be related to a process that means working smarter and greener, not harder and causing damage to the environment.

## Messaging across the Country

Until now, the most popular method of synchronous communication was the telephone. If you needed to speak to someone, you picked up your landline phone, dialed, and were connected. With the advent of cellular phones, it is now possible to reach someone even if he or she is out of the office. Connections might not always be clear, but it is certainly more convenient.

Phones, however, are not the simplest answer; they are expensive. A landline not only charges a monthly fee, but individual nonlocal calls cost by the minute. If your employees regularly call from province to province, the bills can really rack up. Landlines are also inconvenient—if you are not in the office sitting at your desk, you cannot be reached.

Cell phones may seem like the answer but can be even more expensive. Long distance calls may be free, but a plan generally includes a certain number of minutes. If you use more minutes than you have paid for, the overage charges are astronomical. It is unreasonable to expect employees to use their personal cell phone minutes regularly to conduct business.

The solution is instant messaging. Employees will most likely already have a computer with Internet access at their desk, whether they telecommute or work from the main office. Instant messaging programs are generally free to download. Instant messaging is similar to sending e-mails except the response is live. Think of it as the walkie-talkie of the Internet. This is the major form of communication for many young teens, but it can also be a useful tool for nonprofits to communicate across the country for free.

One of the most common instant messaging programs is MSN Instant Messenger, but others include Yahoo Messenger, AOL Instant Messenger, and Google Talk.

SSC utilizes MSN for communication daily between administration in Manitoba and accounting in Ontario. Messages are instant. Employees can keep their status updated so others know at a glance whether someone is at their desk, at lunch, in a meeting, or out for the day. Telecommuters can do the same on their home computers.

Another advantage to instant messaging is that most people are able to message from their cell phones without incurring additional charges; someone on a business lunch can send a quick message back to a coworker at his or her desk to quickly find out a price or fact. Instant messaging is a great money- and time-saving resource for SSC. As a word of caution, however: Never use these types of services for confidential and sensitive information.

## Scanning and File Tagging

Most companies have stacks and filing cabinets full of files. These may include photographs, documents, and archives. Unfortunately, a document can be in only one building at a time. If an employee in Manitoba needs a copy of a document housed in the Alberta office, there is a long process involved.

First the call, then the document must be located, which can take some time if the filing system is not impeccable. Then it must be faxed or scanned. If an original is necessary, it has to be sent through the mail or by courier. It is not a streamlined process and can take a lot of time and expense.

Not only is the process inconvenient; it can create major issues if two people need the same document at the same time. Through the use of a scanner, all documents can be made digital or in pdf format, which is a standard preference for business documents, and easily accessible. Documents, photos, and any other paper item can be saved on a computer, where they are less likely to be damaged. Of course, you still want to find a way to archive hard copies. They can be boxed and put in storage if you need to save space, since the information will always be at your fingertips. The cost of renting storage space will always be at a premium; hard copies files sent to storage need to be sorted properly and identified by type and retention period as required by government regulation. The benefit of scanning documents is that once on a drive or disk, there will always be history of the organization that takes up very little space.

In order to keep files organized once digitized, a specific file-tagging system becomes necessary. By using specific codes to name files with dates, it becomes easy to search them on disk or computer.

For example, for files that deal with client information, such as a letter, you would name them by type, period (.), client name and date, such as Ltr.PAssoc. 04.30.08. Separating an item with a period (.) makes it searchable. Each type of file would have to be saved with a different tag so it could be found at a glance when needed.

Some scanning programs already come with searchable fields and predefined tagging system. Test and see what works best for your organization.

# Document Management

When a document enters a paper system, it goes through a specific process before being filed. In an online document management system, a document must go through a similar process, but instead of going to a filing cabinet, it is filed virtually.

For example, an accounts payable document follows a path. A bill may come in the mail and go straight to the accounting department. At that point, the accounting department may comment on it, then send it to the project manager or the appropriate department for authorization if it was not on the approved budget. The project manager may need special approval from the CEO, at which point the document must be sent back to accounting to be processed.

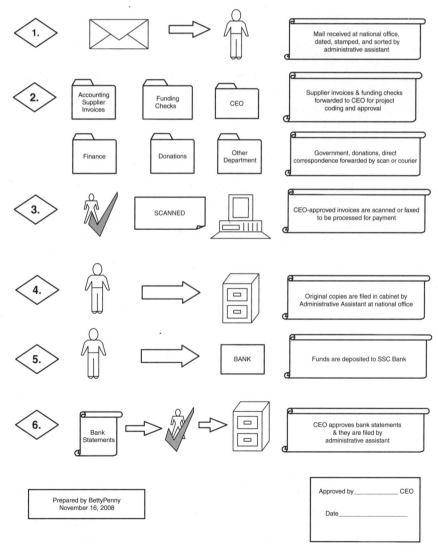

## SSC Document Processing

1. Mail received at national office, dated, stamped, and sorted by administrative assistant

2. Accounting Supplier Invoices / Funding Checks / CEO — Supplier invoices & funding checks forwarded to CEO for project coding and approval

   Finance / Donations / Other Department — Government, donations, direct correspondence forwarded by scan or courier

3. SCANNED — CEO-approved invoices are scanned or faxed to be processed for payment

4. Original copies are filed in cabinet by Administrative Assistant at national office

5. BANK — Funds are deposited to SSC Bank

6. Bank Statements — CEO approves bank statements & they are filed by administrative assistant

Prepared by BettyPenny
November 16, 2008

Approved by_____ CEO

Date_____

For a virtual paperless document system to survive, it must be capable of sending a document on the same workflow path. Online filing systems with document retention processes need to be set up in the same way as in an organized paper filing system office.

Therefore, a document management system is more than a simple online repository, although it ought to have the capability to maintain a backup database of all company files. It needs to be secure from parties who should not have access, inside and outside the company. It also needs to work with the software applications used in the office. The online document management program should be a live system that allows people to access and move documents throughout the office in the same way one would with a hard copy.

A good document management system should do several things.

- It should keep documents in an organized manner that cuts out the need to print documents. While it may not seem like much money to print out a document or two, the amount spent truly multiplies when done repetitively company-wide.
- It should have an organization system with search capabilities. Anyone who has ever lost a document in a brick-and-mortar filing system knows that it is lost forever. If a document is misfiled in a good online document management system, it can be found easily. A good electronic document filing system should basically eliminate the need to print out documents.
- Along with the environmentally friendly reasons, there are financial reasons for an online document management system. Time is money, and anyone who has gone searching for a document knows that a lot of money is lost waiting for a paper document to surface. Also, paper documents take up a huge amount of space.

Many companies even rent storage space to house documents. Some pay employees to manage them. Imagine the money saved in leasing and labor with an online document management system.

## Banking and Payroll Management

The paper bank statement is becoming an item of the past; some banks offer incentives, such as reduced bank charges, for customers to switch from paper to virtual. Almost all banks offer online bank account access, where you can see information on your account. Rather than a monthly paper statement, you can have up-to-the-minute account information. Having an online banking system is important in this day and age. In managing its cash flow, it is critical for SSC to know what is in the bank on a weekly basis.

Banking access online provides instant detail of the transactions; you can expand a debit to see a copy of the scanned check processed through the account. This is another way for both the CEO and the finance department to watch for fraud when bank accounts are in different provinces.

The idea with utilizing technology is that you can find out what is happening financially in another branch with the click of a button. It also means that you can get any answers you need 24 hours a day, seven days a week. Updates and changes are obvious within minutes.

With online payroll systems, government deductions and all payroll are done through the service. Payroll is done virtually with the administrator inputting the data information, such as hours and benefits. Deposits are made directly into the employee's account, and payroll statements are sent via e-mail, where employees can access and download their own information.

Approved hours can be pulled directly from the Hyperoffice system and inputted to the online payroll system, streamlining the process.

Before the payroll is processed, it is approved and authorized by the CEO, as payroll is generally the largest expense of a nonprofit organization. The payroll journal is issued and can be posted on the accounting system, and a copy can be saved in a secure virtual folder. With a good online document flow system, payroll information still must go through the same checks and balances it goes through with a brick-and-mortar system. However, the online process is much quicker and more cost effective, leaving a smaller carbon footprint.

## Selling the Green Process at the National Level

Once you have implemented all these changes at the branch level, the real money savings will not happen until they are brought to the national level. The branches must work together in order to truly reap the benefits. Selling the idea at the national level can make the largest office seem accessible. There are other great aspects of this system; you can save a lot in both money and resources.

You must first determine which changes need to be made and who will implement them. There are bound to be a vast number of changes, and a simple chart can help you delegate responsibilities to different departments and managers. This will help your company work together to transition to the new system.

The national virtual office is also much cheaper than a brick-and-mortar building. Depending on your financial situation, you can use the extra funds to build your reserves or redirect them to other programs. Think about your company; how many employees do you have that complete the same job? By creating a national virtual office, the same job can be handled by one person rather than many. Computer programs also can handle many of the duties that originally were performed by people.

Another great benefit to the virtual office system is that most systems have a front office and a back office. This means that your customers and clients generally can access the information they need from their own home computers. The ease of use will create greater customer loyalty and improve your client base.

The first step to creating a virtual office is to select and implement your software. It is necessary to make sure that all your branch managers are on board and trained on the system. Every branch needs to be included in the process. It may mean some extra work for everyone at first, but it will certainly make everything easier in the long run.

Once you have put the program in place, you will have to hold training seminars to prepare workers to use the system. This may be a time of turnover and change. Some jobs may become obsolete or redundant. Some employees might not be willing to make the switch and will find new places to work. You may find that new positions open within the company that need to be filled by a different kind of employee.

Change is a necessary part of the process. When choosing new employees, you may need to look for prospects with different qualifications from those you have sought before. Applying a positive attitude to the change can make employees more willing to go along. There will, of course, be casualties. Some workers may find that their jobs are no longer necessary. While you will want to reorganize in the most mutually beneficial way possible by taking advantage of technology, some employees will not have the skills to take a different position. Although you want to minimize these changes, you will need to accept that this is a possibility.

In the end, a more profitable and streamlined organization means that it can reach a broader range of people. The technology used to help your nonprofit company make more money does not need to be exceedingly complicated or pricey. Ideally, your software will be as user friendly as possible. This will make the transition as simple as it can be.

## Best Sustainable Business Practices

For a business to be successful, it must be sustainable. This is why the new green technology makes your life so easy. The money saved can make your business much more sustainable. It also lets your company grow in a way that a brick-and-mortar business cannot. A virtual business can be nationwide and even worldwide.

There is no limit to growth in virtual business. You no longer run the risk of running out of office space or resources. The best way to ensure sustainability is to promote growth. Yet another way to save money is to outsource jobs that do not need to be completed by someone within the company. With your company online, you open yourself up to working with employees all over the world. With outsourcing, you save the money that would be spent on health plans and expenses.

It also will be necessary to update job descriptions. Employees who wish to remain with the company may need to learn a new set of skills. One of the best ways to keep the transition friendly and simple is to offer training. Keeping on the same employees provides stability within the company, which makes for better morale, which leads to more productive workers.

In terms of sustainability, however, it is necessary to recognize when an employee is no longer a good fit for the current position. If this is the case, it is necessary to make changes. Loyalty and a willingness to learn are important qualities in a worker. However, your employees must all be capable and ready to work for a common goal.

Nonprofit organizations face a multitude of challenges. Money is often lean, and employees must have different talents and strengths. Dealing with government funding can be unpredictable at best. Rules and regulations change, and funding must be reapplied for and cannot be counted on.

Nonprofits play an important role in society. It is essential to remember that the mission of your organization is one that others can get behind.

## Overcoming the Negative Barriers

Change breeds resistance, even though it is a natural part of the process. Going green and leveraging technology may be easy for some but not for the majority involved with the nonprofit sector. Many baby boomers who hold positions as executive directors in this area are used to dealing with paper. They are accustomed to feeling, touching, and seeing others face to face. Many are still hesitant about the Internet and security and are locked into the old way of doing business.

Without embracing technology and leveraging green initiatives, nonprofits will be in the same category as the automotive sector; labor and administrative costs are just too high to carry on in future years. The focus of any nonprofit needs to be sustainability. Nonprofits are usually the hardest hit when the economy takes a tumble yet are expected to still contribute to society at the same rate.

They are not in a position to downscale as quickly as a for-profit business. Careful strategic planning is one of the many steps required.

Boards and their affiliated associations need to work together to see where cost sharing and savings can be utilized effectively instead of trying to protect their own turf.

There will always be challenges, some based perhaps on personality conflicts, sharing of customer lists, and different goals that may still be considered traditional. Change is evident in any business model, as it must be for nonprofits to succeed. Based on past experiences in dealing with nonprofits, here are some considerations that should be looked at when developing your plan to help others overcome negative barriers.

- People who are involved need to be engaged in the process.
- A common message or mission statement needs to show continuity.

These are important aspects of change because people do not like to feel they are being left behind. You may have some perfectly viable employees who could learn the new system but will resent feeling that they are being edged out. Before implementing changes, you must make sure that your mission statement is clear and uncompromised.

Loyalty is important, and it is a great idea to try to find a place in the company for employees who have shown their loyalty. If they are no longer able to function in the company, however, it may be time to part ways.

A certain amount of resistance is to be expected when working with change. However, this resistance should not be allowed to manifest itself in the form of insubordination or sabotage. Make sure that your employees understand the reasons for change, and you will find it easier to maintain cooperation. Involve them in the process and they will better understand why it is necessary.

Another way to avoid resistance and negative attitudes is through thorough training. Anyone would hate a system that made him or her feel frustrated and stupid. Of course, training should not mean that employees give up their free time or hours after work without compensation. If you want full cooperation, make sure that workers are thanked and compensated for their time. Employees who are part of the process will more likely want to stay after the change.

## Focus on Future Sustainability

Remembering your mission statement or common message is an important consideration. There are people who got behind your company for a reason, and you do not want to let them down or lose their support. With growth, however, you can reach even more people. You do not want to destroy your foundation in the process, so do not let go of your original mission.

Burning bridges can be a huge mistake in keeping your nonprofit going. The people who helped you get there will continue to support you if your mission remains unchanged.

One way to maintain sustainability is to work collaboratively with other organizations in the community. Depending on needs, this process can last for a short while or be permanent. You can share back-office services in order to save money.

Companies can share services in many different ways. Two companies can share shipping or warehouse employees. They can also share accounting and payroll or fundraising personnel. This is especially advisable in smaller nonprofit organizations. Of course, you will want to share with a company that will not cause a conflict of interest.

Another way to save money is to buy in bulk. You can share with another nonprofit organization, which will save cash over time. Even with the tax breaks afforded to nonprofits, the costs of supplies and running businesses can be expensive. Often there are ways to find deals or supply-sharing to save on expenses. Working together with another company can allow you to pool resources and reach more people.

As your business grows, you must always keep your eye on the future. This means that you must be receptive to growth while avoiding growing faster than the business can handle. Adopting new technology is a way to stay with the times and be current. It is also generally a great way to save money and streamline the process of your nonprofit. Keep an open mind toward change.

## Think Outside the Box and on the Grass

The old saying, "If it ain't broke, don't fix it," is really an outdated expression. We are blessed to have grass, forests, fresh air, and oceans. Even during world economic upheaval we still have these wonderful gifts. Yet what would the world be like if in 50 years there was no grass and only dirt and rocks left for our children? It takes innovative thinking and an openness to change to transform the way things are run. This is where we must start to think outside the box and feel the grass beneath our bare feet. Thinking of how we do things now to help the environment will benefit us all, and this is where using technology comes into play.

The creative use of a computer can all but eliminate the need for paper. Children and young adults embrace technology. We are building the best nonprofit green model for them to become leaders to help carry the message into the future. They will improve it. They will not be interested in learning outdated techniques and not being resourceful.

## Reduce, Recycle, Reuse, Realign = Reward

Changing your nonprofit business to a green system can require some major changes and can reap major rewards. The environment is everyone's responsibility, and we all need to do our part to protect the Earth and avoid overusing our nonrenewable resources.

Your motives for going green do not have to be entirely unselfish—you can help the Earth and still improve your business.

Going green saves resources and funds. By realigning the way you think about your office systems, you can make major changes. It is to be expected that you will run into resistance, but you must remember that what is best for the company is best for your clients.

Your nonprofit organization was formed with a mission in mind, and you can best serve that mission by keeping it running efficiently.

## About the Author

**Betty Penny,** MBA, is president and founder of Penny and Associates Inc., an outsourcing accounting and management firm specializing in nonprofits. Betty has been a virtual innovator since 1997, when she attended IBM's first virtual trade mission to Malaysia. Betty's firm has won numerous awards, such as for Chamber of Commerce Business of the Year and for Entrepreneurism in the Community.

She is the founder of the Durham Home and Small Business Association, the past chair of the Durham Economic Development Advisory Committee, a founding director of Women in International Trade Ontario, the past treasurer for Ontario Family Health Networks, and past member of Local Integrated Health Networks (LIHNs). She is a current committee member for Durham Tourism Partners, focusing on economic development and green initiatives.

# Resources and Bibliography

A tremendous number of resources about greening businesses and individual behavior are available on the Web. Even if the information is not geared specifically toward the nonprofit sector, much of it will be applicable. The resources listed here were found in the process of researching and writing these chapters. They can help you green your organization in various ways.

## Resources

**American Association of State Highway & Transportation Officials**
**www.transportation.org**
AASHTO is a nonprofit, nonpartisan association representing highway and transportation departments in the 50 states, the District of Columbia, and Puerto Rico. It represents all five transportation modes: air, highways, public transportation, rail, and water.

**American Public Transportation Association**
**www.apta.com/research/stats/ridership**
APTA is committed to strengthening and advancing public transportation. APTA's diverse membership is united in support of public transportation.

**BAN**
**www.ban.org**
BAN is the world leader focused on confronting the global environmental injustice and economic inefficiency of toxic trade (toxic wastes, products, and technologies) and its devastating impact. BAN is a 501(c)3 charitable organization in the United States, based in Seattle, Washington.

**Bike Portland**
**http://bikeportland.org**
BikePortland.org is a daily news source that covers the Portland bike scene, from street-level activism to the backrooms of city hall.

**Buying Green: The European Commission**
**http://ec.europa.eu/environment/gpp/pdf/buying_green_handbook_en.pdf**
Buying Green has published a handbook that explains in concrete terms how environmental considerations can be integrated into public procurement procedures. Ideas in this handbook can be useful for your nonprofit.

**CarbonFund**
**www.CarbonFund.org**
Carbonfund.org works with over 1,200 businesses and 450,000 individuals to reduce their carbon footprint and solve climate change through education, carbon offsets, and communication.

**Care2**
**www.care2.org**
Care2 provides powerful tools to make a difference in your life, community, country, and world. It is driven by passionate people (just like you) who want to restore the world's balance.

**Clean Currents**
**www.cleancurrents.com**
Clean Currents works with institutions, nonprofits, businesses, and homeowners to reduce their environmental impact and possibly save money through clean energy or carbon reduction strategies.

**Connect the Dots**
**www.connectthedotsnetwork.org**
Connect the Dots is a nonprofit effort dedicated exclusively to helping other non-profit organizations reduce their environmental footprint.

**Community Foundation of Palm Beach**
**www.cfpbmc.org**
Community Foundation of Palm Beach and Martin Counties Nonprofits Going Green Program aims to raise the awareness, capacity, and motivation within nonprofit orga-nizations in Palm Beach and Martin counties to improve the environmental sustain-ability of their operations. The program's Web site offers guidelines and a list of tips and resources, developed to help nonprofit organizations advance their sustainability efforts.

**Consumer Reports**
**www.consumerreports.org.**
Consumers Union is an expert, independent, nonprofit organization whose mission is to work for a fair, just, and safe marketplace for all consumers.

**Earth911.com**
**www.earth911.com**
Earth911.com offers information on how to reduce your environmental impact, how to reuse what you have, and how to recycle your trash. More than 100,000 recycling locations are registered in its recycling database.

**Ecolabels**
**www.ecolabelling.org.**
Ecolabels are available in the categories of buildings, carbon, electronics, energy, food, forest products, retail goods, textiles, tourism, and more. These labels help companies and consumers find green products.

**Ecology Center**
**www.ecocenter.org.**
The Ecology Center is a membership-based, nonprofit environmental organization based in Ann Arbor, Michigan. It was founded by community activists after the country's first Earth Day in 1970.

**Ecoprints**
**www.ecoprint.com**
The word "Ecoprinted" signifies the use of an environmentally responsible printing process. "Eco-ink" products take ink to a new level of environmental sensitivity. Their printing process is 100 percent carbon neutral.

**EcoTuesday**
**www.ecotuesday.com**
EcoTuesday is the Sustainable Business Leaders' Networking Forum. Learn about cutting-edge sustainable business and network with new and old friends.

**EDA Consulting**
**www.edaconsulting.org**
EDA Consulting serves small to midsize nonprofits locally, nationally, and internationally, helping them accomplish their goals and feed their passions. It provides consulting on best practices and capacity building in the areas of communications and outreach, board development, fundraising, next-generation issues, and leadership with special expertise in social media and online philanthropy.

**EHL Consulting Group**
**www.ehlconsulting.com**
The EHL Consulting Group is a full-service fundraising and management consulting firm located in suburban Philadelphia. Resources include grant writing, campaign planning and implementation, leadership development, creative approaches to nonprofit business practices, and strategic planning.

**ENERGY STAR**
**www.energystar.gov**
ENERGY STAR is a government-backed program that helps businesses and individuals to protect the environment through superior energy efficiency. Office equipment that has earned the ENERGY STAR helps save energy through special energy-efficient designs, which allow them to use less energy to perform regular tasks and automatically enter a low-power mode when not in use.

**ENonprofits Benchmarks**
**www.e-benchmarksstudy.com**
ENonprofits Benchmarks is the annual benchmarking survey by NTEN and the consulting firm M+R Strategic Services, providing key sector-wide benchmarks for nonprofits engaged in online advocacy, marketing, and fundraising.

**Enterprise Fleet Management**
**www.enterprise.com/fleets/Home.action**
Enterprise has a comprehensive environmental program in place that includes optimizing the vehicle mix, tapping into alternative fuels, and helping companies purchase offsets so their vehicles can be effectively carbon neutral.

**Environmentally Friendly Hotels**
**www.environmentallyfriendlyhotels.com**
Through Environmentally Friendly Hotels, find lodging worldwide that is committed to sustainable development.

***Environmental Leader***
**www.environmentalleader.com**
*Environmental Leader* is the leading daily trade publication keeping corporate executives fully informed about energy, environmental, and sustainability news.

**Environmental Protection Agency: "Managing Wet Weather with Green Infrastructure"**
**cfpub.epa.gov/npdes/greeninfrastructure/technology.cfm**
This document explains green infrastructure applications and approaches that can reduce, capture, and treat storm-water runoff at its source before it can reach the sewer system.

**Environmental Protection Agency: "WaterSense"**
**www.epa.gov/watersense/**
"WaterSense," a partnership program sponsored by the U.S. Environmental Protection Agency, makes it easy for Americans to save water and protect the environment. Look for the WaterSense label to choose quality, water-efficient products. Many products are available that do not require a change in your lifestyle.

**Environmental Protection Agency: "Be Water Wise"**
**www.epa.gov/region6/water/waterconserv**
Water conservation is the most cost-effective and environmentally sound way to reduce demand for water. There are many effective ways to conserve water.

**EPEAT**
**www.epeat.net**
EPEAT is a system to help buyers evaluate, compare, and select electronic products based on their environmental attributes. The system currently covers desktop and laptop computers, workstations, and computer monitors. EPEAT uses the IEEE 1680 family of standards for electronic product environmental assessment. Products in EPEAT are ranked according to three tiers of environmental performance: Bronze, Silver, and Gold.

**e.politics**
**www.epolitics.com**
e.politics is a Web site devoted to "dissecting the craft of online political advocacy." Lots of Web sites talk about politics—talk and talk and talk—but only a handful discuss much more than a particular point of view.

**European Environment Agency**
**www.eea.europa.eu**
The main clients of the European Environment Agency are the European Union institutions—the European Commission, the European Parliament, the European Council—and member countries. In addition to this central group of European policy actors, the agency also serves other EU institutions, such as the Economic and Social Committee and the Committee of the Regions.

**The Foundation Center**
**www.foundationcenter.org**
The Foundation Center is a national nonprofit service organization recognized as the nation's leading authority on organized philanthropy, connecting nonprofits and the grant makers supporting them to tools they can use and information they can trust.

**Frogloop**
**www.frogloop.com**
Frogloop is a blog for nonprofit professionals engaged in online advocacy, marketing, and fundraising, with a wide variety of practical tools and tips from leading practitioners. Operated by Care2 as a service to the nonprofit sector.

**Fuel Economy and Emissions**
**www.fueleconomy.gov**
Joint Department of Energy (DOE)/Environmental Protection Agency (EPA) fuel economy and emissions Web site. The site helps fulfill DOE/EPA's responsibility under the Energy Policy Act (EPAct) of 1992 to provide accurate miles-per-gallon information to consumers.

**Global Action Plan International**
**www.globalactionplan.com**
Global Action Plan International (GAP International) is a network of nongovernmental organizations that offer expertise in behavioral change for sustainable development. Services range from online calculators (ecological footprint, carbon footprint) to consultancy regarding policy and strategy tools. Their carbon-neutral and sustainable development programs rest on empowerment of individuals and groups.

**Global Standards Organization**
**www.global-standard.org**
The aim of these standards is to define requirements to ensure the organic status of textiles, from harvesting of the raw materials, through environmentally and socially responsible manufacturing, up to labeling, in order to provide a credible assurance to the end consumer.

**GreenBiz**
**www.GreenBiz.com**
*GreenBiz* is the place to go for news and opinion of the green economy. Green business expert Joel Makower is executive editor.

**Green Business Insurance**
**www.greenbusinessinsurance.com**
Green Business Insurance is the place to go for eco-friendly insurance, with Pat Thompson of Dublin, Ohio. The company is a leader in providing insurance policies and services to green and/or sustainable businesses.

**Green Car Institute**
**Www.greencars.org**
Green Car Institute encourages the development and widespread use of alternative and clean fuel vehicles. It emphasizes related areas, such as automotive recycling, environmentally conscious manufacturing, and total environmental load to provide greater understanding of these important and interconnected issues.

**Green Café**
**www.greencafenetwork.org**
Green Café Network is dedicated to bringing sustainability to the mainstream by reducing the ecological impacts of the coffeehouse industry and harnessing café culture for environmental education, inspiration, and action.

**Green Collaborate**
**www.greencollaborate.org**
Green Collaborate is an online portal for Canadian nonprofit organizations and charities used for collaboration among team members, staff, and board. This program can help nonprofits with branded e-mail, an online calendar, fundraising communication, sharing and editing of documents, reminders for due dates, and easy management

of information with secure data storage, virtually at any time, wherever there is an Internet connection.

**Green Drinks**
**www.GreenDrinks.org**
GreenDrinks are organizers of green networking events. Every month people who work in the environmental field meet up at informal sessions known as Green Drinks.

**Green-e**
**www.Green-e.org**
Green-e is the nation's leading independent consumer protection program for the sale of renewable energy and greenhouse gas reductions in the retail market. Green-e offers certification of renewable energy and carbon offset products, and licenses the logo for organizations that purchase or generate sufficient quantities of renewable energy.

**GREENGUARD Environmental Institute (GEI)**
**www.greenguard.org**
GEI is an industry-independent, nonprofit organization that oversees the GREEN-GUARD Certification Program[SM]. As a standards developer authorized by the American National Standards Institute, GEI establishes acceptable indoor air standards for indoor products, environments, and buildings. GEI's mission is to improve public health and quality of life through programs that improve indoor air.

**GreenKeyWest.com**
**www.greenkeywest.com**
This site has some of the very best work done to show how to save energy, reduce waste, and lessen your impact on the environment. It provides prices, formulas, and forms you can use.

**GreenNonprofits.Org**
**www.greennonprofits.org**
GreenNonprofits was founded by Ted Hart to be an accessible global source of practical information about greening your nonprofit workplace and a desktop tool for any nonprofit to become green(er). The Green Nonprofits Certification process is available for any organizations interested in documenting and publicly acknowledging their efforts and progress in becoming greener.

**The Green Office**
**www.thegreenoffice.com**
The Green Office is a provider of green office supplies.

**Green Post Cards**
**www.greenpostcards.com**
Green Post Cards provides green printing services, using recycled papers, soy-based inks, chemistry-free plates, and low-VOC cleaning solvents. It also is 100 percent windpower driven.

**Green Seal**
**www.greenseal.org**
Green Seal provides science-based environmental certification standards that are credible, transparent, and essential in an increasingly educated and competitive

marketplace. Green Seal is a 501(c)(3) nonprofit organization. It issued its first environmental standards in 1991–1992 with the first product certifications completed in 1992.

## Idealist
**www.idealist.org.**
Idealist is an interactive site where people and organizations can exchange resources and ideas, locate opportunities and supporters, and take steps toward building a world where all people can lead free and dignified lives.

## Idealware
**www.idealware.org**
Idealware provides candid and well-researched reviews and information about non-profit software and online tools, including advocacy tools.

## Living Roofs
**www.Livingroofs.org**
Living Roofs is the number-one green roof Web site in the United Kingdom. Livingroofs.org is an independent organization that promotes green roofs and living roofs in the United Kingdom and is the U.K. member of the European Federation of Green Roof Associations.

## McGraw-Hill Construction
**www.construction.com**
McGraw-Hill Construction connects people, projects, and products across the design and construction industry. For more than a century, the company has remained North America's leading provider of construction project information, plans and specifications, product information, industry news, and industry trends and forecasts. In print and online, the company offers a variety of tools, applications, and resources that easily integrate with its customers' workflows.

## National Recycling (NRC)
**www.nrc-recycle.org**
The NRC is a national nonprofit advocacy group with members that span all aspects of waste reduction, reuse, and recycling in North America. The coalition represents advocates from every region of the country, in every sector of the waste reduction field.

## Natural Step
**www.naturalstep.org**
Natural Step is an international nonprofit organization dedicated to education, advisory work, and research in sustainable development.

## NeighborWorks America
**www.nw.org/network/green/default.asp**
NeighborWorks America offers a brochure on its Web site called "Greening Your Non-Profit from the Inside Out: A NeighborWorks Guide for Community Development Organizations." Many of the ideas offered can be of use to your nonprofit organization.

## Network-Centric Advocacy
**www.network-centricadvocacy.net**
This is a blog by Marty Kearns, founder and executive director of the nonprofit Green Media Toolshed. Kearns is an innovator in the field of net-centric campaigning.

**New Organizing Institute**
**www.neworganizing.com**
The New Organizing Institute offers a progressive advocacy and campaign training program focused on online organizing using e-mails, blogs, video, social media, and other techniques.

**Nonprofit Recycling Network™**
**www.recycles.org**
Nonprofit Recycling Network™ links donors together with nonprofit recipients. It is a free, nationwide exchange network that focuses on assisting local teachers, technicians, schools, churches, and nonprofit groups interested in recycling and reusing computers, laptops, and office and school equipment.

**Nonprofit Technology Enterprise Network (NTEN)**
**www.nten.org**
NTEN is an organization of nonprofit professionals using technology to advance causes, sharing solutions and ideas. NTEN's annual conference is extremely helpful to many nonprofits engaged in online advocacy.

**Office Footprint Calculator™**
**www.thegreenoffice.com/carboncalculator/calculator/**
Office Footprint Calculator helps you calculate your carbon footprint. It considers your energy use, waste stream, and purchasing patterns to measure both the global acres required to support your activities and the carbon dioxide emissions that result. The use of exact figures is encouraged, but averages can also be used.

**Organic Trade Association (OTA)**
**www.ota.com/index.html**
OTA is the membership-based business association for the organic industry in North America. OTA's mission is to promote and protect organic trade to benefit the environment, farmers, the public, and the economy.

**PHH Arval Green Fleet**
**www.phharval.com/aboutPHHArval/mediaCenter/articles/greenFleetsurvey 2009.html**
PHH Arval, a subsidiary of PHH Corporation, is a leading fleet management services provider in the United States and Canada. PHH Arval provides outsourced fleet management solutions to corporate clients, including nearly one-third of the Fortune 500 companies.

**Pick Up Pal**
**www.pickuppal.com**
PickupPal provides a global presence on the Internet to intelligently connect drivers and passengers around the world, forming a new transportation marketplace. PickupPal integrates with the most popular social networking tools, making it easier for people to share rides with others who have similar interests or with whom they are already connected via colleagues or friends. PickupPal is a free service and is easily customizable for any individual, group, organization, sports team, corporation, or event.

**PlanIt**
**www.myPlanIt.com**
Planet Leaders Action Network (PlanIt) provides educational workshops and tools to nonprofit organizations interested in reducing their organization's impact on climate

change. Participants learn about renewable energy and carbon offset markets, energy efficiency, carbon footprint measurements, and sustainable purchasing and business practices.

**Progressive Exchange**
**www.progressiveexchange.org**
Progressive Exchange is a lively listserv and discussion forum for thousands of smart online advocacy experts from many nonprofit organizations. It is "progressive"—so conservative organizations would not be a good fit—but participants focus on practical tools and tips, not ideology.

**Pulse Staging**
**www.pulsestaging.com**
Pulse Staging is the first sustainable, eco-friendly audiovisual staging company in the United States.

**Seven-Star, Inc**
**www.sevenstarevents.com.**
Seven-Star, Inc. provides green event production and programming services, exhibit and sponsorship sales, and event greening and consulting for festivals, trade, and consumer expositions, conferences, and concerts. Seven-Star is an EPA Waste Wise sponsor and award winner of the EPA Gold Star.

**ShoreBank Pacific**
**www.Eco-bank.com**
This is the site for the green bank ShoreBank Pacific, which helps green businesses and the communities they are a part of, helping both to succeed. ShoreBank Pacific created and uses a sustainability evaluation system to measure each borrower's impact on community, conservation, and economy.

**SolarCity**
**www.solarcity.com**
SolarCity is a provider of solar power installations and power purchase agreements with businesses with no cost up front. SolarCity is the nation's leading full-service solar provider for homeowners, businesses, and government organizations.

**StartingUpGreen.com**
**www.StartingUpGreen.com**
This is Glenn Croston's site for green entrepreneurs, helping them to succeed with opportunities, strategies, and resources.

**Taproot Foundation**
**www.taprootfoundation.org**.
The Taproot Foundation exists to close the gap between the lack of operational resources nonprofits need to be effective, and to ensure all nonprofits have the infrastructure they need.

**TechSoup**
**www.techsoup.org**.
Similar to NTEN, TechSoup also has a "Green Tech" program with information on ways to work effectively while reducing travel. TechSoup.org offers nonprofits a one-stop resource for technology needs by providing free information, resources, and support. In addition, it offers a product philanthropy service called TechSoup Stock where nonprofits can access donated and discounted technology products, generously provided by corporate and nonprofit technology partners.

**TerraPass, Inc.**
**www.terrapass.com**.
TerraPass, Inc. is an organization dedicated to helping everyday people reduce the climate impact of their car and air travel. This site includes a carbon footprint calculator where you can estimate your personal usage as well as a funding program to help you reduce your carbon footprint.

**Transportation and Housing Costs**
**www.demographia.com/db-cextr.pdf**
This site provides lists of consumer expenditures on housing and transportation in 18 U.S. metropolitan areas for U.S. families, 2006 to 2007.

**Tri-Met Public Transit**
**http://trimet.org**
Tri-Met in Portland Oregon is striving to build a safe, comfortable, reliable, and innovative transit system that delivers transportation options to a growing region.

**Union of Concerned Scientists**
**www.ucsusa.org/cleanvehicles**
Consumers deserve better performance and less pollution than automakers currently provide. Union of Concerned Scientists' experts in diesel, gasoline, and advanced vehicle technologies provide consumers and decision makers with the information they need to build a robust economy based on cleaner transportation choices.

**U.S. Department of Energy**
**www.cityoflancasterca.org/Index.aspx?page=615**
The U.S. Department of Energy has published a brochure packed with tips on saving energy and money at home. Many of the ideas discussed in the brochure can also be useful for your nonprofit organization.

**U.S. Green Building Council**
**www.usgbc.org**
The U.S. Green Building Council is a nonprofit membership organization whose vision is a sustainably built environment within a generation.

**Water Footprint Network**
**www.waterfootprint.org**
Online water footprint calculator.

**Zip Car**
**www.ZipCar.com**
A company that provides shared vehicles for corporate or personal use. Fewer cars, less congestion, and less pollution is good for the environment.

# Bibliography

Anderson, Ray. *Mid-Course Correction. Toward a Sustainable Enterprise: The Interface Model.* White River Junction, VT: Chelsea Green Publishing, 1998.
Barlow, Maude. *Blue Covenant: The Global Water Crisis and the Coming Battle for the Right to Water.* Toronto: McClelland & Stewart, 2007.
Barlow, Maude, and Tony Clarke. *Blue Gold. The Battle Against Corporate Theft of the World's Water.* Toronto: McClelland & Stewart, 2002.

Boschert, Sherry. *Plug-in Hybrids: The Cars that Will Recharge America*. New Society
   Publishers (December 1, 2006).

Bouguerra, Mohammed Larbi. *Water under Threat*, trans. Patrick Camiller. In Black
   Point, Nova Scotia: Zed Books (October 3, 2006), Bass, Brad, and B. Baskaran.
   *Evaluating Rooftop and Vertical Gardens as an Adaption Strategy for Urban
   Areas* (NRCC-46737). Ottawa, Canada: National Research Council Canada, 2003.

Comerford, M. "It Breaks Your Heart," *Daily Herald* (Tondo, Philippines), April 17,
   2005.

De Villiers, Marq. *Water: The Fate of Our Most Precious Resource*, 2nd rev. ed.
   Toronto: McClelland & Stewart, 2003.

Dunnett, Nigel, and A. Clayden. *Rain Gardens: Managing Water Sustainably in the
   Garden and Designed Landscape*. Portland, OR: Timber Press, 2007.

Estes, J. 2009. *Smart Green: How to Implement Sustainable Business Practices in Any
   Industry—and Make Money*. Hoboken, NJ: John Wiley & Sons.

Esty, Daniel, and Andrew Winston. *Green to Gold: How Smart Companies Use Environmental Strategy to Innovate, Create Value, and Build Competitive Advantage*.
   New Haven, CT: Yale University Press, 2006.

Gershon, David. *Water Stewardship: A 30 Day Program to Protect and Conserve Our
   Water Resources*. New York: Empowerment Institute, 2008.

Gleick, Peter H., et al. *The World's Water, 2008–2009: The Biennial Report on
   Freshwater Resources*. Washington, DC: Island Press, 2008.

Gleick, Peter H., et al. "Waste Not, Want Not: The Potential for Urban Water Conservation in California." Report of the Pacific Institute for Studies in Development,
   Environment, and Security, Oakland, CA, 2003.

Hawken, Paul, Amory Lovins, and L. Hunter Lovins. *Natural Capitalism: Creating
   the Next Industrial Revolution*. Back Bay Books; 1st edition (December 1, 2008).

Hirshberg, Gary. *Stirring It Up: How to Make Money and Save the World*. New York:
   Hyperion, 2008.

Lancaster, Brad. *Rainwater Harvesting for Drylands (Vol. 1): Guiding Principles to
   Welcome Rain into Your Life and Landscape*. Tucson, AZ: Rainsource Press,
   2006.

Lohan, T., ed. *Water Conciousness. How We All Have to Protect Our Most Critical
   Resource*. San Francisco: AlterNet Books, 2008.

Ludwig, Art. *The New Create and Oasis with Greywater: Choosing, Building and
   Using Greywater Systems—Includes Branched Drains*. Santa Barbara, CA: Oasis
   Design, 2006.

Masood, Ehsan, and Daniel Schaffer. *Dry: Life without Water*. Cambridge, MA:
   Harvard University Press, 2006.

McKay, Kim, and Jenny Bonnin, with Tim Wallace. *True Green @ Work: 100 Ways
   You Can Make the Environment Your Business*. Washington, DC: National Geographic, 2008.

Mintzer, R. *101 Ways to Turn Your Business Green: The Business Guide for Eco-
   Friendly Profits*. Entrepreneur Press; 1st edition (September 5, 2008).

Morrison, Jason, Mari Morikawa, Michael Murphy, Peter Schulte. *Water Scarcity and
   Climate Change: Growing Risks for Businesses and Investors*. (Report) Pacific
   Institute, February 2009, www.pacinst.org.

Motavalli, Jim. *Forward Drive: The Race to Build "Clean" Cars for the Future*. Sierra
   Club Books for Children (February 29, 2000).

National Energy Education Development Project. *Intermediate Energy Infobook*. Manassas VA: Need Project, 2008.

National Recycling Coalition. *NRC Conversionator*. National Recycling Coalition, 2009.

Nelson, Barry, R. Cohen, and G. Wolff. "Energy Down the Drain: The Hidden Costs of California's Water Supply." New York: Natural Resources Defense Council, August 2004.

Nelson, Barry, M. Schmitt, R. Cohen, N. Ketabi, and R. Wilkinson. "In Hot Water: Water Management Strategies to Weather the Effects of Global Warming." New York: Natural Resources Defense Council, July 2007.

Outwater, Alice. *Water. A Natural History*. New York: Basic Books, 1996.

Pearce, Fred. *When the Rivers Run Dry: Journeys Into the Heart of the World's Water Crisis*. Toronto: Key Porter Books, 2006.

Piasecki, B. The Green Advantage: How Today's Best Businesses Profit by Going Green and Solving Global Problems. ISBN: 1402214502 Sourcebooks, Inc., 2009.

Royte, Elizabeth. *Bottlemania: How Water Went on Sale and Why We Bought It*. New York: Bloomsbury USA, 2008.

Sandford, Robert William. *Water, Weather, and the Mountain West*. Surrey, BC: Rocky Mountain Books, 2007.

Schaeffer, J. *Real Goods Solar Living Sourcebook—Special 30th Anniversary Edition: Your Complete Guide to Renewable Energy Technologies and Sustainable Living*. Gaiam Real Goods (September 1, 2007).

Seireeni, Richard, with Scott Fields. *The Gort Cloud: The Invisible Force Powering Today's Most Visible Green Brands*. White River Junction, VT: Chelsea Green Publishing, 2008.

Sperling, Daniel, and Deborah Gordon. *Two Billion Cars: Driving Toward Sustainability*. New York: Oxford University Press, USA (January 13, 2009).

Steffen, Alex, A. G. *Worldchanging: A User's Guide for the 21st Century*. New York: Abrams, 2008.

Trask, C. *It's Easy Being Green: A Handbook for Earth-Friendly Living*. Gibbs Smith, Publisher; 1st edition (January 23, 2006).

Vaitheeswaran, Vijay, and Iain Carson. *ZOOM: The Global Race to Fuel the Car of the Future*. Twelve; Reprint edition (October 20, 2008).

Ward, Diane Raines. *Water Wars. Drought, Flood, Folly, and the Politics of Thirst*. New York: Riverhead Books, 2003.

"Working the Landfills a Dangerous Occupation," *Honduras This Week,* written by Thomas Debrouwer, Wednesday, October 8, 2008, 14:26.

Wood, Chris. *Dry Spring: The Coming Water Crisis of North America*. Vancouver: Raincoast Books, 2008.

U.S. Environmental Protection Agency. *Guidelines for Water Reuse*, EPA/625/R-04/108. Washington, DC: US EPA, 2004.

Yost, Nick. *The Essential Hybrid Car Handbook: A Buyer's Guide*. Lyons Press; 1st edition (October 1, 2006).

# Instructions and Guides

## Step-by-Step Instructions on Planning a Green Press Event

### Inviting Press to Your Nonprofit's Event

One of the best ways you can generate press for your nonprofit is by inviting press to an existing event or creating an event especially for press—a press conference. Your goal is to generate print, television, radio, and/or online stories about how your group is taking important steps to reduce its impact on the environment and implement the initiatives that will inspire and help other nonprofits to follow your lead.

Here we explain the steps you should take to organize a press event. We use this hypothetical scenario as an example:

*You work for a nonprofit hospital in a midsize American city, and your board has just decided to enact a series of programs that will:*

1. *Improve the building's energy efficiency.*
2. *Increase the building's use of renewable energy.*
3. *Reduce the hospital's paper use.*
4. *Challenge other healthcare facilities, including for-profit and government-run hospitals, to follow your lead.*

*(We're putting a number of possibilities here on purpose; any one of these proposals is a step in the right direction.)*

*You have called other nonprofit hospitals in your city and have found another five that agree to those four principles—and that agree to appear with you at an event at your hospital, along with a doctor researching the effects of pollution on asthma and a local politician who wants to introduce a bill into the legislature that would require every city hospital to reduce its paper use.*

**As soon as possible you should:**
- Pick a date and time for your event. The middle of the week, earlier in the day, is best. Mondays, Fridays, and weekends are usually difficult times to get reporters to turn out. (Yet those may be the only times in which you can ensure that people in the community can come, so it is a trade-off.)

- Gather support from your coworkers, donors, and other health professionals who work in your city. Let people know about the event well in advance.
- Pick a location. The best location would be a hospital, for obvious reasons, but hospitals often seem sterile. Consider using a widely visible area, near a landmark in town, such as city hall or a public park. If you choose a more public location, reach out to your local police immediately to let them know your plans and to ask whether you need a permit. If you encounter difficulties obtaining a permit, you may want to consider an alternative location that does not require one.

### Two to three days before the event, you should:
- Call reporters in your area and inform them that you will be holding an event—tell them you want to make sure they have it on their calendars. (We have provided you with a suggested phone script for this pitch later on in the appendix.)

### The day before the event in the morning, you should:
- E-mail/fax media advisory to your list of reporters to alert them to the event.
- A media advisory is literally just a half-page describing the very basic *who*, *what*, *where*, *when* and *why* of your event, with your contact information at the top.
- Follow-up with pitch phone calls to make sure they received the advisory and to ask them whether they will be attending (script provided).

### The morning of the event you should:
- E-mail and/or fax your media advisory to your list of reporters as a reminder.
- Follow-up with pitch phone calls to any reporters who did not yet confirm or who were on the fence about attending.

### The event:
- At the appointed time, prepare to deliver a short opening statement to the press. If cameras are in attendance, make sure you position yourself with a good backdrop—such as your hospital's logo or a local landmark, if you choose not to host the event at a hospital.
- Introduce yourself, ensure that whatever audio equipment broadcast media is using to get audio is working properly ("test, test..."), and then deliver your opening statement.
- If anyone else is presenting—including leaders or representatives of other organizations, local business leaders, or elected officials—act as the emcee and introduce the speakers in succession. Before the event, ask each speaker to limit comments to about three minutes. That way, when they talk for five, the press and attendees will not be too disappointed.
- Then open up the event to the press for questions and answers.
- After the question-and-answer (Q&A) session, some members of the press may ask you for one-on-one interviews.
- Where possible, ask members of the press when they plan to run a story, and make sure you give each your contact details so they can follow up with you if necessary. If they are willing, get their contact information as well.

### The afternoon after the event:

- Call the reporters who were in attendance. Ask them whether they have every-thing they need, and invite them to call you with any additional questions.
- Update your press list with the names and numbers of the reporters who were in attendance; these will come in handy in the future.
- Call the reporters on your list who were unable to make it. Tell them you are sorry they missed the event but that you hope they will consider covering the issue. Tell them you would be pleased to meet them to discuss it more at their convenience.

### The evening of the event and the day after:

- Watch out for press coverage by the reporters or news outlets that were in attendance. If stories do not appear in a week, follow up with phone calls to ask them whether they need anything else.
- Take note if other hospitals—nonprofit, for-profit, or government-run—call and ask if they can participate in your sustainability initiatives.

## Submitting an Op-Ed to Your Local Newspaper

An op-ed is an excellent way to deliver an unfiltered message to local news con-sumers. Often, however, getting them printed can be challenging.

In the example given earlier, you could write an op-ed on your organization's behalf issuing the four-point challenge on sustainability, laying out the reasons your hospital is undergoing these changes and why other hospitals should follow suit.

Here is some guidance on op-ed writing and submission:

- Often it is often easiest to start off with three simple sentences that represent the three main points you would like to get across in the piece.
- Remember to localize your op-ed as much as possible and place your points within the context of current events. For example, maybe other cities in your state or other sectors are looking at undergoing similar sustainability programs. Use that to your advantage.
- Remember to keep the op-ed to a maximum of 900 words. (Ideally, it should be between 700 and 800 words. Ask your local paper if it has a different word limit.)
- Once you have a final op-ed, e-mail (or, less preferably, fax) it to the op-ed submissions contact at one of your local newspapers.
- A few hours after you submit your op-ed article, call the publication to ensure the piece was received.
- Look for it in the newspaper over the next two to three days. If it does not appear, follow up with your contact to ask them whether he or she intends to run the piece.
- If the newspaper turns down your op-ed, consider submitting it to another paper in your area.
- *Never* submit the same op-ed to two publications at the same time. This will hurt your credibility. All op-ed submissions are meant to be exclusive until a newspaper decides not to run your piece.

## Submitting a Letter to the Editor

A letter to the editor can be a good substitute for an op-ed or another way to get your message out to smaller papers. If your op-ed is turned down by the main newspaper in your area:

- Offer that newspaper a shorter version of the op-ed as a letter to the editor instead—this is our "second best" option.
- Like the op-ed, review the letter and localize it as appropriate. Letters to the editor usually run about 100 to 150 words.
- Once the letter is ready, send it to the contact provided. Note in your e-mail/fax that the newspaper turned down your op-ed but that you are hoping it will accept this letter to the editor instead.

If your op-ed is accepted by the main newspaper in your area:

- Submit your letter to the editor to another print publication.

## Pitching Local Radio Stations

Local news and talk radio have time to fill and are often very popular. Pitching your issue or event—and yourself—to local radio stations is an excellent way to spread your nonprofit's message and to broaden your reach. Resulting interviews are often much longer than television pieces and can give you an opportunity to talk about your issues in your own words.

- Some local radio stations may attend your event and produce a news piece. (If that piece is long and extensive, you probably should not pitch them again, at least for a few weeks. But if they are short pieces, you should make sure to follow up with them as well.)
- In the days following your event, send out a radio advisory (essentially a media advisory) to the radio stations on your press list.
- Follow up with a pitch call to the radio stations to make sure they have your advisory. Ask if they need any more information and whether they would be interested in scheduling an interview.
- If a station expresses interest, it will most likely set up either a live or a taped interview. It will most likely be on the phone (landlines are preferable), but you may be asked to go to the station to do it in person.

# How to Work with the Media

Dealing with the media can sometimes seem daunting or complicated, but it should not be! This guide gives you some helpful hints on how to conduct press outreach and to stay on message.

## The Press Today

You will undoubtedly face some challenges when dealing with the press, and you should remember their state of mind. The reality is that reporters are likely to be:

- **In a hurry.** Reporters often have many stories to work on and tight deadlines. Often they appear rushed or rude—you should be prepared for that. It is just their manner, and you should respect it.
- **Driven by deadlines and competition.** Reporters often face a series of daily deadlines that can make their jobs very difficult and stressful. In addition, they sometimes are competing on a story against other outlets. Sometimes that can make them very eager, even pushy.
- **Generalists, not experts.** A reporter is unlikely to be an expert on the issue of climate change or at least on how to solve the problem. Reporters have to cover many different stories with lots of information—they often do not know the background. This can work to your advantage; remember, everything the reporters will know is based on information they get on the topic. If you dominate the information flow, you are likely to get better coverage.
- **Focused on the negative.** The way news is presented these days, reporters tend to gravitate toward a negative storyline. When news pops about an oceanic cooling trend, or when climate change deniers make news, they may want to focus on those stories rather than your message of sustainability. Your job is to make sure they get the whole story.

But there is good news in all this. In order for reporters to do a story, they will need your help in a number of areas. If you conduct yourself in a professional manner and provide them with the right advice and information, you can be a great success.

Reporters will need:

- **The facts.** You will be providing reporters with a fair amount of their information.
- **Quotes.** Reporters will need quotes from you to legitimize and lend authority to the story. What you say—during the press conference but also when you call to tell them more about it—could be quoted. Remember that at all times.
- **Additional background information, follow-up questions.** Your goal should be to become one of the reporters' go-to sources on the issue of environmental initiatives and nonprofits. You should make clear that if they need any background information on the topic—or have follow-up questions—they should feel free to contact you.

## Preparing for Interviews

Spending some time preparing yourself ahead of your event or any press interview is the single most important thing you can do before you engage in press activities. Obviously, you cannot script an interview or Q&A session, but by practicing, you can prepare to tell your side of the story.

You can do that by:

- **Reviewing your materials: messages, opening statement, fact sheets, and so on.** Most important, have in your mind the top one to three messages you want to get across on your nonprofit and its green work. Practice delivering these short statements.

- **Remembering that repetition is critical.** There is no such thing as being repetitive in an interview of this kind. Television cameras will want you to deliver your sound byte: By repeating it with them, you will have the best chance of making sure the statement you want to deliver is the one they air.
- **Keeping it simple.** Do not overthink the issue or get tied up in complicated background. As you practice, make sure you are thinking of ways to explain this issue simply and directly. Avoid jargon.

## Interview Techniques

A simple list of techniques that should help you think about how to engage the press during the Q&A session of your event is presented next.

- **Get your message across—no matter what question a reporter may ask.** That means that if you get a difficult or irrelevant question, use it as a guide to "pivot" back to your message. In other words, acknowledge that the question is important, but then use it to go back to your important message about urgency and solvability. The next dialogue is a useful example of a reporter asking an irrelevant question and how you can turn the question back to your advantage:
  **Reporter:** But you're just one [hospital] with your environmental agenda—what about all of the [medical waste] you're putting out there? Doesn't that contradict what you're trying to accomplish here?
  **Spokesperson:** It's important to understand just how many other [hospitals] are taking similar, far-reaching steps to create a more sustainable [healthcare] environment. But let's remember the key issue here—the fact is that if we don't act, who is going to take responsibility for the health of our communities and the health of our planet? What we need is a massive and sustained national effort to empower other [hospitals] to become leaders in sustainability. [Hospitals] can [save lives] more than one way, and our sustainability initiatives are consistent with the work we do every day to [make the world a better place].
  - In this example, the spokesperson acknowledges the question but goes back to the key issue as soon as possible. (Words in brackets can be replaced according to your nonprofit's efforts.)
- **Remember sound bytes.** Today, the average sound byte is a tiny *six seconds* long! So, as you answer questions, remember that of everything you say, less than six seconds might be used. Do not say anything you would not like to hear as your sound byte on this issue—and be sure to repeat the key messages in a succinct way.
- **Answer questions one at a time.** If a reporter asks you a long list of questions at once, do not let it throw you off, and do not get bogged down by taking the questions too literally. Pick the one you like most and answer that. Or step back and give the reporter a broader perspective: "I think what you're really asking is..."
- **Tell the truth and do not guess.** Make sure you are being as accurate as possible—this is vital for your credibility. If you do not know the answer to a question, do not make it up. It is perfectly fine to tell a reporter that you will

research something and get back to him or her once you know the answer to the question.

- **Deal with mistakes.** We all make mistakes, and you should be prepared to, as well. If you make a mistake on camera during a taped (i.e., not live) interview, do not worry. Just stop, compose yourself, and say, "I'm sorry, what I meant to say was . . ." or "I should correct that by explaining . . ." Avoid saying something, regretting it, and then saying "Don't quote me on that."
- **Avoid jargon or technical language.** Avoid insider's terms that may be unfamiliar to the general public. Try to simplify your explanations, and use analogies to help explain difficult concepts. Using local examples will help, too—for instance, talk about a large, well-known nonprofit *in a different, noncompeting sector* that is instituting some of the same policies your nonprofit is if your nonprofit is not yet widely known.
- **Maintain eye contact.** Eye contact will hold a reporter's attention and will make you look confident.
- **Be enthusiastic.** You have a great issue to talk about. Now it is time to convey your compelling story to readers, viewers, and listeners. Smile when it is appropriate.
- **Keep your answers succinct.** Do not feel compelled to keep talking. When you have covered your message point, stop talking.
- **Stay away from filling awkward silences.** You should not feel nervous when no one is talking. Wait for the reporter to ask you the next question. Remember the rule: If you have covered your message point, stop talking.

## Your Media List and Pitching the Media

You may know the media in your area very well. Or you may never have done press outreach. Either way, you should now have the tools to start developing relationships with the press.

Here's how:

- **Work with your media list**—television, radio, print, and online outlets in your area. You compile this list using national databases available to public relations professionals or simply by calling news editors and assignment editors at local media outlets and asking who in the newsroom covers which topics.
- **Keep your media list current.** If you use a professional database, it is very likely it is missing some outlets or that contacts have moved on. That is to be expected—media lists are constantly changing. You should seek to update, expand, and correct your media list as much as you can. Each time you make a pitch phone call, be sure to keep notes and follow up with other people whom your contacts suggest: Pitching is all about identifying the appropriate people to talk to and persistence.
- **Find the right person.** When you start pitching your event, your goal should be to find the right person to cover it from each outlet. Start with a news desk contact, but each time you make a call, make sure you ask the reporter or producer if anyone else at that publication or outlet should be getting your materials as well.

- **Respect deadlines.** There are good times and bad times to pitch reporters. Here is a brief guide:
  - **Print.** It is best to call a newsroom between 10 A.M. and 2 P.M. At this time, reporters are most likely not in planning meetings or working against a 5 P.M. deadline.
  - **Television.** Planning editors generally take calls between 10 and 11 A.M. and 1 and 3 P.M. It is best to call the assignment desk after the morning planning meeting, which usually ends between 9:30 and 10 A.M.
  - **Radio.** The best time to call is early—around 7:30 to 8:30 A.M. After that, the staff goes into planning meetings, but you can start calling again after 10 A.M. News directors, reporters, and producers are often gone by the afternoon. If a reporter is not able to attend the event, offer to do a taped interview.

### Dos of Successful Pitching

- **DO** be concise while pitching the story.
- **DO** assume your event is worth a reporter attending.
- **DO** be enthusiastic about your event.
- **DO** be persistent and call back at a later time if you do not get in touch with the reporter right away.

### Don'ts of Successful Pitching

- **DON'T** leave a long phone message with your phone number at the end; leave your name and number immediately after your brief pitch.
- **DON'T** sound like you are reading a script.
- **DON'T** argue with a reporter.
- **DON'T** call during a big news story or at deadline.

## Sample Media, Marketing, and Communications Materials

These materials are provided to give you the tools you need to conduct press outreach. Of course, we recognize that your individual situations are different and we strongly recommend personalizing and localizing all these materials as much as possible.

- Journalist pitch phone scripts
- Actual press release for green nonprofit event

### Sample Phone Scripts for Pitching Reporters

Next is a guide for what to say to reporters when you call them two to three days before the event. Make this call shortly after you send them a media advisory (sample follows the pitch script).

The paragraph breaks shown are there for a reason: They mark where you should wait for a response from the person you are calling—and where to take a breath.

Hi, my name is [NAME] from [YOUR NONPROFIT].

I'm calling to let you know about an event with [OTHER NONPROFIT PARTNERS] and [LOCAL LAWMAKER] that will highlight [NEW SUSTAINABILITY INITIA-TIVES].

At [LOCATION] on [DAY] at [TIME], we will be [ANNOUCING OUR NEW INITIATIVE] because of our commitment to sustainability.

I'll be back in touch [THE DAY BEFORE THE EVENT], but I just wanted to let you know and get this on your radar.

Do you think this is something you'd be interested in covering?

Remember to call back the day before the event!

---

## Actual Press Release for Green Nonprofit Event

For immediate release: July 24, 2008
Press inquiries: Gabe Roth, 202-337-0808, groth@gpgdc.com

### Home Buyers Increasingly Thinking and Buying Green

**IMPROVED AIR QUALITY AND ENERGY SAVINGS CITED AS KEY HOUSING FACTORS FOR ALL FAMILIES, NEW STUDY FINDS**

**Green Homes Seen as Bright Spot for All Income Levels**   *New York, NY*—Lower energy costs, healthier living and improved indoor and outdoor environments are increasingly demanded by and available to home buyers at all income levels, according to preliminary findings from a survey released by the U.S. Green Building Council (USGBC) and McGraw-Hill Construction.

Families and individual homeowners with the lowest incomes are overwhelmingly satisfied with their green home, more likely to recommend a green home to family and friends, and strongly prefer green homes as a purchasing option. The survey found that 78 percent of homeowners earning less than $50,000 per year say they would be more inclined to purchase a green home. The first findings from the study were released at the site of affordable multi-family homes under construction in the Bronx, NY. The development, Melrose Commons 5, is being built with LEED certification as a goal.

"The benefits of green homebuilding must be accessible, and affordable, for every American family," said Michelle Moore, senior vice president, U.S. Green Building Council, which develops and administers the LEED Green Building Rating System for homes, offices, schools, hospitals, and other buildings nationwide.

"Being able to afford your utility bill is as important as being able to pay your mortgage," Moore added. "Green homes are shining through as the bright spot in an otherwise gloomy housing market."

*(continued)*

*(Continued)*

The survey estimates that within the last three years more than 330,000 market rate homes with green features have been built in the United States, representing a $36 billion per year industry. An estimated 60,000 of those homes were third-party certified through LEED or a local green building program.

"Fully committed to sustainability for the long-term, green home buyers and remodelers cut across all demographic lines, regardless of income, zip code, or anything else. Builders are seeing great interest in green across all income levels," said Robert Ivy, vice president and editorial director of McGraw-Hill Construction.

"We're crossing the tipping point for green home building," added Harvey M. Bernstein, McGraw-Hill Construction vice president of Industry Analytics, Alliances and Strategic Initiatives. "Concerns about energy costs, health, and even resale value are adding up green for builders, buyers, and renters. Green homes are here to stay."

The full McGraw-Hill Construction SmartMarket Report will be released this fall. The aim, said Bernstein, is to help builders better respond to the needs of green home buyers and to help product manufacturers and other industry players understand the ever-expanding value of this marketplace.

**Key Study Findings**  McGraw-Hill Construction surveyed a representative sample of one million U.S. households (equating to three million consumers) to find those individuals who had purchased LEED certified and other green homes over the last three years and probe them about their attitudes. The vast majority (83%) said their new homes will lower operating costs; lower energy bills within the first year after purchase (79%); and also lower water bills within the first year after purchase (68%).

Going green was the top reason cited by survey respondents for remodeling their home. Environmental benefits such as lower energy costs and healthier air were identified by 42 percent of respondents as their main reason for home improvements; 34 percent cited increased comfort; only 24 percent said improved appearance was their main benefit from remodeling.

Other key findings of the McGraw-Hill Construction survey include:

- 70% of buyers are either more or much more inclined to purchase a green home over a conventional home in down housing market.
- More than half (56%) of those surveyed who have bought green homes earn less than $75,000 per year; 29% earn less than $50,000.
- Overall, lower-income buyers say they found tax credits and government programs, indoor air quality benefits, and green certifications to be the most important incentives for them to buy green homes.
- Making homes greener is now the number-one reason for home improvement (42%) over remodeling for comfort reasons (34%) or to improve appearance (24%).
- Almost half (44%) of homes renovated between 2005 and 2007 used products chosen for their green attributes.

More than 80 percent of respondents said they believe that green homes are not just more economical, but offer better and healthier places to live. To that end, a new long-term study by the Mount Sinai School of Medicine will track the impact green homes have on childhood asthma in children who will soon live in the Melrose 5 homes. Currently one in six kids in the South Bronx suffers from asthma, one of the highest rates in the nation.

**Going Green in New York** "We can no longer ignore the responsibility of pursuing environmentally sustainable development," said Bronx Borough President Adolfo Carrión, Jr. "As the Bronx and the entire city continue to grow, we must understand that 'economic viability' and 'environmentally friendly' are not mutual exclusive. We have to keep creating a set of conditions in which future generations will enjoy cities that are both economically strong and environmentally sound."

The Melrose Commons 5 development, where highlights of the data were released, will provide 63 rental apartments to families whose income does not exceed 60% of the median income in New York City. The buildings will incorporate 10 wind-powered turbine engines to generate electricity. Each apartment will have individual outside ventilation instead of central ducts. Specially designed window "trickle" vents will bring fresh air into each unit. Energy and water-saving design strategies will be used throughout the development.

"Green affordable housing saves energy and money, while improving the social, environmental, and economic fabric of our communities," New York Secretary of State Lorraine Cortés-Vázquez said in remarks at the event. "Governor Paterson's efforts to make green building accessible to all New Yorkers are a major component of his comprehensive state energy plan. Securing social and environmental equity has been an integral part of my professional and personal life. More importantly, it is an important part of Governor Paterson's agenda and has been since he was Senator Paterson." New York recently passed legislation to provide grants for green home building and renovation and is continuing to offer incentives for green affordable housing.

Blue Sea Development Co. is constructing and will manage the Melrose Commons 5 development. Last year, Blue Sea opened the nearby Morrisania Homes, the first LEED affordable housing development in New York State.

"Building green homes is one of the most important ways architects and developers can make a positive impact on the health and well-being of homeowners of all income levels," said Les Bluestone, president of Blue Sea. "The cost of installing green products into homes is minimal. And direct benefits to homeowners start as soon as they move in."

A school teacher who lives in a LEED Morrisania Homes condominium said homeowners nationwide are benefitting from the move to green. "My home is a special place for two important reasons: first, because my husband and I own the house, which is itself a blessing; and second, because it is a healthy and affordable place to live," said Namiana Filion, who teaches Spanish in Brooklyn. "It's been a wonderful experience for me and my family, for my pocket and for the environment."

*(continued)*

*(Continued)*

For more information and to see a time-lapse video of Melrose Commons 5 construction, please visit www.TheGreenHomeGuide.org/affordable.

**Note to Broadcast and Online Media: Time-Lapse Video Available**  A time-lapse video showing Melrose Commons 5 speeding into shape is available for unrestricted broadcast news and online use. The video was shot over a two-week period in July 2008 as pre-cast wall sections were trucked in from local factories and lifted into place. It can be viewed and downloaded at www.GreenHomeGuide.org/Affordable. For additional information or to request a copy on Beta tape, please contact Gabe Roth at groth@gpgdc.com or 202-337-0808.

**About the U.S. Green Building Council**  The U.S. Green Building Council is a non-profit membership organization whose vision is a sustainable built environment within a generation. Its membership includes corporations, builders, universities, government agencies, and other nonprofit organizations. Since USGBC's founding in 1993, the Council has grown to more than 16,500 member companies and organizations, a comprehensive family of LEED® green building certification systems, an expansive educational offering, the industry's popular Greenbuild International Conference and Expo (www.greenbuildexpo.org), and a network of 78 local chapters, affiliates, and organizing groups. For more information, visit www.usgbc.org.

**About McGraw-Hill Construction**  McGraw-Hill Construction connects people, projects and products across the design and construction industry. For more than a century, the Company has remained North America's leading provider of construction project information, plans and specifications, product information, industry news, and industry trends and forecasts. In print and online, the Company offers a variety of tools, applications, and resources that easily integrate with its customers' workflows. Backed by the power of Dodge, Sweets, *Architectural Record, Engineering News-Record (ENR), GreenSource*, and 11 regional publications, McGraw-Hill Construction serves more than one million customers within the $4.6 trillion global construction community. To learn more, visit www.construction.com.

# Green Event (Venue) Assessment

At the core of planning for greening your event, the first steps begin in venue selection and determination of what sustainability practices the venue is undertaking. A venue with policies and procedures for best practices or environmental responsibility into social respect (eR/sR) will better facilitate the execution of your green plans and may be greatly influenced by the experience of your events practices. Next we present an interview questionnaire that will assess the venue's eR/sR practices, allowing your event team to determine the opportunities to reduce the event's footprint by integrating the venue's current practices with your greening plans. Additionally the venue's best practices will provide a framework for educating your attendees, exhibitors, presenters, and sponsors with the overall responsible environmental and social aspects of the event.

Facility: _____

Contact person: _____

Address: _____

Phone:                    Fax:                    E-mail:

Please provide contact names and numbers for those people responsible for the following operations and services:

Food Service/Caterer: _____

Purchasing: _____

Custodial: _____

Maintenance/Facilities: _____

Event Manager: _____

## Venue Best Practices Questionnaire

### Do you purchase recycled products?
- ☐ Office supplies
- ☐ Copy and printing paper
- ☐ Letterhead, stationery, envelopes
- ☐ Binders
- ☐ Do you purchase reusable, durable products?
- ☐ Do you purchase items in bulk with less packaging?
- ☐ Do you purchase concentrates when possible (e.g., cleaning products)?

### Do you recycle or donate as appropriate the following:
- ☐ Office paper and mixed paper
- ☐ Corrugated cardboard
- ☐ Newspaper and magazines
- ☐ Toner cartridges
- ☐ Computers or electronic equipment
- ☐ Furniture
- ☐ Office supplies

### Do you reduce paper use by any of the following:
- ☐ Double-sided copying
- ☐ Double-sided printing
- ☐ Scrap paper use for notes
- ☐ E-mail for memos
- ☐ Don't print drafts or print them on scrap paper

☐ Print faxes on scrap paper
☐ Print letterhead or forms on demand
☐ Printer drawer for one-sided scrap paper
☐ Use erasable boards/Power Point instead of flipcharts

**Please indicate efforts made toward energy conservation:**
☐ Have you installed compact fluorescent lamps for task lighting?
☐ Have you installed T-8 or T-5 higher efficacy lamps in overhead fluorescent fixtures?
☐ Have you installed HID (high intensity discharge) lamps in appropriate areas?
☐ Have you installed reflectors in fluorescent or other fixtures?
☐ What natural lighting installations are in the venue?
☐ Are thermostats set on timers?
☐ Do you adjust the temperature in the building depending on whether you have an event in progress or not?
☐ Are there any areas in the venue operating with motion-activated lighting?
☐ Are your escalators programmable?
☐ Are your escalators motion activated?
☐ What policies do you have on freight elevator usage?
☐ What energy conservation practices do your employees use?
☐ What back of the house lighting practices do you employ?
☐ Does your office equipment automatically power off if not used for a set time?
☐ Do you have a policy or program to have all office equipment turned off at the end of work time?
☐ What ENERGY STAR appliances and equipment do you use?

## Event Venue: Landfill Diversion Objectives Questionnaire

1. List the number and capacity of each of the following containers that you use:
   _____ Dumpsters _____ Roll-offs _____ Compactors _____
   Gondolas
   _____ Waste Cans and Sizes _____ Toters and Sizes
2. Indicate what type of service you have and if the event planner pays for the service:
   _____ Flat rate: What charges are passed to the event? _____
   _____ Per pull charge: What charges are passed to the event? _____
   _____ Per pull charge + per pound charge: What charges are passed to the event? _____
   We require the Dumpster, debris box, and/or compactor emptied for our event, to determine our landfill diversion weights/volume from the contracted hauler. Is this possible? _____Yes _____ No
3. We require hauling service provider to provide information on certified weights or volume on waste/recyclables/compostables that are collected, processed, and marketed. Is this possible? _____ Yes _____ No
4. Do you collect any materials for recycling, composting, or reuse? If so, please complete the information below.

| Material | Collection Unit: roll-off, gondolas, compactor | Pickup Services: recycler, composter, waste hauler | Costs or Rebates |
|---|---|---|---|
| Mixed paper | | | |
| Cardboard | | | |
| Aluminum | | | |
| Glass | | | |
| Plastics 1 and 2 | | | |
| Plastics 3–6 | | | |
| Shrinkwrap | | | |
| Vinyl | | | |
| Palette | | | |
| Steel bands | | | |
| Gray water | | | |
| Oils | | | |
| Food waste | | | |
| Bio-ware | | | |
| Organic materials | | | |

### I. Landfill Diversion: Goal of >75% diversion of all waste produced and/or brought into event venue.

   i. What recycling can be mingled, and what must be kept separate at the venue?
  ii. Can the facility provide the biodegradable liners or accept ours?
 iii. Can volunteers take items collected in receptacles to back-of-the-house collection units to prevent contamination or incorrect placement by janitorial staff?
  iv. We will want to train all janitorial staff working the event regarding our Resource Recovery plan and efforts to make sure they do not unknowingly contaminate and therefore negate our efforts at landfill diversion. Can we arrange trainings?
   v. Will the facility supplement additional cans (35 to 55 gallon) to meet the minimum Reduce, Reuse, Recycle needs?

### II. Objective: Cardboard, paper, glass, cans, and plastic items will be recycled.

   i. Where is storage area located?
  ii. Is the storage area well lit and safe to be used as a work site for quality control sorting teams?

### III. Objective: Food, beverage, oils, and biodegradable materials items will be composted.

   i. Does the facility handle oils?
  ii. Does the venue sell the oils to vendors, or is it disposed?
 iii. If sold, describe what the sold oil is used for.
  iv. If disposed, can we arrange for pickup?
   v. What oil collection units do you have, and where are they located?
  vi. What experience does the kitchen staff have in composting food waste?
 vii. Does the facility handle compost?
viii. Can we arrange for a compost debris box to be dropped at venue?
  ix. Where would compost debris box be placed?

    x. Can it be placed in the storage/work area mentioned above?

   xi. Do you donate any leftover food—perishable or nonperishable?

  xii. Does your food service area provide reusable service ware?

 xiii. Do you encourage the use of reusable cups and mugs?

 xiv. Do you provide bulk condiments, such as sugar, creamer, ketchup, and mustard?

### IV. Objective: All liquids will be diverted from storm water or sewer system

    i. Has the facility ever used a graywater recovery company?

   ii. Does the facility have a graywater collection system?

  iii. If neither is available, where at the facility can graywater be safely disposed of?

  iv. Where in the facility can we have a graywater tank dropped for collection and pickup?

   v. Can the tank be set up in the same place where compost, recycling, and landfill is being collected?

We would very much like to speak with any existing waste management, recyclers, and commercial composting organizations you have worked with. Please provide contact names and numbers for the following contracted or recommended organizations:

Waste management: _____

Recycler:_____

E-waste recycler: _____

Composter: _____

Graywater collection renter: _____

## Event Venue: Energy Usage and Conservation Questionnaire

    i. What is your average daily estimated or monthly electricity consumption ($ or kilowatt)?

   ii. Can you provide us the kilowatts of energy used from setup through move out?

  iii. What are the primary contributors to event energy consumption?

  iv. At what temperature is hot water maintained? Can the temperature be adjusted for our event?

   v. At what temperature are refrigerators, freezers, and walk-ins maintained? Can the temperature be adjusted for our event?

  vi. Will you adjust the building one degree warmer/colder than standard on show days?

 vii. Do you adjust the lighting in the building depending on the activities of our event?

viii. Will all lights and equipment be turned off in areas where no one is working during nonevent hours?

  ix. Are switches located conveniently so that requests to your employees to power down can be easily made?

x. Are outside lights on timers or light sensors? Can we request setting them for the schedule of our event?

xi. Will you adjust the thermostats to low when our event attendees are not occupying the building?

## Event Venue and *Convention and Visitors Bureau* (CVB): Public Transportation Questionnaire

i. Describe access to public transportation to the venue.

ii. Do you or the city offer transportation alternatives?

iii. Does the CVB offer any transport systems between hotels and venue?

iv. What information do you post on your Web site?

v. What kind of public education campaign do you have promoting public transportation?

vi. Have you worked with traffic safety on traffic flow timing to reduce idling?

vii. What nonprofit or for-profit organizations have collaborated with the venue on traffic reduction and increased public transit?

viii. Have you had a bike valet service before?
   a. Area for bike parking?
   b. Fencing or barricades available?

## Event Venue: Public Water Usage and Conservation Questionnaire

i. Do you have public water fountains?

ii. Is there access to a water main for attaching a water filtration system?

iii. Can we tap into the water port with a filtration system?

iv. Are head tables for speakers provided water pitchers?

v. Can we substitute individual bottled water with pitchers and glasses?

## Event Venue: Product Usage for Custodial and Maintenance

i. Who is responsible for cleaning? _____ In-house crew _____ Contracting company

ii. Are there written guidelines or requirements/specifications for cleaning products used?

iii. Do you specify methods or products they can or cannot use?

iv. Does cleaning staff use bulk concentrate cleaners?

v. Are cleaning supplies nontoxic and are chemical ingredients checked?

vi. Does cleaning staff use reusable rags and other green cleaning methods or products?

vii. Can we provide alternative no-VOCcleaning products for our event?

viii. Can we provide recycled-content bathroom products for our event?

ix. Can we provide organic soaps?

# Event Venue Caterer: Product Usage Food, Beverage, and Services Questionnaire

   i. Do you currently use Styrofoam containers? What alternatives do you offer or will consider getting?
   ii. What local foods can you source?
   iii. Is house catering currently recycling or composting?
   iv. Do you donate to local food banks?
   v. Can you arrange for us to provide training with kitchen and wait staff?
   vi. Do you source any foods that are fair trade?
   vii. Do you have access to local and/or organic beer and wine?
   viii. What kind of bulk service condiments can be offered instead of individual prepackaged units?
   ix. What kind of organically produced foods do you offer?
   x. Do you offer free-range, organic, or natural red meats or chicken on your menu?
   xi. What sustainable guidelines do you use for seafood selection and purchasing?
   xii. Can you provide a menu of vegetarian and vegan options and meals?
   xiii. What are your restrictions on purchases of fresh foods?
   xiv. Do you provide recycled-content paper napkins?
   xv. Can you provide pump or bulk service condiments?
   xvi. What type of disposable food service do you use?
   xvii. Do you have access to biodegradable food service ware?
   xviii. Are you recycling any products in your kitchen production usage?
   xix. Are you currently composting food waste from the kitchen and food scraps?
   xx. What are any limitations to recycling or composting?

# Event Vendor Green Assessment

## Decorator (General Service Contractor) Practices Questionnaire

   i. Do you use online order forms rather than printed?
   ii. Do you research your suppliers to ensure they are manufacturing their products in the most environmentally friendly way possible?
   iii. What green-friendly products are you currently using at events?
   iv. Do you reuse carpeting? If yes, do you track what percentage is reused? Is carpeting that is not inventoried for reuse sent to a recycling facility?
   v. Do you reuse signage? If yes, do you track what percentage is reused? Is nonreusable signage sent to a recycling facility or donated?
   vi. Have you reduced your use of plastic shrinkwrap? If yes, is used plastic shrinkwrap reused or recycled?
   vii. Do you provide an alterative to plastic vinyl tabletops? If no, do you recycle or reuse the vinyl?
   viii. Do you use pallets made of recycled materials? Do you reuse or recycle pallets?
   ix. Do you use biofuels for equipment operations or transportation?
   x. Do any of your vehicles use compressed natural gas, are they electric, or are they hybrid?
   xi. Do you enforce a nonidling policy for all gas-powered equipment? Would you?
   xii. Are cleaning supplies nontoxic and are chemical ingredients checked?

xiii. Does staff use reusable rags and other green cleaning methods or products?
xiv. Are you carbon-offsetting your freight energy usage?

## Exhibitor Practices Questionnaire

i. Do you turn the lights off in your booth outside of show hours?
ii. If you have a walk-away product for sale, do you package it in recycled and reusable paper/plastic/canvas bags?
iii. Are your brochures/pamphlets printed on recycled paper with vegetable-based dyes?
iv. Have you reduced and/or eliminated leftover brochures/pamphlets at the end of the event?
v. Do you separate waste generated at your booth/exhibition for recycling by the facility?
vi. What kinds of packing materials do you use that will not be reused for outbound shipping of your materials?
vii. What kind of food service ware will you use for food sampling?

# Best Practices Guidelines for Events

## Hotel Best Practices Guidelines

i. Provide guests a linen and towel reuse program.
ii. Provide guests a morning newspaper opt-out program.
iii. Provide refillable soap, lotion, and conditioner dispensers.
iv. Provide organic, U.S.-manufactured personal products.
v. Provide recycling in all hotel rooms.
vi. Provide placards in rooms advising guests of best practices.
vii. Provide low-flow showerheads, bath and sink faucet aerators.
viii. Install low-flow showerheads and toilets, bath and sink faucet aerators.
ix. Paperless check-in and- out billing procedures for guests.
x. Room HVAC to be turned down during nonuse hours.
xi. Room lighting to be turned off during nonoccupancy.
xii. Provide recycled content papers: tissues, toilet paper, napkins.
xiii. Cleaning staff to use no-VOC cleaning products.
xiv. Curtains closed or shades drawn during day in nonoccupancy rooms.
xv. Staff instructed to provide water upon request only.

## Exhibitor Best Practices Guidelines

i. Eliminate all Styrofoam packing materials.
ii. Minimize packing materials.
iii. Use recycled and reusable materials in their booths.
iv. Provide promotional products from recycled or sustainable materials.
v. Provide giveaway products that are reusable or made from recycled materials.
vi. Recycle exhibitors' name badges.
vii. Donate leftover flowers, decorations, swag to art organizations, theater company, schools, etc.
viii. Donate leftover food to soup kitchens.

ix. Carbon-offset travel and freight to event.
x. Car ride to event with other exhibitors.
xi. Reduce or eliminate overpackaging products, especially giveaways.
xii. Avoid printing dates on exhibit materials for reusability.
xiii. Comply with a leave-no-trace policy.
xiv. Save and reuse the boxes from the event for repacking leftover materials.
xv. No Styrofoam peanuts.
xvi. Recycle and compost disposal materials.

The realities of events: You must have a face to green. The most effective policies work because of enforcement. Much of our success is due to contractual greening policies. In 2004, we began strict enforcement of a "Leave No Trace" policy with our exhibitors. Our policy is simple:

"Exhibitors are responsible for leaving their booth space just as they found it when they first arrived, clean and free of materials. Booths will be inspected after move out is complete. If booth is not clean and free of materials, with the exception of freight packaged and labeled for shipment, the exhibitor will be charged a fine of $500 to offset the costs associated with resource recovery in the space."

## Decorator (General Service Contractor) Best Practices Guidelines

i. Exhibit information kit to be posted on the Web site.
ii. Eliminate nonreusable materials.
iii. Provide full linen or biodegradable tabletops.
iv. Eliminate vinyl for tabletop covers.
v. Provide recyclable/sustainably produced carpeting.
vi. Provide compliance with your own green standards.
vii. Collection of all steel bands/and vinyl.
viii. Ask for biodegradable shrinkwrap.
ix. Request compliance with all Resource Recovery plans.
x. No equipment idling.

## Food Service Providers Best Practices Guidelines

### List of Restricted Items
i. No poly or plastic-lined cups or plates, such as Sweetheart or Dixie brands.
ii. No plastic disposable forks, knives, or spoons.
iii. No plastic disposable plates, cups, or bowls.
iv. No disposable Styrofoam products.
v. No wax paper products.
vi. No animal bones in foods served; they are difficult to compost and host bacteria.

NOTE: Compostable food wares include cornstarch-based PLA (poly-lactic acid) products, wheat-based products, bagasse (paper product made from pulped sugarcane), or potato-starch–based products.

### Food and Beverage Green Menu Guidelines
These products present many opportunities to lessen the environmental and social impact:

    i. Natural or organic beer.

    ii. Natural or organic sulfide-free wines.

    iii. Organic and fair trade coffee, mate, tea.

    iv. Locally produced and sustainably farmed foods.

    v. Recommend and offer vegetarian menu options.

    vi. Prepare beverages to be served in bulk rather than individually bottled/canned.

    vii. Avoid individually packaged food items.

    viii. Eliminate plastic stir sticks; substitute reusable spoons for coffee and tea service.

    ix. Serve beer from kegs or taps rather pour from bottles.

    x. Provide cloth napkins.

    xi. Do not automatically offer paper napkins with all drinks.

    xii. Minimize the use of processed canned goods whenever possible.

    xiii. Look for the fair trade and organic certification of foods and beverages.

    xiv. Choose alternatives to major brands that are not produced regionally.

    xv. Eliminate all animal bones from items served as they are uncompostable.

    xvi. Serve bulk beverages: beer from kegs, tea, water, juices from pitchers.

    xvii. Provide edible garnishes.

    xviii. Donate untouched surplus food to shelters, food banks, etc.

    xix. Serve smaller portions to reduce food waste.

## Audiovisual Best Practices Guidelines

    i. Consider smart lighting design: reflectors, reflective materials, reflective background paints.

    ii. Incorporate natural light wherever possible.

    iii. Incorporate efficient LED lighting wherever possible.

    iv. Design sets that require reduced lighting.

    v. Check for overlighting sets by testing the lighting levels.

## Marketing, Promotion, and Communication Best Practices Guidelines

### Paper Guidelines

    i. Review the paper standards found on the EPA Web site at www.epa.gov; or 100 percent postconsumer recycled.

    ii. Put on all printed material the paper and ink type.

    iii. Printing and copying should be double-sided (back to back).

    iv. Avoid glossy papers with varnishes and goldenrod or fluorescent colored paper.

    v. Always allow an attendee the option to be removed from event mailing lists.

## Promotional Materials

    i. Avoid mailing printed material. Consider investing in social media marketing, IT advertising and promotion, blogging, Twittering, etc.

    ii. Always use 100 percent recycled or SFC paper for printed material.

    iii. Use online registration and limit the use of paper registration for special needs.

    iv. Self-mailers.

    v. Print with soy/vegetable-based ink and no VOC varnishes.

vi. Produce all material for electronic publication and distribution.

vii. When printed, identify the paper and ink type.

## On-site Materials

i. Use card stock–paper name badge with two holes drilled and elastic lanyard directly holding badge, thereby eliminating the plastic or bio badge holder.

ii. If badge holder is required, set up collection boxes at exits with volunteers to encourage recycling.

iii. Green signs are finally here. Eliminate vinyl—consider reusable templates for signs or the new substrates that can be recycled or composted.

iv. Educate exhibitors and sponsors on bringing minimum paper handouts, and encourage postevent electronic e-mail of literature to attendees.

## Speaker Handouts

i. Post on Web site or download on memory sticks for attendees.

ii. If mandated, print speakers' handouts so that you can control paper quality, and print double-sided.

iii. Suggest that speakers receive business cards from attendees who want a copy of the presentation.

iv. Ensure advance communication to all attendees.

v. When paper copies are preferred, request speaker handouts prior to the event and copy them according to this policy. Ask speakers/moderators who will provide handouts themselves to comply with the policy.

vi. Educate attendees that speakers were asked to comply with this policy.

# Special Event Planners' Best Practices Guidelines

i. Soy candles or beeswax candles are a must.

ii. If organic flowers are not available, consider centerpiece alternatives with a reusable life: herb plants or wheat grass, river rocks in a vase filled with water and floating candles.

iii. Recycle your cardboard into edgy name place cards or invitations—have an embosser made of your name, phone, and address, and use it on any substrate to make a cool recycled card.

iv. Go organic and local. Probably the most sustainable step is to use foods that are in season, grown in the region and whenever possible organic. Select meats that are free range and organically fed. Be sure your fish selection reflects a locally harvested theme.

v. Caviar? If you must choose caviar, select one that is made from soy, which looks, and tastes like the real "endangered animal" thing.

vi. Consider investing in solar-powered tree lights—fabulous year round for the outdoor deck, patio, or garden and available in several colors.

vii. Use as décor items what is natural and reusable, such as large stones, vessels with water and candles, bamboo stocks, lanterns made from old jars or cans. If you need a vase, get one that is fair trade or recycled glass—consider Fire and Light, a recycled glass manufacturer, or Artmosphere, Global Exchange Store, and Ten Thousand Villages, which have wonderful lines of fair trade accessories beautiful for decorating a party.

viii. Serving wine and beer? Be sure that organic or sustainably harvested is on your menu. Frey Vineyards, Organic Vintners, Badger Mountain, and Coturri Wines are some of the many sustainable wines. Beers to consider are New Belgium, Bison, and Wolavers.

 ix. Desserts and coffee and teas: Consider local groceries or bakeries that use organic spelt flour and vegan recipes. Select organic ice cream or rice cream for those cold desserts. Most important is to stay away from processed sugar desserts. For hot beverages, the key words in searching for green products are: fair trade, organic, and shade grown (for coffee). Consider adding Brazilian mate to your list.

  x. Stay away from bottled (glass or plastic) and canned cold drinks and opt for pitcher-prepared beverages, such as exotic organic teas, iced mate, coffee, and acai. Offer natural sweeteners, such as local honey, raw sugar, and Stevia; avoid processed or artificial sugars. If it is from an animal, make sure it is organic. Always choose organic half-and-half and milks for coffee and tea service. Have soy and rice milk for an alternative.

## Set Designer Best Practices

  i. Consider converting into your set design the cool industrial look of recycled materials (some suggestions: Use old automobile tires, oil drums, hubcaps, coffee and tea sacks, PET bottles turned into mobiles, and aluminum cans made into sculptural montages). Consider reclaiming landfill items; once cleaned and assembled, they can create dramatic abstract installations: paint cans, Styrofoam cups, scrap metal. The list is long.

 ii. Consider using materials that connect with nature or are clearly sustainable materials, such as bamboo, local indigenous trees, and natural fabrics or textiles. Stay clear of PVC materials, vinyl, and other plastics that cannot be recycled or reused.

iii. Given the amount of carbon emitted from pyrotechnics such as fireworks, consider lower-voltage (low-carbon) lighting effects. Solar decorative lighting is now widely available and can serve from small sets to theatrical concert sets.

 iv. PVC material for most stage skirting, banners, carpeting is highly toxic and off-gas. Consider investing in or renting these materials made from organic or naturally made materials. Today there is an ever-growing source for corn-, wheat-, and sugar-based materials that are biodegradable.

  v. Consider using water-based paints such as water-soluble latex and thinners, milk paint, and natural minerals paints.

 vi. All that material brought into a set design needs to be diverted from landfill. Store and reuse, rent out, or donate materials. Art schools, local theater groups, and reuse building organizations such as Habitat for Humanity will provide a good outlet for reuse. Recycle all that cannot be picked up by working with Waste Management and wood and scrap metal recyclers.

vii. Consider local products and supplies over those requiring shipping from long distances.

viii. Source products locally to eliminate the need for harmful emissions.

# Live Earth Wish List

| |
|---|
| Organic and/or local sustainably farmed foods integrated into concessionaire menu (Includes replacing red meats and pork by-products with vegetarian options in concession menu.)<br>Catering should add to their menu food products that are organic and/or from local sustainably farmed foods |
| Ensure all plastic beverage products are packaged in #1 and #2 recyclable plastics |
| PLA clear cups for all cold beverage service from concessions<br>Bagasse or recycled-paper paper cups for all hot beverage service from concessions (Our partner Bean Tree and International Paper have a great new hot beverage cup.)<br>Replace commercial paper napkins with recycled paper napkins<br>Replace all plastic utensils with wheat oil or corn oil utensils<br>Substitute all Styrofoam or nonbiodegradable "paper" products with spent sugarcane, used pulped products, or recycled-paper paper plates<br>Biodegradable trash liners used for compostable food collection<br>Biodegradable trash liners used for all waste collection |
| 100% food waste composting<br>100% cup, plate, and utensil composting<br>100% front and back of the house paper and cardboard recycling<br>100% aluminum cans and material recycling<br>100% plastic packaging and bottles #1 and #2 recycling<br>15%+ energy reduction in comparison to traditional commercial concerts/events<br>100% less VOC in cleaning supply residual off-gassing in public spaces<br>50% less VOC in printed signage such as vinyl and foam core<br>10% decrease in gasoline-associated costs for transport of nonlocal foods<br>30% decrease in auto transportation associated with commuting or biking to the event by providing Bike Valet and public transport options |
| Convert all light bulbs to ENERGY STAR–rated bulbs<br>Convert all faucets to low-flow water heads<br>Install motion-sensor lighting into all restrooms and public-use spaces<br>Energy usage assessment for concert to calculate carbon emissions<br>Staff and subcontractor travel audit to calculate carbon emissions<br>Live Earth staff and subcontractor and artist travel audit to calculate carbon emissions |
| Use eco-friendly surface and glass cleaner and disinfectant<br>Replace commercial liquid hand-washing soaps with organic or eco-friendly soaps<br>Replace commercial hand towels with air hand dryers or recycled paper towels |

Developed by Seven-Star and proposed to Live Earth Green Team

## Sample Green Purchasing Policy

This environmental purchasing policy of XYZ Company has been set up to provide guidance in the purchasing of products and services that meet the environmental goals of our company. Purchasing preference (whenever feasible) will be given to products that:

1. Cut back on greenhouse gas emissions or are made with renewable energy (i.e., ENERGY STAR computers, hybrid company cars).
2. Decrease the use of toxins detrimental to human health and to the environment.

3. Contain the highest possible percentage of postconsumer recycled content (a finished material that would normally be thrown away as solid waste at the end of its life cycle and does not include manufacturing or converting wastes).
4. Cut back on air, land, and/or water pollution.
5. Reduce the amount of waste they produce.
6. Are reusable or contain reusable parts (rechargeable batteries, refillable pens, etc.).
7. Are multifunctional (i.e., scanner/copier/printers, multipurpose cleaners) and serve to decrease the total number of products purchased.

Favor will also be given to suppliers who offer environmentally preferable products, who work to exceed their environmental performance expectations, and who can show documentation of their supply-chain impacts.

Environmentally preferable products and services of similar quality and price to conventional counterparts should gain a purchasing preference. When the greenest option is not available, too costly, or impractical, XYZ Company should look at how the products are produced as well as the environmentally and socially responsible management practices of suppliers and producers.

The XYZ Company policy of purchasing environmentally preferable products is one element in our continuing, long-range commitment to the environment. By adopting this policy, we hope to engage the producers and suppliers of office products and services we use to utilize business practices that also reduce their impact on the environment.

## Certification Registration

Go to www.GreenNonprofits.org to start your online profile and begin the Green-Nonprofits Certification process.

NOTE: To be environmentally sensitive, we do NOT advocate printing this document. It should only be read digitally. Applications are always to be submitted online.

---

## Green Nonprofits Certification Application Checklist

### Green Nonprofits Certification Program

Application and Points Checklist

Nonprofit Name: _____

Contact Name: _____ Phone: _____

Address: _____

E-mail: _____ Fax: _____

A Green Nonprofit is a smart Nonprofit, and smart Nonprofits run successful organizations while protecting the environment that sustains our economy. By

*(continued)*

*(Continued)*

assuming leadership and environmental stewardship roles, Green Nonprofits will:

- Reduce solid waste disposal and promote recycling
- Become energy and water efficient
- Purchase products that are less harmful to human health and the environment
- Minimize pollution contributions to the environment
- Help improve indoor air quality and reduce smog formation
- Educate their customers, employees, and other Nonprofits about Green Nonprofit practices

In an effort to recognize and certify outstanding Green Nonprofits and promote their services, GreenNonprofits has established this program. By participating in this program and becoming certified, your Nonprofit will publically declare your commitment to these principles while joining this unique global group of superior organizations.

## How to Get Started

### CERTIFICATION PROCESS

1. Print or download the appropriate Green Nonprofits Certification (GNPC) Program checklist for your Nonprofit. Then simply review the program checklist to determine if this program is a good fit for your Nonprofits.
2. If you decide you want to pursue certification, contact the Green Nonprofit Certification Program Co-coordinator, to register for the GNPC Program: 888-99-GREEN.
3. Perform the self-guided waste assessment using the attached GNPC Waste Assessment Form.
4. Read through the checklist options and check all boxes that apply to your Nonprofit. These can be existing or newly adopted measures implemented in order to meet the GNPC program requirements.
5. **Complete all REQUIRED measures while earning a minimum of 100 points before submitting application.**

    Submit or e-mail 2 copies of your completed checklist with payment to GreenNonprofits:

    Green Nonprofits Certification Program
    1101 15th Street NW
    Suite 200
    Washington DC 20005
    certification@greennonprofits.org

Please make check payable to: GreenNonprofits
Please Note: Payment is nonrefundable.

If you do not pass application verification, you will be granted 90 days to complete corrective measures.

Charter member fee schedule below.

| GREEN NONPROFITS CERTIFICATION FEE SCHEDULE | | | |
|---|---|---|---|
| Type of Nonprofit | | | |
| A | B | C | D |
| Budget Size    <$500,000.00 | $500,000– $2.5 million | $2.5 million– $10 million | >$10 million |
| $250.00 | $350.00 | $550.00 | $750.00 |

6. Congratulations! Assuming your application verification is a success, you are now ready to be certified and recognized for your Green practices. You will receive a Green Nonprofit window decal to market your achievement and an electronic version of the logo to use on your Web site and in promotional materials. Then you'll join a growing number of prominent Green Nonprofits around the world.

   NOTE: GreenNonprofits Certification is valid for two years. If recertification is desired, payment and documentation is required for subsequent 2-year period.

**HONOR SYSTEM/ENFORCEMENT:** The GreenNonprofits Program is based on the honor system. Nonprofits/NGOs are expected and trusted to submit only factual information. However, any member of GreenNonprofits may challenge a certification of another organization, stating specifically why the organization in question is not in compliance with GreenNonprofits standards. GreenNonprofits will then review the matter and take such measures as it feels appropriate to further verify the matter in question. This can result in the certified organization being required to provide additional information and/or make arrangements for site visit. The result may result in extension of certification, suspension, or removal of certification. All decisions made by the GreenNonprofits Board of Directors are final.

## Frequently Asked Questions

- My Nonprofit is not Green. Where can I get assistance?

     GreenNonprofits offers online and offline Greening Your Nonprofit Programs. These programs can put your Nonprofit on the path to becoming certified and receiving recognition for your efforts. To learn more about these programs, visit www.greennonprofits.org/greening or contact the Nonprofit Greening Program at 888-99-GREEN.
- Do I get credit for good things I'm already doing?

     Yes! In fact, your organization may already qualify. Your Nonprofit will get credit for existing Green practices, as well as newly adopted ones implemented to meet the GNPC program requirements.
- Do I have to do everything on the checklist to become certified as a Green Nonprofit?

*(continued)*

*(Continued)*

No! Although you must complete the "Required Measures" in each category to receive certification, the additional "Optional Measures" in the checklist are intended to give Nonprofits flexibility in their approach to becoming Green. Many certified Green Nonprofits have taken their program to the next level using the additional measures as motivation and guidance.

- Does it cost to become a Certified Green Nonprofit?

    Yes. A minimal fee is applied to cover costs to administer certification by GreenNonprofits staff. See the fee schedule listed in the How to Get Started Section.

- How long does my certification last?

    The Green Nonprofits Certification is valid for two years. If recertification is desired, documentation and payment is required for subsequent 2-year period.

- What if I don't pass certification?

    If the measures you selected in the checklist are not verified by documentation presented, you will not obtain Green Nonprofit certification. However, you will be granted 90 days to complete the corrective measures to obtain certification.

## Green Nonprofits Certification (GNPC) Application

General

NOTE: Each measure in this section is worth 2 points once completed.

**Choose a minimum of 4 New or Existing Measures (earning a minimum of 8 points):**

- ☐ **REQUIRED:** Board/leadership of organization formally votes to endorse the GreenNonprofits Pledge.
- ☐ **REQUIRED:** Discontinue use of Styrofoam and nonrecyclable plastic food service containers.
- ☐ **REQUIRED:** Reduce junk mail by removing your organization's name from national databases at: https://www.dmachoice.org.
- ☐ Provide three ongoing incentives or training opportunities to encourage management and employee participation in this Green Nonprofits Certification (GNPC) Program. For example:
    - ☐ Performance appraisals, training programs, job descriptions, new employee orientations
    - ☐ Staff meeting discussion or presentations
    - ☐ Employee reference materials
    - ☐ Company newsletters or bulletins
- ☐ Inform your clients, supporters, and donors regarding your nonprofit's environmental efforts and what you are doing to meet the GNPC standards. For example:

□ Post on your website examples of steps you have taken to become certified as a Green Nonprofit [provide URL for example:
_____]
□ Offer clients, supporters, and donors "Green" service or amenities options.
□ Offer tours that highlight your Green Nonprofit successes.
□ Post your GNPC efforts and/or certification on your website.
□ Upon completion, hang the GNPC decal in a visible location and post to your website.
□ Upon completion of the Green Nonprofits Certification Program, encourage other Nonprofits to participate in the Program and provide their contact information to GreenNonprofits.

Name of Nonprofit: _____
Contact Name: _____
Phone Number: _____
E-mail Address: _____
Total Points Earned (General): _____ (min 8 points)

## Green Nonprofits Certification (GNPC) Application

### Purchasing

Purchasing products made from recycled materials conserves resources and is essential for supporting markets for recycled materials. Close the loop!

NOTE: Each measure in this section is worth 2 points once completed.

**Choose a minimum of 4 New or Existing Measures (earning a minimum of 8 points):**
□ **REQUIRED:** Purchase 100% of office paper—minimum 30% post-consumer recycled content
□ Purchase 100% Letterhead and nonprofit cards—minimum 30% post-consumer recycled content
□ Purchase 100% Envelopes—minimum 30% post-consumer recycled content.
□ Purchase 100% Post-it notes—minimum 30% post-consumer recycled content.
□ Purchase 100% Paper towels—minimum 30% post-consumer recycled content.
□ Purchase 100% Toilet paper—minimum 30% post-consumer recycled content.
□ Purchase only remanufactured toner cartridges.
□ Purchase refurbished, used, or remanufactured furniture and equipment.
□ Purchase refurbished or remanufactured carpet, carpet undercushion, rugs, or floormats.

*(continued)*

*(Continued)*

☐ Purchase refurbished or remanufactured construction materials when building or remodeling: paint, insulation, concrete, lumber/wood flooring, tile, etc.

☐ Purchase refurbished or remanufactured boxes and bags for shipping or retail use.

☐ Formally inform main supplier's sales representatives that you prefer eco-friendly products—request that they start carrying these products if they do not currently do so or switch to a supplier that does.

☐ Replace white napkins and paper towels with one of the following alternatives:

- Recycled content, unbleached paper towels
- Reusable cloth towels and dispenser suitable for washrooms
- Energy efficient air dryers

☐ Purchase at least 50% reusable rather than disposable office items, such as refillable pens, erasable whiteboards and wall calendars.

☐ Request that deliveries come in returnable or reusable containers.

☐ Purchase condiments (milk, sugar, cream, etc.) in bulk.

☐ Purchase supplies (toiletpaper, handsoap, etc.) in bulk.

☐ Retailers: sell products made with recycled content and/or organic materials.

☐ Purchase organic, shade-grown, or fair-trade coffee.

☐ Use biodegradable or compostable "to-go" food containers such as paper or biobased plastics.

　　　　Total Points Earned (Purchasing): _____ (min 8 points)

# Green Nonprofits Certification (GNPC) Application

## Solid Waste

NOTE: Each measure in this section is worth 2 points once completed.

**Choose a minimum of 3 New or Existing Measures (earning a minimum of 6 points):**

**Solid Waste/Reduce:**

☐ Design marketing materials that require no envelope.

☐ Eliminate duplicate mailings of subscriptions by contacting the subscriptions department to request that all but one be removed.

☐ Update your own mailing list annually to avoid duplicate mailing or outdated information being sent to your customers.

☐ When faxing, use fax label on first page instead of full-page cover letter.

☐ Reduce junk faxes by contacting number listed on bottom of fax and requesting permanent deletion of your number.

☐ Purchase or lease copiers and printers that have a duplexing function or retrofit existing printers with a duplexer where applicable.

☐ Make two-sided printing and copying standard practice in your nonprofit. Set printer to default to duplexing mode.

☐ Post staff memos and schedules instead of printing individual copes for each staff member.

☐ Nonprofits with stores, shops, or other retail outlets: Offer an incentive to customers who bring their own shopping bag, coffee mugs, etc.

☐ Replace disposable utensils and tableware with reusable alternatives.

NOTE: Each measure in this section is worth 2 points once completed.

**Choose a minimum of 2 New or Existing Measures (earning a minimum of 4 points):**

**Solid Waste/Reuse:**

☐ Donate or exchange unwanted furniture, supplies, electronics, scrap materials, linens, etc. to other nonprofits like schools, churches, hospitals, libraries, nonprofit organizations, museums, teacher resource organizations, etc.

☐ **REQUIRED:** Reuse packaging (bubble wrap, cardboard boxes, and polystyrene peanuts) or donate to a local shipping company.

☐ Enroll in a local waste exchange program buying and selling reusable and recyclable commodities: www.epa.gov/jtr/comm/exchnat.htm.

☐ Purchase reusable kitchenware (silverware, mugs, plates, etc.) for staff use.

☐ Reuse envelopes and file folders.

☐ Train housekeeping staff to reuse clean trash liners.

☐ Keep a stack of previously used paper for fax machines and/or printers. Use the backsides for notes, drafts, internal memos, etc.

# Green Nonprofits Certification (GNPC) Application

## Solid Waste Cont.

NOTE: Each measure in this section is worth 2 points once completed.

**Choose a minimum of 2 New or Existing Measures (earning a minimum of 4 points):**

**Solid Waste/Recycle:** Implement office-wide recycling programs for:

☐ Office paper—mixed: copy, letterhead, color, glossy, newspaper, junk mail, telephone directories, paper board, magazines, and cardboard.

☐ Cans, plastic, glass.

☐ Green waste: Use Green waste bin or make composting part of the contract with your landscape service.

☐ Food waste: Collect and compost your office food waste.

*(continued)*

*(Continued)*

☐ Recycle toner and inkjet cartridges.
☐ Carpet—many of the leading carpet manufacturers will recycle your old carpet.

Total Points Earned (Solid Waste): _____ (min 14 points)

# Green Nonprofits Certification (GNPC) Application

## Water Efficiency

NOTE: Each measure in this section is worth 2 points once completed.

**Choose a minimum of 3 New or Existing Measures (earning a minimum of 6 points):**
☐ Perform a self-assessment of your waste using the Waste Assessment Form attached.
☐ Identify the types and percentages of waste currently being generated and recycled. Use the assessment information and checklist to create or improve on-site reuse and recycling programs.
☐ Review your water bill for indications of leaks or other problems; report leaks or problems to authorities.
☐ Regularly check for and repair leaks.
☐ Replace pre-1992 toilets which use 3 or more gallons per flush (gpf) with more efficient alternatives that use 1.6 gpf or less.
☐ Replace pre-1992 urinals with more efficient alternative such as 1.0 gpf or water-free urinals.
☐ Clean all outdoor area with a broom and damp mop instead of a hose. This includes parking lots, sidewalks, alleys, or patios. NEVER hose off outdoor hardscapes or use soap outside.
☐ Do not hose off or wash cars, equipment, floormats, or other items where runoff water flows into the storm drain; if possible direct water to landscaped areas.
☐ Keep receiving areas and Dumpsters clear of litter. Ensure tight-fitting lids.
☐ Adjust sprinkler times according to seasons. Sprinkler irrigation runoff is prohibited. No watering between 10 A.M. and 4 P.M.
☐ **REQUIRED:** Obtain an assessment of your facility's water use from your local water authority and provide specific steps you are taking to improve water efficiency. Review annually to identify additional opportunities to improve water savings. (Provide narrative of your plan to improve water efficiency.)
☐ Install standard faucet aerators or flow restrictors facility-wide. (2.5 gallons/minute is standard.)

Total Points Earned (Water Efficiency): _____ (min 6 points)

# Green Nonprofits Certification (GNPC) Application

## Employee Practices

NOTE: Each measure in this section is worth 2 points once completed.

**Choose a minimum of 2 New or Existing Measures (earning a minimum of 4 points):**

☐ **REQUIRED:** Regularly remind all staff members to power down all computers when work is completed.

☐ **REQUIRED:** Designate time at staff meetings or other employee gatherings to cover existing new and environmental efforts.

☐ Place "use water wisely" stickers near faucets. Educate staff on the need for water efficiency. (Members may download forms from the GreenNonprofits website.)

☐ Educate staff regarding the hazards caused by run-off and how to prevent them.

☐ Use dishwasher only when full. Post signage to remind employees.

☐ Regularly clean litter and debris in front of your organization. Attempt to minimize the amount of litter entering the storm drain.

Total Points Earned (Employee Practices): _____ (min 4 points)

# Green Nonprofits Certification (GNPC) Application

## Landscape

**If you do not have or do not manage your landscape, you are exempt from these measures.** However, if you are able to influence the landscaping around buildings you use, you are encouraged to take these measures and document your efforts for certification.

☐ Check box if exempt; if not:

☐ In place of turf, install water efficient shrubs or ground cover.

☐ Remove hardscapes and install permeable paving, such as porous concrete, decomposed granite, or pavers.

☐ Install drip irrigation.

☐ Install a smart irrigation controller that uses weather data to irrigate appropriately.

☐ Plant environmentally friendly and native plants.

☐ Annually apply mulch to all exposed landscape to increase moisture retention, reduce weeds, and prevent soil erosion.

*(continued)*

*(Continued)*

☐ Redirect downspouts toward landscaped areas where possible.

☐ Install a cistern or rain barrel to catch rainwater.

☐ Install a graywater system (where permitted, check with local authorities).

☐ Test irrigation system to ensure proper operation and watering schedule. Ensure all spray heads are functioning and not overspraying onto hardscapes.

☐ Instruct landscapers and staff NOT to hose off hard surfaces. Simply dry-sweep the area.

Total Points Earned (Landscaping): _____ (no minimum points)

## Green Nonprofits Certification (GNPC) Application

### Energy Efficiency

NOTE: Each measure in this section is worth 2 points once completed.

**Choose a minimum of 4 New or Existing Measures (earning a minimum of 8 points):**

ENERGY EFFICIENCY/EQUIPMENT AND FACILITIES   Special note: Check for rebates with your local energy provider for any energy conservation steps taken. Rebates may be available for many of the energy-efficient measures listed below.

☐ **REQUIRED:** Place "turn off light" labels on appropriate switches facility-wide. (Members may download labels from the GreenNonprofits website.)

☐ **REQUIRED:** Program computer monitors to sleep mode after 15 minutes or less.

☐ Convert at least 50% of all lighting fixtures to energy-efficient alternatives, such as ENERGY STAR–qualified compact fluorescents lights (CFLs), low-voltage track lighting, halogen or high-intensity discharge lighting. Install occupancy (motion) sensors or times in low-traffic areas such as storage, bathrooms, and offices.

☐ Obtain an assessment of your facility's energy use. Review suggestions annually to identify additional opportunities to improve energy savings.

☐ Upgrade existing fluorescent tube lighting with T-8 or T-5 lamps with electronic ballasts.

☐ Reduce the number of lamps and increase lighting efficiency by installing optical reflectors or diffusers in fluorescent fixtures.

☐ Replace all exit signs with LED or high-efficiency alternatives.

☐ Set the Energy Save feature on photocopier to default.

☐ When replacing equipment and appliances ensure that they are ENERGY STAR rated and/or equipped with energy-saving features (www.energystar.gov).

□ Purchase renewable energy for your organization through the purchase of renewable energy certificates (RECs), or through direct purchasing by a renewable energy supplier. (www.green-e.org/base/re_products?cust=b)

□ Insulate water heater, storage tanks, and hot-water pipes.

□ Use a thermos or pump pot instead of electric burners to maintain hot liquids (coffee and/or tea).

□ Install solar panels.

□ Implement an office-wide policy that encourages staff members to turn off equipment and lights when not in use.

□ Clean light fixtures and diffusers regularly for optimal light output.

□ Clean skylights annually in late spring to maximize incoming light.

□ Rearrange the workspace to take advantage of areas with natural sunlight; design future spaces with natural lighting opportunities in mind.

□ Use "task" lighting where extra light is needed, rather than lighting an entire area.

□ Instruct all employees to unplug equipment that is not being used.

## ENERGY EFFICIENCY/HEATING, VENTILATION, & AIR CONDITIONING (HVAC) UNITS
NOTE: Each measure in this section is worth 2 points once completed.

**Choose a minimum of 2 New or Existing Measures (earning a minimum of 4 points):**

- Use natural ventilation instead of mechanical air conditioning. Open windows at opposite ends of room to facilitate cross breezes.
- Install ceiling fans.
- Install programmable thermostat and set to 68 degrees in winter and 78 degrees in summer with a nighttime setback of 55 degrees.
- Replace leaky, inefficient, or broken windows with double-pane, low-E, energy-efficient windows.
- Apply window film to reduce solar heat gain.
- Shade sun-exposed windows and walls during the warm season: use awnings, sunscreens, shade trees, or shrubbery.
- Use caulk and/or weather-stripping around windows and doors.
- Perform regular maintenance on your HVAC (heating, ventilation, and air conditioning) system. If leasing your facility, ask the building owner or property manager to do the following:
  - Clean or change filters every 2–4 months.
  - Check entire system for coolant and air leaks, clogs and obstructions of air intake.
  - Provide a copy of HVAC service records or Property Management contract to the GNP.

Total Points Earned (Energy Efficiency): _____ (min 12 points)

# Green Nonprofits Certification (GNPC) Application

## Chemical Use & Pollution Prevention

**EQUIPMENT AND FACILITIES**    NOTE: Each measure in this section is worth 2 points once completed.

**Choose a minimum of 4 New or Existing Measures (earning a minimum of 8 points):**

☐ Stock one nontoxic, biodegradable cleaner for daily use; for example, multipurpose cleaner, glass cleaner, etc.

☐ Install filtered water tap at your sink for drinking water, instead of purchasing bottled water.

☐ Use recycled content or low-VOC paint products available from local paint suppliers.

☐ Use nontoxic, low-VOC office supplies, such as Wite-Out, whiteboard pens, etc.

☐ Use low-mercury fluorescent lamps—most lighting suppliers carry a line of low-mercury, energy-efficient, long-lasting lamps.

☐ When remodeling, use low-emitting/low-polluting building materials, carpets, furniture, and other materials to improve indoor air quality and reduce downtime. Look for products certified by GreenGuard or the Carpet and Rug Institute.

☐ Educate and inform cleaning staff of your eco-friendly preferences.

☐ Discontinue purchase of glass cleaner and replace with vinegar and water for cleaning windows.

☐ Use less-toxic graffiti removers.

☐ Use less-toxic cleaning products that are safer for staff and the environment.

☐ Consider Green Seal–certified products available from most cleaning product suppliers.

☐ Store all chemical products in their original containers or properly labeled secondary containers with tight-fitting lids. Chemical products should be stored in secure, controlled areas, away from ignition sources and food storage areas.

☐ Utilize proper government-authorized Hazardous Waste Drop-off facilities (search in your community for keyword: Hazardous Waste Drop-off). These materials should never be thrown in the trash or poured down a drain:

- Batteries—rechargeable and alkaline
- Paint
- Used toner and ink-jet cartridges
- Cleaning and maintenance chemicals
- Compact fluorescent lamps and fluorescent tubes
- Electronics
- Aerosol cans that are not completely empty of contents

You may list up to 3 products (from the list above) you have disposed of accurately, for a total of 3 credits:

☐ _____

☐ _____

☐ _____

☐ _____

☐ Use unbleached and/or chlorine-free paper products; for example, copy paper, paper towels, coffee filters, etc.

☐ Retailer—stock/sell products that are less toxic or less polluting than conventional ones.

☐ Purchase organic or shade-grown coffee and teas.

☐ Use rechargeable batteries instead of disposable alkaline.

☐ Have materials printed using soy or vegetable-based ink.

## CHEMICAL USE & POLLUTION PREVENTION /INTEGRATED PEST MANAGEMENT

NOTE: Each measure in this section is worth 2 points once completed.

**Choose a minimum of 2 New or Existing Measures (earning a minimum of 4 points):**

☐ Request that your pest control or landscape contractor reduce use of pesticides and/or use less toxic pesticides. Get their commitment in writing.

☐ Use less toxic insecticides, such as soaps, horticultural oils, and microbials.

☐ Pick weeds by hand rather than using herbicides (weed killers).

☐ Correct situations that attract and harbor pests, such as improperly stored foods, open trash bins, and dense foliage around your building.

☐ Use traps, containerized baits, gels, and/or barriers for ants and cockroaches.

☐ Request pest control company or property manager apply pesticides on an "as-needed" basis instead of on a set schedule.

☐ When chemical pesticides are necessary, use those labeled "caution" rather than "warning" or "danger."

Total Points Earned (Chemical Use & Pollution Prevention): _____ (min 12 points)

# Green Nonprofits Certification (GNPC) Application

## Transportation

NOTE: Each measure in this section is worth 2 points once completed.

**Choose a minimum of 5 New or Existing Measures (earning a minimum of 10 points):**

☐ Provide a secure location for staff to store bicycles or install a bike rack in or near facility.

*(continued)*

*(Continued)*

☐ Cover rideshare programs at new employee orientations.

☐ Provide bus and metro maps and information (where available).

☐ Encourage alternative modes of transportation via incentives; for example, bus pass or small bonus.

☐ Provide ridesharing information on carpooling, vanpooling, bicycling, walking, and public/mass transportation on a bulletin board. Distribute rideshare information monthly.

☐ Offer telecommuting opportunities and/or flexible schedules so workers can avoid heavy traffic.

☐ Incorporate a "How to Get Here via Alternative Transportation" page into your employee manual and provide information to employee upon hiring.

☐ Perform local errands on bike or foot.

☐ Shop at local businesses within close proximity.

☐ Maintain fleet to optimize miles per gallon, including adjusting tire pressure, filter, oil, etc.

☐ Provide company commuter van.

☐ Provide shower facilities for employees who walk, jog, or bike to work. Consider contracting with a nearby health facility for the use of their showers.

☐ Provide preferential parking for alternative modes of transit such as carpools, electric, hybrid or biodiesel vehicles.

Total Points Earned (Transportation): _____ (min 10 points)

---

**GreenNonprofits Solid Waste Assessment Form is available online at www.greennonprofits.org.**

# Notes

## Chapter 1

1. http://nccs.urban.org/statistics/quickfacts.cfm; accessed April 29, 2009.
2. www.councilofnonprofits.org/?q=newsrelease/2006/ussector; accessed April 29, 2009.
3. Ibid.
4. http://en.wikipedia.org/wiki/Direct_mail_fundraising; accessed April 29, 2009.
5. Ibid.
6. Holly Hall, "Direct-Mail Appeals Suffer, New Survey Finds," *Chronicle of Philanthropy,* January 8, 2008; http://philanthropy.com/news/index.php?id=3734.
7. www.cfpbmc.org/page10003707.cfm?CFID=34757010&CFTOKEN=95f29c53439 1c172-F4058A47-188B-4F65-9AE9C64C4B1BC2EE&jsessionid=4430bf088eed$00 $CAj$; accessed April 29, 2009.
8. www.jfsg.com/donor_cultivation.phtml; accessed April 29, 2009.
9. http://majorgivingnow.org/launch/cultivation.html#management; accessed April 29, 2009.
10. "Donor Commitment Continuum," developed by Advancement Resources, LLC.advancementresources.org
11. www.fleet.ucdavis.edu; accessed April 29, 2009.

## Chapter 2

1. Dan Esty and Andrew Winston, *Green to Gold* (New Haven: Yale University Press, 2006).
2. U.S. Green Building Council, in collaboration with Capital E, October 2003, "The Costs and Financial Benefits of Green Buildings."
3. www.eere.energy.gov/buildings/commercial/hvac.html.
4. Third *UN World Water Development Report*, 2009.
5. Gary Hirschberg, *Stirring It Up: How to Make Money and Save the World* (New York: Hyperion, 2008).
6. Richard Seireeni, *The Gort Cloud: The Invisible Force Powering Today's Most Visible Green Brands* (White River Junction, VT: Chelsea Green Publishing, 2008).

# Chapter 3

1. Seventh Generation Corporate Web site, Seventh Generation's *2007 Corporate Consciousness Report*, www.seventhgeneration.com/corporate-responsibility/2007; accessed March 25, 2009.
2. Green Nonprofits Certification Application and Checklist, www.greennon-profits.org; accessed March 28, 2009.
3. Libby Johnson McKee, Desiree Williams Rajee, Manan Shukla, and Stephen Yogi Rueff, "The Time Clock Revolution: Creating Sustainable Work through Engagement and Choice," www.betterworldtelecom.com; accessed April 5, 2009.
4. Libby Johnson McKee, Desiree Williams Rajee, Manan Shukla, and Stephen Yogi Rueff, "BetterWork: A New Strategy for Work: Lower Costs and Carbon Emissions while Increasing Profits and Employee Morale," www.betterworldtelecom.com; accessed May 12, 2009.
5. www.actnowproductions.com/assets/files/PSP_onesheet_final.pdf; accessed April 5, 2009.
6. www.worldblu.com/organizational-democracy; accessed April 15, 2009.
7. Adapted from WorldBlu, www.worldblu.com/organizational-democracy/principles, accessed April 15, 2009.
8. www.worldblu.com/worldblu-list/worldblu-list?company=takingitglobal.
9. www.worldblu.com/worldblu-list?company=takingitglobal; accessed April 15, 2009.
10. Jim Collins, *Good to Great* (Harper Business, 2001).

# Chapter 4

1. How and why is *MJ* a nonprofit? According to its Web site: "Being a magazine that investigates everything, including corporations, and takes a pass on celebrity fluff doesn't exactly scream 'ad friendly' or 'giant profits.' So the founders decided to diversify the income stream. This way, we're not beholden to any conglomerate. And since our donor pool is broad, we're not beholden to any person or foundation, either." www.motherjones.com/about; accessed September 17, 2009.

# Chapter 5

1. Bowers, C. A. "The Culture of Denial: Why the Environmental Movement Needs a Strategy for Reforming Universities and Public Schools."
2. Ibid.
3. American Institute of Biological Science report by Myers and Knoll.
4. Environmental Science by D. D. Chiras.
5. EPA—Stratospheric Update on Ozone Depletion.
6. United Nations Population Division.
7. Green Meeting Industry Council and Meeting Professionals Industry.
8. EPA, Green Meeting Industry Council and Meeting Professionals Industry.

## Chapter 6

1. Organization for Economic Co-operation and Development, www.oecd.org. Specifically, the report states that transport accounted for 27% of all emissions in 1998 and projects that the contribution of the transport sector to total $CO_2$ emissions in OECD regions will increase to 31% by 2020. So, between 1998 and 2020, it will increase to 31% (nearly 1/3). The report also says that $CO_2$ accounts for the overwhelming majority of increasing emissions from transport.
2. Association of Corporate Travel Executives, February 13, 2009.
3. Guardian Unlimited, February 8, 2001.
4. "A Consumers' Guide to Retail Carbon Offset Providers," Clean Air–Cool Planet, 2006.
5. GreenMoney Journal, Fall 2009, www.greenmoneyjournal.com/article.mpl?newsletterid=48&articleid=677.

## Chapter 7

1. United States Green Building Council Web site, www.usgbc.org/DisplayPage .aspx?CMSPageID=1718; accessed April 17, 2009.
2. Ibid.
3. www.breeam.org/page.jsp?id=13; accessed April 24, 2009. BREEAM (BRE Environmental Assessment Method) is the leading and most widely used environmental assessment method for buildings.
4. The National Building Institute of Sciences, Whole Building Design Guide, www.wbdg.org/design/sustainable.php; accessed April 25, 2009.
5. California Integrated Waste Management Board Web site, www.ciwmb.ca.gov/ greenbuilding/Materials; accessed April 25, 2009.
6. www.scscertified.com/ecoproducts/products; accessed April 10, 2009.
7. Western Area Power Administration Web site, www.wapa.gov/es/pubs/techbrf/ oandm.htm; accessed April 8, 2009.
8. United States Environmental Protection Agency Web site, www.epa.gov/osw/ conserve/rrr/imr/cdm/whatyoucan.htm; accessed April 29, 2009.
9. Your Building Web site, www.yourbuilding.org/display/yb/Ten+questions+ answered+for+designers+of+sustainable+commercial+buildings; accessed April 16, 2009.
10. The California Integrated Waste Management Board website, from www. ciwmb.ca.gov/greenbuilding/Materials, accessed April 25, 2009.
11. United States Department of Energy Web site, www.energysavers.gov/ your_home/space_heating_cooling/index.cfm/mytopic=12640; accessed April 29, 2009.
12. United States Department of Energy Web site, www.eere.energy.gov/de/ wind_power.html; accessed May 2, 2009.
13. City of Santa Monica, Office of Sustainability and the Environment, from www01.smgov.net/epd/residents/Water/saving_tips.htm; accessed April 24, 2009.

# Chapter 9

1. PHH Arval is the second largest provider of commercial fleet management services.
2. Daniel Sperling and Deborah Gordon, *Two Billion Cars: Driving Toward Sustainability* (New York: Oxford University Press, 2009).
3. Irwin Kellner, "Free Ride," February 9, 2009, *MarketWatch,* www.marketwatch .com/story/mass-transit-systems-taking-wrong-turn.
4. Jim Motavalli, *Forward Drive: The Race to Build Clean Cars for the Future* (San Francisco: 2000).
5. "Compressed Natural Gas (CNG) Conversions," About.com, http://alternative fuels.about.com/od/naturalgasvehicles/a/cngconversion.htm.
6. Amory Lovins to author, 2008.
7. Felix Kramer to author, 2008.
8. Jim Motavalli, "The Costs of Owning a Car," *New York Times,* March 22, 2009, http:// query.nytimes.com/gst/fullpage.html?res=990CEFDA1E3FF931A15750C0 A96F9C8B63.

# Chapter 10

1. U.S. Census Bureau (n.d.), *World Population 1950–2050*, www.census.gov/ ipc/www/idb/worldpopgraph.html; accessed June 14, 2009.
2. J. Hoffman, "Business Decisions and the Environment: Significance, Challenges, and Momentum of an Emerging Research Field," in Garry D. Brewer and Paul C. Stern, ed., *Decisionmaking for the Environment: Social and Behavioral Science Research Priorities* (Washingon DC: National Research Council, National Academies Press, 2005).
3. European Environmental Agency, "Climate Change" (n.d.), www.eea.europa.eu/ themes/climate; accessed June 14, 2009.
4. Association of British Insurers, "Preparing the UK for Climate Change. ABI's New Adaption Strategy" (January 2009), www.abi.org.uk/BookShop/Research Reports/Adaption%20Strategy%20final%20draft%20updated%2021st%20Jan%20- %20formatted2%20(5).pdf; accessed June 15, 2009.
5. A. J. Hoffman, *Competitive Environmental Strategy. A Guide to the Changing Business Landscape* (Washington, DC: Island Press, 2000s).
6. TheGreenOffice, "Products: What Makes a Product Green?" (n.d.), www.thegreenoffice.com; accessed June 24, 2009.
7. Planet Green, "How to Go Green: Furniture," July 22, 2008, http://planetgreen .discovery.com/go-green/green-furniture/green-furniture-top-tips.html; accessed June 17, 2009.
8. Charity Guide, "Encourage Better Use of Paper and Supplies at the Office" (n.d.), www.charityguide.org/volunteer/fewhours/paper-recycling.htm; accessed June 24, 2009.
9. U.S. Department of Energy Efficiency and Renewable Energy, "Home Office and Home Electronics," 2009, www1.eere.energy.gov/consumer/tips/home_office .html; accessed June 21, 2009.
10. 1E Energy Awareness Campaign, "PC Energy Report US 2009" (n.d.), www.1e.com/energycampaign/index.aspx; accessed June 17, 2009.

11. "City of Gothenburg Bans Bottled Water," *The Local*, September 19, 2008, www.thelocal.se/14440/20080919; accessed June 18, 2009.
12. Eutrophication is the process by which a body of water becomes rich in dissolved nutrients, thereby encouraging the growth and decomposition of oxygen-depleting plant life and resulting in harm to other organisms. www.savetheplasticbag.com; accessed June 17, 2009.
13. Savetheplasticbag.com, "Schottish Report" (n.d.), www.savetheplasticbag.com/ReadContent486.aspx; accessed June 17, 2009.
14. HowStuffWorks.com, "How to Clean Your Bathroom" (n.d.), http://home.howstuffworks.com/how-to-clean-bathroom2.htm; accessed June 24, 2009.
15. Global Ecolabelling Network, "What Is Ecolabelling?" 2008, www.globalecolabelling.net/whatis.html; accessed June 21, 2009.
16. U.S. Environmental Protection Agency, "Reduce & Reuse," February 18, 2009, www.epa.gov/waste/conserve/rrr/reduce.htm; accessed June 24, 2009.
17. Earth911.com. (2008). "Create a Workplace Recycling Program," http://business.earth911.com/green-guides/workplace-recycling-program-guidelines; accessed June 21, 2009.
18. City of Portland Beuro of Planning and Sustainability, "Start a Green Team" (n.d.), www.portlandonline.com/bps/index.cfm?a=110278&c=49793; accessed on June 26, 2009.
19. California Integrated Waste Management Board, "Electronic Product Management: What Is E-Waste? June 13, 2008, www.ciwmb.ca.gov/electronics/WhatisEWaste; accessed June 24, 2009.
20. Basel Action Network, "What Is Basel Ban?" (n.d.), www.ban.org/about_basel_ban/what_is_basel_ban.html; accessed June 24, 2009.

## Chapter 11

1. www.gartner.com; accessed May 18, 2009.
2. www.energy.gov; accessed March 28, 2009.
3. www.energystar.gov/ia/partners/prod_development/downloads/EPA_Report_Exec_Summary_Final.pdf.
4. www.datacentermanagementguide.com.
5. U.S. Department of Energy.
6. www.cisco.com/en/us/solutions/ns708/networking_solutions_products_genric content0900aecd806fd32e.pdf; accessed May 5, 2009.
7. "Dawn of New Data Center," TechWise TV, http://cisco.com/en/US/netsol/ns340/ns394/ns224/index.html; accessed May 5, 2009.
8. www.mckinseyquarterly.com/Data_centers_How_to_cut_carbon_emissions_and_costs_2255; accessed May 15, 2009.
9. Gabriel Roy, "Green Data Centers," *Green IT* (Summer 2008).
10. www.edf.org/home.cfm; accessed April 17, 2009.
11. www.neenahpaper.com/ECOPaperCalculator/index.asp?ft=Home; accessed May 9, 2009.
12. http://en.wikipedia.org/wiki/Paperless_office#cite_note-economist-1; accessed June 3, 2009.
13. Canadian Broadcasting Corporation Web site, www.cbc.ca/technology/story/2006/11/10/tech-paperless.html; accessed June 12, 2009.

# Chapter 12

1. OSHA Hazard Communication Standard, Subpart Z, "Toxic and Hazardous Substances," 29 CFR 1910.1200, http://www.ilpi.com/msds/osha/1910_1200.html; accessed April 6, 2009.

2. American Chemistry Council, "What Should Chemical Management Systems Address?" (May 2008), www.americanchemistry.com/s_acc/bin.asp?CID= 316&DID=7476&DOC=FILE.PDF; accessed April 6, 2009.

3. Executive Order on the Health and Safety Activities of an Enterprise 575–21-J, www.at.dk/sw12592.asp; accessed April 7, 2009.

4. University of Arizona, Risk Management and Safety, chemical management best practices homepage, http://risk.arizona.edu/healthandsafety/ chemicalmgmtbestpractices/index.shtml; accessed April 7, 2009.

5. Executive Order for Work with Substances and Materials (Chemicals)–292, www.at.dk/sw12444.asp; accessed April 7, 2009.

6. "Workplace Assessment Guidelines for Denmark," www.at.dk/sw12485.asp; accessed April 7, 2009.

7. UHSW Procedure 12, "Chemical Process Risk Identification and Assessment," www.unisa.edu.au/ohsw/forms/docs/ohsw12.doc; accessed April 7, 2009.

8. Lean Enterprise Institute, www.lean.org; accessed April 7, 2009.

9. James P. Womack and Daniel T. Jones, *Lean Thinking* (1996). Free Press; 2nd edition (June 10, 2003).

10. J. Womack, "Mura, Muri, Muda?" Lean Enterprise Institute, www.lean.org/ common/display/?o=743; accessed April 7, 2009.

11. One such work available in book form is Robert J. Alaimo, ed., *Handbook of Chemical Health and Safety* (New York: Oxford University Press, 2001). Another is *The OECD Guiding Principles for Chemical Accident Prevention and Response,* 2nd ed. (2003), www.oecd.org/document/61/0,3343,en_2649 _34369_2789821_1_1_1_1,00.html; accessed April 7, 2009.

12. The United Nations Environmental Programme Strategic Approach to International Chemical Management www.saic.org accessed April 9th 2009.

13. See the Health and Safety Executive homepage for CHIP: www.hse.gov.uk/chip; accessed April 9, 2009. Ravi Govindaradjalou and George Dyson, "Chemicals (Hazard Information and Packaging for Supply) Regulations in Great Britain," *Chemical Health and Safety* 10, no. 3 (May–June 2003): 5–7.

14. http://ec.europa.eu/environment/chemicals/reach/reach_intro.htm; accessed April 9, 2009.

15. The Rotterdam Convention homepage www.pic.int/ accessed April 9th 2009.

# Chapter 13

1. For the Philippines: See Comerford, M. (2005, April 17). It Breaks your Heart. Retrieved April 2009, from Daily Herald: www.dailyherald.com/special/ philippines/part1.asp.

For the Honduras: See Debrouwer, T. (2008, October 08). Working the Landfills a Dangerous Occupation. Retrieved April 2009, from Honduras This Week: www.hondurasthisweek.com/component/content/article/412- dangerous-occupation.

2. National Recycling Coalition, 2009. *NRC Conversionator*. Retrieved April 2009, from www.nrc-recycle.org: www.nrc-recycle.org/theconversionator/shell.html

3. National Energy Education Development Project, 2008. *Intermediate Energy Infobook*. Retrieved April 2009, from www.need.org: www.need.org/needpdf/Intermediate%20Energy%20Infobook.pdf.

4. Jason Morrison, February 2009. Water Scarcity and Climate Change: Growing Risks for Businesses and Investors. Retrieved April 2009, from www.pacinst.org: www.pacinst.org/reports/business_water_climate/full_report.pdf.

5. National Recycling Coalition, 2009. Retrieved April 2009, from www.nrc-recycle.org/theconversionator/shell.html.

# Chapter 14

1. Peter H. Gleick et al., *The World's Water 2000–2001: The Biennial Report on Freshwater Resources* (Washington, DC: Island Press, 2000).

2. www.waterfootprint.org/?page=cal/waterfootprintcalculator_national.

3. http://ga.water.usgs.gov/edu/qahome.html.

4. United Nations Environment Programme/Division of Early Warning and Assessment/Global Resource Information Database—Europe, http://www.grid.unep.ch/product/publication/freshwater_europe/consumption.php.

5. Gleick et al., *The World's Water 2000–2008*, 202–210.

6. Ibid.

7. Habiba Gitay, A. Suarez, D. J. Dokken, and R. Watson, *Climate Change and Biodiversity*, Intergovernmental Panel on Climate Change Technical Paper V (April 2002), 11–34.

8. Ibid., 11–13.

9. Gary Klein, M. Krebs, V. Hall, T. O'Brien, and B. Blevins, "California's Water-Energy Relationship: Final Staff Report," California Energy Commission, Sacramento, CA (November 2005), 8.

10. www.epa.gov/WaterSense/pubs/toilets.htm.

11. www.epa.gov/WaterSense.

12. http://ga.water.usgs.gov/edu/sc4.html.

13. U.S. Environmental Protection Agency, U.S. EPA *Guidelines for Water Reuse* (EPA/625/R-04/108) (Washington, DC, produced by Camp Dresser & McKee, Inc. under a Cooperative Research and Development Agreement with the U.S. Environmental Protection Agency, 2004).

14. www.watersavertech.com/AQUS-Diagram.html.

15. www.sinkpositive.com.

16. HOG Works PTY Ltd., www.rainwaterhog.com.

17. www.bluescopewater.com.

18. City of Chicago, Department of Environment, http://egov.cityofchicago.org:80/city.

19. G-Sky Green Walls and Roofs, www.g-sky.com.

20. Brad Bass and B. Baskaran, "Evaluating Rooftop and Vertical Gardens as an Adaption Strategy for Urban Areas," NRCC-46737, National Research Council Canada, 2003.

21. Amanda Suutari, "Arcata's Constructed Wetland: A Cost-Effective Alternative for Wastewater Treatment," *Earth Island Journal* 22, no. 2 (2007): 26–31.

22. City of Portland, Oregon, Portland Bureau of Environmental Services, "Portland's Innovative Wet Weather Program (IWWP)," www.portlandonline.com/bes/index.cfm?c=35941.

## Chapter 15

1. AWEA, "Wind: Electricity without Emissions," www.awea.org/pubs/factsheets/Climate_Change.pdf.
2. www.ipcc.ch/pdf/assessment-report/ar4/syr/ar4_syr.pdf, 30, 36; accessed June 26, 2009.
3. M. Goodsite, R. Armstrong, and O. J. Nielsen, *Technoetic Arts* (forthcoming). National Environmental Research Institute Department of Atmospheric Environment, Denmark.
4. U.S. Department of Energy, "Department of Energy—Coal," www.energy.gov/energysources/coal.htm.
5. U.S. Department of Energy and the U.S. Environmental Protection Agency, "Carbon Dioxide Emissions from the Generation of Electric Power in the United States" (July 2000), www.eia.doe.gov/cneaf/electricity/page/co2_report/co2emiss.pdf.
6. L. D. Hylander and M. E. Goodsite, "Environmental Costs of Mercury Pollution," Science of Total Environironment 368 (2006): 352–370.
7. Energy Information Administration, "Coal Energy," www.eia.doe.gov/kids/energyfacts/sources/non-renewable/coal.html.
8. U.S. Environmental Protection Agency, "Mid-Atlantic Mountaintop Mining," www.epa.gov/region3/mtntop/index.htm.
9. U.S. Environmental Protection Agency, "Carbon Dioxide—Geological Sequestration," www.epa.gov/climatechange/emissions/co2_geosequest.html.
10. U.S. Department of Energy, "Department of Energy—Oil," www.energy.gov/energysources/oil.htm.
11. John A. Veil, Markus G. Puder, Deborah Elcock, and Robert J. Redweik Jr., "A White Paper Describing Produced Water from Production of Crude Oil, Natural Gas, and Coal Bed Methane," U.S. Department of Energy, National Energy Technology Laboratory (June 2004), www.ead.anl.gov/pub/doc/ProducedWatersWP0401.pdf.
12. Energy Information Administration, "Natural Gas and the Environment," www.eia.doe.gov/pub/oil_gas/natural_gas/analysis_publications/natural_gas_1998_issues_trends/pdf/chapter2.pdf.
13. National Governor's Association, "Securing a Clean Energy Future, Greener Fuels, Greener Vehicles, A State Resource Guide," www.nga.org/Files/pdf/0802GREENERFUELS.PDF.
14. Ibid.
15. Energy Information Administration, "Natural Gas and the Environment."
16. Department of Energy, Office of Civilian Radioactive Waste Management, "What Are Spent Nuclear Fuel and High-Level Radioactive Waste?" www.ocrwm.doe.gov/factsheets/doeymp0338.shtml.
17. Kentucky Deparment for Energy Development & Independence, "Hydroelectric Power," www.energy.ky.gov/dre3/renewable/Hydropower.htm.

18. "Hydropower: Licensed to Protect the Environment," *ORNL Review* 26, Nos. 3&4 (1993), www.ornl.gov/info/ornlreview/rev26-34/text/hydmain.html.

19. Lydia Grimm, "Certifying Hydropower for 'Green' Energy Markets: The Development, Implementation, and Future of the Low Impact Hydropower Certification Program," Low Impact Hydropower Institute (May 2002), http://hydropower .inel.gov/techtransfer/pdfs/greenenergy.pdf.

20. U.S. Department of Energy, "Department of Energy—Bioenergy," www.energy .gov/energysources/bioenergy.htm.

21. Biomass Research and Development Board, "Increasing Feedstock Production for Biofuels: Economic Drivers, Environmental Implications, and the Role of Research," www1.eere.energy.gov/biomass/pdfs/brdi_feedstock_wg2008.pdf.

22. Ibid.

23. Ibid.

24. U.S. Department of Energy, Energy Efficiency and Renewable Energy, "Solar Energy Technologies Program: PV Physics," www1.eere.energy.gov/ solar/pv_physics.html.

25. U.S. Department of Energy, Office of Energy Efficiency and Renewable Energy, "Solar Energy Technologies Program: The Crystalline Silicon Solar Cell," www1.eere.energy.gov/solar/crystalline_silicon_cell.html.

26. U.S. Department of Energy, Office of Energy Efficiency and Renewable Energy, "Solar Energy Technologies Program: Solar Water Heating," www1.eere.energy.gov/solar/sh_basics_water.html.

27. U.S. Department of Energy, Office of Energy Efficiency and Renewable Energy, "Solar Energy Technologies Program: Concentrating Solar Power," www1.eere.energy.gov/solar/csp.html.

28. NREL, "Solar Energy Basics," www.nrel.gov/learning/re_solar.html.

29. AWEA, "Wind: Electricity without Emissions."

30. "Wind Power Today: Building a New Energy Future," U.S. Department of Energy, Energy Efficiency and Renewable Energy, April 2009, www.nrel.gov/docs/ fy09osti/44889.pdf.

31. Ibid.

32. U.S. Department of Wind Energy, Office of Energy Efficiency and Renewable Energy, "Wind and Hydropower Technologies Program: Frequently Asked Questions about Wind Energy," www1.eere.energy.gov/windandhydro/ faqs.html#question11.

33. AWEA, "Wind Power Myths v. Facts," American Wind Energy Association Web site, www.awea.org; accessed September 18 2009.

34. "Bats and Wind Turbines," American Wind Energy Association Web site, www.awea.org; accessed September 18 2009.

35. AWEA, "Utility Scale Wind Energy and Sound" (updated March 2009), www.awea.org/pubs/factsheets/Utility_Scale_Wind_Energy_Sound.pdf.

36. U.S. Department of Energy, Office of Energy Efficiency and Renewable Energy, "Geothermal Technologies Program: Geothermal Basics," www1.eere.energy .gov/geothermal/geothermal_basics.html.

37. U.S. Department of Energy, Office of Energy Efficiency and Renewable Energy, "Business Energy Investment Tax Credit," Database of State Incentives for Renewables & Efficiency, www.dsireusa.org/incentives/incentive.cfm?Incentive _Code=US02F&re=1&ee=0.

38. U.S. Department of Energy, Office of Energy Efficiency and Renewable Energy, "DSIRE: Summary Maps," Database of State Incentives for Renewables & Efficiency, www.dsireusa.org/summarymaps/index.cfm?ee=1&RE=1.

39. U.S. Department of Energy, Energy Efficiency and Renewable Energy, "Energy Savers: Small Solar Electric Systems," www.energysavers.gov/your_home/electricity/index.cfm/mytopic=10710.

40. U.S. Department of Energy, Energy Efficiency and Renewable Energy, "Energy Savers: Siting Your Small Solar Electric System," www.energysavers.gov/your_home/electricity/index.cfm/mytopic=10830.

41. Ibid.

42. Ibid.

43. U.S. Department of Energy, "Modified Accelerated Cost-Recovery System (MACRS)," www.dsireusa.org/incentives/incentive.cfm?Incentive_Code=US06F&re=1&ee=0.

44. U.S. Department of Energy, Energy Efficiency and Renewable Energy, "Energy Savers: Siting Your Small Solar Electric System."

45. See    http://apps1.eere.energy.gov/states/maps/renewable_portfolio_states.cfm for a map of states with RPS or an up-to-date listing.

46. Ryan Wiser and Galen Barbose, "Renewables Portfolio Standard in the United States: A Status Report with Data through 2007," Lawrence Berkeley National Laboratory (April 2008), http://eetd.lbl.gov/ea/ems/reports/lbnl-154e-revised.pdf.

47. Maryland    Energy    Administration,    "Solar    Energy    Grant    Program," www.energy.state.md.us/incentives/residential/solargrants/index.asp.

48. E. Lantz and S. Tegen, "Economic Development Impacts of Community Wind Energy Projects: A Review and Empirical Evaluation," National Renewable Energy Laboratory (April 2009), www.nrel.gov/docs/fy09osti/45555.pdf.

49. U.S. Department of Energy, Energy Efficiency and Renewable Energy, "Energy Savers: Buying Clean Electricity," www.energysavers.gov/your_home/electricity/index.cfm/mytopic=10400.

50. U.S. Department of Energy, "Distributed Energy Program: Grid Architecture and Function," www.eere.energy.gov/de/grid_architecture.html.

51. Kevin Porter, "The Implications of Regional Transmission Organization Design for Renewable Energy Technologies," National Renewable Energy Laboratory (May 2002), www.nrel.gov/docs/fy02osti/32180.pdf.

52. U.S. Department of Energy, "Distributed Energy Program: Regulation of Electric Utilities," www.eere.energy.gov/de/electric_utility_regulation.html.

53. Ibid.

54. U.S. Department of Energy, Office of Energy Efficiency and Renewable Energy, "Energy    Savers:    Green    Certificates,"    www.energysavers.gov/your_home/electricity/index.cfm/mytopic=10430.

55. U.S. Environmental Protection Agency, "Renewable Energy Certificates (RECs)," www.epa.gov/grnpower/gpmarket/rec.htm.

56. U.S. Environmental Protection Agency, "Certified and Verified Products," www.epa.gov/grnpower/buygp/certified.htm.

57. U.S. Environmental Protection Agency, "Renewable Energy Certificates (RECs)."

58. Western Area Power Administration, "Energy Services Bulletin—Technology Spotlight: Selling Voluntary Carbon Offsets from Your Energy Project," www.wapa.gov/es/pubs/esb/2009/jun/jun094.htm.

## Chapter 16

1. In the first paragraph of the first chapter of his book, *Rules for Radicals* (New York: Random House, 1971), Saul Alinsky writes: "What follows is for those who want to change the world from what it is to what they believe it should be. *The Prince* was written by Machiavelli for the Haves on how to hold power. *Rules for Radicals* is written for the Have-Nots on how to take it away."

2. Clay Shirky, *Here Comes Everybody: The Power of Organizing without Organizations* (New York: Penguin, 2008). The quote is from Shirky's first chapter, "It Takes a Village to Find a Phone," in which he adds: "By making it easier for groups to self-assemble and for individuals to contribute to group effort without management (and its attendant overhead) these tools have radically altered the old limits on the size, sophistication and scope of unsupervised effort."

3. Seth Godin elaborates on his theories of peer-to-peer marketing in his free e-book, *Flipping the Funnel*, available for free download from his blog at http://sethgodin.typepad.com/seths_blog/2006/01/flipping_the_fu.html.

4. From Chesapeake Bay Foundation Web site, www.cbf.org/Pag.aspx?pid=929.

## Chapter 17

1. www.wateryear2003.org.

## Chapter 18

1. http://eetd.lbl.gov/paper/html/concept.htm.

## Chapter 19

1. Conversion based on the U.S. Environmental Protection Agency Greenhouse Gas Equivalencies Calculator, www.epa.gov/cleanenergy/energy-resources/calculator.html.

# Index